THE
GLASNOST
READER

OTHER BOOKS BY JONATHAN EISEN

THE AGE OF ROCK

UNKNOWN CALIFORNIA
(with David Fine and Kim Eisen)

UNKNOWN TEXAS
(with Harold Straughn)

THE NOBEL READER
(with Stuart Troy)

THE GLASNOST READER

Compiled and Edited
by Jonathan Eisen

With an Introduction by
Wilson Carey McWilliams

NAL BOOKS

NEW AMERICAN LIBRARY

A DIVISION OF PENGUIN BOOKS USA INC., NEW YORK
PUBLISHED IN CANADA BY
PENGUIN BOOKS CANADA LIMITED, MARKHAM, ONTARIO

NAL BOOKS ARE AVAILABLE AT QUANTITY DISCOUNTS
WHEN USED TO PROMOTE PRODUCTS OR SERVICES.
FOR INFORMATION PLEASE WRITE TO PREMIUM MARKETING DIVISION,
NEW AMERICAN LIBRARY, 1633 BROADWAY,
NEW YORK, NEW YORK 10019.

NAL BOOKS TRADEMARK REG. U.S. PAT. OFF. AND FOREIGN COUNTRIES
REGISTERED TRADEMARK—MARCA REGISTRADA
HECHO EN DRESDEN, TN, U.S.A.

SIGNET, SIGNET CLASSIC, MENTOR, ONYX, PLUME, MERIDIAN
and NAL BOOKS are published *in the United States* by New American Library,
a division of Penguin Books USA Inc.,
1633 Broadway, New York, New York 10019,
in Canada by Penguin Books Canada Limited,
2801 John Street, Markham, Ontario L3R 1B4

LIBRARY OF CONGRESS CATALOGING-IN-PUBLICATION DATA

The Glasnost reader / compiled and edited by Jonathan Eisen.
    p. cm.
Includes bibliographical references.
ISBN 0-453-00695-7
1. Soviet Union—Politics and government—1985– 2. Glasnost.
I. Eisen, Jonathan.
DK28G.5.G53   1990
947.085′4—dc20   89-13376
                                                        CIP

First Printing, March, 1990

1 2 3 4 5 6 7 8 9

PRINTED IN THE UNITED STATES OF AMERICA

ACKNOWLEDGMENTS

Heartfelt gratitude is herewith extended to the numerous people who gave me their help and encouragement along the way. The task would have been much more difficult without them, perhaps impossible. They include my mother, Miriam Eisen, who kept me up to date with the unfolding story when I was traversing the far corners of New Zealand; Mr. Oleg Benyukh, former counselor at the USSR Embassy in Washington, for his unhesitating moral support and initial encouragement when the idea for the book was gestating (Oleg, a novelist of great popularity in the Soviet Union, was astute enough to know that sometimes encouragement at the outset is manna that can last through many deserts of subsequent frustrations); my longtime mentor, Wilson Carey McWilliams, professor of political science at Rutgers University, who helped as always to maintain and develop perspective on the unbearable lightness of being when one is faced with overdosing on too many issues of *Pravda*; my translator and friend Julia Malkovskaya-Tarshis, whose keen sense of humor and intimate knowledge of life in the Soviet Union enabled me to develop a book that could resonate on many levels; my dear and loving friend, Katherine Joyce Smith, whose constant support always metamorphoses into inspiration (her fearless good humor and willingness to pursue the logic of the heart was a source of strength to me and continues to be so); all the librarians at the Council on Foreign Relations (their contribution to this book is perhaps the greatest of all, and their patience as well. Somewhere their names are noted in the Akashic records, that great library "out there" where good deeds are noted forever); Virginia Etheridge, Janis Kreslins, Barbara Miller, and Marcia Sprules; my partner, Harold Straughn, whose love is matched only by his intellect; and lastly, my editor and catalyst, Alexia Dorszynski.

CONTENTS

PREFACE

You hold in your hands a representative sampling of writings from what is arguably the most hopeful social revolution of our time—the outpouring of an entire people learning to breathe and think freely, to exercise their democratic rights.

Perhaps the words of poet Naum Korzhavin sum it up: "The meaning of language has been restored. Words now mean what they really mean. People are communicating again. The line by Mandelshtam, which recently expressed the reality of our everyday existence—'We live without sense of country'—does not express reality today. Freedom of thought is returning to our country. I don't believe that we have achieved full democracy, but we have gained some intellectual freedom, a substantial amount."

Although one could argue that "historical necessity" required that this revolution should happen, this argument can be made only after the fact. Certainly economic pressures threatened across-the-board disaster, and certainly major dissatisfaction with the Communist Party had reached unprecedented volatility. But still, major reform was not a foregone conclusion. "History" cast Mikhail Gorbachev as instigator and initiator, emancipator and catalyst—the one who returned to his people *the meaning of language.*

Since his ascendency to power in 1985, Gorbachev has prodded not only his own country but in many ways the entire world out of its period of "stagnation." Indeed, the measure of his success is counted in numerous ways, not the least of which is that people are actually coming to grips with the fact that the Cold War appears to be coming to an end—with neither bang nor whimper but with the joyful, hopeful, yet still cautious celebration of a world that can scarcely believe that it's true.

This is not to imply that Gorbachev's policies have an instantaneous success on all levels. As the world's news media have testified and as you will find in these pages, *glasnost* and *perestroika* have unleashed decades' old frustrations and anxieties, age-old animosities and blood feuds. Being able to express the truth for the first time in recent memory, the Soviet people are whelmed in revelations, many of them very unpleasant. Still, all this is undertaken with the spirit of exorcism and expiation, set against the backdrop of hope. Regardless of the backsliding into "command and administer" forms of administration, the society as a whole seems to be lurching, sometimes kicking and screaming, into the strong light of reality, beginning to find its legs again after so many, many years of being tossed about in the sickening swells of Stalinism.

Much of the backsliding is quite understandable. People tend to look for anchors of certainty, sometimes not minding the harshness in which that certainty is often clothed. Stalinism was unmitigated brutality, governance by threat and intimidation, and for millions, unimaginable horror and death. Still, as we have learned from landmark studies of concentration camps and other "total institutions," there is often a tendency on the part of the inmate to identify with the captor, and we find this having occurred in Stalinist USSR. Years after his death, the institutions of repression created by Stalin continued his legacy. Finding the right combination to unlock this legacy has been the major challenge facing Mikhail Gorbachev—and he seems to be succeeding.

More than anything else, *The Glasnost Reader* is a chronicle of this unlocking process, and the reader will be both shocked and delighted by what is revealed about the struggle for freedom in this tormented country, where perhaps 40 million people perished by the hand of "Father" Stalin, leaving the survivors cringing in fear or numbed for the duration of their lives, accommodating wherever they could to the exigencies of the times. The one notable exception, of course, were the refusniks, the dissidents—those for whom cringing and accommodation were worse than jail or torture or "psychiatric" incarceration. The words of many of them are represented here, though we have passed over much of the underground writing so important in the pre-*glasnost* era since this is primarily a book about what's happening *now*.

Where *glasnost* is leading is anybody's guess at this point, but even so, the real question is not the end goal, but the continuing legitimation of the process of *glasnost* and, with it, true democracy. The Soviet Union, along with much of the rest of the world, seems to be acknowledging, albeit slowly, that the cure for a little democracy is more democracy. And the country seems to be developing its long-dormant democratic instincts with an enthusiasm and vigor both sincere and refreshing to cultures such as our own, which seem to be jaded and often paralyzed in the face of real and present dangers. We can only cheer a society that seems to have learned that it's all right to speak out and create a democracy—and has gone ahead and *tried* to do so.

Gorbachev is the helmsman in all this, and perhaps it's a good thing that he, like Stalin, is a father figure. The Soviet Union is a profoundly conflicted society, without a strong tradition of political compromise. Power in the Soviet Union has historically been an all-or-nothing proposition, and learning the virtues of toleration and mutual respect, compromise and pluralism, with civic institutions that exist independently alongside the political institutions, is a slow process. But reform *is* continuing, though the lessons are being learned with difficulty.

Without the father figure—the strong leader—the Soviet Union and the movement in general would lose its moral leadership; and *glasnost* and *perestroika* are, if nothing else, a lesson in morality. Gorbachev is trying to teach his country that Stalinism was an aberration, a radical departure from the teachings of Lenin, who is increasingly portrayed as the true father of *glasnost*, a humanist who would never have condoned the brutality that followed on his death. Whether that is objectively true or not, saying so was the only logical choice for Gorbachev to have made, since his radical reforms could then be presented as the true legacy of the founding father. He thereby has been able to accomplish the twin goals of rousing the opponents of communist rule at the same time that he preserves it. The analogy might be to Franklin Roosevelt, who preserved capitalism at the moment of its worst crisis by adopting some of the lessons of socialism.

In all, *glasnost* has been a success, and the world eagerly awaits its codification—the recognition of *glasnost* and democracy as *inalienable rights*, set down as law and upheld by the courts. Already we can see signs that this is coming, and the results of the remarkable elections of 1989 indicate that this is precisely where the momentum is taking the country.

What *The Glasnost Reader* portrays is a veritable sea-change in history. What you will read is what the Soviet people themselves are reading—and writing—as this debate proceeds, and the questions you will be left with are the same ones that they are asking. And some of those questions have no answers but are, in a way, answers themselves.

—JONATHAN EISEN
New York City
May, 1989

INTRODUCTION

Like most Americans, I am no expert on Soviet politics or culture, but for years I could get by. Americans learned to regard the U.S.S.R. as a land of menace, full of dreadful secrets but also predictable, a totalitarian bureaucracy colored gray. Today, all of those givens are shaken. The Soviet Union has become mercurial and astonishing, a place of political prodigies and the source of paradox.

Glasnost, John Le Carré has written, is "an hour in history as momentous as 1917," and this book lets us feel the sand in the glass.* *The Glasnost Reader* lets Soviet citizens speak for themselves, in the full diversity of their political vocabularies, which is as it should be. A revolution in speech, glasnost is an effort to reconnect words and meanings, a quest for the recovery of politics.

Politics is shaped by words, and *political* power depends on authority, the right to rule. A state enjoys a "monopoly of the legitimate use of force"—Max Weber's definition—only when it is regarded *as* legitimate; totalitarian regimes aim to control the very source of legitimacy, the distinction between political right and wrong. As Solzhenitsyn sought to remind the Soviet intelligentsia, "violence quickly grows old; a few years and it is no longer sure of itself, and in order to hold its ground, to look decent, it has to adopt Lie as an ally." Since this is true, glasnost could begin with a refusal to say "what we do not think." However, a refusal to lie falls short of telling the truth. Along with Gorbachev, Soviet officialdom is "learning a new tongue"— and the same is true of Soviet citizens. Democratic dialogue is an art unpracticed in Soviet experience. Relative freedom of speech is "heady" for Soviet citizens, as Daniel Bell has observed, but for that reason dangerous, uncertain of the limits of prudence or civility.

The stakes and the difficulties are both titanic. The sounds of glasnost are discordant, and any reader of this book will hear a

---

*The New York Times, September 29, 1989, p. A35

cacophony of clashing memories, cultures and aspirations. Despite that, glasnost rests on the conviction that it will be possible to find or forge a public language, a common way of talking about political things. In this respect, glasnost is on the battle line of contemporary philosophy as well as politics.

Democracy relies on the doctrine that all citizens are, in some decisive respect, the same and that deliberation can transcend differences of interest and experience—in other words, that speech can rule culture. Relativism, the cultural countercurrent, denies this, holding that human beings are shut into their distinct cultures or selves, imprisoned by uniqueness, so that language itself is only an imposition forced on us by others. Rule, in this view, is at bottom force, and cultural hegemony, constraint overcoming the anarchy of things. It is in that tradition that Nina Andreyeva, Stalin's defender, appeals to "Great Russian national pride" and attacks "cosmopolitan tendencies." Struggling on behalf of speech, glasnost upholds the possibility and dignity of both politics and philosophy, democracy and reason.

But if speech and law can transform a political society, they do so slowly, and glasnost and Gorbachev do not have much time. Even friends of reform are inclined to think that perestroika will fail and Gorbachev will be ousted. For that matter, Gorbachev—both Luther and the pope, as one observer described him—could feel compelled to lead his own counter-revolution.*

Everywhere, nationalism seems to threaten Soviet unity. In the Baltic republics, the Caucasus, the Ukraine and Moslem Central Asia, people suddenly sense an opportunity to overcome captivity and subordination. Nationalistic vitalities, so apt to become virulent, confirm the fears of hardliners that freer speech will lead straight to Babel. And the strength of separatist sentiment may tempt Gorbachev to postpone the local elections scheduled for February and March, 1990. Meanwhile, Pamyat and its imitators are always ready to offer their sewer-broth of antisemitism and Russian chauvinism.

Economic success, of course, could moderate discontent and even ease old resentments. So far, however, perestroika has not significantly reduced shortages or eased the perception that Soviet consumer goods are generally second-rate. Moreover, unemployment is escalating—over 27% in some regions and republics. Economic gains are bound to come slowly. The Soviet Union

*Michael Dobbs, "Eliminating Excuses Along With Opponents," *Washington Post National Weekly*, October 2-8, 1989, p. 16.

needs entrepreneurial skills and habits; it must heal the weakness in agriculture that began with Stalin's decimations; it will have to enter into the "information revolution." As Leonid Albakin remarks, reform in the Soviet Union requires the building of an economic culture, creating and nurturing the "social forces" necessary to growth, a "social humus" that can be accumulated only over years or generations.

The pressure for economic results is doubly troubling because it is not at all clear that democracy is inherently linked to economic growth. The success stories of recent years have been regimes which combine a market economy with political authoritarianism, using state power against any popular effort to soften the market's rigors. In the Soviet Union, the slow pace of economic gain—combined with strikes, disorders and the unsettling of old securities—inevitably inspires some nostalgia for the totalitarian dynamism of Stalin's era. Even defenders of glasnost sometimes reinforce this mood. General Dmitry Volkogonov, Stalin's most recent biographer, contends that Stalin "recklessly forced the pace" of development, paying a price so high that even Stalin's defenders "would not agree that the success which is so eagerly desired should be achieved by using his methods." Perhaps not, but more than one Soviet citizen probably sympathizes with the assertion that "Stalin issued orders only once."

It does not help that Soviet society is unaccustomed to excesses and irresponsibilities of liberty familiar in the West. Even routine Western practices undermine or endanger glasnost: commercial advertising, now beginning to appear in Soviet life is yet another form of speech in which words do not say what they mean, and even polling emphasizes private expressions of opinion rather than public deliberation.* Solzhenitsyn is not alone in harboring the dark suspicion that political democracy may be inseparable from degeneracy.

For glasnost and perestroika, nothing will come easily or quickly. Soviet reform can rely on few external sources of support, especially if America's leaders persist in their tepid response. Glasnost depends on inner resources, the strength of commitment and the force of ideas. As Sigmund Krancberg observes, while Westerners are apt to see glasnost as part of the "decline of ideology," from a Soviet point of view, ideology is

---

*And polling obviously upsets Soviet officials. On October 18, 1989, *The New York Times* reported that Gorbachev, disturbed by a mildly critical poll, had called for the resignation of Vladislav Starkov, editor of *Argumenty i Fakty*.

critical. Hence the importance of efforts to develop a *socialist* basis for perestroika, like Aleksandr Yakovlev's relatively orthodox appeal to Marxist humanism or, more imaginatively, Lavroskiy and Skoptsov's shrewd contention that bureaucratic control over property alienates workers quite as much as capitalist ownership. The strongest voices of glasnost recognize, however, that its promise does not rest on ideology but in the soul, on moral virtue rather than the laws of history. As Aleksandr Levikov wrote, "A moral person goes into battle—even a dangerous and hopeless one—guided by his conscience and convictions."

Yet "conscience" is a relatively insubstantial term, and the courage of one's convictions can lead to fanaticism, imprudence and repression. Ultimately, glasnost will depend on beliefs and souls that are specifically democratic. As Fazil Iskander contends, the Soviet public needs to learn democratic habits of speech and mores of self-government. The idea of legitimate and loyal opposition is unfamiliar; in Russian and Soviet history, the stakes of dissent have regularly been mortal. Civility requires longer practice and greater security than can be provided by *Izvestiya*'s sermons on moderation. Above all, the supporters of glasnost—and its critics, for that matter—need assurances that they will not be the victims of the next swing to repression. The immediate goal of Soviet politics is not democracy but the rule of law, the indispensable ground of civil speech.

The constraints of Soviet experience and culture, Andranik Migranian maintains, argue for authoritarian rule as a step toward the development of democracy, a personal dictatorship limited in term and held to standards of accountability.* At least partly conned from Jeane Kirkpatrick, this line of argument aims to create civil *society* as a kind of preparatory school for a future democratic state. But this authoritarian version of Madison's *Federalist Number 10* walks a tightrope, since the powers necessary to enforce civil speech are obvious dangers to it. And it is not at all clear that the widespread eagerness for liberty and self-government in the Soviet Union admits of any extended period of tutelary rule.

As Sergei Zalygin points out, habit is the foundation of civility in Western democracies (although, if our recent experience is any test, that foundation may be showing signs of wear). By contrast glasnost is exciting precisely because it is new, at odds with the old Soviet habits of secrecy and suspicion. Soviet citi-

*_The New York Times_, Sept. 11, 1989

zens will learn to trust the law to protect their personal and political security only if the law proves trustworthy. For generations, Soviet civility will be as fragile as sobriety among reformed alcoholics, depending on the conscious commitment of leaders and citizens.

The very idea that law can and should rule requires a revolution in Soviet thinking. It presumes that some principles and rules of right are superior to history and to will. It implies the subordination of socialism to the human, the historical to the perennial.

Accordingly, the mayor of Moscow warns that the appeal to universal values suggests the disparagement of "socialist values." Glasnost and perestroika may, in fact, be attempting to square a political circle, abandoning Leninism while clinging to Lenin as the founder and symbol of Soviet political legitimacy. The debunking of his successors may actually have increased Lenin's relative stature; at any rate, the indignation at the suggestion that Lenin's body be buried is an indication of his still-sacred status. At the same time, it is now possible to observe that Lenin failed to see that capitalism had not yet exhausted its possibilities. But public discussion of Lenin's errors of judgment may invite sharper critique. In symbol as in substance, Gorbachev is a fiddler on the roof, precariously playing for time and hoping to be justified by results.

Americans have a stake in the success of glasnost that goes beyond calculations of great power politics. From East Germany to China, glasnost and perestroika have unleashed a yearning for democracy that stands as a challenge to our own weak ardor. Beyond calling for our sympathy and support, the difficulty of the struggle for democratization and its uncertain prognosis ought to remind us that democracy is embattled, threatened by bureaucratic and technological power and dependent on human devotion. *The Glasnost Reader* helps us see that the Soviet Union, racing to establish civility and citizenship, is running for our future as well as its own.

—Wilson Carey McWilliams
Professor of Political Science
Rutgers University

THE
GLASNOST
READER

ADVERTISING

Moscow Radio Offers Advertising Slots
Moscow Domestic Service in Russian, November 3, 1988

Attention, directors of enterprises: Mayak [Moscow radio second program] is opening a new advertising and information slot: Enterprise Seeks Partner. You have changed to financial autonomy and have started counting your money. You need a customer for marketing your output, to get rid of surplus equipment, or you need to buy materials. From Vladivostok to Brest, Mayak will announce this to your future business partners. If your offer is announced on the radio, it reaches an audience of millions throughout the country instantly. Send your advertisement by registered mail, the envelope marked: Mayak—Enterprise Seeks Partner, to the following address: 127-427 Moscow Radio Mayak. The telephone number for information is: 217-90-29.

So, by means of a paid advertisement on Mayak and other radio channels, enterprise heads can establish commercial and scientific-technical contacts with partners in any sector. The same applies to the developmnet or introduction of inventions and projects. If you wish, advertisement offers can be broadcast several times a day on six channels.

AFGHANISTAN

A Lesson Which Should Be Learned
by V. Skosyrev, *Izvestiya*, May 4, 1989

FOR ALMOST TEN YEARS, Afghanistan, for us, has been a wound that would not heal. But let us be honest with ourselves. Though the Soviet soldiers, sent over the Amu-Dar'ya, selflessly carried out their duty, as it is expected from the loyal sons of their Homeland, our involvement in Afghanistan caused a lot of doubts at home. Our people did not accept this war. The proof of that is the letters sent to the editor, whose authors ask for the explanation of how the Soviet Army was sent beyond the borders without the sanctions of the Supreme Council, and without any attempt whatsoever to find out the opinions of the majority, beforehand. The readers are also interested in the present situation in Afghanistan and the perspectives of regulating the conflict.

Today our guest is the doctor of history, senior scientist of the department of the Eastern Studies of the Academy of Sciences of the USSR, Yu. V. Gankovsky.

The Afghasistan war through the eyes of the historian.

Q: Yurily Vladimirovich, before everything else, in your opinion, why did the Soviet Union become so deeply involved in the Afganistan situation?

A: We can not be unconcerned with the fate of Afghanistan. We share with them a common border of about 2,400 kilometers. Ever since 1919, we provided Afghanistan with extensive aid. For example, by 1978 we took the first place among nations in providing the economic aid to Afghanistan. Over three thousand Afghani officers have gone through basic training in our country even before the April revolution of 1978. All of this can not be erased from history.

Q: I agree. But it is one thing to work together with the neighbor in different fields, including the military, but it is totally different to send your troops in to support him. In the last ten years, you have been in Afghanistan on many occasions. You participated in the conventions dealing with developing the new politics in that country. Please explain what made our leadership step over the fateful border in 1979?

A: It is not an easy question. It is known that at that time, there was a high-level committee dealing with Afghanistan. It had to give a recommendation on how to act when armed troops of extremist right groups infiltrate the territory of the neighboring country with which we have an alliance pact. I must say that following the April revolution the Pakistani influence started to increase, though it can not in essence be compared to that of the present time.

We could have used political and diplomatic means. I am

convinced that they were not fully exhausted. Unfortunately a different policy prevailed. Do you remember that the cannons of Louis XIV were decorated with the sign "King's last argument"? That was the "argument" they turned to. Not taking into account the particularities of Afghanistan, they were planning to stabilize the situation and to bring the soldiers home. It turned out to be quite different. The 40th Army was there for nine years and seven weeks. This is the longest war that Russia has been involved in since 1813.

Q: But wasn't there anyone who stood up against the move which consequently brought about such strenuous effects both militarily and internationally?

A: It was not in vain that those times were called the "period of stagnation." I will remind you of something that already came out in the press. Namely, the decision to send in the troops was taken behind closed doors by a few top leaders of the government.

It is true that doubts were expressed, but the last word was L. I. Brezhnev's.

Q: Today, such practice is frowned upon. Yet it is important to establish another point. Namely, was the information which was going "up" becoming the basis for the governmental decisions sufficiently accurate?

A: Unfortunately not always. I want everyone to understand me correctly. We had people, working on the Afghanistan question, extremely competent in the question of the East. But their opinions were not listened to.

On the other hand, the quality of the information was not alway adequate for the events. Apparently the lack of a scientific center for the Afghanistan studies was also felt. It does not exist even today (while there are such centers in the USA and other Western countries). As a result, there was not a timely development of an overall scientifically based policy in relation to Afghanistan.

It also happened that the information was given by not fully competent people. Here's an example. One time, I had a chance in Moscow to read a report on the situation in the area of the Pushtun tribes in Pakistan, through which came the main flow of arms to the rebels. This report was totally unsatisfactory. In three days, I went to Kabul and in the counsulate met with the author of the report, sent from the USSR by an official from one of the DRA ministries. He was a man of about thirty, but very pleasant. Since the facts from the report obviously did not match reality, I had to give him a sort of an exam. At it turned out, he did not know the area of the tribal zone, nor the population there. At the end of the conversation I asked: "What university did you finish?" He faltered and then named a medical school in one of the regional cities in Russia.

Q: Was it not for that reason that we were too optimistic in our evaluation of the perpectives of the April revolution? We even called it "socialist" . . .

A: I am familiar with only one article in the Soviet scientific journal, where it was asserted that following 1978, Afghanistan would start socialist reformation. In other scientific publications, the April revolution was characterized quite correctly as national-democratic. The April revolt truly played a key role in the history of the country. It has been in the making for a long time. It was not in vain that the American Afghanistan specialist Luis Dupre predicted a year before that if the Daud's regime would not undergo reforms, revolution was unavoidable.

Unfortunately, under Amin, this little Afghani Pol Pot, the authority of the new rule was jeopardized by mass arrests, executions of undesirables, quick reforms which were not consistent with the national traditions, executions of the Moslem theologians. The number of compounds in the Afghani army went down three to four times and of officers ten times.

Q: Amin's regime brought great hardships to Afghanistan. There is no question about that. But who in our country took upon himself the question of liberation of the foreign country from the dictator? The events related to this were presented in our country quite tendentiously, to put it mildly. Let us try to open the curtains a bit. Firstly, did you get to meet with our military personnel who were sent to Kabul at the end of December of 1979?

A: Of course I met with them. Though to tell the truth I arrived in Kabul two weeks after. I was now witness to the operation. What can I say? Under the terror and repressions established by Amin, many active participants and supporters of the April revolution were forced to seek political asylum in the foreign consulates (including our own). Others accepted illegal status and actively fought against the regime headed by Amin and obviously asked for help. After his downfall they came into the leadership of NDPA and the DRA government.

There are Afghani publications that say it was these people who planned the storming of the president's palace. However, from the conversations with our officers, I found out that our subdivision participated in the operation. The battle did not last long. No one except Amin's personal guards made an attempt to defend the regime.

I think it is time to tell the truth no matter how bitter it is. After all, across the border there are books written about this. Failing to mention this only gives birth to speculations.

Q: Withdrawing our troops from Afghanistan was not merely an act of state wisdom. It is a concrete and tangible result of Perestroika. It is approved by our people. On the other hand, when the discussion of the beginning of the war begins, there are a lot of different suppositions. Since it has been admitted that it is impossible to regulate a problem in a military fashion, it would also seem that the sending of Soviet soldiers into Afghanistan was a mistake. Nevertheless, the commander of the land troops, Army General V. I. Varennikov, in an interview with the magazine *Novoye Vremia*, said that in view of the threat to our southern borders which originated in 1979, the decision was adequate . . .

AGRICULTURE

The Lessee Must Be Protected
I. Avakumov, *Izvestiya*, January 19, 1989

After the vigorous support for the lease system from the very top, one might suppose it has no opponents. Everyone is now for it. And that is the danger: How not to suffocate the trusting creature in our embrace. Because there is abundant experience of this . . .

We do not have to look far; **let us recall what one generation can remember. In the past 20-30 years there have been repeated attempts to revive the peasant.** Remember the self-planning system and the emergence of various forms of contracts. Their creators intended that farmers would have extensive economic, and not just labor independence. As you will probably recall, on each occasion the introduction was a big and noisy affair. And what came of it? Only the exclusive collectives that obtained this independence on an experimental basis survived. All the rest gave up the ghost, because no one created special conditions for them; indeed, no one could because there was no provision for altering the principles of the administrative-edict system of management. What we got was a nominally progressive but essentially palliative form of production organization that had been merely adapted to the system. This contract did not produce a food miracle, and people stopped believing in the word. Something similar may happen to the lease system. It is already happening. . . .

We have come face to face with a phenomenon whereby an unsuccessful attempt is being made to call hired workers lessees. Moreover, the widespread view that the lessee should exist only within the confines of the sovkhoz or kolkhoz constantly multiplies these errors. We know all too well what operating a plot by "remote control" means, but how persistent are the attempts to maintain control of the farmer. And unless the farm which is to have lessees itself changes, unless the people at the top change, and if there is essentially no change in production relations, then . . . Right! You get the familiar smell of palliative, which once destroyed the contract system. The lease system must not suffer the same fate, because we have endured too much getting this far.

Technical Hitch
by Alexander Shumsky, *Moscow News*, August 31, 1988

How can a farmer work without a plough? The ploughs being used throughout the country today hinder farmers more than help: they don't plough evenly and leave either crests or ditches, which means great losses. Tractors are no good on such uneven fields, land has to be cultivated. All this calls for extra fuel, time and resources.

The rotation plough does not have all these shortcomings, and it is by no means a new invention. I visited Britain this spring and saw that this was practically the only type of plough they used.

What about in the Soviet Union? The Ministry of Agricultural Machinery knows all about these ploughs, but this "knowledge" doesn't seem to change anything. Where are the brakes being applied and why? Is our most acute problem being cast aside as an unnecessary headache? I repeat: we have nothing to plough with; not only do we lack rotation ploughs, we don't have any efficient ploughs at all. Will it take us long to move just a little away towards progress?

—Alexander Shumsky,
chairman of the
Kazminsky collective farm,
Kochubeyevsky
District, Stavropol
Territory, deputy to the USSR
Supreme Soviet

(Mikhail Zlatkovsky, *Soviet News*)

The Great Interminable Food Supply Debate

MOSCOW TELEVISON SERVICE in Russian at 1845 GMT on January 16 in its Restructuring Spotlight" program presented by Valeriy Golubev carried a 15 minute report on debates conducted by the USSR Council of Ministers on January 14 concerning the food supply problem.

Introducing recorded excerpts of the debate, Golubev, in the studio, says that over the last few days, there have been many reports on the problems in the supply of fruits and vegetables to the population. Golubev describes the depressing situation with the cultivation and consumption of many vital crops and states that not a single Union republic, with the exception of Armenia, has fulfilled the production quotas as stipulated in the food program, and Golubev cites figures to demonstrate the poor performance. Golubev states that "procurement, storage, processing, and trade are in a most neglected state. Participants in the USSR Council of Ministers session, which took place on 14 January, had yet another opportunity to see that at a photographic exhibition. It shows vividly the obsolete mechanism of procurement that developed during the period of stagnation."

The report then moves on to a video recording of excerpts of the Council of Ministers debates with offscreen comments by Golubev.

———————————————

RYZHKOV: The prices are absolutely . . . strongly fluctuating, up to five times, according to data reported here. From the point of view of quality, does it correspond to the fluctuation in prices or not?

MURAKHOVSKIY: Yes, it does. Why do people buy at markets potatoes which are four times more expensive then in shops? Because they find choice potatoes there, they buy it and know that it is a potato.

RYZHKOV: But there are two reasons there: either shortage—the shop simply does not have the product and therefore the buyer goes to the market—or, indeed, the increased price at the market corresponds to the consumer appeal for the product. Could you please explain this to us?

MURAKHOVSKIY: Nikolay Ivanovich, I think that, of course, there are the two fundamental factors. If there is no trade going on in the shops, then the market is simply dictating its price. If the shops sell potatoes but their quality is inferior to that of potatoes on the market, then the price on the market rises accordingly.

RYZHKOV: So is it still the shortage that dictates the prices or the quality?

MURAKHOVSKIY: The quality.

RYZHKOV: The quality.

MURAKHOVSKIY: Nikolay Ivanovich, just look: we procure potatoes in September and we will be selling them at 10-12 kopecks until January and spring. Is this right or wrong? I think it is wrong. If we said to our trade organizations in charge of storage: sell them at 10-12 kopecks in September, at 20 kopecks in January, and at 30 kopecks in March, then farms would start storing them properly. But now not a single farm wants to store them in their facilities. They delivered their products in September and do not want to know anything more about it. And then there are production and maintenance costs; potatoes will be rotting. So a price should be set which would make it profitable for the farm to store them. . . .

RYZHKOV: All right, what kind of system do you have to face mass deliveries of, say, cabbage? This means there are no long-term contracts with those comrades from republics.

SAYKIN: There is a system of contracts, and by and large we conclude them, but this system is not being complied with today, it is not being complied with either in terms of uniform deliveries or in terms of the quality of products. Therefore, some new economic levers are required.

RYZHKOV: We have been discussing this system already since the summer, last summer, when Moscow was yet again having difficulties with fruit and vegetables. We spoke with you then: Of course, the Agroprom must set some sort of definite quotas, respectively, but there must be a system of working. But it looks like there is no system. Right?

GOLUBEV: There are no flexible prices, there is neither a system nor the desire of farms to cultivate crops. This was stated unequivocally by Shtepo, general director of the Volga-Don Association.

SHTEPO: Take, for example, the vegetables that are being sent to Moscow. I do not mention the issue of prices. There are such wise men in Moscow, I do not know—you just try to come here and they will strip you of all you have got. Over the last 2 years, we have been losing R500,000 yearly on our deliveries of tomatoes to Moscow.

RYZHKOV: What amount of your products have you been sending to Moscow, what percentage?

SHTEPO: We have dispatched nearly 5,000 tonnes to Moscow . . . 5,000 altogether and of them in Moscow. . . .

RYZHKOV: What percentage?

SHTEPO: Percentage? In terms of percentage, we dispatch 60 or 70 percent of tomatoes.

RYZHKOV: Have you been dispatching your products to nobody in specific, or to Richin, Ivanov, and so on?

SHTEPO: Nikolay Ivanovich, we have already become like those soldiers, we have been given assignments for everything. We sent them where we were told.

On Government Agenda
by E. Gonzalyez, *Izvestiya*, January 10, 1989

In brief, it is obvious that the system targeted to the plan, and not to the consumer, is successful in providing citizens with work at the fields and bases but not in providing them with vegetables. It is gratifying that in the production sphere this system is not changing radically—leasing is entering rural life. But will the new economic relations extend further along the "vegetable conveyor?" If they do not, then will the harvest increase we expect not bypass the consumer?

These are the difficult problems that form the background to a discussion of the question formulated in a mundane and simple way: "On measures to provide the population with fruit and vegetable produce." It is scarcely possible to overcome these problems by "conventional" measures—by reprimands and rebukes and the replacement of leaders. **Even the transfer of individual organizations from one department to another, as the practice of recent years has shown, does not increase the quantity of vegetables and fruit.** The kolkhoz markets have been handed over to consumer cooperatives, but to be honest little has changed since then. In Kiev fruit and vegetable trade has been subordinated to the agro-industrial committee, but, in the specialists' opinion, things have become not better, but worse.

The shrinkages and spillages are surrounded, as though encased in cotton padding, by the norms for "natural" loss, and the intermediaries between customer and producer successfully reduce harvests. They will obviously do so until they, too, are affected by economic responsibility, self financing, and economic accountability [khozraschet].

Tonya the Milkwoman
by Lev Voskresensky, *Moscow News*, January 3, 1988

I met the milkwoman from Protasovo at the Butyrsky Market in Moscow where she has gone every Saturday for thirty years to sell her curd, cream and milk which are fresher than the finest "dairy products" from Gosagroprom (the State Agro-Industrial Committee).

Antonina (Tonya for short) Chernyayeva, a veterinary assistant at the Menzhinets state farm, retired two years ago. Her husband Nikolai is a forest ranger.

The couple had a hard start in life. They built their own house and relied mainly on home-grown vegetables and fruits and on their cow while raising two sons, since their wages were so small. Then came the 1961 "anti-cow" campaign.

The official decision sounded appealing: if villagers gave up their personal livestock, especially cows, they could work more efficiently on collective farms. After work, there would be fewer chores to do on their own small-holdings. The press praised those who relinquished the burden of individual small-holdings.

Prescient heads of collective and state farms encouraged subsidiary farming at their own risk. But, in most villages, especially near urban areas, owners of cows were harassed. The number of livestock in personal possession plummeted as did the private production of meat and dairy products. This, however, did not start rivers of milk flowing from collective farms. Villagers joined the lines outside foodshops in towns and market prices skyrocketed.

Strictly speaking, there was no law against keeping livestock or selling your products at market. It's just that you couldn't mow the hay. Even on waste land, in ravines or along the roadsides. If you did mow hay, militiamen would seize it.

Every family in the village of Protasovo had always had a cow. In 1961 more than half the families gave up their cows. The Chernyayevs decided to keep their cow no matter what the cost. They used every square metre of their plot and saved every food scrap and bread crust to feed their cow. At night they quietly mowed the sedge on the bog and along the village canal. They often denied themselves to keep their cow alive.

And they hung onto their cow despite everything.

In the 1970s it became easier: you could make hay on waste land. As a forest ranger, Nikolai was allowed to mow hay in the woods. So they bought a second cow.

Their cows have afforded the Chernyayevs all they have, including two cars (a Zhiguli for their son and a Volga for them), a "Russian stove", and money to reconstruct their house. Another benefit is the fresh milk for their grandchildren who stay with them in the summer.

Today the Chernyayevs have four cows, two of them for milk. They don't keep pigs, sheep or poultry. Their plot of land is exclusively used to grow mangel-wurzel and potato. They also grow vegetables and greens for themselves and their sons, who live in the city. Each cow produces at least 5,000 litres of milk a year, twice the country's average yield and not bad as far as private cattle farm standards go.

What are the overheads? They pay nearly 500 roubles per cow for insurance, insemination, the cow herder, mixed feed and so on. They also have to provide all the hay, mangel and potato.

Each Saturday, the Chernyayevs take their produce to the market. Even if the market prices are three times those in the state-run shops, they don't have to spend much time behind the counter. Many of their customers are regulars of ten or twenty years' standing. Some make personal orders for curd the way they like it. In return the customers bring crusts and stale bread for their cows.

Their Saturday takings might be 150-160 roubles, while Nikolai's pay as a forester is 85 roubles and Tonya's pension 62 roubles.

If you consider all the effort that goes into it, you become less enthusiastic about the money. Milking three times a day, cleaning the yard, procuring the feed, keeping up the vegetable plot and attending daily to the milk—a steady string of work without days off or vacations, up at 4:30 in the morning to work through to late night.

For what? Money? Yes, of course. But this work habit is also something you were born with, something which proves wrong those physicists who deny the possibility of perpetual motion.

While we were talking, Nikolai got up from his chair now and again to get rid of the cramp in his feet. "If I don't work, this will get worse," he grumbles.

What do the neighbors say about the Chernyayevs' income, of which they make no secret, and about their brand new Volga and renovated home?

Some may be envious. But no great occasion is complete without them: Nikolai plays the accordion and Tonya is a fine singer. If someone's cow falls sick, or if calving is difficult, they run to fetch Tonya. All in all the attitude of the villagers to the couple is one of concern. "Take it easy, Tonya," her neighbours try to tell her, "give up that cow business. Why not wise up in your old age and take some rest?"

There remain thirty or so cows per one hundred households in Protasovo, and the number has been steadily declining with each year. Milk is delivered to the shop every other day. It is not quite the same as the milk from their own cows, but it is still milk, and costs only 28 kopeks a litre.

Today you can live without keeping a cow. Take my childhood friend Marusya, who used to sell milk in our village and who says she is OK. She was very unhappy when she parted with her cow, while today she never gives it a thought: it's twenty-five years since she was a milkwoman.

How many former milkwomen are there? We can guess the number, because there remain less than 13 million cows in private possession, including those of Tonya. Thank goodness she did not part with her cows despite the harsh campaigns. Instead she has set a glowing example for others, which they can consider when deciding the future of the village.

AIDS

Diagnosis: The Hypodermic. Criminal Negligence by Medical Workers Led to the Infection of Young Children with AIDS
by B. Belitskiy, *Trud*, January 27, 1989

Perhaps it would be appropriate to begin with some emotionally colored phrase: "My blood ran cold" or "the teletype brought horrifying news" . . . But the facts are such that they do not need "embellishing"—merely to report them is horrifying. So let us, for the moment, stick to the bare facts, so to speak, without emotion.

In the city of Elista, at the republican children's hospital, it was discovered that many of the young children being treated are infected with human immunodeficiency virus—AIDS, in short. The initial figures were confirmed by a second, more rigorous investigation. That means that those young lives could be cut short at any moment.

It was discovered quite by chance. At the end of November last year the AIDS prevention laboratory at the Central Scientific Research Institute of Epidemiology in Moscow received a report that a child had been found to be infected with the virus in Kalmykia. Almost simultaneously another report arrived from the same place—about a woman who had presented herself voluntarily to give blood, but was found to be infected. Both the child, with its mother, and the woman were brought into the laboratory for investigation. But the source of infection could not be established in either case. The child's parents were healthy. So was the husband of the infected woman. And—what a coincidence!—suddenly it emerged that she too had a child who died quite recently, and the two little ones were together in two departments of the hospital for nearly a month . . .

"And then," V.V. Pokrovskiy, chief of the AIDS laboratory, says, "we decided to check the other children in those departments, where there were very small children, babes in arms . . . Out of the first series of 19 analyses that were sent to us at our request, 4 were positive. Immediately after the New Year a team from the Epidemiology Institute flew to Elista, and we began to investigate all the children who had been near to these little ones—the one who was infected and the one who died. Every day more infected children were found, and so the number of their neighbors who had to be checked also increased. So far, 300 have been investigated, and 27 have been found to be infected—most of them under the age of 2. The analyses have not yet been completed, they may need to cover around 1,000 children. The sphere of investigations also takes in other hospitals in the republic where all these kids have been treated from time to time—we are talking about children who are very weak and who have spent a large part of their short lives thus far in clinics."

Searching for the cause, they checked all the donors whose blood the young patients had received and 100 medical workers at the hospital—nothing. But when they checked the mothers who had stayed in the department with their children, they found that four of them were infected. A theory sprang up: They were breast-feeding, and the infection could have travelled back from the children through a split in the nipple. This phenomenon had not previously been described anywhere in the world. But no other possibility remained. Out of 12,000 inhabitants of Kalmykia who had been tested for AIDS prior to that time, not one carrier of the virus had been found. And with such a low level of infection in the population, it is impossible that five women should suddenly have appeared in the same place, at the same time, who had picked up the infection somewhere else . . .

"I believe we can say unequivocally that the medical workers and nurses are to blame; they probably used nonsterile hypodermics to inject the children, or else they used the same syringe and only changed the needle, which amounts to the same thing," Academician V.I. Pokrovskiy, director of the Epidemiology Institute, stated. "That means that in all probability we are dealing with an outbreak of hypodermic infection within the hospital. The final answer will emerge only after the investigation that is now beginning, and the trial."

It is hard to believe that medical personnel were almost universally violating all the rules of hygiene. But Ye.N. Belyayev and V.I. Starodubov, chiefs of main administrations at the RSFSR Ministry of Health, cite figures that demonstrate this convincingly. For instance: Out of the annual complement of logbooks in which hypodermic consumption is recorded, only one could be found, for August. The others . . . perished in a "natural disaster"—they got flooded. Nothing can be learned from another log, the one for the sterilization of hypodermics in the department, because although the log exists, there are no entries in it. According to the figures provided by the republican health and epidemiology station, last year instruments that were recorded as being sterile were not in fact sterile in 14 percent of cases. And that is just one of a long line of similar statistics . . .

Those are the facts. Let us try to evaluate them.

There is no need to use many words to describe the despair of parents who surrender their children to the hospital in the hope of a cure, but find themselves facing something irreparable. Of course, anyone can put himself in their place, with horror. Our words will be useful for something else: to find out the source of our astonishing, foolhardy laxity that does not let us down even in the face of mortal danger, and where it develops. And it is not only a question of laxity.

Compassion, concern for others, the heartfelt longing to help people in trouble—these are certainly signs of a moral, civilized society. For many years, alas, we strutted around persuading ourselves that we had created the "new man." Meanwhile morality was flouted, while ostentation and servility were encouraged, leading to irresponsibility and mass indifference to everything. An appropriate slogan even appeared: "The most important thing in our day is not to lose your equanimity."

The cynicism that was instilled over the decades can produce nothing but more cynicism. Can we be surprised at the irresponsibility, equanimity, and cynicism of medical workers who calmly dispatch beyond the pale of life little ones whose only sin in this world is a soiled diaper? No, we should not be surprised. We should try to grasp what to do next.

To this end, I would like to remind the readers of a few things. On 1 December last year, in the article "Portrait of the Enemy," devoted to the problems of combating AIDS, we cited as an example of striking laxity the resolution of the then (in 1985) deputy minister of health and USSR chief state health inspector, Academician P. Burgasov, on the first item on AIDS that was compiled for TRUD from American sources. Imposing a ban, he wrote: ". . . The roots of its spread are the American and Western way of life, unrestrained and flourishing homosexuality. This item is not necessary, it will misinform and frighten the Soviet reader. Who needs a vaccine? Who should be inoculated?"

The other day we received an angry letter from the offended academician. He insists: Yes, the main means by which the AIDS virus spreads is homosexual relations, and nothing else is significant. The editorial office asked a group of scientists to review the letter. Because of the lack of space, I will not quote verbatim their opinion, which is based on weighty statistics and the conclusions of the WHO. It will be sufficient to say that the "Burgasov theory" arouses nothing but perplexity and extreme regret. All the recent cases of AIDS infection—in Leningrad and Odessa, and now in Elista, when women and children suffered, show that the virus did not obey Burgasov's instructions, and is already actively circulating not somewhere overseas, but here at home. But we are not yet ready to seriously combat it. The reason for the laggardness is laxity and the games of "ideological struggle" engaged in by those who should instead, by virtue of their professional duty (I cannot bring myself to write "according to their conscience as doctors"), be sounding the alarm. "Who needs a vaccine? Who should be inoculated?" the chief state health inspector passionately cried . . . The parents of the little patients at the Elista hospital could explain it to him very clearly today.

Did P. Burgasov have to answer for these impassioned remarks that had such bitter reverberations? No, he was removed from his post for something entirely different, but he is still active at sessions of the USSR Academy of Medical Sciences and is not giving ground; on the contrary, he is gaining ground: He has transferred to a job at the USSR Ministry of Medical and Biological Industry. As a consultant. On AIDS problems, perhaps?

It looks very much like it. After all, this ministry—as well as the USSR Ministry of Instrument Making, Automation Equipment, and Control Systems, incidentally—has responsibility for the production of disposable syringes and spectrophotometers, and (sole responsibility, in this case) for the production of test systems used to detect the virus. The leaders of both departments made all kinds of excuses in their attempt to explain to the newspaper, after criticism, why there is an acute shortage of the first, the second, and the third! Nonetheless, there were no syringes, and there still are virtually none: Having failed to reach agreement with associates or organize their own production, the two ministries . . . buy them for foreign currency. Naturally, there is not very much of that available, and naturally what is purchased is hardly likely to get as far as Elista.

I don't know about anyone else, but I found these excuses insulting. Because at about the same time that the replies came in from the ministries, a comrade told me how, while working in Czechoslovakia, he went to the veterinarian to have his dog injected. You've guessed it, reader? Of course! The dog was treated with a disposable syringe, which then went straight into the garbage can . . . Is the juxtaposition of these two facts not an insult to morality, common sense, and patriotism? And ultimately to a parent's feelings? Once again I invite you to imagine you are in Elista . . .

But I am not only inviting you to weep with the mothers and fathers who suffered this terrible blow. I also want us to take a little trip into the future, that future that the two aforementioned ministries paint for us in the promises. Let us suppose that the day has come when everything medicine asks for is available. Hypodermic syringes, needles, instruments, equipment, drugs . . . So will the Kamlyk story then be impossible?

Alas, I do not believe in that bright future. Let us give a disposable syringe to that same nurse who only yesterday did not give a damn about professional duty or the sterilizer. Where is the guarantee that tomorrow she will not start injecting the kids repeatedly with one disposable syringe and selling the rest, say, to drug addicts? There is no guarantee. Just as there was none in Leningrad or Odessa . . .

Belitskiy on How, Where AIDS Virus Originated
Moscow World Service, March 11, 1989

Moscow World Service in English at 1031 GMT on 11 March broadcasts an item during which Boris Belitskiy answers the latest batch of listeners' questions about AIDS. The questions are read by an unidentified announcer. Belitskiy replies to a U.S. listener's question on how many cases of AIDS exist in the USSR, saying: "Some 20 foreigners and 30 Soviet citizens have been found to be AIDS carriers. The actual number of people who have developed the disease does not exceed 40. A screening of 1 million blood donors revealed only 1 AIDS case." Belitskiy goes on to say that well over 10,000 people have applied for AIDS tests; a few of them were found to be infected—5 Soviet citizens and 10 foreigners.

The announcer says that several listeners have asked about the theory that AIDS is a man-made virus and if there are any facts to support it. Boris Belitskiy replies: "Several U.S. Administration officials, such as USIA Director Charles Wick, have accused the Soviet Union of having invented this theory for propaganda purposes. But actually it is not Soviet scientists at all who first came up with this theory. It was first reported in Western journals by Western scientists, such as Dr. John Seale, a specialist on venereal diseases at two big London hospitals and one of the first scientists to point to the viral nature of AIDS."

The announcer asks if there has been any new evidence lately to support this theory. Belitskiy says: "Just recently a Soviet journalist in Algeria, Aleksandr Zhukov, managed to interview a European physician at the Moustapha Hospital there, who made some relevant disclosures on the subject. In the early seventies, this physician and immunologist was working for the West German Otrag Corporation in Zaire. His laboratory had been given the assignment to cultivate viruses ordinarily affecting only animals but constituting a potential danger to man. They were particularly interested in certain unknown viruses isolated from the African green monkey, and capable of such rapid replication that they could completely destabilize the immune system. These viruses, however, were quite harmless for human beings and the lab's assignment was to develop a mutant virus that would be a human killer."

The announcer asked: "Did they succeed?"

Belitskiy replies: "To a large extent, yes. But when they innoculated the inhabitants of several jungle villages with such a mutant virus on the pretext of giving shots against cholera, this did not produce the immediate results required of the lab. Now, it is well-known that people infected with the AIDS virus can live for several years without developing the disease but at the same time the result was summed up as proving the unsuitability of the virus as a biological warfare agent. The lab was ordered to wind up the project and turn the results over to certain U.S. researchers, who had been following this work with keen interest, to such an extent that some of the researchers believed they were in reality working not for the West German Otrag Corporation but for the Pentagon. In fact, two U.S. assistants had been with the lab throughout the work on this project. Several years after the lab had turned over its findings to the Americans, back came the news of the first AIDS cases in San Francisco. The researcher believes that the Pentagon had tested the mutant virus on convicts in California.

ALCOHOLISM

Alcohol Output to Increase to "Prevent Turmoil"
by Nikita Demidov, *Tass*, February 29, 1988

The number of road accidents resulting from drunken driving last year fell by 6,000, or 14 percent, and the rate of deaths due to heavy drinking in the past two years plummeted by 52 percent, a senior militia officer said here today. Major-General Vyacheslav Ogorodnikov, first deputy chief of the Soviet Interior Ministry's main directorate for protecting public order, was speaking at a news conference on the results of the anti-drink drive since anti-alcoholism legislation was enacted in 1985.

Describing the increasingly hard line taken on illegal home brewing, he said more than 500,000 people, or twice as many as in 1986 and 13 times as many as in 1984, were brought to administrative and criminal responsibility for moonshining last year.

The scope of illicit distilling exceeds that of government-run operations by 40 to 50 percent.

The sharp reduction of liquor production (by 44 percent, as compared with 1984) has led to a situation where 3.6 million liters of home brew and 167,000 home stills were confiscated in the country last year.

It has not been decided, the general said, to somewhat increase the output of some categories of alcoholic drinks, including brandy, grape wines and beer, so as to prevent unhealthy turmoil.

ALIENATION

Letter from Teacher N. Radyakin: "Tell the Truth and Only the Truth . . ."
Komsomolskaya Pravda, November 5, 1988

Novokuznetsk—I am following attentively the progress of restructuring, but a sense of my own powerlessness rarely leaves me here.

The halfheartedness of decisions taken on high. We are emphasizing economic accountability [khozraschet] but there is no material basis for it—for instance the sale, and not the distribution, of the means of production and raw material. Ecological questions have arisen in all their magnitude and binding documents with the force of orders are adopted, yet the real results are minimal. Indeed, where could real results come from if enterprises and sectors have no economic interest in nature conservation, after all they are made answerable not for people's health but for the plan fulfillment percentage!

We speak of the democratization of the political system and we are taking real steps, but it seems to me, for instance, that the uniting of the posts of first secretary and chairman of the soviet of deputies is also more like autocracy than democracy. Perhaps I fail to understand something, but in my opinion we have already had this.

And quite recently. And again. For how long will people in our country be afraid of criticizing their top leaders? Perhaps these are trivial details. But they often have decisive importance. Yet on the whole I trust Comrade Gorbachev and I believe that he will be able to lead our country out of failure. (Believe me, I did not add that phrase "for safety's sake").

The party itself should set an example of real glasnost. It seems to me abnormal that in many respects internal work in the party organizations is "classified." And what is a "party secret" anyway? A secret from whom, from its own people? The CPSU is the sole and ruling party. Therefore everything taking place in it affects everyone—him and me. Glasnost should exist primarily within the party itself, in the Politburo, in the Central Committee, and in the primary organization. Otherwise the party will not become closer to the people and the slogan "the people and the party are united" will remain an empty sound.

Now about my own powerlessness. I can feel it almost physically in the solution of any important questions of our life. The only thing within my power is to work honestly—if I make a mistake in my work the harm will be relatively small. But when a "big," important person makes a mistake? How can I influence him as long as these people, in my opinion, are in no way dependent on ordinary people, on simple citizens? The elections of deputies are still fictitious, at any rate in our region. Leaders live their lives, in a kind of "twilight." They have their own circle of people needed for communication, their own sources of supply (I do not believe they stand in line), and their own transport, most often official transport. How can this be changed, how can we achieve a situation where they really live the life of the people? After all in the final analysis where people are to live, what kind of air there will be in the city, and what there will be in the stores largely depends on these enterprise, city, and regional leaders. Believe me, it is not the envy of an aggrieved man in the street which is talking, no. It is simply that I cannot rest for asking the question: What can I do?

And finally one last point. Fear. I considered how to sign myself: Using a false name or only my initials . . .

—N. Radyakin, teacher,
24 years old

N. ANDREYEVA

Nina Andreyeva "Letter to the Editorial Office from a Leningrad VUZ Lecturer" under the rubric "Polemics": "I Cannot Waive Principles"
Sovetskaya Rossiya, March 13, 1988

THE FOLLOWING "letter to the editor" appeared to the Soviet reader as an indication that glasnost was running into serious— Stalinist—trouble. There was intense speculation that the letter was really the work of Mr. Ligachev, known to be at the core of hard-line opposition to Gorbachev's policies of liberalization and de-Stalinization. For three weeks after the letter was published—Gorbachev was out of the country—the entire country held its metaphorical breath, and glasnost shut down as peoople waited to see which side would predominate. Andreyeva/Ligachev apparently lost, and glasnost continued, albeit in a lurching fashion. The legacy of the episode, however, was one of continued caution as it became quite evident that glasnost was not yet institutionalized or legitimated as ongoing "irreversible" policy.

I decided to write this letter after lengthy deliberation. I am a chemist and I lecture at Leningrad's Lensovet Technology Institute. Like many others, I also look after a student group. Students nowadays, following the period of social apathy and intellectual dependence, are gradually being charged with the energy of revolutionary changes. Naturally, discussions develop: About the ways of restructuring and its economic and ideological aspects. Glasnost, openness, the disappearance of zones where criticism is taboo, and the emotional heat in mass consciousness, especially among young people, often emerge in the raising of problems which are, to a greater or lesser extent, "prompted" either by Western radio voices or by those of our compatriots who are shaky in their conceptions of the essence of socialism. And the variety of topics that are being discussed! A multiparty system, freedom of religious propaganda, emigration to live abroad, the right to broad discussion of sexual problems in the press, the need to decentralize the leadership of culture, abolition of compulsory military service ... There are particularly numerous arguments among students about the country's past.

Of course, we lecturers have to answer the most controversial questions and this demands, in addition to honesty, also knowledge, conviction, broad cultural horizons, serious reflection, and considered opinions. Moreover, these qualities are needed by all educators of young people and not only by members of social science department staffs.

The Petergof Park is a favorite spot for the strolls I take with my students. We stroll along the snow-covered paths, enjoy looking at the famous palaces and statues, and—we argue. We do argue! The young souls are eager to investigate all complexities and to map out their path into the future. I look at my ardent young interlocutors and I think to myself how important it is to help them discover the truth and shape a correct perception of the problems of the society in which they live and which they will have to restructure, and how to give them a correct perception of our historical past, both distant and recent.

What are the misgivings? Here is a simple example: You would think that plenty has been written and said about the Great Patriotic War and the heroism of those who fought in it. Recently, however, a student hostel in our Technology Institute organized a meeting with Hero of the Soviet Union Colonel of the Reserve V.F. Molozeyev. Among other things, he was asked a question about political repressions in the army. The veteran replied that he had never come across any repressions and that many of those who fought in the war with him from its beginning to its end became high-ranking military leaders. . . . Some were disappointed by this reply. Now that it has become topical, the subject of repressions has been blown out of all proportion in some young people's imagination and overshadows any objective interpretation of the past. Examples like this are by no means isolated.

It is, of course, extremely gratifying that even "technicians" are keenly interested in theoretical problems of the social sciences. But I can neither accept nor agree with all too much of what has now appeared. Verbiage about "terrorism," "the people's political servility," "uninspired social vegetation," "our spiritual slavery," "universal fear," "dominance by boors in power" . . . These are often the only yarns used to weave the history of our country during the period of the transition to socialism. It is, therefore, not surprising that nihilistic sentiments are intensifying among some students and there are instances of ideological confusion, loss of political bearings, and even ideological omnivorousness. At times you even hear claims that the time has come to take Communists to task for having allegedly "dehumanized" the country's life since 1917.

The Central Committee February Plenum emphasized again the insistent need to ensure that "young people are taught a class-based vision of the world and understanding of the links between universal and class interests. Including understanding of the class essence of the changes occurring in our country." Such a vision of history and of the present is incompatible with the political anecdotes, base gossip, and controversial fantasies which one often encounters today. . . .

Take for example the question of I. V. Stalin's position in our country's history. The whole obsession with critical attacks is linked with his name and, in my opinion, this obsession centers not so much on the historical individual itself as on the entire highly complex epoch of transition. An epoch linked with unprecedented feats by a whole generation of Soviet people who are today gradually withdrawing from active labor, political, and social work. **The industrialization, collectivization, and cultural revolution which brought our country to the ranks of great world powers are being forcibly squeezed into the "personality cult" formula. All this is being questioned.** Matters have gone so far that persistent demands for "repentance" are being made of "Stalinists" (and this category can be taken to include anyone you like). . . . There is rapturous praise for novels and movies which lynch the epoch of storms and onslaught, which is presented as a "tragedy of the peoples."

. . . Let me say right away that neither I nor any members of my family are in any way involved with Stalin, his retinue, his associates, or his extollers. My father was a worker at Leningrad Port, my mother was a fitter at the Kirov Plant. My elder brother also worked there. He, my father, and my sister died in battles against the Hitlerites. One of my relatives was repressed and then rehabilitated after the 20th party congress. I share all Soviet people's anger and indignation about the mass repressions which occurred in the thirties and forties and for which the party-state leadership of the time is to blame. But common sense resolutely protests against the monochrome depiction of contradictory events which now dominates in some press organs.

I support the party call to uphold the honor and dignity of the trailblazers of socialism. I think that these are the party-class positions from which we must assess the historical role of all leaders of the party and the country, including Stalin. In this case, matters cannot be reduced to their "court" aspect or to abstract moralizing by persons far removed both from those stormy times and from the people who had to live and work in those times. And to work in such a fashion as to still be an inspiring example for us today.

For me, as for many people, a decisive role in my assessment of Stalin is played by the candid testimony of contemporaries who clashed directly with him both on our side of the barricades and on the other side. It is the latter that are quite interesting. For instance, take Churchill, who, back in 1919, boasted of his personal contribution to organizing the military intervention by 14 foreign states against the young Soviet republic and, exactly

40 years later, was forced to use the following words to describe Stalin, one of his formidable political opponents:

"He was an outstanding personality who left his mark on our cruel time during his lifetime. Stalin was a man of exceptional energy, erudition, and unbending willpower, harsh, tough, and ruthless in both action and conversation and even I, brought up in the English Parliament, could not oppose him in any way. . . . A gigantic force resounded in his works. This force is so great in Stalin that he seemed unique among the leaders of all times and all peoples. . . . His effect on people is irresistible. Whenever he entered the Yalta conference hall, we all rose as if by command. And, strangely, we all stood to attention. Stalin possessed a profound, totally unflappable, logical, and sensible wisdom. He was a past master at finding a way out of the most hopeless situation at a difficult time. . . . He was a man who used his enemies to destroy his enemy, forcing us—whom he openly called imperialists—to fight the imperialists. . . . He took over a Russia still using the wooden plow, and left it equipped with atomic weapons." This assessment and admission by the loyal custodian of the British Empire cannot be attributed to either pretense or political timeserving.

The main elements of this description can also be seen in the memoirs of De Gaulle and the reminiscences and correspondence of other European and American politicians who had dealings with Stalin both as wartime ally and as class adversary.

Considerable serious food for thought on this question is provided by Soviet documents which are available to anyone wishing to consult them. Take the two-volume "Correspondence Between the Chairman of the USSR Council of Ministers and the U.S. Presidents and British Prime Ministers During the Great Patriotic War, 1941-1945," published by the Political Literature Publishing House back in 1957. There is no doubt that these documents evoke pride in our state and its position and role in a stormy and changing world. I recall the anthology of Stalin's reports, speeches, and orders dating from the last war on which the heroic generation of the victors of fascism was raised. It could perfectly well be reissued to include documents which were secret at the time, like the dramatic order No 227, which some historians are indeed pressing for. Our young people are familiar with none of these documents. Particular importance for the cultivation of historical awareness attaches to the memoirs of military leaders Zhukov, Vasilevskiy, Golovanov, and Shtemenko and aircraft designer Yakovlev, who all knew the Supreme Commander personally.

There is no question that this period was extremely harsh. But is also true that personal modesty bordering upon asceticism did not feel ashamed of itself and that potential Soviet millionaires were still afraid to peck away in the quiet of minor offices and trading centers. Furthermore, we were not so businesslike and pragmatic and prepared young people not for the finer points of consuming wealth accumulated by their parents but for Labor and Defense, without demolishing young people's spiritual world with masterpieces imported from "the other side" or home-grown imitations of mass culture. Imaginary relatives were in no hurry to invite their fellow-tribesmen to "the promised land," turning them into "refuseniks" of socialism.

Long and frank conversations with young interlocutors lead us to the conclusion that the attacks on the state of the dictatorship of the proletariat and our country's leaders at the time have not only political, ideological, and moral causes but also a social substratum. There are quite a few people interested in expanding the bridge-head for these attacks, and they are to be found not just on the other side of our borders. Along with professional anticommunists in the West who picked the supposedly democratic slogan of "anti-Stalinism" a long time ago, the offspring of the classes overthrown by the October Revolution, by no means all of whom have managed to forget the material and social losses incurred by their forebears, are still alive and prospering. . . .

I was puzzled recently by the revelation by one of my students that the class struggle is supposedly an obsolete term, just like the leading role of the proletariat. It would be fine if she were the only one to claim this. A furious agrument was generated, for example, by a respected academician's recent assertion that present-day relations between states from the two different socioeconomic systems apparently lack any class content. I assume that the academician did not deem it necessary to explain why it was that, for several decades, he wrote exactly the opposite—namely that peaceful coexistence is nothing but a form of class struggle in the international arena. It seems that the philosopher has now rejected this view. Never mind, people can change their minds. It does seem to me, however, that duty would nevertheless command a leading philosopher to explain at least to those who have studied and are studying his books: What is happening today, does the international working class no longer oppose world capital as embodied in its state and political organs?

The first and most swollen ideological current which has

already manifested itself in the course of restructuring claims to offer a model of some sort of left-wing liberal intellectual socialism which allegedly expresses the most genuine humanism, "cleansed" of class accretions. Its champions counter proletarian collectivism with the "intrinsic value of the individual"—modernistic quests in the cultural sphere, God-seeking tendencies, technocratic idols, homilies to the "democratic" charms of contemporary capitalism, and kowtowing to its real and supposed achievements. Its spokesmen claim that what we have built is supposedly not proper socialism, and that apparently "an alliance between political leadership and progressive intelligentsia has been formed for the first time in history" only today . . .

It is the champions of "left-wing liberal socialism" who shape the tendency toward falsifying the history of socialism. **They try to make us believe that the country's past was nothing but mistakes and crimes, keeping silent about the greatest achievements of the past and the present.** Claiming full possession of historical truth, they replace the sociopolitical criterion of society's development with scholastic ethical categories. I would very much like to know who needed to ensure and why that every prominent leader of the party Central Committee and the Soviet Government—once out of office—was compromised and discredited because of actual and alleged mistakes and errors committed when solving the most complex problems in the course of historical trail-blazing? Where are the origins of this passion of ours to undermine the prestige and dignity of leaders of the world's first socialist country?

Another peculiarity of the views held by "left-wing liberals" is an overt or covert cosmopolitan tendency, some kind of non-national "internationalism." I read somewhere about an incident after the revolution when a delegation of merchants and factory owners called on Trotskiy at the Petrograd Soviet "as a Jew" to complain about oppression by the Red Guards, and he declared that he was "not a Jew but an internationalist," which really puzzled petitioners.

In Trotskiy's views, the idea of "national" connoted a certain inferiority and limitation compared with the "international." This is why he emphasized October's "national tradition," wrote about "the national element in Lenin," claimed that the Russian people "had inherited no cultural heritage at all," and so on. We are somehow embarrassed to say that it was indeed the Russian proletariat, whom the Trotskiyites treated as "backward and uncultured," who accomplished—in Lenin's words—"three Russian revolutions" and that the Slav peoples stood in the vanguard of mankind's battle against fascism.

This, of course, is not to denigrate the historical contribution of other nations and ethnic groups. This, as it is said nowadays, is only to ensure the full historical truth. . . . When students ask me how come thousands of small villages in the non-Chernozem Zone and Siberia are deserted, I reply that this is part of the high price we had to pay for victory and the postwar restoration of the national economy, just like the irretrievable loss of large numbers of monuments of Russian national culture. I am also convinced: Any denigration of the importance of historical consciousness produces a pacifist erosion of defense and patriotic consciousness, as well as a desire to categorize the slightest expressions of Great Russian national pride as manifestations of great power chauvinism.

Here is something else that also worries me: The practice of "refusenikism" of socialism is nowadays linked with militant cosmopolitanism. Unfortunately, we remember it suddenly only when its neophytes plague us with their outrages in front of the Smolnyy or by the Kremlin walls. Moreover, we are gradually being trained to perceive the aforementioned phenomenon as some sort of almost innocent change of "place of residence" rather than as class and national betrayal by persons most of whom graduated from VUZ's and completed their postgraduate studies thanks to our own nationwide funds. **Generally speaking, some people are inclined to look upon "refusenikism" as some sort of manifestation of "democracy" and the "rights of man," whose talents were prevented from flourishing by "stagnant socialism."** And if it so happens that people over there, in the "free world," fail to appreciate bubbling entrepreneurship and "genius" and the special services are not interested in the trading of conscience, one can always return. . . .

It seems to me that the question of the role and position of socialist ideology is extremely acute today. The authors of timeserving articles under the guise of moral and spiritual "cleansing" erode the dividing lines and criteria of scientific ideology, manipulate glasnost, and foster nonsocialist pluralism, which objectively applies the brakes on restructuring in the public conscience. This has a particularly painful effect on young people, which, I repeat, is clearly sensed by us VUZ lecturers, schoolteachers, and all who have to deal with young people's problems. As M.S. Gorbachev said at the CPSU Central Committee February Plenum, "our actions in the spiritual sphere—

and maybe primarily and precisely there—must be guided by our Marxist-Leninist principles. Principles, comrades, must not be compromised on any pretext whatever."

This is what we stand for now, this is what we will continue to stand for. Principles were not given to us as a gift, we have fought for them at crucial turning points in the fatherland's history.

Struggling and Believing
by Aleksandr Levikov, *Moscow News*, March 27, 1988

When we take a pen in hand or join a discussion, we always present ourselves as advocates of perestroyka—regardless of whether we are or not. I've never met anyone who spoke out against perestroyka. Those who urge that Stalinism be exposed and those who ascribe resounding victories to Stalinism, those who advocate the socialist market and those who reject the market economy as a threat to socialism, those who vote for a consistent type of democracy and those who say democracy will lead to "impending anarchy"—they all pledge allegiance to perestroyka.

What is one to make of it?

I don't think there is something unnatural going on. In the past we often judged our unity solely on the basis of this monopoly of official opinion. The first, even furtive taste of glasnost established that we are all different. We want something "different" varies from one person to the next. These social contradictions aren't new to us, they've simply stopped being an area where people fear to tread. History and how to proceed are the topics of heated discussions and debate. These discussions have revealed many different groups—even groups within groups. A struggle between "advocates and advocates" (not just "advocates and opponents") is inevitable in the process of perestroyka, even necessary. But what sort of struggle should it be?

According to Nina Andreyeva—in her long letter "I can't give up my principles" to *Sovetskaya Rossiya* (March 13)—this struggle should be viewed from the dogmatic position of "aggravating the class struggle". Once this approach provided a theoretical basis for repressions, but Andreyeva even today sees "enemy" intrigues in critiques of Stalinism, rather than the intellectual rebirth of a nation after the tragic events in its history, or the deep-seated need to squeeze the slave out of the people, to free them from the fear and submissiveness cultivated with demagoguery and terror.

ANTI-SEMITISM

Lexical Nuance
by Boris Berman, *Moscow News*, March 6, 1988

Who is Zurab Tsintsadze? You don't know him? Naturally. He lives, let's say, in Kutaisi. So what is he? An engineer? Probably. A worker? Quite possible. But on top of everything else he is a "person of Georgian nationality". Rubbish, you will say, this Tsintsadze is a Georgian—not a "person of Georgian nationality". And you will be right. In this sense everything is simple regarding all the nationalities inhabiting our multinational country. With one exception.

Reading newspapers, listening to the radio and watching televison, one discovers that our country is populated not by Jews, but by "persons of Jewish nationality". This is the kind of lexical nuance we have. Therefore, it appears, I am also a "person of Jewish nationality". Like my late father who fought through the whole war and became a party member at the front, like my mother and sister and her six-year-old daughter. . . .

This is not a linguistic question. The lexicon, as we all know, is nourished by life and its realities. So from whence did this red-tapism enter into our life? In whose hearing mustn't one say "simply" Jews? Who has offended whom and in what respect?

This term, "person of Jewish nationality", was widely used at the end of the 1960s and beginning of the 1970s when many Jews went abroad to be reunited with their relatives. Some of them really wanted to be reunited, but others profited by the "wave" to quit the country. For various reasons. But there were consequences. One of them was this term invented evidently by some official representative who, wittingly or otherwise, expressed his scorn for those who had left. The expression was extended to those who never even planned to leave. When they were referred to as "persons of Jewish nationality" in their own country, doubts inevitably sprang up in the mass consciousness as to the loyalty of these "persons".

And yet, I think, these are merely events on the surface. If we trace the plot back, it will lead, I believe, to the early 1950s. The clumsy formula-euphemism recalls other euphemisms for those "persons" ("displaced" ones, for example) whom Stalin's bureaucratic machine flatly denied the privilege of loyalty. Much, you will agree, too much is still with us from those times. I don't know whether the choreographers of the "doctors' case" wanted to implant the "presumption of guilt" with respect to the Jews in people's minds, but they largely succeeded regardless. Only recently my mother told me about the nasty looks people gave her in a store where she had come with me, then five, the morning newspapers reported the arrest of Vovsi and other "doctors-wreckers".... The "doctors' case" was settled a long time ago, but the term "persons of Jewish nationality" is still being given wide currency.

Even in *Moscow News*, in an article entitled "Shadows Off Screen" criticizing the jingoistic views of leaders of the Pamyat society, the Jews are again referred to as—of all things—"persons . . ."

Once I came across a documentary episode dating back to the Patriotic War. Two popular singers, who became members of a partisan detachment, "legalized" themselves on occupied territory, gave concerts and, naturally, fulfilled combat missions. Both died deaths of heroes. Both were Muscovites—one was a Russian and the other a Jew. When I shared my intention to write a script with a well-known scriptwriter whom I sincerely respected, he began to persuade me—with cautious kindness, like his own son—not to touch that theme.

And persuade me he did. I am still ashamed when I think of this. I feel ashamed both in respect to myself and in respect to the memory of those who, defending my Motherland, were in a single formation with all the peoples of this nation. There were no "persons of Jewish nationality": the formation was made up of Soviet people.

As far as that theme is concerned, there were those who, thank goodness, were not scared by it. Much has already been written about Aleksandr Askoldov's film "Commissar" in which Yefim Magazannik dreams about a "kind international". Magazannik is a Jewish tinsmith, whose poor family is entered—not without some difficulty—by a Russian woman, Klavdiya Vavilova, a stern commissar of the civil war. Banned for twenty years, "Commissar" is now being released. Justice triumphs beyond all doubt. But reading a thorough, clever review of the film in a popular youth newspaper, I find no mention of the family Vavilova joined or the nation she discovered for herself. I phoned the author of the review (we are good friends) and it turned out that he had called a spade a spade: Russians were called Russians, and Jews—Jews. What tactical considerations guided the editor, when he crossed out all the references to "Jews" and replaced them with the abstract "people"?

We, of course (as a TV humorist brilliantly put it), do "more reading between the lines than any other people in the world". But isn't it time to give up this dubious priority? There are no abstract "people". Every one of us is such as he is—with his own name, his own profile and colour of eyes. Which is why we are people. "Little cogs" alone are abstract. But we have already studied this, we have already been given this name. Little depends on "little cogs", but everything depends on people. And if we're fighting for the new thinking, let's not forget about lexical nuances. People are behind them.

All of us are co-citizens. What a remarkable word. What a weighty meaning a mere two letters impart to it.

Pamyat's Vasilev: Jews, Zionism "Evil Force"
Interview with Pamyat leader Dmitriy Vasilev by Fiammetta Cucurnia in Moscow, *La Republica*, February 26, 1988

Moscow—Pamyat (Memory) is the strongest of the approximately 30,000 unofficial organizations whose existence in the USSR is acknowledged by *Pravda*. It seems to be the only one now with the potential to become a genuine mass opposition party. Perhaps this is why it is the most feared and publicly attacked. Nevertheless it is constantly winning new members. Indeed, its undisputed leader, Vasilev, says that "whenever any Soviet newspaper publishes an article criticizing Pamyat we gain more members." It is often criticized by *Pravda*, which describes it as "a group of extremists that incite national hostilities." It is feared, criticized, and opposed by prominent newspapers representing Gorbachev's restructuring policy, from *Moskovskiye Novosti* and *Ogonek*, which accuse it of petty anti-Semitism, and by *Znamya*, which describes it as an organization that "actually discredits restructuring." They deny it, however, and describe themselves as "strong supporters of restructuring."

It was not easy to find them or, rather, to track them down. Pamyat does not seek out foreigners, does not seek publicity abroad. Their battleground is here at home, in the Great Russia where, Vasilev says, "we will fight until the last drop of blood." Before receiving us he sought guarantees that we were not "dirty liars in the pay of cosmopolitans and of the U.S. dollar." Eventually, however, he did admit us to his home, which is where most of the group's meetings take place.

CUCURNIA: Tell me, Mr. Vasilev, how many members does Pamyat have?

VASILEV: There are approximately 20,000 monitored members, that is, members that we are able to monitor. Each of them has his own circle, however. If the state were to register us normally, there would be millions of us.

CUCURNIA: How do you manage to maintain contacts between the organization and members throughout the country?

VASILEV: That sounds like a KGB-type question. I will answer you by saying that we maintain only personal contacts, partly because an outright campaign of persecution is being organized against us. Pamyat members are being expelled from the Komsomol and party and bear in mind that there are numerous party members in Pamyat's ranks. They prevent us from speaking on television and from holding public meetings with the press. It is because they fear us.

CUCURNIA: What is your platform?

VASILEV: We want to tackle and resolve the problems of our nation, by which I mean the Russian nation, since Pamyat was born in Russia. In fact these problems are international problems since there are evil forces that would like to build their power on the ruins of the world's loftiest cultures. So whereas Lenin once said "proletarians of the world unite", now Pamyat says "patriots of the world unite." We have reached the conclusion that it is no coincidence that we have been witnessing for years the destruction of our historic monuments, our traditions, and the customs of our peoples—in this specific instance, of the Russian people. There is clearly some evil force wanting to rob the peoples of their memories and their material, historical, and cultural wealth in order to prevent their moral progress.

CUCURNIA: Pardon me, but mankind can certainly not be said to have made no progress in recent years.

VASILEV: I am talking about moral development, not technological and scientific development, which is in fact a blind alley for mankind. It is technological and scientific progress that creates weapons. It is technological and scientific progress that brings closer the time of a sudden conflagration that will engulf us. Chernobyl has taught us this. This is why we are struggling for the protection of the environment, which is mankind's living space, against nuclear energy and against alcohol, which has inebriated the Russian people. This is clearly all part of a plan carefully devised by somebody. . . .

CUCURNIA: Who?

VASILEV: A terrible force active here and in your country, trying to destroy our culture—a force of whose existence we became aware during our work to protect Russia's cultural heritage: Zionism and freemasonry.

CUCURNIA: Mr. Vasilev, there is already much confusion in this regard. Please explain: When you say "Zionists" do you mean the Jews?

VASILEV: Yes, always these Jews, as though there were nobody else in the world. The Jews live everywhere, own the capital, live like parasites throughout the world, emigrate freely from country to country, and are always depicted as the most unfortunate nation. Nobody is concerned about the Russian people, who are now the worst off and most unfortunate of all peoples. It is enough to read the "Protocols of the Elders of Zion" to realize who created this situation. However, not all Zionists are Jews and not all Jews are Zionists. This is why we are not anti-Semitic. Tell me, who invented the gas chambers? The Jews. The freemasons, on the other hand, are the material executors of the Zionists' plans. It is a very serious matter. . . .

CUCURNIA: Tell me, what exactly is your attitude toward the Jewish population in the USSR and Moscow?

VASILEV: I will tell you just this: The ideologue of the destruction of our monuments and our culture was Yaroslavskiy, whose real name was Gubelman. He was a Jew. Who carried out this destruction? Kaganovich—a Jew. Moreover, Trotskiy, Zinovyev, and Kamenyev were all Jews.

CUCURNIA: I do not understand.

VASILEV: You do not understand because you do not live here. You do not understand because you do not earn R120 a month, because you are a foreigner. We have nothing against the Jews: There are some decent people even among them. However, our analysis of the facts always confronts us with the Jewish nationality. Were Beria and Yagoda not Jews? Were the administrators of many of the Stalinist prison camps not Jews? We are not anti-Semitic, but the truth must be told. Now 20 percent of the state's leadership posts are held by Jews, who represent only 0.69 percent of the population. This actually goes against the constitution. No less than 50 percent of doctors of science and candidates are Jews too. The majority of members of professional unions—composers, writers, movie makers, jurists, medics, and so forth—are also Jews, and they are supposed to be persecuted. There is never any mention of the persecuted Russians. In any case all Jews who have wanted to do so have emigrated with their pockets full of money, while the Russians have always been, and remain, poor. Nobody is concerned about them.

CUCURNIA: Be that as it may, there are no Jews within the Politburo and Secretariat now.

VASILEV: You are mistaken. I have my suspicions.

CUCURNIA: Sure it is not the case, is it, that Communists, Marxixts, are Zionists?

VASILEV: I did not say that but since you suggest it, I will bear it in mind. . . .

ARMENIA

Telephone interview with *Glasnost* Chief Editor Sergey Grigoryants
by Basile Karlinsky, Paris, *Liberation*, March 11, 1988

LIBERATION: You have just returned from Yerevan. What was the situation on Wednesday evening?

SERGEY GRIGORYANTS: The situation is much more tense than it was in February. The process of radicalization has been very rapid.

LIBERATION: What about the strike scheduled for Friday?

SERGEY GRIGORYANTS: The idea of a 1-hour strike has been superseded. The movement may spread. The Organizing Committee had not made a decision by the time I left Yerevan on Wednesday evening.

LIBERATION: Can we believe the reports given during the meeting last Monday in the Armenian cemetery in Moscow about the atrocities committed by the Azeris?

SERGEY GRIGORYANTS: Yes, but they underestimate the real situation, which is much more terrible. The most unfortunate effect of the anti-Armenian "pogroms" in Azerbaijan is that the

Americans have now lost confidence in the Russians. They say that the Azeris were manipulated, whereas they did not and will not allow themselves to be provoked. It is dangerous to continue discussing this subject on the telephone.

LIBERATION: Were official meetings held in Azerbaijan to stir up the population against the Armenians?

SERGEY GRIGORYANTS: No, but there was a series of provocative programs on Azerbaijani television which constantly stated: "We will never give up the Nagorno-Karabakh." The chairman of the Azerbaijani Writers' Union even stated: "The border (with Armenia—*Liberation* editor's note) is open and those who do not feel comfortable in Nagorno-Karabakh can go home.". . .

LIBERATION: What are the party grass-roots organizations doing?

SERGEY GRIGORYANTS: They are out of their depth and paralyzed, but the leadership is trying to infiltrate the committee in order to take control of it. It is not having much success because the party has lost all authority. It is incapable of formulating proposals likely to be taken up by the Organizing Committee or the grass-roots committees.

LIBERATION: What about the Writers' Union?

SERGEY GRIGORYANTS: It is more active and closer to the people's positions.

LIBERATION: What about the university?

SERGEY GRIGORYANTS: The students are on the same wavelength as the rest of the city. They are participating in all actions but their role will probably increase further.

LIBERATION: What do you expect to happen in the next few days?

SERGEY GRIGORYANTS: Nothing good. Bloodshed is still possible. That must be prevented at all costs. The only thing we can do is report what happens.

Baku, 26 November
by R. Lynev and A. Stepovoy, *Izvestiya*, November 27, 1988

Izvestiya's SPECIAL CORRESPONDENTS arrived in Azerbaijan 25 November. We publish their first report. The first impression is that everything is as it always is in the city. The stores and institutions are open and there are many people in the streets, hurrying about their affairs. But then we reach the first intersection, where

(Sergei Tyunin, *Soviet News*)

armored carriers stand, with soldiers with submachine guns beside them. The closer you come to the center, the more keenly you feel it—the city is, alas, not as it always is. In the center, surface public transport has stopped.

All the approaches to Government House and the adjacent Lenin Square are closed, yet groups of people with flags and banners approach the square itself in an endless stream, on foot and in cars. Many of them, especially the young people, have their hair tied up with red ribbons bearing the legend "Karabakh." Immediately before the square is another cordon. Or rather, two: a chain of soldiers, and in front of them young people controlling the entrance to the square. Some of them have their symbol on their lapels—labels from "Karabakh"-brand cigarettes. They are volunteers. They check everyone who they think looks suspicious. They inspect bags and they asked us to show our passports. Later, we had to produce them on a number of other occasions. Why?

"To prevent provocations," we were told.

Throughout the days leading up to our arrival here, the telephones in the editorial office were buzzing with agitated calls: "Why are you not writing about what is happening in Baku? Why are you hiding the truth from the people?!"

But this is a fact: On arriving in Baku we learned that subscribers did not receive *Izvestiya* for 25 November. The reason? The first short report on the rallies in Azerbaijan and Armenia, the content of which was not to the liking of the workers at the local publishing house and printing plant. Where is the truth; where is glasnost under that kind of censorship?

In Kirovabad people have been wounded. Three servicemen were killed. In connection with this a special situation was imposed in Baku, Kirovabad, and Nakhichevan. An appeal by S.B. Tatliyev, chairman of the Azerbaijan SSR Supreme Soviet Presidium, said that the holding of rallies, demonstrations, and strikes is prohibited at any time of day. . . .

As for the people in the square—they are all different. Guseyn Mamedov, a 28-year-old fire service chief at a plant, explains why he is here in the middle of the working day: "We demand compliance with the law. I do not want a repetition of Sumgait, or of Kirovabad, where blood flowed a few days ago. This time it was the blood of Russian soldiers who had come to maintain order. That is why I am here."

Murat Amirov, until recently a tank man and now a student in the 1st year at the polytechnical institute, says: "I am explaining to everyone that a soldier is not an enemy of our people, but a defender."

Senior Lieutenant Aleksandr Sandalov remembers Sumgait well. He says: "When we were sent here, to Baku, we were afraid it would all happen again. But here the situation is entirely different; everything is organized. People are friendly to the soldiers. It would be nice if we could continue to avoid excesses."

Now, as we write these lines, the voices of successive speakers, amplified by a megaphone, ring out over the square.

Baku, Yerevan: Autumn of Anxiety
by A. Romanov and A. Teplyuk in Baku,
Komsomolskaya Pravda, November 27, 1988

We did not recognize the road from Bina airport. We had never seen anything like it before, except, perhaps, on "International Panorama." Armed patrols, military hardware. But this is still Baku. Here and in several places in the republic there is a special situation. A curfew has been imposed. Rallies, demonstrations, and strikes are banned. But even on the 3d day after the imposition of the special situation, little has changed in this city—many enterprises are not working, transport operations are subject to interruptions, rallies are constantly being held.

On Lenin Square there is a large crowd, with armored carriers forming barriers. There is a strong smell of smoke. When we realize why, we feel slightly relieved. It is not from conflagrations. A dozen camp fires are burning in the square. The square is closely surrounded. The soldiers look impressive: submachine guns, helmets. Despite the late hour and our lack of a special pass, we are able to pass through—by way of a narrow approach guarded by volunteer militia details.

There are comparatively few people outside Government House—about 20,000 (in the daytime there are about half a million). The majority of them are spending the whole night here. Tents, stacks of firewood, a cluster of people around the camp fires. Suddenly, as if at a signal, the surroundings shake as tens of thousands of people chant the word "Karabakh!"

Some stern-looking guys (they have combat orders and medals on their green parkas) carefully check our documents. Someone volunteers to escort us—a young historian. Several more people come up to us. And we immediately start hearing complaints about all the central press—for its long silence and for its coverage of events in connection with Nagorno-Karabakh, which is not the kind of coverage our new acquaintances would like.

Further into the square there is a kind of center. It is a tent where those taking part in the rally have their headquarters. It operates round the clock. Our guide calls in there for permission, gets the "go-ahead," and leads us to another, bigger tent. It is enclosed by benches and access to it is barred by an unofficial patrol. We are told that six young Azerbaijanis began a hunger strike here on 17 November. On folding beds in the tent there are four guys (we were told that the student Aida

Zulfigarova and the worker Akif Aliyev called off their hunger strike because of their deteriorating health and the admonitions of their relatives, and are now in the hospital). The other four—Faramaz Allakhverdiyev, Rafaddin Nuriyev, Aliaga Iskenderov, and Elshan Kuliyev—have so far resisted the pleas of their parents, clergymen, and participants in the rally.

A brief interview with F. Allakhverdiyev. He looks a little brighter than the others.

"When the American Professor Hyder was on hunger strike, the central newspapers wrote about it every day. We have been on hunger strike for 9 days, drawing attention to the fact that the Nagornyy Karabakh problem is not being resolved, but no interest is being shown in us," Faramaz says in an injured tone.

For all the babble, the square lives according to laws of its own. Thousands of people obey the man with the megaphone. At a words from him, a table was laid for us next to the hunger strikers' tent, and we were fed well. Food is free for those taking part in the rally.

There is a special situation in the city. But it apparently does not extend to the central square. We recognize the former "Afghaners" from afar by their erect figures. They have come here at a difficult time to help ensure order. As soon as more than five or six people begin to gather around us, the "Afghaners" tactfully ask the curious to more on. We are completely safe here.

But alas, the same cannot be said confidently of absolutely all the inhabitants of Baku. In Lenin Square hundreds of thousands of people have sworn a solemn oath: Nothing will make them take an ill-considered step, and emotion will not prevail over reason. But the words of the oath did not reach everyone: Several dozen drivers who went out on the roads were stopped.

The trigger for the deterioration in the situation, *Azerinform* explained, was the start on construction of a branch of the Armenian SSR's Kanakerskiy Aluminum Plant in the village of Topkhana on the territory of Nagorno-Karabakh Autonomous Oblast. As activists in the square told us, this place is a site of historic and national significance for the Azerbaijanis. Be that as it may, according to the latest reports from the autonomous oblast construction work and the shipment of materials to Topkhana have been stopped.

There are still many rumors about the tragic events in Kirovabad, where as a result of disturbances 3 servicemen died and at least 160 inhabitants sought medical help. *Azerinform* has refuted rumors that the disorders began after "a small girl died after falling under an armored carrier." No such incident occurred.

It must be noted that relations between the inhabitants of Baku and the servicemen are markedly friendly. We saw this for ourselves, observing many scenes of peaceful conversation in the city streets.

But it would be wrong to conclude with this reassuring picture. The situation remains serious.

Izvestiya did not come out in Baku on Friday or Saturday. Apparently the issue did not pass the strikers' unusual form of "censorship." As we transmit this report, we hope that people in Baku will read it.

L. BERIA

Beria: Some Episodes from a Criminal Life
by Nikolay Zhusenin, Moscow *Nedelya*, February 22-28, 1988

YES, STALIN was guilty of repressions and lawlessness, no one is denying that or justifying it. But everything cannot be "blamed" on him alone: everything that happened under Stalin cannot be disparaged wholesale. In any case, after Stalin's death nowhere, neither in official documents nor in speeches by state and party figures, was there or is there any talk of the blame being Stalin's alone. That is only natural: Behind Stalin there were many henchmen and adventurists like Yezhov, Beria, and possibly others. I say "possibly" because far from everything has yet been studied and researched about those repressions. This too must be written about.

A.G. Zavrazhnykh, Verkhniye Polany, Kirov Oblast.
ZHUSENIN: Many legends exist about how he became people's commissar of the NKVD [People's Commissariat for Internal Affairs]. But not one of them is supported by documentary evi-

dence. In general very few documents survive about Beria's life, especially before his "rise." This man, who assembled enormous files on every more or less significant state figure, and even—rumor has it—on Stalin himself, knew the value of testimonies and witnesses. That is why it is so hard today to discover the truth and recreate a reliable, living portrait of this terrible, fateful personality in our history.

The biography of a true comrade in arms of the "leader of the peoples"—the official version for the millions, on the one hand, and muffled, nightmarish rumors, any one of which could cost you your life, on the other—that is the canvas on which we can today compose a portrait of this man.

But a few witnesses are still alive; testimonies exist about his last days, his arrest and death. Here Beria no longer had it in his power to rewrite or destroy.

But how did his rise begin? One version is this: Stalin placed infinite trust in Beria after the latter had averted an attempt on the leader's life by shielding him with his own body and dealing quickly with the attackers. That was while Stalin was on vacation on Lake Ritsa. At the time some people speculated that the assassination attempt was only a masquerade that later ended in bloody reprisals against the "players," that Beria was skillfully playing on Stalin's morbid suspicions . . . But nobody dared to uncover the deception or even simply to hint at it to Stalin. It would have meant mortally insulting and humiliating him. Thus the masquerade was elevated to the rank of an act of heroism which became one of the cornerstones of Beria's phenomenal career.

"He started work in his new post diplomatically," Sergey Anastasovich Mikoyan says, recalling his father's stories. "The first thing he said was: Enough 'purges,' it is time to get down to real work. Speeches like that prompted sighs of relief from many people who were living in constant fear that someone would come for them any minute. At the time few people entertained the idea that Beria was simply slackening slightly the reins that Yezhov had held so tight. He needed time to find out how to start up and operate the repressive machinery that was created before his time, to understand why it had suffered the breakdowns that eventually led to Yezhov's fall. He needed time to perfect this machinery, make it omnipotent and universal, and at the same time not only to avoid alarming Stalin, but, on the contrary, to convince him that only in that form would the NKVD be a reliable shield for the leader, **whatever aims he**

might pursue. This was the nature and ultimate goal of that 'real work.' It took exceptional diplomatic and organizational capabilities and the ability to weave a web of intrigue to restart the repressive machine in a very short space of time (even with Stalin's tacit encouragement)."

No, this man was not, like Yezhov, merely a loyal henchman ready to remove anyone on orders from above, with no particular concern for the semblance of justice. Beria was the champion of Stalinist policy who could make total tyranny over people who got in the way look like a struggle for the people's good. Such a person was precisely what was needed, and for this he was forgiven much that no one else would have gotten away with.

Beria succeeded in his intentions. The day was to come when Stalin would confer on him the title of Marshal of the Soviet Union and elevate him to the Hero's star for his "ultradevoted" service.

Sergey Nikitovich Khrushchev, son of N.S. Khrushchev, described the indignation of his father and many other senior party and state figures when they recalled the blackmail and intrigues with which Beria bound literally every member of Stalin's government. Everyone knew that Beria was spying on them, and everyone surmised that all this was to Stalin's liking.

Nothing was sacred to Beria. Communists with prerevolutionary service, Ilich's comrades in arms, young men, Komsomol workers, students, eminent scientists and cultural personalities, women and children—all became victims of the machinery of destruction. Even his native Georgia suffered cruelly. The entire flower of the republic's party organization, the entire flower of the intelligentsia was mercilessly destroyed. The same can be said of literally every region of the country. It was not only the "enemies of the people" who were subjected to repressions, but also their families, close and distant relatives, colleagues, and friends.

Today as we confront in all its importance the question of the need to write a truthful, complete history of the Soviet people's life and struggle, we should not bypass these chapters in silence. . . . People are alive to this day—I was able to meet with them while working on this item—whose hands begin to shake at the very mention of Beria's name. Why is he so terrible? Why do I see in their eyes just one desire—to see me off as soon as possible? After all, it is 34 years since Beria was shot. What do these people carry in their souls today? A sense of complicity in such great crimes, of dire sin against their people? Or the feeble self-consoling feeling (so that they can continue to live and look people in the eyes today) that they were blind tools in the hands of a villain? Or the certainty—worst of all—that there was no alternative. These last are still repeating a proverb that has acquired a sinister meaning: When you cut down trees, splinters fly.

People from Stalin's entourage are still alive. I tried to meet with them too, in the hope of learning more about Beria's activity. But in vain.

Those who were Beria's victims or unwilling witnesses of his crimes recall their meetings with him with indignation and with anger that never fades, even for a moment.

Glafira Lukinichna Blyukher, widow of the marshal who was shot in 1938, recalls: "I spent 7 months in solitary confinement in the Lubyanka. I will never forget the first interrogation, which Beria himself conducted. They did not beat me or torture me, as they did many wives of military men, to extract from them fabricated evidence against their husbands. But that did not make it any easier for me. They took away the person who was dearest to me. Later I realized why there was no need to torture: All the documents on Blyukher had already been concocted. They simply isolated me, as someone close to the famous marshal. Beria himself conducted the interrogation, evidently simply from sadistic curiosity."

"Glafira Lukinichna, how do you remember Beria?"

"He held himself arrogantly. He did not look at you, he seemed to examine you, like someone examining a little insect through a magnifying glass. His appearance was repellent. He exuded coldness, indifference to everything human in his victim . . . It was a time when we, who were physically destroyed and morally humiliated, were not the only ones to suffer. It was no better for those who were living and working, were even held in honor, but were constantly waiting: any moment . . . Talk to them, to their relatives."

Lieutenant General Igor Borisovich Shaposhnikov, retired: "In the war, all our people's thoughts were directed toward the speediest routing of the enemy. My father, Marshal of the Soviet Union Boris Mikhaylovich Shaposhnikov, made his contribution to this sacred cause. Although, to be honest, I am amazed that he found the strength to do useful work after one of our closest relatives was arrested on Beria's personal orders . . ."

Colonel Ilya Grigoryevich Starinov, retired, recalls: "While working in the state security organs, I was far removed from Beria's affairs, because he did not concern himself with so-called operational work. But of course, some things did reach me. The following story was told my by a comrade in the service. After the war Stalin decided to remove Chief Marshal of Artillery Voronov. Beria was worried: Who would provide compromising evidence against the marshal? They urgently hunted out Nora Pavlova Chegolayeva, an interpreter who worked with Nikolay Nikolayevich in Spain. The intention was for her to testify on Voronov's long-standing links with the Trotskiyists. That courageous woman spent a year in prison without breathing a word against the illustrious military leader. She was only released after Stalin's death.

"No less than the military," Ilya Grigoryevich continued, "many NKVD staffers also suffered under Beria. These were people who would not make a deal with their conscience, who tried to save the innocent. In saving others, they perished themselves, sentenced to shooting or to a slow death in the camps . . ."

A prominent Soviet construction worker, who, in his youth, worked on the Baykal-Amur Railroad, and later worked within the NKVD system, recounts: "In those days a powerful incentive for the prisoners was the so-called 'reckoning of work days,' whereby for particularly important, hard, and urgent work they counted 2 days of your sentence for 1 day's work, or 3 days of sentence for 2 days' work. But once, about 2 years before the war, the chief of the railroad construction camps came to Moscow. He reported to Beria on 'outrages involving the reckoning of work days.' Sentences were being reduced by one-third to one-half . . . Beria reported it to Stalin. Soon the reckoning system was abolished. A ray of hope was extinguished for thousands of people . . ."

It is well known how fussy Stalin was about any manifestations of immorality or unscruplousness in the personal life of people in his entourage. Nonetheless he "did not know" (did not want to know) anything about something that brought grief to dozens of families.

"Do you remember Beria, at least from pictures?" Svetlana Vasilyevna Sh. asked me. "Bulging eyes, behind the glass of his pincenez. A half-grin that looked as if it was stuck on . . . I remember the women in my circle looked at that face in the newspapers and in pictures with terror. At that time persistent rumors were going around in the capital about the disappearance without trace of beautiful young women, after a car had approached them, clinging insinuatingly to the sidewalk, and stopped alongside them. You could believe the rumors, and not believe them, too. When believing was terrifying, you tried to shrug them off. That was what I did, until . . . One day I was walking along the Arbat with a fellow student. All at once a car stopped nearby, two muscular thugs got out, and rapidly approached us. We did not have time to realize what was happening before they seized my friend by the arm and forcibly shoved her into the car. I felt ill when I suddenly realized where they were taking her and why. Shout, weep, complain? We knew it was useless and dangerous, then . . ."

"Yes! It's all true," Mayya Ivanovna Koneva, daughter of the well known Soviet military leader who was in the chair at Beria's trial, bitterly confirmed this story. "I remember my father was filled with hatred of that villain, partly because of what he heard from the weeping mothers of those girls who were the debauchee's victims. I will never forget my father's impassioned words: 'I suffered in the war for the fate of every young woman, devoutly remembering that after the war she would be someone's sweetheart, wife, mother . . . And he, that scum, treated them so inhumanly.' "

. . . That is how this man lived, until Stalin's death. In the new government Beria became USSR minister of internal affairs. Perhaps he would have held onto that post for a while, but he himself hastened his fate.

"He met with Bulganin and Khrushchev one after the other," Andrey Geogiyevich Malenkov says, sharing the reminiscences of his father, then chairman of the USSR Council of Ministers, "and tried to incite them to seize power. Why them? Probably because they both had influential posts in the government and the CPSU Central Committee. But Beria miscalculated. Both Bulganin and Khrushchev went to my father and told him everything. Their report was sufficient reason to take urgent measures . . . "

"My father told me," A. Malenkov went on, "how they arrested this dangerous and still very strong adversary. Beria was invited to a routine session of the Politburo. He clearly had no idea what was to be discussed.

" 'Lavrentiy,' Georgiy Maksimilianovich Malenkov asked him, in the presence of everyone, 'did you want to accomplish a coup d'etat? How?' Everyone present never forgot how Beria paled and lost the power of speech . . ."

There are so many myths of all kinds among the people about how Beria was arrested! Fate led me to the sole surviving participant in this arrest, Major General Ivan Grigoryevich Zub, retired, and gave me an opportunity to dispel the myths once and for all.

"On that hot day I was at my dacha," the general recalls. "All at once my adjutant telephoned and told me that Defense Minister Nikolay Aleksandrovich Bulganin had summoned me urgently. I admit I was surprised that the minister was interested in me, chief of the political directorate of Moscow District Air Defense Forces. I went. . . .

"First Bulganin checked on my biographical data, asked after my health, and inquired how I could handle weapons. Finally he asked whether I was prepared to carry out a responsible government mission. I answered strictly according to the book. The conversation ended there."

ZHUSENIN: Why, in your view, were you and your comrades entrusted with the arrest of Beria?

ZUB: I suppose Nikita Sergeyevich Khrushchev, who knew Moskalenko well from the war years, proposed him as a candidate, and Kirill Semenovich obviously wanted to be accompanied by people he knew to be tried and tested combat comrades. First Deputy Defense Minister Georgiy Konstantinovich Zhukov led the entire arrest operation and played a most direct part in it.

ZHUSENIN: How did you get into the Kremlin, which was guarded mainly by Beria's men?

ZUB: Bulganin and Zhukov took us through the Borovitskiye Gate in their cars, which had dark glass. In Malenkov's reception room, so as not to arouse suspicion, we were put down as people who had come with the minister for a conference . . .

ZHUSENIN: How did subsequent events develop?

ZUB: In the break, Bulganin and Khrushchev came into our room and explained our task. They said we would have to go into the hall of sessions in response to an agreed signal—a bell. When the bell rang, we went in through the three doors in pairs, pistols in our hands. Some comrades started to get up from their seats in alarm. It seems far from everyone had been informed about the possible events. Well, after that everything was simple. Malenkov explained the crux of the matter and then, in our presence, proposed a vote: "Who is in favor of arresting Beria?" Everyone raised their hands. Georgiy Konstantinovich went up to Beria, who was still sitting motionless, and said: "Hands up. You're under arrest."

We stayed in that room until the Kremlin guard was changed. Only when measures had been adopted for Beria to be dispatched secretly to the place where he was to be held, at about 4 in the morning on the following day, did we set off.

ZHUSENIN: How did Beria behave during those hours?

ZUB: He tried to distract us, to weaken our vigilance, so as to get to the telephone somehow and contact some of his people. But we were on the alert.

ZHUSENIN: One last question. Later you were one of those responsible for Beria's fate until the trial. How did he behave in his imprisonment beforehand?

ZUB: He did not confess to anything. Then he went on hunger strike, which lasted 11 days. We made considerable efforts to make that villain "hold out" until his trial, where he would have to answer for his crimes . . .[Zub ends]

It has already been said that Beria, aware of the value of testimonies and witnesses, tried to do everything possible to make sure they were kept to a minimum. All the same, in the course of investigation it emerged that back in 1919, while in Baku, Beria became an agent for the counterintelligence service of the courterrevolutionary Musavatist government in Azerbaijan, which operated under the control of the English intelligence organs. In 1920, in Georgia, he cooperated with the Georgian Menshevik government's secret police.

Did Stalin know about that? That thought gives me no rest.

The trial lasted from 18-23 December 1953. With Beria in the dock were six of his colleagues. They were tried by a Special Judicial Body of the USSR Supreme Court. It was a special court, and it has to be discussed in a special way, because it took place behind closed doors.

The hour of retribution struck.

"The Special Judicial Body of the USSR Supreme Court has resolved: L. Beria, V. Merkulov, V. Dekanozov, B. Kobulov, S. Goglidze, P. Meshik, and L. Vlodzimirskiy are sentenced to the supreme measure of punishment—shooting, with confiscation of their personal property and deprivation of military titles and awards. The sentence is final and not subject to appeal."

That same day, 23 December, the sentence was carried out.

BLACK MARKET

Five Rubles to the Dollar: The Exchange Rate on Moscow's "Black Market"
by Yelena Khanga, Leonid Miloslavskiy, and Aleksandr Kabakov, *Moscow News*, October 16, 1988

The militia confiscated 130,000 dollars from black marketeers and detained 5,881 persons for illegally trading with foreigners—all in the first half of 1988. Though these detainees paid a total of 185,000 roubles in fines to the state, this illegal business keeps expanding.

Our Zhiguili and a tourist bus drew up to the Maurice Thorez Embankment almost simultaneously. The special Moscow militia unit which had organized our "excursion" to the busiest points for "fartsovka" (illegal trading for foreigners) parked round the corner. "We're too well known around here," the militiamen explained. "We're even on a first-name basis with some of these guys." As for us, disguised in jeans and animated tourist-like expressions of expectation, we melted into the crowd pouring out of the bus.

While the tourists snapped pictures of the Mrelin across the Moskva river, we also pretended to be enraptured by the city-scape. Then three young men cropped up out of nowhere. One approached a grey-haired lady and whispered something. He dived into his bag, the lady into hers. Our "guide" suddenly appeared at our side.

Aleksandrv Khalfin, of Moscow's special militia unit: "See that one, in the grey pullover? He's trying to make a deal. He's not a big-time 'fartsovshchik': I don't even know him. He'll offer a badge, a matreshka doll, and if these tourists were Americans, he'd offer our state flag or something from a military uniform. In return, he'll take anything—from chewing gum to clothes to dollars. No big deal? Just wait. . . ."

Exactly what is "fartsovka"? There's probably no foreign equivalent. It is based on the high prestige of anything foreign—from a fountain pen to a car. And on the fact that the official exchange rate for the rouble doesn't coincide with realities in the world of commodity-money relations. For many of us "fartsovka" is just a worthless hobby for dumb teenagers who needle foreigners for worn-out jeans or plastic bags. How far that cliche is from reality becomes clear when one remembers the case of Rokotov and Faybishenko, large-scale currency dealers, thirty years ago. Since then cases of this kind have become routine in our courts, though not on so grand a scale. Anton D., a minor, was tried by the People's Court of Moscow's Kievskiy District on October 5. He was accused of buying 50 dollars from Italian tourist V. Sardi for 200 roubles which his grandmother had given him. Anton said he wanted to buy jeans, and 50 dollars was what he needed to do that. Anton's mother, his legal representative, wept; she couldn't understand what sort of pants one would pay 200 roubles for and what sort of dollars those were which, at the official exchange rate, cost a bit over 29 roubles. . . . The prosecutor asked that the defendant, who pleaded guilty and fully repented, be punished but not deprived of his freedom.

The fellow in the grey pullover glanced over his shoulder and immediately moved away from the lady he'd been talking to. Could our appearance have made him suspect something or was he just being cautious? The tourists continued clicking their cameras, we continued admiring the view, the cautious young men continued to stare thoughtfully at the river. Altogether it looked like some children's game. It was, however, neither a game nor childish mischief.

Aleksandr Khalfin: **"Just like any market, the black market is not adverse to small change, to kopeks—and they add up to thousands of roubles. What makes it so hard to fight 'fartsovka' is our lack of efficient legal levers.** What can we do? Note the 'badgering of foreigners for purposes of trading.' Under the Decree, the first-offense fine is 100 roubles, for a second offense it's 200. But first we have to prove the 'badgering' and the tourist must confirm it. The guy usually says he was just talking about unemployment in the tourist's country, while the tourist hurries away. At best we manage the purely symbolic punishment of very small fry. Though we are completely convinced that behind this small fry is a well-organized large-scale operation. We estimate the worth of one 17-year-old 'fartsovshchik' at 17,000 roubles! But I can't give you his name— until we've caught him red-handed he's not a 'fartsovshchik' . . . ."

Not far from the observation platform on Lenin Hills, we talked to a fashionable-looking blond fellow. One of the men accompanying us spied him among the people crowding the platform and beckoned to him. He wandered over to us and nodded at the man: "Hi, Sergey Ivanovich. . . ." In the same free and easy manner he agreed to talk to us—as long as we didn't use his name.

N., 19, a professional "fartsovshchik" (unemployed):

"I'll tell it to you straight—you'll never be able to put an end to this. I'll pay any fine, I can 'earn' it in one day. I'm already something like a reckless gambler. It's like a disease. See what I mean? Today 200, tomorrow 300. . . . I've been doing this for four years and don't regret anything. Risk? Of course there's risk, but not much. My future? Someday I'll marry—probably a foreigner, and not a poor one, you can be sure of that. . . ."

We asked how often foreigners refused to deal with him or his colleagues. He smiled: "Maybe one in five." There are no barriers between the "fartsovshchiks" and their partners—neither linguistic nor ethical barriers—while the dollar stretches both ways, from here to somewhere beyond our borders. In the self-styled "bank" that roams from the hotel to the observation platform, from the museum in Kolomenskoye to Red Square, the "fartsovshchiks" give foreigners five roubles to the dollar. Middlemen pay the small fry seven roubles to the dollar, then resell those dollars for 10 roubles apiece to other foreign visitors, for some of whom buying and selling currency is the principal purpose of their frequent visits to the USSR.

Aleksandr Khalfin: "The main thing is the law. And the law is so flawed it tempts more and more violators. Thus my doubt— strange as it may seem, whether such a law is necessary. Should the punishment be harsher? I'm sure that wouldn't help. Should it be less harsh? That's absurd. Now kids are brought to me whom we'd overlooked five or ten years ago because of the shortage of jeans and chewing gum. In five years I'll be seeing the kids we're overlooking now because of a shortage of common sense. In the meantime the bigwigs, the bosses who pocket thousands of dollars, remain out of sight—as do their foreign partners who, as a rule, are not tried."

. . . By the Bolshoi Theatre life was bustling. In between the famous columns, where we're so used to hunting for extra tickets, the same fashionable-looking young men are offering those tickets to foreigners for ten and twenty dollars. Where on earth does that, say, young fellow in the green shirt get these tickets, which ordinary mortals can never get? The system functions. It has its executives in every link, while the militia manages, with really great difficulty, to get its hands on the very tip of this dollar iceberg.

One of the recent big-time cases involved a gang in Leningrad. I. Kogan, a senior research associate at one of the city's scientific institutes, and A. Semeynov, a chief porter at the Pulkovskaya Hotel, sold paintings to Finnish tourists for markkas. They even sold a painting by Ayvazovskiy. Their receipts were 2,000 marks, 4,000. . . . But even that case doesn't show the true scope. The Finns, of course, were never brought to trial. . . .

Now that we're restructuring our legal system, it might be worthwhile putting some hard-and-fast rules in place of the ineffective prohibitions. Why not set up special shops that would take on commission or simply purchase all sorts of things from foreigners? These shops could be state-owned or cooperative and they'd be profitable both for our society and for a foreigner who wants to make a little money on an extra pair of pants.

Much more serious, however, is another question—what is the real exchange rate of the dollar? The black-market rate or the official one? It seems to me it's the real market rate. So shouldn't the rate offered in the state exchange bureaus be as near as possible to that one? No matter how one tries, one can't fool life. . . .

L. BREZHNEV

Legal Club: The Young Heirs
by Yevgeny Dodolev, *Nedelya*, July 18-24, 1988

Last summer in the Crimea, I overheard a heavy-set young man and a visibly tipsy older fellow arguing in a restaurant.

"Well, Andryusha, your time has passed, hasn't it?" the older man said. "The train has left the station, eh?"

To which the young man replied: "You're an idiot. My grandchildren and I both will have more of everything than a hundred morons like you ever will."

I remembered the young man—Andrei Yurevich, L. I. Brezhnev's grandson—because I happened to see him again the next day as he carefully parked his silver Mercedes on a Yalta street.

The young man's antagonist I had met previously; he's a well-known photojournalist. And I had come across his name earlier this summer while examining some of the exquisite artifacts uncovered in the corruption probe under way in Uzbekistan. The photographer had recorded the sumptuous wedding of Tamara Kamalova, daughter of Kallybek Kamalov, the "father of the Kara-Kalpak people" and First Secretary of the Kara-Kalpak Province Party Committee from 1963 to 1984.

The hundreds of color photographs record the impressive feast, the smiles, the goblets, the women's diamonds, the men's gold cuff links. We see the confident bridegroom, the son of Sh. Rashidov, former First Secretary of the Uzbekistan Communist Party Central Committee. And the numerous medals on the guests' jackets, in the Brezhnev style. No expense was spared. The bride's portrait was painted by one of our most prominent painters. The guest list included the most popular film actors and most famous athletes.

The whims of these pampered children of the elite were the talk of the town, and their romantic affairs did not always remain secret. They "go crazy because there's nothing left for them to want," sings Boris Grebenshchikov of these golden— and diamond—youth.

Friends called Boris Buryatsa, Galina Brezhneva's notorious "friend," Boris Diamond; Galina Leonidovna was invariably addressed as "Madam." A former actor, Boris had met "Madam" in the Crimea, not long before her last legal husband, Yury Churbanov (now in custody), became Deputy Minister of Internal Affairs to N. Shchelokov. Boris was 18 years younger than Galina (Churbanov nine years younger), but they shared a passion for diamonds, which became Boris's undoing.

"Madam" herself, however, speculated in precious stones with utter impunity. Diamond prices more than doubled during Brezhnev's rule. Galina Leonidovna found out about impending price increases ahead of time and bought up diamond jewelry by the lot. When she didn't have enough cash, she issued IOUs.

Her partner in the diamond business was Yu. Sokolov, manager of the Yeliseyev Food Store (Sokolov was executed for massive embezzling during Yu. V. Andropov's tenure as General Secretary). Circus performers who collaborated with the two smuggled diamonds through customs in the cages of their most fearsome beasts.

Galina Leonidovna occasionally accompanied the circus performers abroad, albeit unofficially. For after taking her on a trip to Yugoslavia, Galina's father never dared take his daughter along again—she had provided journalists with more than a little grist for their publications.

These overgrown "children" lived above the law. For example, the son of former Politburo member Kirilenko used to spend scarce foreign currency on breathtaking African safaris. Nor was money ever a concern for Kamalov's oldest son. After his father was arrested, Bulat started living more modestly. Kallybek Kamalovich had left him just 900,000 rubles. Forced to adopt "austerity measures," Bulat spent 184,000 rubles in an 18-month period—on video-cassettes, clothing, restaurants and resorts.

Meanwhile, the younger Kamalov and his ilk see the steps being taken against their families as unjustified interference in the "natural way of things." They clearly hope for a return to better days.

And are their hopes all that unjustified? After all, Molotov was reinstated in the Party in the mid-1980s. Yet this man was involved not in mere embezzling but in carefully planned mass killings and unprecedented repressions. And didn't the broad silhouette of "Madam" reappear at Kremlin receptions after Yu. V. Andropov's death? And weren't the criminal cases against Shchelokov and many others, started under Andropov, stalled until the March and April (1985) Central Committee plenary sessions?

So there is some basis for these hopes. Kamalov and his cohorts still have sufficient friends in high places. After all, aren't these friends the ones who pushed through a general's pension for Galina Leonidovna? (The special personal pensions for G. and Yu. Brezhnev were recently revoked.)

Why do we know so little about all these things? Why are we content with mere rumors? We now discuss the painful chapters of our past more and more openly. But why do we find it so hard to speak about the negative aspects of the 1980s? The reason is that we know that some of those involved still hold high positions. And that they will not surrender them without a fight.

Needless to say, the "five-star" leader bestowed awards liberally. Galina Brezhneva's precious husband, the circus performer Yevgeny Milayev, was named USSR People's Artist and Hero of Socialist Labor. The children of the "untouchables" were admitted to the most prestigious schools and given degrees and positions. Galina Brezhneva, for example, was made a doctor of philosophy, while Yury, her brother, was appointed Deputy Minister of Foreign Trade. Before his father's arrest, Bulat Kamalov headed a 2,000-man collective.

The Brezhnev lifestyle: drinking; bribe-taking; allowing others to do as they pleased, provided they were "our people"; pre-

tence; hypocrisy; and the repugnant motto "Après nous le Chernobyl."

Kallybek Kamalov can't even remember how many millions of rubles he turned over to relatives for safekeeping. Of 73 valuable antiques confiscated from an inveterate swindler by police, N. Shchelokov, Brezhnev's close friend since their student days, kept 53 for himself and donated the remaining 20 to museums. And this was standard practice.

Special prosecutor Nikolai Ivanov told me that efforts to recover the ill-gotten wealth of former high-ranking officials are dropped in the event of the officials' deaths. Why, he asked, should their families be allowed to keep their enormous fortunes? Now this wealth is being passed on to their "heirs," though it rightfully belongs to the people.

There is every reason to believe that the former high-ranking Young Communist League official Igor Shchelokov (whose parents, fearing the inevitable disclosures, committed suicide), Galina Brezhneva, former employee in the archives of the USSR Ministry of Foreign Affairs, and many others like them are not sitting around impassively. Though deprived of the protection of their high-ranking fathers, they still enjoy the backing of "foster" fathers.

There are many such people, and they include not just the elite, or high-placed bureaucrats, but jewelry store directors, private photographers, architects, etc. They yearn for a return to the good old days, when, like Yu. Churbanov, one could simultaneously be a bribe-taker and embezzler and the author of a book entitled "Political Education Work in Internal Affairs Agencies," which is still to be found on library shelves. But those days must never return. This is why we need legality and glasnost so badly.

NCO with Stripes on His Pants: Sensational and Logical Features of the Recent Trial
by Yu. Feofanov, *Izvestiya*, January 2, 1989

It was a "No 1" sensation—the arrest of a first deputy minister of internal affairs, a colonel general, only recently an RSFSR Supreme Soviet deputy and a candidate member of the CPSU Central Committee. The arrest and committal for trial of Churbanov and another eight top militia officials of Uzbekistan. But the real sensation, in my view, was the verdict. To see why, we will have to take a closer look at it and tell our readers about the course of events at the trial and before.

Let us not pretend: The figure of Churbanov and his "case" aroused worldwide interest. Long before the trial began, myths had already grown up about the sums stolen. And when, in private conversations, I mentioned the figures cited in the charge, people were disappointed, although the sums are considerable. Especially since magazines "over there" had already published photomontages of Churbanov with millions of rubles and piles of gold, while our newspapers were ranking him with Yezhov and Beriya.

But even notoriety was not enough to make Yuriy Mikhaylovich glamorous. In himself he was small fry, and he sank into the kind of criminal activities that are typical of corrupt circles. All the same, whatever anyone may say and however hard we may try to convince ourselves that this is an ordinary trial of a corrupt careerist who stooped to bribery, all the same there is no getting away from the fact that he was not simply a high-ranking official, but somebody's son-in-law. That was the paradox of the situation, and posed great difficulty for the court.

Before fortune smiled on this outwardly attractive man, he served as a Komsomol functionary, and then began little by little to move up the ladder in the internal troops. Then, all of a sudden, a general's stripes were sewn onto this senior lieutenant's pants. It was enough to turn a weak head. He would hardly have been capable of organizing, say, a criminal gang or heading a mafia clan. He was only capable of becoming a son-in-law. But that was enough for people to start handing him sums of 10,000, 30,000, and 50,000 at a time.

His own evidence and the evidence of those who handed it over, as well as other proof, provided grounds for charging Churbanov with receiving bribes totaling R650,000. (The sum admitted in the verdict was 90,000, but at the moment I am talking about the preliminary investigation.) First he admitted everything, then he started changing his evidence: He denied the charge of receiving 220,000 through Begelman, and some charges were lifted in the course of the investigation. What about the rest? Let me quote this evidence, which is recorded in the indictment.

January 24, 1987: "I wish to purge my conscience before the party and the state, and I understand that I can prove my decency only through my own concrete actions."

January 25, in a letter to the general prosecutor: "The money is at the dacha in Zhukovka; a diagram of the hiding places is attached."

January 26: "I gave false information about Zhukovka; I do not remember where the money is."

July 16: "I gave 300,000 to my wife Galina Brezhneva as a gift from Rashidov. She spent it on jewelry."

The next day: "My earlier evidence was precipitate. I did not give my own wife any money except my wages."

July 23: "The question of money is very difficult. The point is that I have no right to compromise the family of my late father-in-law, still less his memory."

December 4, 1987: "I gave the money to Vashkov—R300,000, in two leather cases. Vashkov told me he 'had to sort things out with someone from the business world' and that he would give me the money back soon. But 2 months later Vashkov suddenly died, and he did not give me back the money." The Vashkov in question was chief of the USSR MVD trade department at the time. . . .

On 27 April 1983 the Uzbek SSR KGB instituted proceedings with regard to the apprehension red-handed (for bribery) of A. Muzaffarov, chief of the Bukhara Oblispolkom Internal Affairs Administration Department for Combating Embezzlement of Socialist Property. The case went to the USSR Prosecutor's Office, and a tangle of actions that was to give the Soviet public a real shock began to be unraveled. Criminal proceedings were taken against the chairman of the republic council of ministers, secretaries of the Central Committee, obkoms, and raykoms, soviet staffers, and employees of law enforcement organs. Including the present defendants.

In the course of the investigation R42 million was confiscated; 6 million from one person, 6 million from another, 4.5 million from a third, 2 million from some people, and "various trivial sums," reckoned in tens and hundreds of thousands, from many people. Naturally, none of this was earned by honest labor; all of it was stolen from you and me. Bribes "for nothing" flourished, although this "nothing" took the form of official patronage, appointments, career moves, and promotions, as well as connivance and protection. People benefited from entertainment and gifts, taxation of subordinates, allocation of apartments, cars, and other things in short supply, places in VUZ's, and so forth.

J. BRODSKY

The Trial of Joseph Brodsky
Published by A.A. Raskina, commentary by E.L. Beznosov,
Ogonyek, **December 1988**

"STOP WRITING!" the judge demands.

Frida Vigdorova does not stop.

"Take away her notes!" shouts someone from the audience.

Vigdorova continues writing, at times hiding it, at times openly.

"Hey you! The one writing! Take away her notes and that's that."

Frida continues stubbornly. And how can one not write? Restrain himself? Every character here is from Gogol, Saltykov-Shchedrin, or Zoshchenko; the jury, the judge, the prosecutor. Every word uttered by the judge is an example of lawlessness. Every word of the prosecutor is an incoherent roar of militant ignorance. Every certificate is forgery. A writer is being tried while the audience gathered here is least of all prepared to comprehend literature.

Life is a great artist but it is rarely able to create such a phenomenon of expression, of irreproachable finality. It is not just anyone who is being tried, but a poet and for nothing more than idleness and parasitism. Two powers collide at the trial, powers which have been forever opposing each other—intellect and bureaucracy; the power of the inspired word and that of banality.

In the center of the collision, probably as a visual aid, life placed a poet, while the role of the witness of this mockery, it assigned to a woman as talented as she was honest, energetic, unsparing toward herself, and courageous.

The name of Frida Abramovna Vigdorova (1915–1965), a teacher, a writer, a journalist, became widely known at the end of the 1950s, beginning of the 1960s. Her articles in *Izvestia, Komsomol'skaya Pravda, Literaturnaya Gazeta* often brought about restoration of justice.

Yet the transcripts of the two trials were not to be printed.

Not a single newspaper would risk exposing them to the public. The document connecting the verbal art with irreproachable precision went from one person to the next. It was retyped many times by the fans of Brodsky's poetry. It became one of the first works published by the newly formed *Samizdat* ("self-press"). It was read by hundreds in its homeland and then came over to the West. Its role grew by the day. Frida Vigdorova sent legal appeals to every office attaching a copy of her notes with each of the appeals, complaints, and requests.

The notes taken by F. Vigdorova made everyone who had read the document relive the trial with anger and bitterness as if the reader himself was insulted. Such is the power of art. I think that the modern reader, reading into the text, will take it with the same pain.

Brodsky's fate is to defend the honor of Russian poetry at home and across the border. The honor of arming the intellectuals in order to fight the bureaucracy had fallen upon F. Vigdorova. Brodsky's ardent defenders did not allow the bureaucrats to finish him off. Brodsky returned from exile in a year and a half instead of the five years.

Joseph Brodsky and Frida Vigdorova never met. She died of cancer August 7, 1965, a month before his release.

The following transcripts were recorded by Frida Vigdorova in spite of the judge's prohibition against doing so.

The first trial of Joseph Brodsky.
Dzerzhinsky courtroom
Vosstanie St.
Leningrad
February 18, 1964
Judge Savelieva, presiding

Judge: What do you do?
Brodsky: I write poetry. I translate. I suppose . . .
J: No supposing. Stand up straight! Do not lean against the wall! Look at the court! (To me) Stop writing immediately or I'll have you removed from the courtroom! (To Brodsky) Do you have a permanent job?
B: I thought that it is a permanent job.
J: Answer the question precisely!
B: I wrote poetry. I thought it would be published. I suppose.

J: We are not interested with what you "suppose." Answer why you were not working?

B: I did work. I wrote poetry.

J: We are not interested in that. We want to know what organization you were affiliated with.

B: I had contracts with publishing houses.

J: Then say that. Do you have enough contracts to earn your livelihood? List their dates and the amounts they are for.

B: I do not remember exactly. My lawyer has all my contracts.

J: I am asking you.

B: In Moscow, two books with my translations were published . . . (lists)

J: How long is your work record?

B: About . . .

J: We are not interested in "about."

B: Five years.

J: Where did you work?

B: At the factory, in the geological teams . . .

J: How long did you work at the factory?

B: A year.

J: Your position?

B: A metal cutter.

J: And what is your occupation in general?

B: Poet, poet-translator.

J: And who recognized you to be a poet? Who put you in the ranks of poet?

B: No one. (Unprovoked) And who put me in the ranks of humanity?

J: Did you study it?

B: What?

J: How to be a poet? Did you attempt to finish an institute of higher learning . . . where they prepare . . . teach . . .

B: I did not think that it is given to one by education.

J: By what then?

B: I think it is . . . from God.

J: Do you have an appeal for the court?

B: I would like to know why I was arrested?

J: That is a question not an appeal.

B: In that case, I do not have an appeal.

J: Does the defense have any questions?

Defense lawyer: Yes. Mr. Brodsky, do you contribute your earnings to your family?

B: Yes.

D: Are your parents also working?

B: They are retired.

D: Do you live with them?

B: Yes.

D: So your earnings were a part of the family budget?

J: You are not asking questions. You are making assumptions. You are helping him answer. Do not assume. Ask.

D: Are you registered at the psychiatric clinic?

B: Yes.

D: Did you go through treatment?

B: Yes. From the end of December of 1963 until January 5 of this year in the Kashchenko hospital in Moscow.

D: Do you not think that your illness prevented you from working regularly in one place for a long time?

B: Maybe. Probably. Actually, I do not know. No, I don't know.

D: Did you translate poems for an edition of the Cuban poets?

B: Yes.

D: Did you translate the Spanish romanceo?

B: Yes.

D: Were you affiliated with the translators' department of the Writers' Union?

B: Yes.

D: The defense wishes to submit the review of the office of the translators' department . . . A list of published poems . . . Copies of contracts . . . A telegram: "We ask to speed up the signing of the contract" . . . (lists) Even from one listing it is obvious that all the accusations of parasitism are nonsense. And I request that Mr. Brodsky be sent for medical evaluation to determine whether or not his health prevented him from holding a job on a regular basis. Besides that I ask that he be immediately released from the custody of the court. I do not think he has committed any crime, therefore his detention is unlawful. He has a permanent place of residence and can come back to court at any time.

(The court goes into deliberation. Upon return the judge reads the following decision):

Brodsky is to be sent for a psychiatric evaluation to determine whether or not he suffers from any illness which should prevent his being sent away for forced labor. His documents should be sent to the police for an additional check of his earnings. Taking into account Brodsky's refusal to be hospitalized, he will be brought in for psychiatric evaluation from police precinct #18.)

J: Do you have any questions?

B: I would like to request paper and a pen for my cell.

J: That you should talk about with the chief of police.

B: I asked but he refused. I am asking for paper and a pen.

J: (Softening) All right. I'll tell him.

B: Thank you.

(When we walked out of the courtroom, there were a great number of people in the hall, especially young people.)

J: Look at all the people. I did not think there would be this many people.

From the crowd: It's not every day that a poet is on trial.

J: We do not care if it is a poet or not.

(In the opinion of the defense attorney Z. N. Toporova, Judge Savelieva should have released Brodsky from custody, so that he could go himself for the psychiatric evaluation to be determined by the court hospital. The judge, however, left him in the custody of the court and so he was sent to the hospital under guard.)

The Second Trial of Joseph Brodsky
Builders' Club Hall
22 Fontanka
Leningrad
March 13, 1964
Judge Savelieva

The psychiatric evaualtion stated: "Possesses psychopathic traits but remains able to work. Therefore, official measures may be taken." Those entering the courtroom are met with the sign: The trial of Brodsky, the Parasite, Continues. The large hall of the Builders' Club is full of people.

"Please rise. The court is now in session."

Judge Savelieva asks Brodsky if he has any appeals for the court. It is discovered that Brodsky was not informed of the charges against him either prior to the first trial, or now. The court is in recess. Brodsky is taken away to be informed of the charges against him. He comes back after a while and states that the poems on pages 141, 143, 155, 200, 234 (lists) are not his. Besides that he requests that his diary of 1956 not be included in the case since at that time he was only sixteen years old. The defense attorney stresses this request again.

J: As far as the poems go, the court takes the request into account. However, as far as the personal diary, there is no need to exclude it from the evidence. Mr. Brodsky, as of 1956 you changed your place of work thirteen times. You worked for a year in a factory. Then you did not work for half a year. In the summer, you were a member of the geological team. Then you did not work for four months. (Lists all the employments and the breaks between them.) Explain to the court why you did not work during the breaks between your jobs but led the life of a parasite?

B: I worked during the breaks. I was doing the same thing I am doing now. I wrote poetry.

J: That is to say, you were writing your so called poetry? And what was the use of changing jobs so many times?

B: I began working at the age of fifteen. Everything interested me. I was changing jobs because I wanted to learn more about life and people.

J: How did you benefit your country?

B: I wrote poetry. This is my work. I am convinced ... I believe that that which I wrote will serve people and not only now, but future generations as well.

Voice from the crowd: Imagine that!

Another voice: He is a poet. He must think that.

J: So you think that your so-called poems benefit people.

B: Why are you calling the poems "so-called"?

J: We are calling the poems "so-called" because we have no other concept of them.

Sorokin (prosecution)†: You talk about the future generations. Do you think that you are not understood today?

B: I did not say that. Simply my poems had not yet been published and people do not know them.

S: You think that if they would be known, they would be accepted?

B: Yes.

S: You claim that you have a well-developed curiosity. Why then did you not want to serve in the Soviet Army?

B: I will not answer such questions.

J: You will answer.

B: I was excused from the service. I did not "not want;" I was excused. Twice. The first time, when my father was ill and the second time because of my illness.

S: Can you live on the money that you earn?

B: I can. Being in jail, I signed a paper every day that forty

---

†F. Sorokin was made a participant in the process in spite of the objections of both Brodsky and the defense attorney.

kopeks a day have been spent on me. I earned more than forty kopeks a day.

S: But you have to buy clothes, shoes.

B: I have one suit, an old one, but that is the one I have. I do not need another one.

D: Were your poems evaluated by experts?

B: They were. Chukovsky and Marshak spoke very highly of my translations. Better than I deserve.

D: Were you affiliated with the translation department of the Writers' Union?

B: Yes. I was presented in the almanac, which is called "In Russian for the First Time" and read translations from Polish.

J: You should ask about the useful work that he has done and you are asking about his appearances.

D: His translations are the useful work that he has done.

J: Brodsky, why don't you tell the court why you were not working in the breaks between your jobs.

B: I did work. I wrote poetry.

J: But that did not prevent you from working?

B: But I did work. I wrote poetry.

J: But there are people who work in the factory and write poetry. What prevented you from doing so?

B: But all people are not alike. Even their hair color, facial expressions . . .

J: You did not make any startling discoveries with that. Everyone knows that already. Why don't you tell us how to judge your participation in our great progressive movement toward communism?

B: Building of communism does not only mean standing at a machine or ploughing the fields. It is also intellectual work which . . .

J: Leave the grand ideas alone. Why don't you just answer how you are planning to build up your working experience in the future.

B: I wanted to write poetry and to translate. But if it goes against some established norms, I will get a permanent job and will continue writing poetry.

Jury member Tiagly: In our country everyone works. How could you remain a loafer for such a long time?

B: You do not consider my work to be work. I wrote poetry. I consider that work.

J: Did you draw any conclusions for yourself from anything that came out in the press?

B: Lerner's article was libelous. That is the only conclusion that I have reached.

J: So you have drawn no other conclusions?

B: I have not. I do not consider myself a parasite.

J: You have said that the article "A Near-literary Drone"* published in the newspaper *The Evening Leningrad* is not reliable. In what way?

B: Only the name and the last name in it are correct. The age is not. The poems are not mine. In the article people whom I either barely know or do not know at all are called my friends. How can I consider such an article reliable or draw any conclusions from it?

D: You claim that your work is useful. Would the witnesses whom I will be calling be able to attest to that?

J: (Ironically to the defense lawyer) Is that the only reason that you are calling the witnesses?

S: (To Brodsky) How could you translate from Serbian independently without using someone else's work?

B: This is an ignorant question. Sometimes the contract includes an interlinear [translation]. I know Polish. Serbian, I know less but the languages are related, therefore I was able to translate using . . .

J: The court calls Witness Grudinina.

G: I have been directing the work of aspiring poets for eleven years. For seven years, I was a member of the committee, working with young writers. Now, I direct the upperclasssmen-poets in the Young Pioneer Club and the society of young writers at the plant "Svetlana." I was asked by the publishing house to compile and edit four collective volumes with the poetry by young writers. That included over two hundred names. Thus, I am familiar with the work of all young poets in the city.

Brodsky's work, as that of a starting-our poet, is known to me from his 1959 and 1960 poems. These poems were still rough, but they had some vivid ideas and images. I did not include them in the collective volumes, yet I found the author to be talented. I had not had a chance to meet Brodsky in person until the fall of 1963.

After the publication of the article "Near-literary Drone" in *The Evening Leningrad*, I called Brodsky in to talk to me since

---

* The article was published November 29, 1963, and was signed by A. Ionin and M. Medvedev, along with Ya. Lerer. January 8, 1964, in the same *Evening Leningrad*, a selection of readers' letters was assembled under the title "There is no room for parasites in our city."

the youth was bombarding me with requests to intercede on the behalf of the slandered man. To my question, what is he doing now? he replied that he has been studying languages and doing literary translations for about a year and a half. I took from him the manuscripts of his translations in order to get familiarized with them.

As a professional poet and as someone who knows literature, I maintain that Brodsky's translations are done on a highly professional level. Brodsky has a special and a rare talent for the literary translation of poetry. He showed me a project of 368 poetic lines. Besides that, I read 120 lines of his translations published in the Moscow editions.

From personal experience of having done literary translations, I know that the work of such volume requires from a writer at least a year and a half of intense involvement and that not counting the hassles related to the publication of the poems and consultations with specialists. Time required for something like that can not be measured, as you well know. If one is to estimate his income, using the lowest publication prices, from his translations which I have seen with my own eyes, Brodsky has earned about 350 new rubles and the only question remaining is when the rest of his work will be published.

Other than the translation contracts, Brodsky showed me his contracts with the radio and television. That work has already been completed but not yet paid for in full.

From talking to Brodsky and the people who know him, I am aware of his very modest life-style. He refuses himself clothes and entertainment and spends most of his time at the work desk. The money that he earns for his work he brings into his family.

D: Is it necessary for literary translators of poetry to be well acquainted with the author's work in general?

Gr: Yes. For good translations, like those of Brodsky, it is necessary to know the author's work and to truly understand his voice.

D: Does the payment decrease if one works using the interlinear?

Gr: It does. When I was doing a translation from Hungarian using the interlinear, I was receiving a ruble (old currency) less per line.

D: Is such method of translation common among the translators?

Gr: It is. One of the most prominent Leningrad translators, A. Gitovich, uses this method with translating from the Old Chinese.

D: Is it possible to learn a language on one's own?

Gr: I learned two languages on my own in addition to those I learned at the university.

D: If Brodsky does not know Siberian, can he still produce a highly literary translation?

Gr: Of course.

D: Do you consider using a word for word translation as using someone else's work?

Gr: God forbid.

Lebedeva, a member of the jury: I am now looking at the book. There are only two short poems by Brodsky in it.

Gr: I wish to explain a few things about the specifics of the literary work. The thing is that . . .

J: Don't. So what is your opinion of Brodsky's poetry?

Gr: In my opinion, as a poet, Brodsky is very talented, a lot more so than many of those who are considered to be professional translators.

J: And why is he working alone and does not go to any literary organizations?

Gr: In 1958 he asked to be accepted into my literary organization. However, I heard him to be a hysterical young man and did not accept him, pushing him away with my own hands. That was my mistake, which I greatly regret. I will gladly accept him now and will work with him if he so desires.

Tiagly, a member of the jury: Did you yourself ever see him work or did he use someone else's work?

Gr: I never saw Brodsky sitting and writing. At the same time, I have never seen Sholokhov sit at a desk and write. And yet that does not mean . . .

J: It is indecent comparing Brodsky to Sholokhov. Didn't you ever explain to the youth that the government demands that they study? After all Brodsky only finished seven grades.

Gr: His knowledge is extensive. I am convinced of that after reading his poetry.

S: Did you ever read his bad, pornographic poems?

Gr: No, never.

D: I would like to ask you something. The results of Brodsky's work for 1963 is as follows: Poems in the book *Dawn Over Cuba*, translation of Galichinsky's poems (though not yet published), poems in the book *Yugoslavian Poets*, the gaucho songs and publication in *The Flame*. Can this be considered serious work?

Gr: Absolutely. It is a full year's work. As for the money, this work may not necessarily produce profits today, but in a few years. It is wrong to judge a young poet by the sum that he had received. He may not be lucky in the beginning and additional work may be required. As the joke goes: The difference between a parasite and a starting-out poet is that the parasite eats but does not work, while the poet works but may not always eat.

J: The court does not appreciate that remark. In our country, a man earns according to his work. Therefore, it can not be that a man who works a lot does not receive much. In our country where young poets are treated with such regard, how can you say that they starve? Why did you say that the young poets do not eat?

Gr: I did not say that. I simply suggested that there is truth to every joke. Starting-out poets' earnings are not at all proportional.

J: That depends on them. Besides, the court does not need such clarification. You have however explained that your comment was a joke. We will accept that.

(The next witness is called.)

J: Let me see the passport. Your last name is not very clear. (Takes the passport) Etkind . . . Yefim Gershevich . . . Go ahead.

Etkind: (A member of the Writers' Union and an instructor at the Gertsen University.) In my position in the literary sphere and connected with the education of young translators, I often had to read and listen to the translations of young artists. About a year ago, I had a chance to get acquainted with the works of Brodsky. These were the translations of a wonderful Polish poet, Galchinsky, whose poems were barely known to our readers and were almost never translated prior to this. I was tremendously impressed by the clarity of the poetic images, the musicality, the passion and the energy of the verse. I was also amazed by the fact that Brodsky mastered the Polish language on his own, without anyone's help. He read Galchinsky's poems in Polish, with the same enthusiasm with which he read his Russian translations. I realized that I was dealing with a man of rare talent, and what is not any less important, with capacity for work and assiduity. The translations which I had the chance to read later on, confirmed that opinion. These were, for example, the poems by the Cuban poet Fernandes, published in the book *Dawn Over Cuba*, and those of the contemporary Yugoslavian poets, printed in the edition of the State Literary Publications. I had many conversations with Brodsky and was amazed at his knowledge of American, English, and Polish literature.

Poetry translation is the most difficult job, which requires diligence, knowledge, and talent. On this path an artist may encounter numerous disappointments while the material gain is a thing of the distant future. One may translate poetry for a number of years without earning a ruble. Such work requires selfless love for poetry and work in general. Language, history, other cultures' studies, all that does not happen right away. Everything I know about Brodsky convinces me that he has a great future as a poet-translator ahead of him. This is not merely my opinion. The bureau of the translators' department, after finding out that the publishing house dissolved their contracts with Brodsky, made a unanimous decision about appealing to the director of the publishing house about giving Brodsky work and restoring with him the contracts.

I also know for a fact that this opinion is shared by the greatest authorities in the field of poetic translation, Marshak and Chukovsky, who are . . .

J: Speak only about yourself.

E: Brodsky must be given a chance as a poet-translator. Away from the big city, where there aren't the needed books nor the literary sphere, this is very difficult, almost impossible. I repeat that in my opinion this path holds a great future before him. I must say that I was very surprised when I saw the announcement "Brodsky—the parasite, on trial."

J: You did know about such a combination?

E: I did. However I did not think that the court would accept this. Keeping in mind Brodsky's poetic technique, there was nothing to prevent him from hack work. He could have easily translated hundreds of lines if he were doing that in a relaxed manner. The fact that he did not earn much does not at all mean that he is not a hard worker.

J: And why is he not a member of any organization?

E: He attended our translators' seminars.

J: Well, seminars . . .

E: He fit into the seminars in the sense . . .

J: And without sense? (Laughter from the public) That is, I meant to ask, Why did he not belong to any organization?

E: We do not offer membership, that is why I can not say "belonged." He came to us and read his translations.

J: (To Etkind) Did you have any problems at work or in your personal life?

E: (Puzzled) No. Actually I have not been at the university for the last two days. Perhaps something had happened.

(The question was perplexing for the public and apparently for the witness as well.)

J: Why is it that when you were talking about Brodsky's

knowledge you emphasized foreign literature? Why did you not speak of our literature?

E: I spoke with him as with a translator, and for that reason I was interested in his knowledge in the spheres of American, English, Polish literature. In those areas his knowledge is vast, diverse, nonsuperficial.

Smirnov: (A prosecution witness, in charge of the house of defense) I do not know Brodsky personally but I wish to say that if all citizens treated material earnings as he does, we won't have communism for long. Intellect is a dangerous weapon for its possessor. Everyone was saying how bright he is, practically a genius. Yet nobody said what kind of man he is. He grew up in a cultured family, but had only finished seven grades. I would like to know how many of those sitting here today would want to have a son with a seven-grade education? He did not serve in the army, for the reason of being the sole provider for his family. So what kind of provider is he? It was said that he is a talented translator, but nobody is saying that he is confused. And what about his anti-Soviet lines?

B: That is not true.

Sm: He should change many of his ideas. I also question that excuse that he had received from the psychiatric clinic. It was simply that his mighty friends began ringing all the bells and asked: Oh, save the young man! He should be treated with forced labor, and then no mighty friends will be able to help him. I don't know him personally, but I know of him from the press. And I have heard excuses. I question the medical excuse which released him from military service. I am not a doctor, but I question it.

Brodsky: When I was released from the service, I was released as the sole provider. My father was ill, in bed after a stroke, and I was working and earning a living. How do you know me to talk that way about me?

Sm: I got acquainted with your private diary.

B: On what grounds?

J: You do not have to answer that.

Sm: I read his poetry.

J: There are poems brought in evidence, which were not written by Brodsky. How do you know that the poems which you have read are really his? After all, you speak of poems not yet published.

Sm: I just know.

J: The next witness. Logunov.

L: (Assistant director of Ermitage, of the financial department.) I do not know Brodsky personally. I met him for the first time here in court. One can no longer live the way he does. I do not envy the parents of such a son. I've worked with writers and moved in their circles. I compare Brodsky with Oleg Shestinsky. Oleg traveled with the agitation brigade. He graduated from Leningrad State University and a university in Sofia. He also worked in the mines. What I wanted to say is that one must work, share all the cultural experiences. Then Brodsky's poetry would be real poetry. He must start his life over again.

D: Witnesses should talk about facts. They . . .

J: You will evaluate their testimonies later on. Next witness, Denisov.

Den: (Pipe layer from the CPD-20) I do not know Brodsky personally. I know of him from our press. I am here as a citizen and the representative of the community. I was appalled by what I read about Brodsky in the press. I wanted to get familiarized with his work. I went to the library, his books were not there. I asked my friends whether they have heard of him. No one has. I am a worker. In my life, I only changed two jobs. I am not satisfied with Brodsky's statement that he knew many trades. . . . You can not learn a trade in such a short period of time. I heard here that Brodsky has some ability as a poet. Why, then, was he not a member of any organization? Does he not accept the theory of dialectical materialism? Engels after all maintained that work makes a person. Brodsky, however, is not satisfied with such a formula. He thinks otherwise. Perhaps he is very talented, then why does he not find recognition in our literature? Why is he not working? I wish to express my opinion, that I find his work activity unsatisfactory.

J: The court calls Mr. Nikolayev.

N: (Retired) I don't know Brodsky personally. I just want to say that I know about him for the last three years by the detrimental influence that he has on his peers. I am a father. I have learned from personal experience what it's like to have a son who does not work. I have often seen Brodsky's poetry in my son's possessions. There is a forty-two-part poem and separate poems as well. I also know Brodsky from the case of Umansky. There is a saying: Tell me who your friends are and I will tell who you are. I knew Umansky personally. He is renowned for being anti-Soviet. Listening to Brodsky, I heard my son. My son also says that he considers himself a genius. Like Brodsky, he does not want to work. People like Brodsky and Umansky have a detrimental influence on their peers. I am surprised at Brodsky's parents. It seemed that they supported him in unison. From the style of his poems it is apparent that Brodsky can write poetry. However, these poems caused nothing but harm. Brodsky is not merely a parasite. He is a militant parasite. People like him should be treated without mercy. (Applause)

Tiagly, the jury member: So you think that Brodsky's poetry influenced your son?

N: Yes.

J: In a negative manner?

N: Yes.

D: And how do you know it was Brodsky's poetry?

N: There was a folder. On it, it was written "Joseph Brodsky."

D: Did your son know Umansky?

N: Yes.

D: Then why do you think that it was Brodsky and not Umansky who had the detrimental influence on your son?

N: I consider Brodsky and the likes of him to be of the same cloth. Brodsky's poems are shameful and anti-Soviet.

B: What are my anti-Soviet poems? Recite at least one line.

J: I forbid it.

B: But I would like to know what poems he is talking about. Perhaps they are not mine.

N: If I knew that I would be speaking to the court, I would make copies and bring them in.

J: The court calls Romashova.

R: (An instructor of Maxist-Leninst theory at the Mukhina School) I do not know Brodsky personally, but I know of his so-called activity. Pushkin said that talent is above all work. But look at Brodsky. Does he work? Does he do anything to make his poems comprehensible for the people? I am surprised that my colleagues are creating such a halo around him. After all, it is only in the Soviet state that the court speaks to him so benevolently, advising him to study in such a friendly manner. I, as a secretary of the party organization, of the Mukhina School, can honestly say that he influences the youth in a negative way.

D: Did you ever see Brodsky?

R: No. But his so-called activity allows me to judge him.

J: Can you give us more facts?

R: Being an educator of youth, I know their opinions of his poetry.

D: Are you yourself familiar with his poetry?

R: I am. It is horrible. I can not repeat his poems. They are awful.

J: The court calls Mr. Admoni. May I see your passport since the last name is quite unusual?

Admoni: (A professor at Gertsen University. A linguist, a man of literature, a translator.) When I heard that Joseph Brodsky is being tried for parasitism, I felt it my duty to express my opinion to the court. I consider myself to have every right to do so, since I've worked with the youth for about thirty years now as a university professor and also in view of the fact that I have been doing translations for many years.

I barely know Joseph Brodsky. We greet each other but have never exchanged more than two phrases. However, in the course of the last year, perhaps a bit longer, I have been following his translations intently, through his appearances at the translators' evenings and in publications. I was doing that because these translations were competent and expressive. Based on the translations of Galchinsky, Fernandes, and others, I can wholeheartedly say that they demanded tremendous work from the author. They serve as proof of the great skill and culture of the translator. Miracles do not happen. Neither skill nor culture come by themselves. They require constant and persistent work. Even if the translator is using the interlinear he must have a good conception of the language from which he is translating, feel the structure of that language, know the life and the culture of its people, etc., in order for the translation to be of real value. Besides doing all that, Brodsky was also studying the languages themselves. It is therefore clear to me that he worked, worked intensely and persistently. And after finding out today that he has only finished seven grades, I understood that his task of acquiring such skill and culture, which he possesses, was truly immense. One may use the words of Maiakovsky, "You exhaust one word for the sake of a thousand tons of verbal ore," when one speaks of the work of a poet-translator.

The statute used in the accusation against Brodsky is directed at those who do not work a lot, rather than those who do not earn a lot. For that reason the accusation of parasitism against Brodsky is absurd. A man who works as much as Brodsky, who works persistently without thinking of large profit, who is ready to restrict himself to the necessities so that he could only master his art and create true literary works, can not be accused of being a parasite.

J: What is it that you said about not judging those who do not earn a lot?

A: I said that according to this statute those judged should not be the ones who do not earn a lot but those who do not work a lot.

J: What do you mean by that? Did you read statute 4 which says that communism is achieved only through the work of millions?

A: Any work which benefits the society should be respected.

Tiagly: Where did Brodsky read his translations and in what languages did he read?

A: (Smiling) He read in Russian. He translates from foreign languages into Russian.

J: If a simple person asks you a question, you must answer him and not smile.

A: I am explaining that he was translating from Polish and Serbian into Russian.

J: Address the court not the public.

A: I apologize. It is a habit of a professor to speak to the audience.

J: Mr. Voyevodin (a witness), do you know Brodsky. . . .

CONVERSATIONS IN THE COURTROOM

"Writers. We should get rid of all of them."

"Intellectuals! They sit on our back."

"What about the intellectuals? Don't you think they work also?"

"And what are you? Look how she is working using someone else's labor."

"I can also get an interlinear and start translating poetry."

"Do you know what an interlinear is? Do you know how a poet uses it?"

"Big deal."

"I know Brodsky. He is a good man and a good poet."

"He's anti-Soviet. Did you hear the prosecutor?"

"Did you hear what the defense attorney said?"

"She spoke for money, the prosecutor did it for free. That means he is right."

"Of course. All those defense attornies want is the money. The more the better. Everything else does not concern them."

"That is nonsense."

"Are you insulting me? Careful or I'll call the bailiff. Did you hear what the prosecution recited?"

"He wrote that a long time ago."

"So what?"

"I am a teacher. If I did not believe in education, what kind of teacher would I be?"

"You see what is happening to our children?"

"But Brodsky wasn't even given a chance to defend himself."

"That's enough. We have heard enough of your Brodsky."

"Hey you! You are the one who was taking notes. Why were you taking notes?"

"I am a journalist. I write about education, and I want to write about this."

"What's there to write about? Everything is clear here."

"All of you are in this together. We should take away your notes."

"Try it!"

"So what will happen?"

"Try it and you'll see."

"So you are threatening me! Bailiff! I'm being threatened!"

"He is a bailiff and not a policeman, to jump at every word."

"Bailiff, you are being called a policeman! You should all be thrown out of Leningrad! Then you'd find out what it is all about. You parasites!"

"Comrades, what are you talking about? He will be vindicated. Didn't you hear the defense attorney?"

The judge comes back and the verdict is read:

"Brodsky systematically did not perform the duties of Soviet man of producing material good and providing for himself. That is apparent from his numerous changes of jobs. He was warned by the department of Moscow State Security in 1961 and by police in 1963. He promised to find permanent employment but did not. He continued not working. He continued writing and reading his decadent poems. From the deposition of the Committee working with the young poets, it is apparent that he was not considered a poet. He was criticized by the readers of *The Evening Leningrad*. For those reasons the court in accordance with the statute of 5.4.1961 sentences Brodsky to five years of internal exile and hard labor."

The bailiffs passing the defense attorney: So? Guess you lost the case, comrade attorney.

BUKHARIN

The Measure of the Law and the Excesses of Lawlessness
by Lev Ovrutskiy, *Sovetskaya Kultura*, February 27, 1988

The political lexicon tends toward unambiguity and therefore avoids figurative language. About restructuring they say—a "fresh wind," a "wind of change." At best, bordering on poetic license, a "fresh wind of change." Wishing to make what contribution I can to the process of metaphorization, while continuing the meteorological theme, I would compare restructuring to spring rain washing away the gray film of cataracts from our crystalline lenses, making our vision sharper and more detailed.

On recovering our sight we notice that life has gotten bigger. Ordinary events used just to disappear; today each has acquired a distinct significance and meaning. But one recent event stands out amid this unusual sequence. I am talking about the 4 February USSR Supreme Court resolution quashing the sentences passed on N.I. Bukharin, A.I. Rykov, A.P. Rozengolts, M.A. Chernov, P.P. Bulanov, L.G. Levin, I.N. Kazakov, V.A. Maksimov-Dikovskiy, P.P. Kryuchkov, and Kh.G. Rakovskiy. In March 1938 they were convicted in the case of the so-called anti-Soviet "right-wing Trotskiyist bloc."

The old dogmas, desiccated herbarium dwellers, are crumbling. Increasingly social justice is becoming historical justice. I believe that the majority of readers will have straightened their shoulders and sighed with relief and hope. And made some atheist's equivalent of the sign of the cross: "At long last." They had believed and waited. Nigh on 50 years had passed.

The waiting was over.

BUREAUCRACY

Secrets of the Peace Fund
Izvestiya, March 31, 1988

At our enterprise it was proposed that a day's wages be deducted for the Peace Fund. But this proposal generated no enthusiasm and it was not for nothing that people started saying that it was "an enforced voluntary measure." People are frankly saying that the Peace Fund organization has become surrounded by a bureaucratic apparatus and we do not want to finance trips abroad for its officials and the payment for this apparatus. Why are reports on the expenditure of Peace Fund assets published only irregularly? At general meetings it was decided to deduct money for the children's fund and specifically for a children's home. Please understand us correctly: People do not begrudge money for specific measures connected with the struggle for peace. People do not begrudge money for orphans and underprivileged children. Nor are there any problems with aid to the victims of Chernobyl or natural disasters. But everyone is sick of bureaucracy!
—A. Chizhov, Leningrad

Problems and Opinions Rubric:
On State Ownership and Pluralism
by Ye. Proshechkin, *Sovetskaya Litva*, January 29, 1989

State ownership of the means of production is a great gain for the Soviet people! This postulate from the "Short Course [of the History] of the All-Union Communist Party (Bolsheviks)" was accepted by us a long time ago as an axiomatic term giving rise to no doubts. Nonetheless, I will take the liberty of expressing a few doubts. . . .

Ever since Lenin's time and to this very day, a struggle against bureaucratism has been waged in the country but so far—let's be blunt—without any particular success. What is happening, what is the reason for bureaucratism's tenacity of life? What provides its economic basis? The answer to this question is to be found with the classics of Marxism. **In his work "Toward a Critique of Hegel's Philosophy of Law," K. Marx remarked that a bureaucrat perceives state property as his own property and considers it the source of his prosperity and of the immutability of his situation. In other words, the struggle against bureaucratism is a pointless occupation as long as state ownership in the country occupies such a colossal position in social production.** The supercentralization of economic management is an ideal breeding ground for the flourishing of bureaucracy. . . .

What happens when all other forms of ownership—apart from state ownership—are abolished? Forms are abolished, but property remains in the form of specific articles, commodities, means of production, natural resources, and so on. At whose disposal are they now? The state's? But the state is not a living person, it cannot issue instructions. This is done by people, by a small group of administrators with hitherto unprecedented economic might concentrated in their hands and with all the ensuing consequences for the people (violence, personality cult, and so on).

The fact that, in conditions of the development of commodity-money relations and the combination of different forms of ownership, the owners's influence on policy is indirect, is certainly a restraining element as regards the intensification of state bureaucracy. **"Every monopoly inevitably leads to stagnation," V.I. Lenin wrote.** It seems that we should have realized at least this, if nothing else. For many years on end we have been led by one single party following one single general line.

I can expect to hear voices of indignation: Look at him, what a target to pick! Was it not the party that launched restructuring? Yes indeed, who else should have launched it if not the most sober-minded people belonging to the one and only real political force in the country? But the point now is that the party should become the leading, inspiring—and so on—force, not just in declarations but actually in reality! What is needed for this purpose is not some amorphous mass, not a submissive and unanimous crowd but a creative multitude of voices; in other words a fundamental opportunity must be created to form freely competing organizations expressing different shades of public opinion. Otherwise there will be nobody to be "inspired" and nobody to be "organized," since the sum of even millions of zeros is still nothing but zero. Struggle between social forces and opinions does not weaken the party but, on the contrary, verifies its course and gets rid of gross mistakes and deformations. As a matter of fact, the multiparty system is a phenomenon which exists in socialist countries and gets on very well with socialism. . . . The argument that the single-party system is an "historical development" in our country is also unconvincing. What a fatalistic view of history! History is made by people, and if historical experience teaches them that a certain option has not proved its worth, they are free to seek an alternative. As a matter of fact, neither the USSR Constitution nor any other legislative act prohibits the multiparty system; all they speak about is the CPSU's leading role. But these are different matters. To lead—not in conditions of a no-loser lottery but in conditions which exclude any monopoly of the truth—is the meaning of the system of pluralism. I think that both the leading party's prestige and our whole society will gain from this.

Unhealthy Instructions
by Natalya Loginova, *Moscow News*, March 8, 1989

Lyudmila Lunina flew in to Moscow from Yakutsk, 3,000 miles away. In the Far North, where she lives, people are entitled to longer holiday leave, and she had big plans to spend part of her vacation in Bulgaria and then to visit her mother in Kiev. On her first day in Moscow Lyudmila was hit by a car and ended up in hospital with a broken arm. Three weeks later, her arm in plaster, she was discharged and told to return to Yakutsk.

Why? Because her sick leave could be extended or ended only by officials at her place of residence. The doctors said she could only spend three days travelling, after which the sick leave slip entitling its bearer to extend leave and payment become invalid, a mere scrap of paper.

The young woman didn't believe that doctors could send patients on long flights across the length of the country and phoned **MN. MN** called the Ministry of Public Health to find out why Moscow doctors had urged their patients to take a plane to Yakutsk to endorse her sick-leave slip when she, despite her plastered arm, wanted to go to Kiev? And if she flew, who would refund the cost of the return air ticket—268 roubles?

There was a heavy sigh on the other end of the line: "It's silly, of course. But that's what the All-Union Central Council of Trade Unions' instruction says. Many people simply can't abide by it: they can't reach their homes in three days' time. This riles everyone who finds themselves in such a situation. But this instruction is law for us. We violate it by calling the Council and going down on our knees, because we understand the anger of the patients who complain to us."

It's hard to find someone at the Council who can explain the existence of this instruction. Many people I talked to knew about the silly rule but could not see why Lunina should fly to Yakutsk instead of to Kiev. One resolute female said over the phone: "Is the patient in plaster? Right, this means she isn't on vacation. If she has sick leave, she is supposed to stay at home!"

I tried to explain that her home was halfway across the world, that she was going to her mother who was to take good care of her. "But is she in plaster? Yes. So this makes her on sick leave! If she goes to Kiev, it would mean she is on both sick and annual leave!" Further reasoning was futile.

We managed to help Lunina "by way of exception."

We spent some time at the **MN** office trying to fathom why the trade union body should, without any benefit for itself, curtail freedom and dip into the purses of those unfortunate enough to land in hospital away from home. We concluded that it was obviously not a matter of a conspiracy with the transport people—they were not interested in taking anyone anywhere—nor of people's recovery. It all stems from the fact that inventing instructions is the only way of receiving a salary for a large section of the able-bodied population. The more there are instructions, the harder it is to invent new ones. But they must not, at any cost, lose their jobs. As for any other logic, there is none.

CENSORSHIP

The More Freedom, the Greater the Responsibility. Will Censorship and Glasnost Get Along?
by Master of Laws Mikhail Fedotov, *Moscow News*, October 23, 1988

"I proposed taking this phrase out, for it might make the reader think that censorship exists in this country," was how a representative of the Chief Administration for the Protection of State Secrets in the Press, attached to the USSR Council of Ministers

(V. Rozantsev, *Soviet News*)

(Glavlit), tried to formulate his argument five years ago when he spoke before the editors of a prestigious magazine. But even though his words sounded strange, no one at the editor's briefing even smiled. And he himself had no desire to joke either, because the organization he represented protected state secrets, while it had somehow happened that the very existence of preliminary censorship had become a secret, too. But for whom was it really a secret? It's a familiar scene from our past life—we know that some phenomenon exists, but maintain that it doesn't.

Answering the questions of a *L'humanité* correspondent, Mikhail Gorbachev said quite definitely that yes, we do have censorship. Its task is to prevent the divulgement of state and military secrets, and the illegal propaganda of war, violence, cruelty, offending an individual or pornography. The habitual mist that shrouded censorship for so many years is just beginning to lift. Today we're already able to judge what sort of an institution it is, and whether there aren't other, alternative possibilities for dealing with the same problems.

Censorship has existed for many centuries and has engendered a variety of different types. One type is the preliminary censorship which was widely used in the last century. The most critical things said about it were probably those said by young Karl Marx. He thought that the introduction of censorship was an expression of mistrust of the press, of public opinion and of the people. Censorship acts secretly and, because of this, it tries (and quite often succeeds) in remaining outside the bounds of criticism. Lastly, censorship by its very nature leads to a condemnation of the opinion of anyone who thinks differently than the censor and his bosses. The paradox is that censorship, without desiring to do so, makes any work which it forbids seem attractive, regardless of its real value. Marx noted that by hiding unfavourable facts and contradictory opinions from glasnost, thus creating a false picture of well-being, censorship does not bring well-being nearer to all, but turns the people into a "rabble of private individuals". . . .

After the victory of the October Revolution, given the continuing struggle, to tolerate the existence of the counter-revolutionary press would mean, as Lenin said, "allowing Kaledin's Bombs to be reinforced by the bombs of falsehood". That's why a decree was issued on the second day of Soviet power, which established that the organs of the press that call for open resistance and disobedience to the government, or sow trouble through an obviously slanderous distortion of facts, or call for activities of a criminal nature, are to be closed down either temporarily or permanently. But censorship was not introduced. **I think that to the majority of the professional revolutionaries, who had themselves experienced the humiliating feeling of making speeches in Aesopian language, the very idea of "red censorship" seemed alien.** Lenin's position was clearly expressed in the Decree on the Press—"as soon as the new system is firmly established, all administrative influences on the press will be ended; it will enjoy complete freedom within the limits of responsibility to the court, according to the broadest and the most progressive law relating to the particular case."

However, we've had to wait for this law on the press for seven decades, while the idea of preliminary censorship was quickly implemented by a budding bureaucracy. In May 1919, the press department of the Moscow Soviet obligated all publishers in the capital to ask its permission before publishing any manuscript. The Council of People's Commissars was angry—what grounds did they have for this? And it annulled the resolution.

Preliminary censorship was introduced throughout Russia by

the November 12, 1921 Decree on Private Publishers—permission from Gosizdat (state publishers) or Gubpolitprosvet (regional political enlightenment organization) was needed in order to publish any manuscript. This decree was adopted by the Smaller Council of People's Commissars and signed by Aleksandr Tsyurupa. Several months later, on June 6, 1922, the Council of People's Commissars approved—with the signature of Alexey Rykov, its Vice-Chairman—a Statute on the Main Administration of Literary and Publishing Affairs, attached to the People's Commissariat for Education (Glavlit).

At first it was authorized to issue permission for setting up new organs of the press and publishing houses, to compile lists of forbidden editions, and to subject manuscripts to preliminary read-throughs. Certain publications by Comintern, the State Publishers, Glavpolitprosvet, the newspaper *Izvestiya Vtsik*, the entire Party press and the works of the Academy of Sciences were free from this control. In these publications, Glavlit succeeded in securing only the interests of subsequent military censorship by looking over already-printed publications. There were few cases when a work was forbidden. If it found in a manuscript something going against soviet power, a divulsion of military secrets, anything which might excite nationalistic or religious fanaticism, pornography, or any provocation of public opinion by giving false data, then Glavlit vetoed the work.

Not too long after that the concept of "military secrets" was replaced by the broader "data not to be divulged," and instead of "anti-Soviet agitation" there appeared "works containing hostile ideology concerning social life, religion, the economy, national relations, the arts, etc." It is easy to understand that these "flexible" formulas provided boundless opportunities for advocates of the administrative-command methods of management in ideology and culture.

Soon Glavlit was enjoying the right of giving consent to the appointment of editors and changing members on editorial boards. And at the beginning of the 1930's it was entrusted with drawing up the list of the data that it intended to protect. Then the situation with those publications which had previously been free of control also changed. The only things Glavlit couldn't control were secret documents, forms, account books, office books and wall newspapers.

So stood matters in the mid-1930's—there is absolutely precise and available data about that.

Now let's take a look at today. Restructuring, especially in its second period, makes known the need for a reasonable combination of the forms of society's control over the mass media with glasnost, openness and socialist pluralism. I think that this control must discard what are obviously obsolete organizational forms and reinstate Lenin's concept of "responsibility to the court, according to the broadcast and most progressive law relating to the particular case." The notorious blue (or red?) pencil is more suitable in the hand of an editor than it is in the hand of an official. Although there are journalists behind these officials' backs who prefer not to stick their necks out to defend public interests, justifying this with "the censors won't let it through anyway."

Today the CPSU is building its relations with the media in a spirit of mutual respect and trust. Against this background the essentially bureaucratic, preliminary censorship looks like a monument to the style of administrative command.

Of course, we cannot help but take into account the need for protecting state and other secrets. But why censorship? Such secrets aren't born in editorial offices. They can only reach editors through the negligence of the officials to whom they were entrusted. Wouldn't it be more sensible to guard such secrets at the places where they're supposed to be, and not at the places they accidentally find their way to?

Lastly, the very list of secrets, especially of classified information, has grown to unnatural proportions. It looks like it's time to reduce such lists to the necessary minimum. And to openly publish the lists of state secrets (without disclosing them). By the way, that's exactly how it was in the 1920's, and the list itself fitted easily on a single page. That way it will be known beforehand exactly which information should not be used in the press, and what punishment the court would impose on the journalist who violates the ban.

If it is possible to protect secrets without the aid of preliminary censorship, then it is even easier to do without it when we deal with, say, calls for war or violence. There are always a responsible editor, an author and the Criminal Code. The system of internal newspaper editorial control and subsequent responsibility to the court is quite capable of keeping our press from being saturated with publications containing war propaganda, pornography, calls for violence and any items insulting individuals—in other words, containing anything punishable by law.

The very development of the media is forcing preliminary censorship to gradually give up its hold. There are more and more "live" programmes on the radio and TV, and fewer and fewer subjects forbidden to the press. And now there's this article, too. If, of course, they let it through. . . .

Airwaves Free from "Black Holes"
by B. Pipiya, *Pravda*, March 15, 1989

Moscow—For about 50 years there was a secret department at the USSR Ministry of Communications, which in recent years was known by the staffers, among themselves, as the "Krestyaninova service." Nataliya Yevgenyevna Krestyaninova was for 25 years in charge of radio transmitting devices designed to create artificial interference to foreign radio stations throughout the USSR's territory.

The practice of subversive radio broadcasting by one country to another began as long ago as the twenties. Radio countermeasures began at about the same time. Thus in Paris in 1923 radio transmitters installed on the Eiffel Tower were jamming Berlin radio. Austria tried to jam Nazi Germany's transmissions. In 1934 a station in Klaypeda was active against subversive broadcasts against Lithuania from Koenigsberg.

In 1937 an intergovernmental conference in Geneva, under the auspices of the League of Nations, drew up a convention on the use of radio broadcasting in the interests of peace. The articles of the international treaty confirmed, in particular, the right of every state to ban and immediately stop all broadcasts that might incite the citizens of the territory in question to acts contrary to internal order and security. The convention was adopted by 22 countries. Among those who did not sign were Germany, Italy, Japan, and the United States. Two years later a special service was created in our country to jam the "radio voices." Communications experts were on duty around the clock in every union republic and in kray cities and the majority of oblast cities, jamming foreign broadcasts.

In Moscow, for instance, it worked like this. The so-called control and positioning point was situated on Taganka. Work was done in four shifts. The operator found the voice of Radio Liberty, for instance, on professional receivers, and gave a command by way of a direct link to the radio broadcasting station: "Switch on the first transmitter with antenna number one at a frequency of 5955 kilohertz." Interference appeared on the air.

Depending on current events and the political situation in the world, the center received special instructions on which broadcasts to "kill" and which not to touch.

N. Krestyaninova showed me the now unnecessary documentation of her service. There is a map, "Areas of Operation of Foreign Radio Stations Broadcasting to the USSR." It shows the positions of radio transmitters. For instance, the Voice of America broadcasts to us from the United States, Britain, the FRG, Greece, Morocco, and the Philippines. The BBC from Britain, Cyprus, Oman . . .

Radio Liberty and Free Europe broadcasts in all the languages of the Soviet republics. The Voice of America broadcasts in Russian, Ukrainian, Uzbek, and the languages of the peoples of the Baltic region and the Transcaucasus, and the Voice of Israel in Russian and Georgian. In all, 38 radio stations from 28 countries broadcast to the USSR today. Radio Liberty ranks first in terms of the volume of broadcasts. It is on the air for 71 hours in every 24 hours, the Voice of America for 23 hours 45 minutes, Radio Beijing for 15 hours 35 minutes. . . .

And now the service for radio countermeasures to foreign broadcasting has been entirely abolished. But it would be naive to think that with our restructuring and new thinking, the tasks of certain foreign "voices" have changed and they now operate exclusively in the interests of the struggle for peace, freedom, and mutual understanding. As before, alongside honest, objective, and well-intentioned broadcasts, one can encounter lies, falsifications, and distortions on the air. All these methods from the "psychological warfare" arsenal do not, of course, promote trust between countries.

Nonetheless it was decided to abolish the "Krestyaninova service." One feels this decision is fully in accordance with the policy of glasnost and openness pursued by the Soviet leadership. First, the majority of radio listeners are capable of deciding for themselves what is true and what is a lie, what is information and what is the cunning manipulation of "facts." Second, from now on there is no need to spend money on the maintenance and operation of the "jammers."

How will the radio transmitters and equipment thus made available be used?

"Some of the former 'jammers' will, it has been decided, be used to relay radio broadcasts from all the union republics in Moscow," A. Varbanskiy, first deputy chief of the USSR Ministry of Communications Main Administration of Space and Radio Communications, says. "From 14 March the voices of the Ukraine,

Belorussia, Moldavia, and the Baltic republics came on the air on the short-wave frequencies of 31 and 49 meters, from 21 March Azerbaijan, Armenia, and Georgia will join them, and a week later Kazakhstan and the Central Asian republics. A list of frequencies for the new radio broadcasts will be published in the weekly *Govorit I Pokazyvayet Moskva*.

"The question of the use of short-wave communications in the state geophysical system is now being studied in conjunction with the USSR Ministry of Geology. This would make it possible to transmit geophysical field data from the sites to the center, for subsequent processing and decisionmaking."

Letters "Not for Publication": New Blank Spots, *Izvestiya*, August 17

Just recently we, the employees of city public libraries, were summoned to a special seminar and, after being told that these were the instructions of higher authorities, were ordered to remove from our collections the works of Brezhnev, Grishin, Suslov, Chernenko and a number of other authors, as well as all the political and economic literature published prior to March 1985, as material that is outdated and no longer relevant. It was recommended that we remove the documents of the 22nd through the 26th Party Congresses from our shelves and tell any patrons who ask for them that they are currently in use.

Doesn't this mean that, while granting access to the archival documents of 50 years ago, we are creating new "blank spots" in our most recent history?

—I. Zavgorodnyaya, Crimea Province

More Democracy—Fewer Secrets
Izvestiya, February 10, 1989

E. PARKHOMOVSKIY FEATURE comprising readers' letters to Doctor of Economic Sciences V. Boldyrev, chief of the Main Administration for Safeguarding State Secrets in the Press, and his responses to them under the rubric "Readers' Dialogue with Chief of the USSR Main Administration for Safeguarding State Secrets in the Press."

Since the publication of our *Izvestiya* correspondent's conversation with Doctor of Economic Sciences V. Boldyrev, chief of the USSR Council of Ministers Main Administration for Safeguarding State Secrets in the Press (USSR Glavlit), under the heading "More Democracy—Fewer Secrets" (*Izvestiya* No 308, 1988), the editorial office has been flooded with mail. Noting the frankness of this conversation with satisfaction, and the fact that democratization has also affected the work of Glavlit, the letter writers have particularly drawn attention to V. Boldyrev's idea that "it is essential to overcome the force of inertia preventing certain departments—including our own, it must be confessed—from shaking off the old approaches and stereotyped attitudes." We selected several letters, which seemed to us to be the most typical and principled, and asked V. Boldyrev to answer them in the same spirit of frankness. This produced the dialogue we publish below.

I. TETEREV, candidate of technical sciences and lecturer from Tyumen: For every item which we wish to publish we are forced to complete a so-called expert's report (we are talking about publications of a technical nature—editor). Previously, this consisted of two pages, but now there are four. It contains every bureaucratic obstacle imaginable. **If you do not confirm that you are a fool and that your article contains nothing new, you should not hold out too much hope of publication. So we lie every hour of every day.** This is because any scientific article naturally contains new elements. It goes without saying that these elements will not go unnoticed abroad. Just as anything new they publish does not go unnoticed. Such is the nature of scientific development. So why do we have to practice self-deception, hiding behind the mania for secrecy? Why do we waste so much paper on filling out "reports" which no one needs? I propose that we simplify the procedure by which scientific articles undergo examination by experts, abolish these so-called expert reports, and give the author the right to publish his own results.

V. BOLDYREV: I. Teterev obviously works in one of those organizations where the new procedure for preparing material for the press has yet to become established, and so he claims that this procedure has not been simplified in any way. In reality, however, a new interdepartmental regulation on the procedure for preparing material for publication came into force early last summer. It envisages a fundamentally new type of expert's report that is no more than half a page long and only needs one signature. In the past this report would be signed by every member of the commission—often five or more people. Moreover, the experts' decision can now be registered by putting the appropriate stamp on the item. The range of people with the right to carry out an expert examination is now broader. The size and composition of the expert commission, its work procedure, and also the form of the author's involvement in the examination of his material are no longer decided from above but by the leaders of the organization concerned. I cannot share the opinion that these expert commissions should be abolished and the right to assess the possibility of publication given to the author himself. The practice of Glavlit's work shows that a considerable amount of secret information has hitherto had to be removed from material we have monitored that has not been through a commission of experts. The author often simply does not possess the necessary information to establish the possibilities for utilizing his results. He also cannot know all the press restrictions. That is the responsibility of the experts, who undergo special training for this purpose.

Reader Complains of Letter Interception
Letter under the rubric "Letters . . . Not for Publication": Letter to BBC, *Izvestiya*, January 4, 1989

I have sent several letters to the BBC and VOA. Have they stopped jamming the two radio stations? They have. That means they are not banning them. What is not banned is permitted. That is what we have been told for all to hear. Everything would seem to be clear. Not one of my letters has reached its destination or been returned. If the letters had reached their destination, I would have known from the broadcast. They list all the letters they have received.

Not so long ago there was a program on the BBC about the work of the Soviet mail. The presenter said that he was prepared to supply British mail service receipts for mail items which had left the country although the addressees in the Soviet Union had not received them and nothing had been returned. A direct line was set up on this program. You could telephone to London and talk with the presenters. There were a great many telephone calls and everyone complained that they had sent letters, registered letters with notification documents. But neither the former nor the latter [as published] arrived or were returned, and that includes the notification documents. As for simple letters, we cannot prove their existence: Receipts are not issued for such letters.

If the loss of letters addressed abroad is just a matter of chance, these cases are being repeated somewhat too often.

—D. Shesterkin, Krivoy Rog

A Game of Monopoly That Goes Against Lenin
Letter to the editor of *Ogonyek*
by Y. Vakhtin and M. Golubovsky

The government monopoly of the press in the Soviet Union today has not always existed. In a decree on December 12, 1921, the government allowed private publishing houses, which could own offices, print shops, warehouses and so on.

By 1923 there were over 70 such private publishing houses in Leningrad alone. But then, together with the other forms of co-operative enterprise, all of them were banned and closed down.

The ban on co-operatives was only lifted after the 27th Congress of the CPSU (in 1986), which declared a course of comprehensive democratisation of our society as a foundation for its radical economic and cultural rehabilitation.

But the government decree on December 29, 1988, restores the ban on co-op "publishing activities to turn out works of science, literature and art". It makes these activities as inadmissible as producing firearms, poisons and drugs, or private dealings in foreign currency.

Who can possibly benefit from having fewer "works of science, literature and art" published in the Soviet Union? No-one can answer that. Could it be prompted by fear of a loss of government control? But the co-ops have never published a single book without the permission of the government censorship bodies, and never will.

Or could it be the limited capacity of the printing facilities? If so, the situation can be quickly improved by co-ops manufacturing copiers and other printing machines—assuming they are not hamstrung by legal snags, of course. The decree, however, places these co-ops under the control of agencies which have proved their total lack of interest in products of that category.

Perhaps the problem is the paper shortage then? But co-op publishing houses would quickly galvanise other co-ops to produce recycled paper from the wastepaper incinerated, or just sat on, by various ministries and departments.

We would like competent lawyers to say whether the decree of December 29, 1988, is even lawful in the first place. After all, it aims not only to "regulate some forms of cooperative activities" as its official title says, but to directly ban many such activities. It empowers the governments of the 15 republics to ban any forms of co-op activities, as before. So what is left of the Law on Co-operatives?

It is also unacceptable that a sweeping ban on co-op publishing and the manufacture of copying equipment should be imposed before the draft Law on the Press has been published.

The government decree of October 27, 1917, signed by Lenin, clearly states: "As soon as the new political system settles in, all administrative leverage on the press will be stopped, and it will be granted full freedom within the limits of responsibility before the courts, in accordance with the broadest possible and most progressive laws in this respect."

We urge the new parliament to revise the latest decree, to cancel the ban on co-op publishing and to pass the promised fully democratic law on the press.

COLD WAR

We Are All in the Same Boat
by Nikolay Popov, *Literaturnaya Gazeta*, March 1, 1989

THE AUTHOR IS a doctor of historical sciences.

In all of our discussions on a foreign political theme we have proceeded from the notion—a kind of constant in the U.S.-Soviet equation—of the "consistent peace-loving Soviet foreign policy." "Their presidents and parties in power change and along with them their policies, but we have collective leadership, consistently carrying out ..." The world is black and white, bipolar:

the "camp of socialism and peace" and the "camp of capitalism and war." The West has repeated the same stereotypes, investing them with different meaning. The situation is clear, although alarming, and at times, as during the Caribbean crisis, it leads us to the brink of nuclear disaster. Correspondingly, the military doctrine also assumed our complete victory in any conflict, in any encounter with the enemy camp: And if the aggressor were a nuclear power, it would suffer a crushing attack from our armed forces.

The seventies brought a certain softening of the rhetoric. The term "sober thinking" appeared in regard to our enemies: These are the capitalists who, seeing the inevitability of their "decay" and departure from the world arena, do not intend to subject mankind to war and are ready to quietly wait out their time.

But the truth, it seems, has gradually made its way into the awareness of both camps: In modern war there will be no winners, it will be mutually destructive; and, consequently, confrontation must be lessened and diluted by various kinds of cooperation. Perhaps it is also necessary in and of itself—each can also live without help from the other side—but it would be desirable if only for the sake of getting used to one another and to reduce the mistrust. It goes without saying that in general we are still enemies, and were it not for the threat of the nuclear apocalypse we would not experience any special pleasure from communication and would try to do as much harm to one another as we could.

In this respect our relations remind one of the intelligent spiders in the bank who cooperate out of necessity in order to get out of there, or the representatives of the Montekki and Capuletti clans who ended up on an uninhabited island and built a boat together so they could escape and continue their hostilities under more convenient circumstances. Peaceful coexistence in the traditional interpretation meant the competition of two firms trying to force each other out of the market but at the same time trading with one another. In both cases the initial hostility is assumed; incompatibility, just as tissues from different organisms are incompatible, like matter and antimatter. What is the main reason or reasons for our conflict with America, which has sucked the last juices from us and led the whole world to the verge of destruction and at the same time has become a necessary evil for many generations of people both in the Soviet Union and the United States? Energetic attempts are now being made to reduce the danger of a nuclear standoff and normalize relations, both political and economic and cultural. The first successes have been achieved in disarmament, and the danger seems to be decreasing. But the profound mistrust of us remains and, correspondingly, along with the rapprochement there continue to be arms, particularly SDI; the danger of war is decreasing slowly, and billions are being cast to the winds. For example, an influential conservative observer, G. Will, writes that Gorbachev's policy is an attempt to "camouflage a tank with sugar coating" and that his policy is based on a "belief in the inevitability of a final conflict between the socialist and capitalist camps." What is the reason for this conflict, and what do we share and what can we never share in this world?

Any school child will tell you that the reason for the discord between our socioeconomic and political systems is that capitalism and socialism are irreconcileable enemies—our progressive system must replace the capitalist system, which has outlived its time. And peaceful coexistence is a peaceful form of competition, of struggle between them, so that the "elimination" will take place without wars.

In general we have tried to divide the world into zones of influence: the capitalist zone according to the American model and the socialist according to ours. What have we achieved? The capitalist world, in spite of all American efforts after World War II and the billions of dollars that have been spent, is departing more and more from the "American" model. The ungrateful Japanese, whom for a fairly long time the Americans called "cheap imitators," not only have begun not to copy the American model, but also have surpassed their teachers in many ways, including labor productivity and such branches as electronics and automotive construction.

We "sell" abroad a model, an item which we ourselves have not completely tested, have not brought, as it were, to the point of industrial production: This is still the experimental model of socialism. We, who have persuaded Asia and Africa to follow our example, are ourselves actually beginning a new experiment. We have already gotten a long way away from Saint-Simon, Fourier, Marx, and Engels. What we have are the dreams of the great utopians and Marxists, the fourth dream of Vera Pavlovna, and other models from artistic literature. The closest thing we have had to the real plans was the NEP, Lenin's cooperative socialism which its author did not manage to realize, although there was plenty of promise of world revolution and the victory of communism on a world scale. This was also burned into the memories of the rest of the people.

We are practically beginning all over again. We should construct socialism at home without a lot of noise and fanfare and achieve slow and modest but real successes. We should not construct endless Intourist Potemkin villages to show to the foreigners, but construct roads and pipelines; we should not put on a grandiose show, which leads the country to the brink of crisis, but raise the standard of living of the people just a little bit. We are called a "superpower," but in many respects we are a poor and developing superpower. All the statistics in the service of the cost economy and the self-reproducing political elite and its propaganda apparatus were directed at the production of advantageous figures that show "further successes" and the "flourishing of the socialist economy"—ore, iron, fertilizers, combines; behind them were concealed relatively "insignificant" indicators— the real provision of the people with housing, food, clothing, and conveniences—and the "discrediting" data completely evaporated —the infant mortality rate, which is among the highest in developed countries, pollution of the environment, and social problems such as drug addiction and prostitution. Moreover, as the song goes, "we are making missiles and damming up the Yenisey."

We must see our country through the eyes of the rest of the world, both a half century ago and now, in order to understand the sources of the policies of the Western states with respect to us. In general it is difficult to look at oneself from the outside, and it is frequently painful, but if we have mustered to resolve to "figure out the society in which we live," as M. S. Gorbachev said at the February (1988) Plenum of the CPSU Central Committee, "having suffered and having allowed to pass through our consciousness and spirit the experience and lessons of the past," in exactly the same way we must straighten out our foreign political past and the roots of our problems with the rest of the world.

For [prerevolutionary] Europe and the United States our country was not only and not so much the country of the DneproGES, 5-year plans, the elimination of illiteracy, and the Stakhanovite movement, Gorkiy, Eisenstein, and the Chelyuskin crew; it was primarily a country of bloody forced collectivization, mass persecutions and camps, a country of terror and dictatorship, the country of Stalin. In the eyes of many Europeans and Americans "Stalin's Russia" stood right alongside "Hitler's Germany," and for some the reputation of the Soviet Union was even lower since Stalinism as a state policy began before fascism did. It is naive or hypocritical to be surprised or indignant about the intractability of England and France in their relations with us during the thirties—the reason for this was not only the inconsistency, the cowardice, and the short-sightedness of the leaders of these countries who participated in the collusion treaty in Munich but also the people of these countries had placed us on the same level with fascist Germany and had to make a choice between the two evils. How, for example, could the military figures of England and France hope that the Stalinist government would be true to its word and what could their military delegations expect from the leader of the Soviet delegation, K. Ye. Voroshilov, who along with Stalin and his stooges destroyed the best of the Soviet Army? . . .

When speaking of the "cold war" with the West, historians frequently note that among our allies the talks concerning opposing the Soviet Union right up to the point of joining with Nazi Germany were taking place already in 1943. Actually, our confrontation with the West took place in the twenties and thirties. In the eyes of the world community two unprecedented colossuses had been formed: Hitler's Germany and Stalin's Soviet Union. The differences in the ideological slogans—the supremacy of the German race and the inevitability of its expansion on one hand, and the reign of brotherhood and justice under socialism on the other—did not do much to mask the political practice—a military dictatorship, bloody terror, and a regime of the personality cult.

Much of our tragic past is becoming known only now, but the main landmarks of Stalinism have been known to the world community for a long time: forced collectivization with millions of victims and the subsequent famine. . . . In our history books and articles we frequently read that the political leaders of the West, "blinded by anticommunism," "proceeding from narrow class interests of the bourgeoisie," rejected the hand extended by the Soviet Union and did not enter into an alliance against fascism. But every time we recall and analyze the reaction of the West to the Soviet foreign policy we must try to look at our country of that time from the outside and understand that this was an attitude primarily toward the Stalinist foreign policy, the Stalinist Soviet Union, and Stalinist communism. Sometimes people say that many political figures in the West took advantage of the repressive measures in the USSR as another reason for their initial class anticommunism and anti-Sovietism.

This is probably true. But this does not change very much: Stalinism reinforced the anticommunism of some of them, created anticommunism for the first time for others, and repulsed still others who had sympathised with socialism and our country.

In the West it is generally thought that the Soviet-German agreement of 23 August 1939 led to World War II, and the "agreement on friendship and boundaries" of 28 September caused a state of shock among antifascists in Western countries. At the same time one should keep in mind that the concept of "appeasement" of the potential aggressor enjoyed the support of broad segments of the population of England, France, and other European countries who remembered well the horrors of World War I and thought they should do everything to avoid getting into another war, which would be fatal for Europe. These attitudes contributed to the situation where the Western countries did not help republican Spain in its fight against the Franco revolt, which was supported by Hitler and Mussolini, and did not stop fascist Italy's aggression against Abyssinia. And when Chamberlain returned to London from Munich, the majority of Englishmen greeted him as a peace maker. F. Roosevelt sent him a rush telegram: "Good chap." . . .

The psychology of "appeasement" came to an end with the occupation of all Czechoslovakia in 1939. It became clear to the majority of Europeans that the Munich game had failed, that war could not be avoided, and that the only solution was to repulse the aggressor. But even after the fascist forces attacked Prague the prospect of an alliance with the Soviet Union did not attract the "Western democracies." Consequently, they were even cool in conducting the negotiations concerning the creation of an anti-Hitler military alliance with the USSR. America looked at all this from the sidelines since isolationist moods and the deep crisis kept both politicians and the broad public from understanding how real the threat of fascism was for the United States as well. . . .

There is no doubt that the bolshevist revolution in Russia and its first transformations evoked a hostile attitude toward it from the West and attempts to "nip socialism in the bud." What had happened here threw the gauntlet to the entire established system of capitalism and its norms and values. But to no small degree the anti-Sovietism of the West was based on ideas about the Soviet political system as a repressive dictatorship that was hostile to democracy, a "left-wing despotism" that had replaced the "right-wing despotism" of tsarism. Since the end of the twenties ideas about the Stalinist regime have become central in the image of our country abroad.

Under these conditions only the attack by fascist Germany on the USSR changed the attitude toward us. In the eyes of the world community we changed from an aggressive, dangerous country into a victim of aggression, the main burden of which lay on the Soviet people. The attitude toward us during the war and after it continued to be ambiguous, and one can feel this to this very day. On one hand there is sympathy for our people, compassion, and support for their struggle against Nazi aggression. On the other—as before—hostility and suspicion for the Stalinist regime and its heirs. The excitement about the victories of the Red Army carried over to Stalin as its formal leader, including from Churchill and Roosevelt. Many leaders of the West understood that victory over Hitlerism would not change the essence of the political system created by Stalin. Looking back, many of us recall with bitterness and indignation that the leaders of the United States and Britain were in no hurry to support us at the beginning of the war, wanting to see first who would get the upper hand and then to help the weaker side, and that they began to create the atom bomb, keeping it a secret from their blood-covered allies. Perhaps what they knew about Stalin cannot be discounted when evaluating their actions? It was impossible to predict his behavior within the country, and you could expect anything in his foreign policy as well. But through all the unpredictable steps one can trace a general pattern—egoism, cruelty, and suppression of any hint of different thinking.

In this connection, the "cold war," which began in 1946—many link it to Churchill's Fulton speech in which he spoke of the "iron curtain" that separated the USSR from the rest of the world—was another round of confrontations between capitalism and socialism and a continuation of the opposition to Stalinism of the thirties. It came very close to being a "hot" war between the two opposing blocks, as, for example, during the Berlin crisis of 1948–1949, the Korean War of 1950–1953, and, later, during the Cuban crisis.

We now say that our foreign policy was inadequate and we reacted too sharply to provocations from the West. Obviously, the same thing can be said about the actions of the West, and above all the United States, with respect to the foreign political actions of Stalin, Malenkov, Khrushchev, and Brezhnev. But an important reason for the fear, suspicion, and hostility in Western policy and psychology regarding us was the revulsion for Stalinism and its equation with communism as an ideology and political practice.

Therefore our main task today, in addition to an honest analysis of our past and an elimination of the remanants of Stalinism in our domestic policy and psychology, is to divorce Stalinism from communism in the eyes of the world.

At the cost of incredible effort we created an atomic bomb and then a hydrogen bomb and an arsenal of missiles, and by the end of the sixties we reached parity with the United States and the West. But we did not manage to protect ourselves from danger with a fence of missiles, and the danger of war increased. It is possible to avert it, as our present government constantly emphasizes, only through political and not military means. In this sense glasnost is our parity, restructuring is our weapon, and destalinization is our main ammunition.

It is difficult to separate oneself from Stalinism even within the country. It is even more difficult before the world audience, for which much that takes place in our country is as much of an enigma as it was before, attractive but not very comprehensible, or else even a "propaganda trick." This is the more difficult since we have created an entire art of confrontation, a constant battle with the "world bourgeoisie" and their rotten influence. It has its own establishment, its own bureaucracy, its own science, and its own language, and—the main thing—its own client, since the foreign enemy was necessary in order to justify the domestic problems, the shortage of resources, machines, food, and housing, the general slovenliness and poverty, and—the main thing—the strong authority and lack of openness for the people under the conditions of a "hostile environment."

The renunciation of Stalinism is a long and painful process, since a tumor has appeared in the healthy tissue of the society. It will not be easy to cut it out. In order to dissociate ourselves from Stalinism, from the crimes it committed against mankind, we shall need a court trial of Stalinism as a criminal political system and organization as well as a trial of it main leaders. It is impossible to impose sentences on the dead, and this is not a question of punishment—it is a matter of nationwide condemnation of the criminal political practice based on verified facts, a moral sentence passed against Stalinism. If we want to break the ice of disbelief we must provide an example of self-purification, of deep criticism of our own vices of the past, including the quite recent past.

Now when it comes to America, confidence in us is growing

slowly. According to data of last year's public opinion polls, only 2 percent of the Americans feel "great" confidence in us, 33 percent—"some" confidence, 24 percent—"little" confidence, and 37 percent—no confidence at all. And although confidence has increased in recent years, one must not think that everything changed with the beginning of restructuring. The Americans are looking at us with a great deal of interest, sympathy is growing, and they rate M. S. Gorbachev very highly. But the mistrust is still great. We are still the main military threat to the United States according to the ideas of Americans, and 60 percent of them rate this threat as "extremely serious" and "serious," and only 37 percent rate it as "weak" or see no threat in us at all. Even more concretely: 56 percent think that the Soviet Union would attack the United States if the United States were militarily weak (37 percent doubted this).

For many in the United States glasnost and restructuring mean mainly allowing the emigration of Jews, the return of Academician A. D. Sakharov from exile, and the decision to withdraw our troops from Afghanistan. We are not drawing our own portrait for the rest of the world, but a good deal depends on the expression on our face. Foreign policy has never been the prerogative of diplomats alone. In the final analysis we have dealt not with ambassadors but with the country. It is no wonder that our people and the residents of other countries have been unable to understand how something so incomprehensible and uncivilized could come from the "country of Schiller and Goethe."

We are offering the world more and more peace initiatives, we want to rid the planet of nuclear weapons altogether, we are prepared for unilateral steps, and we are striving to radically change foreign political thinking in the world. But with the prejudices that have developed over the decades we do not have complete faith, proposals are accepted with difficulty and only partially, and as usual we are pursued by the reputation of being Danaideans. A unique situation has now developed in which people are ready to believe us if we go all the way in the restructuring of our country and our thinking, having rid ourselves of the burden of the past, having clarified the human value of our goals, regardless of what we may now call our society, just so that not only will President Reagan no longer call us the "evil empire" but also future leaders can say with a straight face upon meeting that "our societies are based on common human values."

CONSUMER AFFAIRS

Our Letters
by M. Zhvanetsky

We receive letters and marvel at the growth of interests of our readers. Semenov is concerned about when there will be hot water in his building. The letter is written in a lively manner with an original ending. Lipkin, a retired citizen, should be resting but nevertheless he is writing, expressing interest in when the elevator will be fixed in his house. The letter is written in beautiful language with old expressions and expressive examples. A whole group of readers in a wave of inspiration wrote about the assortment of produce in the neighborhood store. It is not every writer who can find such soul-captivating words, put the accents in all the right places. This is literature already. We have a passionately convincing letter about a collapsed ceiling. The style is evident. One can tell that a lot of authors are writing.

The concerns of the readers can be divided seasonally. In the winter, most people are interested in the central heating system, cleaning of the streets. In the fall the interests turn to gutters, and plumbing. In the summer the subjects in question are vegetables, train tickets. There isn't one single area which has been ignored by the curious minds of our readers. Just think about the growth in the level of culture. When before were city dwellers concerned with the winter conditions for cattle, preparation of feed. Now, these people insist on observing the laws governing cattle-rearing. They beg to improve the living conditions of the cattle. There is particular interest in the slaughter of large horned animals. Also, when before were our citizens so concerned with harvest? Now they ask what grows, how much was planted, and where exactly does it grow. We read the letters and are happy at the variety of your questions. We hope that the readers will be equally happy with the variety of our answers.

"We've invested all our collective farm money into this railway, and now food supplies are no longer a problem: half an hour and you are in the city!" (G. Ogorodnik, originally published in *Krokodil*)

COOPERATIVES

Curbs Imposed on Cooperatives
Izvestiya, December 31, 1988

USSR COUNCIL OF Ministers 29 December 1988 Resolution on the Regulation of Certain Types of Cooperative Activity in Accordance with the USSR Law "On the Cooperative System in the USSR"

In accordance with Articles 3 and 54 of the USSR Law "On the Cooperative System in the USSR," regulating possible types of cooperative activity, the USSR Council of Ministers resolves:

To establish that cooperatives do not have the right to engage in the types of activity laid down in Appendix No 1.

Appendix No 1 to the USSR Council of Ministers 29 December 1988 Resolution

Types of activity which cooperatives have no right to engage in are:

- The manufacture of any type of weapons, ammunition, explosives, or fireworks, as well as the repair of weapons; the teaching of karate and other types of combat for which the permission of the relevant bodies is required; the performance of blast-hole drilling operations;
- The manufacture and sale of drugs and offensive and toxic substances;
- The sowing, cultivation, and sale of crops containing narcotic, offensive or toxic substances:
- The administering of the following types of medical assistance: treatment of cancer patients; treatment of patients with infectious diseases, including venereal and contagious skin diseases; treatment of drug addiction; treatment of mentally ill people whose state of health requires immediate

(R. Grabauskas, *Soviet News*)

hospitalization; the issuing of findings on people's mental condition; supervision and treatment of pregnant women; invasive methods of investigation and treatment; surgical intervention, including abortion; the conduct of statutory periodical and preliminary checkups and examination of citizens;
- The manufacture and sale of medicines;
- Activity to establish hygienic environmental norms for chemicals substances;
- Wine and vodka production;
- The organization and maintenance of gambling establishments and the organization of games of chance and the taking of bets at athletic and other competitions;
- The manufacture, buying up, and sale of articles made from precious metals and precious stones or articles in which these materials are used (including the manufacture of dental prostheses from precious metals);
- The manufacture and sale of public catering products in unsanitary conditions and the use of food additives prohibited by sanitary norms and rules;
- The organization of general education schools;
- Publishing activity for the production of works of science, literature, and art;
- Making of movies and videos, organization of exchange, sale, renting, and public showing of movies and videos and foreign economic activity associated with this;

- The reproduction of movies, films, and programs on video and all activity associated with it;
- Servicing of the technical facilities of the unified national automated communications system and of television and sound broadcasting and cabled transmission facilities;
- The manufacture of orders and medals and stamps and dies;
- The performance of all types of cash transactions involving foreign currency; the taking on commission or acquisition of goods belonging to foreign citizens;
- The manufacture and use of registered trademarks and tradenames of Soviet and foreign enterprises and organizations without their permission;
- The organization of pawnshops;
- The organization and holding of lotteries;
- The manufacture and restoration of icons, church plate and articles of religious symbolism and use; the manufacture of candles (apart from decorative ones).

Reading the Mail: Once Again About Cooperatives
by Yuriy Orlik, *Izvestiya*, February 27, 1988

THE AUTHOR is deputy editor for the *Izvestiya* letter department.

The mail about cooperatives and individual labor activity divides into two unequal parts. I will begin with the bigger one.

Letters are full of indignation, anger, and insulting remarks about "private operators" and serious accusations against those "who allowed all this to happen."

"By introducing individual and cooperative labor activity in conditions of developed socialism, we are taking two steps backward," L. Verkhoglyad (Moscow) is convinced. "Money at any price, this is the goal of the cooperatives," A. Tarasov from Sevastopol believes. "What do we need newfound millionaires for?"—Yu. Chekmenev from Ulan-Ude asks. "What do you think I, a sovkhoz tractor driver earning R2–3 per day during repairs, feel like when I read that somewhere a dealer who makes bra fasteners makes R100 a day?"—N. Yelkin from Rostov Oblast's Semikarakorskiy Rayon vents his indignation. "Not even government members earn that much!" Lisova from Odessa exclaims. "Maybe our cooperative campaign is a gesture to the West," V. Shekhovtsov writes from Shchelkino settlement in Crimea Oblast. "A stratification of society into the rich and the less well-off is under way, the living standard of individual groups of people is falling. Is our government not aware of these negative phenomena and deformations?" V. Zotkin from Leningrad asks. "The family contract in rural areas is a shortcut to bring back the kulaks, and the cooperatives in cities will lead to a revival of the bourgeoisie," I. Sigachev from Tashkent Oblast's Krasnogorskiy settlement believes, and in his mind he already sees signs like "Petrov's Diner" and "Watchmaker. Synovya and Co." appearing in the streets of our cities.

And so the main accusations leveled at the individual and cooperative sector are: incompatibility of the said forms of labor activity with the principles of socialism, excessively high—not according to labor—earnings in this sphere, and the resultant stratification of society. Are there any grounds for these accusations?

Over many, many years a suspicious, wary attitude to all types of labor outside the state enterprise was instilled in us. We even regarded kolkhoz-cooperative ownership as in some way inferior, promising to "elevate" it in the future to the level of state ownership. The accepted system of remuneration, divorced from the end results of labor, and the predominance of wage leveling meant that the craftmanship, talent, and skills of thousands upon thousands of people were wasted. Economically accountable relations and the development of various forms of contract work are changing the situation in the economy and are designed, in particular, to lead to higher wages and the elimination of constraints and pay "ceilings." Hand in hand with this goes the expansion of opportunities for individual and cooperative labor.

"Yes, the textbook notion of socialism engendered by the poverty of our economy and the resultant need to distribute everything—be it energy, raw materials, machines, or food—by means of ration cards, is changing." Kh. Nabokov writes from Vologda. "Scope is being provided for the development of commodity-money relations and the management of the economy in accordance with its laws. And we are shouting: Leave us in peace, give us back the past."

"Cooperatives and individual labor activity must be viewed without prejudice and we must rid ourselves of the habit of rejecting anything new out of hand," S. Shabanov writes from Tuapse. We must rid ourselves of the habit, let me add, of

clapping political labels on anything new and frightening everyone with pictures of an impending degeneration of socialism.

"The return to and revival of these types of socialist economic activity can only be welcomed," Candidate of Medical Sciences I. Manoim writes from Leningrad. "After all, it is perfectly obvious that in many spheres the state sector has proved sluggish and insolvent. Anyway, it should not be expected to bear the whole burden ... Naturally, new problems are bound to arise with the development of individual labor activity, including negative problems. Some are afraid that people with big incomes might emerge. However, is there not a considerable difference in the level of incomes even now? Furthermore, high incomes are by no means always earned by honest labor, and this definitely is a deviation from socialism. I am convinced that someone who works conscientiously and hard, someone who is talented and enterprising, deserves to be richer than the statistical average worker."

Reading the mail, you cannot fail to notice how eagerly we count other people's money but often fail to take into account that the labor productivity of workers in cooperatives is 3, 5, and even 10 times higher than in ordinary production. I would like to remind the critics of the favored status of cooperatives and individual labor activity that the population's deposits in savings banks now total R250 billion. What does money in savings books represent? It is postponed, unsatisfied demand. It is a mass of money which is not backed up by a mass of goods. And now an opportunity has emerged—albeit a small one—to enrich our counters with much needed everyday goods, even if some people may thereby earn big money, but we turn away in disgust.

"I am an installation worker with 23 years' experience," V. Nikitin from Dzhambul Oblast's Energetik settlement writes. "I have worked at construction sites in the North, in Siberia, and the Kara-Kumy. And the result? True, you get paid well, but besides vodka there is nothing you can buy with your money. All stores at remote construction sites are run by the Worker Supply Department and the clothes that are sold are simply hideous. Recently I and my friends spent a short holiday in Tashkent. We saw the goods on offer in the cooperatives. And I am not ashamed to admit that for the first time in my life I bought clothes that I actually liked. Trousers, jackets, shirts—everything fashionable, attractive, and relatively inexpensive. I am not interested in what the tailor earns, all I want is to be well dressed. However, the opponents of cooperatives are very skilled in counting up other people's money."

When, on reading this kind of admission, you start looking into the reasons for the rejection of cooperatives, you find that most often this is connected with the work of cooperatives in the sphere of public catering. People object to kebabs being sold at exorbitant prices "as if by passing under the grill they had been gilded." (A. Ivashin, Zaporozhye). Cooperatives of all kinds are operating in the country: cooperatives for the construction and repair of housing, procurement of agricultural produce, teaching of computer literacy and provision of information, the organization of concert and performing arts activity, and household gadget repairs. Yet the letter writers assess the cooperative movement on the basis of an encounter with a kebab or cotton candy seller in the bazaar. This is the result of a distorted view, a wrong picture in public consciousness of what workers in the individual labor and cooperative sphere can do and what they actually do.

It is true, of course, that the cat-shaped money boxes, photographs of girls with big biceps, and other curios available at market stalls are an embarrassment. "However, every good cause attracts undesirable elements" (V. Bokov, Smolensk Oblast). Can they be dealt with? "By means of different tax rates favorable conditions could be created for cooperatives which offer vitally important services, cooperatives, for instance, which build summerhouses or carry out housing repairs, and so forth," N. Poluektov from Moscow suggests very sensibly. "Differentiated deductions from profit will sort everything out, including the pay of cooperative members," V. Slastin from Nakhodka believes.

Many readers complain that the cooperative prices are exorbitant. What can be done? A. Nikitenkov from Magadan demands that local authorities draw up a price list. Yu. Plyusnin from Pionerskiy city in Kaliningrad Oblast voices the same demand. However, attempts at administrative price regulation are pointless, as we well know from our rich experience. N. Poluektov, who writes that the cooperatives must be given the greatest freedom and made to work in conditions of tough competition, is much closer to the truth. Because at the moment "some cooperatives are turning into monopoly producers, much more so than state enterprises. They dictate conditions, inflate prices, and obtain undeserved profit." The way out of this situation is the expansion of the network of rival cooperatives and the improvement of the work of state enterprises which produce the same goods or offer the same services.

Another accusation must be mentioned. "The cooperatives will damage the state sector," Yu. Shaferov from Tashkent believes, "because they will siphon off efficient and energetic cadres and good specialists and will introduce mercenary motives into the moral atmosphere."

Is there a real danger of cadres being siphoned from one sphere to the other? There are only 13,000 cooperatives in the country at the moment, and just over 300,000 people engage in individual labor activity. This is very little for a country like ours. "More and more people must be drawn into this work," Yu. Flerov from Sverdlovsk believes. Especially if you take into account that there is overstaffing at many, if not most, enterprises and institutions. We have started seriously discussing effective employment of the population, which, incidentally, presupposes releasing 16 million people by the year 2000. It is envisaged that many of them will take up work in the service sphere or will engage in the production of consumer goods, including in the cooperative and individual labor sector.

One last point. I, like the readers, am still largely dissatisfied with the work of the cooperatives and the quality of their services, and I view with suspicion the greed and the search for easy money which threaten to undermine confidence in the individual worker almost before it emerges. But I absolutely cannot accept the appeal sent in by the Kravtsov family from Voroshilovgrad: "The cooperatives are not for us. It is time to stop."

A Case Involving Millions—or The Confession of an Honest Soviet Millionaire
Moscow News, March 13, 1989

Artyom Tarasov strode into our editorial office and introduced himself: "I'm a millionaire." He said this without any pride or fear, as if he were announcing that he was a trade union member.

No, he was not one of those underground, stagnation-era businessmen who stole everything that could be stolen. He was a perestroika-age millionaire. A Candidate of Science, a co-op member and an honest person, I believe, who is disgusted by any kind of machination. No one made him advertise his wealth. After all, tens of others keep silent. Maybe even hundreds by now? But Tarasov declared himself.

"To begin with, I am distinguished from other millionaires by the fact that the bank refused to pay my wages: the bank had no cash. True, this didn't prevent a colleague of mine from paying Party dues to the tune of 90,000 roubles (I am not a Party member). It is these actions that sparked such negative reaction in Moscow when the press reported this fact.

"We didn't boast about our incomes, but we didn't try to hide them either. Although according to the Law on Cooperatives earnings may not be limited, Soviet society is still convinced that that much money cannot be earned legally. For this reason many cooperative members prefer to conceal their incomes. This isn't difficult: just divide a million among 20 or 30 people and the sum won't seem so terrible. This is why almost every cooperative has aunts, uncles, mothers- and fathers-in-law on its payroll. Items of expenditure screen the real incomes of cooperatives. We, however, want to live within the law and were the first to announce the sum at our disposal. Our cooperative consists of scientists, technologists and programmers who have come here to test their inventions. I worked at a research institute for 18 years. During my first three years I received 29 author's certificates. Over the next 15 years, only one of them was accepted for production. We have collected people with similar problems from all over Moscow.

"There is only one yardstick for their selection: the superiority of their inventions on the world market. For instance, the technology of ionoplasma spraying, foam metal (a new ultralight construction material), a chemical-technological installation that accelerates the reaction of liquid from 10 to 12 times, early cancer-detection methods, a sewing machine (developed in only three months) which surpasses Japanese models. We want to introduce these and other inventions: this would help close the gap with the Western market (the above-mentioned inventions are all superior to similar projects in the West).

"Having announced our incomes, we came under enormous pressure. A commission was sent to our cooperative at the end of last year—but found no violations. Now we're being assailed by the Ministry of Finance, the City Financial Department, People's Control and a commission of deputies. We are being summoned for friendly chats to the Department for Combatting Thefts of Socialist Property . . .

"For nearly a month the cooperative has stood idle. But we can count. If we have earned 23 million roubles since last November, it isn't difficult to estimate the 'cost' of our doing nothing. But everyone is out of work.

"Whence the millions? The press has directly or indirectly

accused us of illegal or speculative activies which boil down to obtaining money with a mere stroke of the pen. In fact, this is not so. Imagine mountains of sawdust, waste and unsold goods which have been abandoned and are not being used by anyone, including those which are worthless after a month and liable to be destroyed. We use these raw materials and sell them to the West—not for foreign currency but for modern equipment, notably computers. Our contract with these Western partners is signed not by us, but by organizations from the Ministry for Foreign Economic Relations which takes 10 to 12 per cent of our profits as commission.

"We have already brought 10 million dollars' worth of equipment into the USSR. The computers thus received are supplied by the cooperative with a package of license-clear programmes developed by us, making it possible to use them in the work of any Soviet enterprise. We guarantee our customers training and currency-free service.

"We make a profit on the sale of computers at the lowest possible market price, which is twice as low as the official one. The price fixed by the State Committee for Material and Technical Supplies is 96,000 roubles, our price is 48,000. (On the 'black market' a computer costs 175,000.) Even the verifying commissions were struck by 'such rare disinterestedness'.

"Could we lower the price still more? Yes, we could. But we need millions. What for? In order to organize production based on the inventions with which we came to the cooperative.

"A standard reproach: but you don't produce anything. But what does that mean—to open a factory and start manufacturing goods? To get it on lease? Try and do it. Very soon you will understand that no one is interested in this. It means that the factory has to be built. That's why we need money, our millions. For the time being we get them from trade.

"We sell computers to the State Committee for Material and Technical Supplies, the Institute of Space Research, the Institute of Cybernetics and other 139 similar organizations—all those who cannot obtain computer equipment in any other way. They are prepared to pay any amount of money, but we take only the minimum fixed by us.

"I would like to refute the claim that we have obtained our capital by exploiting thousands of people. In our trade service we employ a mere 20 people (the cooperative's total membership is 241). But could any other state-owned organization, for example, do what we are doing? I am sure that it couldn't. The state monopoly on foreign trade has meant that our vast and very rich country has been selling only a few billion currency roubles' worth a year of manufacturing industry goods on the world market. But our exports, products which are worthless here, could reach 50 or 60 million dollars by the end of 1989 if we are allowed to spend our millions. That is, to export whatever no one needs here, whatever will inevitably spoil and damage the environment besides.

"Can all of this be done by a person sitting at the Ministry of Foreign Economic Relations? No, it can't. Why should he all of a sudden go to Magadan to look for sawdust which no one needs or start collecting mineral fertilizers abandoned in the fields, load and transport them to the port of dispatch?

"What have we done to shock society? We have transferred a tiny fraction of our profits into wages. If we hadn't done this, we would have been without ready cash and unable to go on operating. The cooperative's quarterly profit is 70 or 80 million roubles, which are deposited in a bank account. Part of this goes to pay the wages of the workers. A little over 7 million roubles we have earmarked for ourselves. Three million went to the chairman, three million to the commercial director, one million to the managing director and 280,000 to the bookkeeper.

"What for? Not for pocket money, of course. It's an attempt to set up our own monetary fund with which to freely operate. After all, what is an entrepreneur? It's a person who quickly analyzes the economic situation and finds a rational solution for obtaining an income. But in so doing, forgive me, he has a cheque book in his pocket. In our case its analogue is money. After all, it's absurd to start an enterprise with no money in your pocket.

CREDIT CARDS

To Save Money and Nerves
by G. Charodeyev, *Izvestiya*, August 2, 1988

Payment by [credit] card has become an important part of the modern payment system in dozens of the world's countries. So far, however, Hungary is the only socialist country that has the system. But it will soon go into operation in the Soviet Union as well. That, at any rate, is the belief of representatives of the USSR Bank for Foreign Economic Activity and of Eurocard/Mastercard/Eurocheque, the world's largest payment system, who signed an unprecedented cooperation agreement in Moscow's International Trade Center on Saturday, July 30.

"Our work will proceed in a number of stages," said N. Sviridov, a leading consultant to the USSR Bank for Foreign Economic Activity's administration for export and import transactions and nontrade operations, in a conversation with *Izvestiya*'s correspondent. "First the credit cards themselves will be produced. We will initially issue them to citizens traveling to our country from abroad. They will be able to use the cards to pay for goods and services in hotels, restaurants and stores. We will be tied into the Eurocard/Mastercard system by then.

"In the second stage, credit cards will be issued to Soviet organizations. For example, *Izvestiya* journalists traveling abroad on business will no longer have to take foreign currency with them. Your organization need only maintain an account with our bank, which is tied into the international payment system. The cardholder enjoys certain privileges. For example, he can obtain an immediate cash advance when needed."

"What do the credit cards look like?"

"There are two basic types of cards—a 'Gold Card' and a 'Silver Card.' The cards are small. The gold (or personal) card has special codes, a magnetic tape and a hologram that guards against counterfeiting. When a transaction is made, powerful computers will verify within seconds that the card is yours and rapidly check it against a 'blacklist.'

"The silver card is for the specialized business needs of companies, firms and organizations."

A. Ziegler, Chairman of the Board of MasterCard, said: "The agreement is very important both economically and politically. Soviet citizens are traveling abroad more and more. Why take cash along?—it could be stolen or lost. We offer an effective means of safeguarding a person's money, nerves and time."

CRIME

Under Siege
by Dimitry Likhanov, *Ogonyek*, January 1989

HE CAME TO US, to the editorial office. He lowered himself into the chair, tired, and said, "I am prepared to tell all. It's just too much already. After all, if you think about it, many of us are already under siege."

He is a little over thirty. There was a time when he, in the company of so called "corporators," organized his own enterprise. Since at that time, such activity was not welcomed, to put it mildly, and more than that, it was mercilessly punished not merely by the law but also by public opinion, one had to work "underground," experience everyday fear and uselessness in one's own country. It is only now that he has opened a cooperative and perhaps for the first time feels that he does not live in vain. Yet the problems remain, just as fear does. It is precisely for that reason that he asked that his name not be mentioned.

Q: So what are you afraid of? After all, it seems that the "underground" is no longer necessary. The activity of your cooperative is completely legal. It is welcomed by the government in every way. What is the problem?

A: The thing is the racket, both criminal and state.

You see, in our country there were always people who considered Ostap Bender* their father. What I mean is that thieves were always interested in those who had money. They always tried taking that money away. Those who had the cooperatives were included.

Q: Let's take it one step at a time. Is it possible to approximate the time when the racket was formed in our country?

*An expert con artist in the novels by Ilf and Petrov, *Twelve Chairs* and *The Golden Calf.*

A: That depends on what you mean by that. If one can now finally speak of the racket on governmental levels, then as far as the "bouncers," the "extortionists" and the prostitutes go, the racket exists for as long as they do. They all pay from day one. Ever since underground business has existed, so has the racket.

Then the situation changed. Due to the closing of the "Beryozka,"* a whole lot of unoccupied petty criminals have been freed. After all, thousands of citizens occupied themselves with the "extortionists" of the checks.† A number of small-time profiteers have been left with nothing to do. They too were around in quite large numbers. A good portion of these people have gotten used to a nice profit. But not one of them will go to work in a factory, or to work in construction. He may serve fifteen years in prison, he'll still not come close to a factory. What I mean is that these were the commercial outlaws. The moment they faced problems with earnings, they all headed straight for the racket and things like that. Then all of a sudden, it came together, the cooperatives were beginning to open. So these people grabbed on to that.

Q: So the racketeers asked for payoffs from these cooperatives right away? Is that what you're saying?

A: As far as the cooperatives of communal feeding go, yes. In any case, our cooperative was hit when it was merely five months old.

Q: And how did it happen?

A: Well, what do you mean how? A plain-looking man came up to our saleslady and said that if she does not bring two thousand the next day, both she and her family . . . Well we could protect ourselves. We called a friend. He put them in their place. From that time on everything is quiet. But firstly, I don't think that it's going to last and secondly it's not the best protection.

I just want to emphasize that the first ones who suffered and will suffer from the racket are the commercial and food cooperatives. They are visible and they have a ready flow of cash. If a stranger comes to me, it's noticeable, but when thousands of people come through the cafes every day, how can you know which one of them brought a knife or a bomb and will kill you right on the spot? How can you? Does that mean there should be

*A hard currency store.
†When a Soviet citizen travels out of the country, upon return he is given checks for the amount of hard currency that he has with him. Those checks could be used to make purchases in a "Beryozka."

three armed militia men put into every cooperative? Besides you have to be sure that they will not join the plans . . .

In a word, according to the information I get, almost all cooperative cafes and restaurants, many tailors and commercial shops are under the control of the racketeers. If this is to continue, all the cooperative movement will be under that control. I am not exaggerating.

Q: I don't doubt that. Once I went to the Riga market and it seemed as if everything there has been bought and rebought a long time ago. Plus some shady characters are walking around . . .

A: In the Riga market everyone pays. But the way I see it the profiteering that takes place there is from things like cigarettes, contraceptives, alcohol, imported clothes, possibily weapons and narcotics.

Q: How are the prices?

A: Cigarettes are ten rubles a pack, a bottle of whiskey is forty or fifty, caviar, thirty rubles for a jar, contraceptives, twenty-five.

Q: I heard that women are sold there as well.

A: Women too. Women are sold everywhere, by the "National" and the "Continental," but in those places they are a special sort of prostitute. They are not particularly thrilled with the Soviet rubles. But here, they are for the general consumer, right on the market, like potatoes.

As far as the individual sellers go? You know, at first the profits one could make here were pretty decent. Even now they are not too bad. People come here from the entire country. After all, the fame of the market is widespread. But at the same time, many of my friends had to get out of there. They were as we say "caught."

Q: What does that mean?

A: Well, let's assume that someone made ten pairs of pants using his own money. That required three hundred rubles. He bought himself a sewing machine, fabric, spent his own time, and then went on to sell them. At the market he was approached by someone and they said, "Give us five hundred." He refused. They took everything away. Just took it away and left. And beat him up. That happens most often. If he, for example, pays the five hundred, the next time somebody else may come and ask for money. Anyone can come up to you. At the Riga market it's limitless.

Besides that they have to pay for the spot. But in order to buy it you have to be out there at six to get your place in line, after all, there are a lot of people who want to get in. There is another story. For example, they sell places in line. I do not know how it worked out but it seems that the people in the market are always the same.

That's the situation. It doesn't even make sense to come there. That's what I heard from a lot of people.

Q: And who controls the Riga Market today?

A: I heard a number of names, the Dolgoprudenskie, the Luberetskie. They make up quite a strong force. I am sure that eventually, the market will be taken over by the stronger ones.

Q: What about other places?

A: Well, Luzhniki, for example. I don't know who operates there. They came, beat up all those who refused to pay. As a result everybody paid. Thirty rubles per person. Multiply that by forty. A thousand plus profit. And that's every day.

Q: Speaking of profits. To tell you the truth I can't even imagine what are the figures in which they operate. After all, if there are only a few thousand cooperatives in the country . . .

A: Oh yes. They work in six-digit figures or close to that. Let me give you an example. At the end when the "Beryozkas" started to close down, special stores opened for the Afghanistan veterans. Prices went up on both TV sets and VCR's. An acquaintance of mine, decided to make a little profit. The "Afganistan Beryozka" received three hundred TV sets. He was among the first five but did not get one set. The racketeers took everything.

Q: What did they do, buy places in line?

A: No. They simply walked in and took everything. They did whatever they wanted. There were a lot of them and they were big. As my friend told me, they just threw the disabled out of the stores. People without legs, they simply threw them out. They are animals.

Anyway as I said earlier, three hundred TV sets were received. They were then being sold right outside of "Beryozka." People from the East were paying fifteen hundred checks over the actual price, the Moscovites were paying a thousand over. Now add it all up; three hundred sets for three hundred thousand checks. If you exchange that according to the minimum rate, a ruble and a half for a check, that comes to four hundred fifty thousand rubles. And that's in one day. Even if there are many racketeers, they still have something to divide. They have something to stick their necks out for. You understand?

Q: What are the numbers involved in the racket? A hundred? A thousand?

A: A lot more. Especially in Moscow, because people come here from all over the country. Moscow is a very big city. You can get lost here. You can live here for years without being registered, drive someone else's car. And if you observe all the traffic laws everything will be fine. If worst comes to worst, you can try to pay someone off. It does not matter what you did. So under these conditions, I presume that a few thousand people are involved in the racket in Moscow alone. Of course it exists everywhere, but in Moscow it has reached the peak. Someone told me that in Lubertzy, he can gather up eight hundred people in one hour. I wondered for a long time how he could do that. Apparently it is very simple. All you have to do is call the gyms. And there are plenty of them in Lubertzy.

I saw these guys. Apparently they were going somewhere for a "job." You get scared looking at them. They are all big, tall, with necks this big. These are people who hearing the command "go" will tear a man apart.

But the ones at the top are not the ones who carry out the orders. The ones who do the dirty work are merciless and stupid. They don't even understand the consequences. They don't realize what they are doing. They are paid a thousand and they work for that. The whole thing lies with the organizers.

Q: I think we have reached an important question here. What do the leaders of the criminal world think of the racket??

A: According to them a lawful thief should not lower himself to extortion. It discredits him and it is incompatible with the "thieves' code of honor." Now, however, nothing is beneath them. Perhaps there is an elite of thieves which does not participate in racketeering but simply receives the money, though the money comes from thieves. I don't know. Everything has changed. With time, the racket will become more subtle, without the blood and the beatings. Here is an example. A friend of mine needs fur for the manufacturing of jackets. He started looking for ways to get it. Of course he found nothing through the official channels. A few days ago a man came to him. Obviously from some organization. All his offers were of a very unofficial nature. He said something like this: "I can get you fur, the one you want costs forty rubles, we can get it for twenty rubles per skin." They are smart. They'll be looking for every possible way to catch you, to grab things for themselves knowing the deficiencies in the system, and to play on them. And if they succeed they will be making money, as much as they want. If a man is smart, he will try to get in on it. If he is stupid, he'll try to take everything.

In the very near future, the most unimaginable things will start. I am completely sure of that. Here is why. At the end of the year each cooperative has the right to take its profits out of the banks and divide it among the employees or do with it whatever it wishes.

Take my word for it, something awful will start. They will be forcing people to take the money out. Even if someone wants to trick them and keep the money, it will not work. And I am sure that to scare people, they will kill somebody.

Q: So what can be done? Isn't there any way at all to stand up to the racket? Let's take the recent events at the Vnukovo Airport, where there are a lot of private taxis. By the way, what did happen there?

A: As far as I know, this is the story. Taxis are a profitable business, As a rule the people who gather there are the same people. They come with their own cars. They make deals with the security so that they are not bothered and so they get good passengers. Anyway, the racketeers came to them and said, "You'll pay." The amounts were different in every place. I heard figures from a hundred and fifty to three hundred. But taxi drivers are not cooperators. This is a different breed. So they decided to stand up to the racketeers in an organized manner. About a thousand people gathered in Vnukovo. Apparently they said something like: "You know our cars, we know yours. For every one of our cars that will be burned, one of yours will be burned. For every one of our men whose head will be broken, one of yours will get the same." Still I think that the racketeers will not give up. They'll be catching one at a time.

For example, they come and say, "You'll be paying us." All right. Then another group comes and says, "No, you'll be paying us." He says, "Come on guys, decide among yourselves. I can't pay all of you." But in order to resist one gang, his gang has to be stronger. That means that he'll be gathering people around himself, building up strength, arming himself. And what if he has to get a bodyguard, they also have to be paid. Only to one of your own you have to pay more. At the same time, where is the guarantee that nothing will happen to your family? You see, the cooperatives simply have no choice. They have to pay. Let's take our cooperative for example. We do not steal. We do everything through the official channels. We have no money to pay the racketeers. We simply have no place to get it from. That means that in order to pay we have to steal, from ourselves. That means we have to buy fabric "underground" not registering it anywhere, sew, and pay. That means that if the government can not provide its citizens with protection, it will lead to unfortunate consequences. Many cooperators will once again go into illegal business, since it is becoming more dangerous to stay legal.

CULTURE

A New Customer
by Viktor Slavkin, *Ogonyek*, December 1987

Around four o'clock, a new customer stepped over the threshold of the second-class restaurant. "Greetings." He crossed the room diagonally and sat down at an empty table.

About twenty minutes passed. Volodia, the waiter, gave his unfinished cigarette to one of his colleagues to hold, with his right hand smoothed over the piece of a Russian folk ornament hanging off his left sleeve, and moved toward the customer. Having approached the table, he silently pointed to a napkin lying in the center of the table, on which was written "This table is not being served."

The customer looked at the waiter with the eyes of a kind dog who had just heard from its master the words, "Time for a walk."

"Move to a table where there is already someone," Volodia explained patiently. "I won't serve you alone."

"Please do not chase me away," the customer said timidly.

"Don't you understand Russian? I said this table is not set."

"I'll wait."

"As you wish. You'll sit." Volodia lost all interest in the conversation.

"I'll sit," said the customer. "Thank you."

"Only there is no need to be rude," the waiter warned.

"I'll sit. Don't worry. It's nothing."

"Besides, how can there be accusations? Just sat down, and already . . ."

"What is your name?" asked the customer.

"Are you going to cause a scene? Watch it."

The other waiters, smoking by the manager's table, felt the trouble brewing.

Their loose jackets filled out by young muscles, the lapels flared up.

"I don't want to cause a scene." It seemed as if the customer was about to cry. "I just want an introduction."

Volodia waved his friends off and their jackets loosened up once again.

"Volodia," said he.

"My name might seem strange to you."

"So, what do we want to eat?" asked the waiter and took out his writing pad.

"Don't rush, Volodia. Go, finish your cigarette. Give the other table their bill. Besides, you don't even have a menu with you . . ."

"It's not been printed yet."

"Wonderful. Then I'll just sit. The people who were at this table before me left some bread, there is mustard. What else does one need? After all, it is inconvenient for you to take care of me now."

"Inconvenient," agreed Volodia, but for some strange reason, he did not walk away.

The customer took a piece of bread out of the basket, covered it with a thick layer of mustard, sprinkled it with salt, and bowed his well-groomed head over this dish, deeply inhaled the scent.

"What, you've never seen food?" the waiter snickered.

The customer choked and began coughing. Volodia hit him hard on the back.

"Volodia, I'd like to ask you . . . that is, could you promise me . . . anyway, if I admit something to you, give me your word that your benevolence towards me will not change."

"What are you coming back from, prison?" The waiter guessed.

"I am a . . . foreigner . . ." the customer said quietly. Then in a completely morbid voice he added, "from a capitalist country."

Volodia's Adam's apple bobbed as if he had swallowed an apricot pit, and he asked hoarsely:

"May I be allowed to change the tablecloth?"

"I thought this might happen." The customer hung his head and his thin fingers began running spasmodically over the dirty tablecloth. "This stain reminds me of the shape of my poor country."

Volodia glanced with interest at the stains from the sauce "piquant."

"Gee, I'm not aware of such a country."

"And a good thing it is." The customer covered the stain with his hand. "It is a pygmy country with no particular significance in the world. The name is Grand-Carlo. Have you heard of it?"

"No."

"We're the richest country in the world," the customer said sadly, and bit off another piece of bread.

"But I bet you don't have mustard like this!" Professional pride spoke in the waiter.

"We have everything, except economic problems. Or any problems. None whatsoever."

"Whatever you say," said the waiter somberly. "I have to go to work."

He tried walking away from the table.

The foreigner held him back by his jacket.

"Volodia, my dear! You can't imagine what it's like."

"We can. Saw it in a movie."

"Oh no! What you saw in a movie can not compare to what is happening in our country. It is awful! Awful! Our muscles wither, our brains freeze, our instincts vanish, our immune system disintegrates—the nation is becoming extinct."

Bread trembled in the customer's hand.

"Only here in your country do I feel like a human being." Suddenly the customer smiled. "You know, the moment I crossed the border, I tore off all my clothes and bought clothes made in your country in the nearest Manufactured Goods store. I bought a shirt, shoes, a suit . . . Volodia, buy yourself one like it; there are more. The collar cuts into the neck and under the arms, it pulls in the crotch, the waist is too tight . . . But I feel them. I am in constant contact with them, I fight them! This fills me up with energy and belief in my eventual victory. I know that you dream of getting Cardin clothes. No, Volodia. Don't. Get them only from Manufactured Goods Store."

"Your wealth is making you mad. You know this saying that we have."

"It's not a saying, Volodia, It's a proverb." Once again the customer became sad. "In any case, such is the view of Vladimir Ivanovich Dal'."

"Are your parents Russian?"

"That's another one for you. I am a native Grand-Carlean, but the moment I expressed the desire, our travel agency in two weeks, only two weeks, instilled in me the vocabulary of four volumes of Dal' as well as the total absence of an accent. They have worked out a method. I had to make no effort. But where is the happiness that comes from work, the marvel of comprehending something new? Can one live like that, Volodia?"

"You know what," squinted the waiter, "if you are so sick of it, send all you have in excess to Africa. They'll use it there and you'll be able to relax a bit."

The customer looked at him with respect.

"You have the mind for government, Volodia. But you don't know our immoral industry. We can give away everything. Burn everything. It will all be reproduced immediately, doubled in volume."

"Well, then, I don't know what to tell you." Volodia shrugged his shoulders, and his face showed the utmost concern.

The customer began speaking excitedly.

"This is not my first time in your country. I come here not without reason. Not at all. I walk down the streets, visit stores, cafeterias, other places of communal usage, and everywhere, everywhere I see burning eyes, goal-striving faces, thought-out movements. Life is in full swing, people act, everything around is changing for the better. Man struggles, meaning he exists, damn it! I feel it myself, right now. For example, if I were to walk into one of our Grand-Carlo restaurants, immediately I would be attacked by our service sharks, our courtesy gangsters, our terrorists of communal feeding. In a moment they turn a person into a well-fed satisfied beast. Now let's take your blessed establishment, your soul-saving Greetings. I crossed its threshold experiencing a sharp pang of hunger, a feeling I haven't had in a long time. And you so keenly comprehending my state did not rush over to me. I sat at the table and with nothing to do, my stomach empty, began thinking over my life. The memories came to me by themselves. I remembered how I skinned my knee as a child. I remembered my mother, my father . . . It has been a long time since I've thought of them."

"That's not good," Volodia said strictly. "I personally always bring my mother some goodies once a week."

"And when you came up to me," the customer continued, "you did not spoil my mood. On the contrary, you obliged me with your so pleasant refusal to serve me. Thank you. But how do we teach *our* dummies to do that?"

"That's easy," said the waiter. "How do you say, 'This table is not served' in your language?"

"It's an untranslatable play on words."

"So let your dummy write this play on words on a piece of paper and put it on the table."

"And that's it?"

"That's it."

"But what is the purpose?" It was apparent that the customer had difficulty grasping the novel idea. "After all, the seat is not being used, profits are lost, the earnings . . ." He was reasoning out loud.

"Well, if you think like that, it won't work for sure."

"The kitchen is still preparing food. It must realize . . ."

"So let the kitchen staff consume what they make."

"How's that?"

"Or take it home."

"I don't understand."

"What's there not to understand? Every cook must have a bag with him. He comes in the morning with it empty and goes home with it jammed."

"Jammed? What does 'jammed' mean?"

"So much for your celebrated knowledge of Russian."

The customer's head dropped onto his chest.

"Come, come now, What's the matter? What's with you? . . . Oh come now, stop crying!" Volodia shook the customer by the shoulder, and the customer once again regained control of himself.

"These are not tears my friend. It's a type of contact lenses that we have. They have neither weight, nor thickness, just sparkle to rejuvenate a person. I am old, Volodia. It is only this physical shape that we are in. Don't believe it, Volodia, don't! I am an old and a sick man. But they, our killers in white coats, they made me young and healthy. I play tennis, I swim. I am loved by young girls. But Volodia, I want to sit in the park with people my age, play chess, stand in line for cottage cheese, and if it's not there or it has run out, to go to another one and another . . . with friends, with a crowd, with company. Or maybe to ride the bus to the other end of town during the traffic hour. How many stories we can tell each other on the way there! All of us together, jointly, all at once, in cohoots, all of us, en masse . . . Do you respect me, Volodia? Do you? Tell me, Volodia, do you respect me?"

"I respect you, pops, I do. But only . . ."

"What!!!" exclaimed the customer tragically. "What!!!"

"Be quiet." Volodia threw a glance around. The restaurant was almost empty. "I'm trying to say that the kitchen is about to close. Nobody here is hired to serve you until all hours of the night."

The customer became depressed.

"Then, Volodia," he said, "I have a last request for you. Bring me something as bad as possible."

"That we'll do." The waiter scribbled something on his pad and started toward the kitchen. He came up to the serving window and shouted:

"Vasia, one burned steak with yesterday's potatoes."

"O.K.," replied Vasia, "O.K.," and carried out the order diligently.

DEMILITARIZATION

Disarmament and the Economy
Interview with USSR Deputy Foreign Minister V. Karpov
by correspondent D. Makarov, *Argumenty I Fakty*,
February 4–10, 1989

HOW WILL the disarmament process now under way affect the development of the Soviet economy? *Argumenty I Fakty* Correspondent D. Makarov discusses this with USSR Deputy Foreign Minister V. Karpov.

MAKAROV: We now say that we are switching to a defensive doctrine. Does this mean that our military doctrine was offensive in nature in the past?

KARPOV: Well, I would not unequivocally say this about the nature of the doctrine just because we now say that a defensive configuration must be imparted to it, as though drawing the conclusion from this that it was not previously defensive. . . .

Under the conditions now, when the world has changed, when the new political thinking is making headway, and when the tasks of preserving modern civilization and defending common human values are coming to the fore, it has also become necessary to change the strategy of the USSR Armed Forces.

This does not mean we want to unilaterally reduce everything that can shoot and thus turn our Armed Forces into something like a pacifist organization. But we are taking the path of restructuring them. Take the unilateral measures announced by M. S. Gorbachev at the United Nations on 7 December. What is their import? People might say that reductions were also implemented under Khrushchev, at the end of the fifties. However, the present reductions are connected with a change in the very structure of the USSR Armed Forces. It is not just a reduction of the Army by 500,000 men; it is also a restructuring of the military by reducing the number of offensive arms and consequently increasing the defensive potential. That is, a motorized infantry division, for example, will now have fewer tanks, and it will have its large-caliber artillery pieces and assault river-crossing equipment designed to overcome obstacles during an offensive removed from it.

However, we will not, of course, be able to continue alone in this direction and totally eliminate, for example, our Armed Forces' potential for conducting large-scale operations. For this, corresponding accords with NATO are needed with regard to reductions in their armed forces commensurate with and essentially corresponding to our reductions—that is, reductions leading to the same result: a reduction in the offensive potential of the NATO Armed Forces and the imparting of a defensive nature to them.

MAKAROV: An old stereotype is still current in the West: Do not trust the USSR because it totally conceals everything concerning its Army. Is it not time to lift the veil from this sphere, too?

KARPOV: I believe that the policy of glasnost simply obliges us to do so. The reform of the structure of state power, the creation of a new Supreme Soviet, and the granting of new functions to it in accordance with the changes to the Constitution, which have already been approved and which are still just the first part of the reform, must entail questions of military building, defense spending, and appropriations for the military industry all becoming topics of discussion and decision-making after a comprehensive debate in the country's supreme organ of power. Spending which, under conditions of secrecy, goes to military needs is not always dictated precisely by those needs but might result from the inertia of the administrative apparatus or from some political guidelines that are already obsolete and need serious correction.

Take, for example, the decision to produce SS-20 missiles. It was adopted in the seventies. But we are now engaged in destroying all the missiles we have produced over these years and on which we have spent billions. We are now investing money in destroying them. Maybe we should have stopped at some time in the past and ceased production, particularly since the strategic situation, as is now coming to light, did not demand such mass deployment of SS-20 missiles. FRG Chancellor H. Schmidt proposed to us at the time, in the mid-seventies, a freeze on the deployment of our SS-20 missiles. In that instance Schmidt raised the question of the possibility of preventing deployment of Pershings and U.S. cruise missiles in Europe. But our conveyor belt was running, the stagnation period was at its height, and we thought and acted out of inertia. It seems to me that now, under conditions of glasnost and openness, we can no longer keep totally secret the problems of military spending, the strength of the Armed Forces, or even, perhaps, the tactical and technical data of the main types of arms the Soviet Union possesses.

DECISION-MAKING

Let's Fly
by Mikhail Zoshchenko, *Ogonyek*, March 1989

For two years, the ninth united handicraftsmen's artel collected money for an airplane.

It put ads in the papers, put up particularly colorful billboards, and organized friendly propaganda. What didn't it do! Just as far as special meetings went, there were at least ten.

The enthusiasm was indescribable, as were the dreams, the plans! You can't imagine how much imagination and strength was spent just on the proposed name of the airplane.

At the meetings, the chairman of the artel was simply drowning in questions. Mainly the handicraftsmen wanted to know whether the plane would be the property of Dobrolet* exclusively or would it be the property of the artel? Also, would every handicraftsman who contributed some money be able to fly on it in the air?

*State air ministry.

The excited and happy chairman spoke in a hoarse voice: "Of course, comrades! Of course you will! Fly! . . . Only let's get the money together . . . It'll be such wonder! Such freedom . . ."

"The main thing is that we'll be flying on our own plane." Members of the artel spoke excitedly. "Don't know why, but there's just no desire to fly on someone else's plane. It's no fun to fly on someone's plane."

"That's true. What kind of flying is it if it's on someone else's plane?" agreed other members of the artel. "If you fly on your own, even dying is great."

The chairman was interrupting separate outbursts of excitement and asking that the feelings be expressed in an orderly fashion.

And all the handicraftsmen, excited by the new idea and the ability to fly in the sky, kept asking for permission to speak, painted upcoming possibilities in bright colors, and branded with inexpiable shame those small-minded ones who had not yet contributed for the machine.

Even the secretary of the artel, a rather depressed and melancholy individual who was poisoned by gas twice during the tsar's war, in response to the chairman's request to speak of the essence, said:

"Comrades, being without a plane is just like being without hands. What do you suggest to fly on? You can't fly on a table. Just imagine that you want to fly somewhere, so you get on your plane and fly. And that's that."

For two years, the artel collected money with enthusiasm and excitement. In the third year, it began counting the collected capital.

It came to seventeen rubles and some kopeks.

At an extremely important meeting the chairman gave a short but a powerful speech.

"In view of the fact," he said, "that the airplane costs immeasurably more, what do the honorable comrades suggest that we do with the above-mentioned sum? Do we give this sum to Dobrolet or are there any other suggestions? I request that we decide this question by the show of hands."

The votes were divided.

Some suggested giving the money to Dobrolet. Others suggested buying a small but sturdy propeller out of Corellian birch and hanging it on the wall of the club above the portraits of the leaders. The third group advised buying some gasoline and keeping it ready. The fourth pointed out the necessity of fixing up the kitchen. Only a few small-hearted people asked for their money back.

They were given seven rubles.

As for the remaining ten rubles and some kopeks, it was decided to give the money to Dobrolet. But the treasurer had his own ideas.

One foul autumn evening, Ivan Bobrikov, the treasurer of the artel, lost this money in a game of cards.

At an extremely important meeting everyone was informed that the bastard-treasurer would be arrested, his property confiscated, and the money made off it donated to Dobrolet with a letter containing personal good wishes.

The chairman of the artel spoke in a slightly puzzled tone:

"And why, may I ask you, do we really need our own airplane? In essence, what the heck do we need it for? Where would we fly on it?"

"That's true. There's really nowhere to fly," agreed the members of the artel.

"That's what I am saying," affirmed the chairman. "There is nowhere to fly. We'll send the money to a powerful organization like Dobrolet. We don't need our own machines."

"Of course we don't need it," the handicraftsmen were saying. "There're only problems when it comes to a plane."

"An airplane is not a horse," the secretary said despondently. "With the horse, you get on it and go. Try that with an airplane. You got to put the gasoline in, get the propeller spinning . . . and what if you pour the gasoline down the wrong hole; the whole machine's history, the end of the people's money . . ."

"And the main thing, comrades, we've got no place to fly to," the chairman mumbled, puzzled.

Having finished the matter of the air force and deciding to give the money to Dobrolet, the handicraftsmen began discussing current issues.

The meeting came to life.

DEMOCRACY

Increasing Responsibility for the Course of Restructuring
Pravda, December 17, 1988

Perm, 16 Dec.—Dissatisfaction with the pace of restructuring and the realization of the region's potential were the main themes of the oblast party conference which opened here today.

Taking part in the conference was A.N. Yakovlev, member of the Politburo and secretary of the CPSU Central Committee. [His comments:]

Today our society and the party are sharply critical of the times of authoritarianism and stagnation and realize with distress how much was lost. It is clear that we could have moved faster, lived purer and more honest lives, and worked better. We were hindered by arrogance, a belief in our own infallibility, and deformations which, once tolerated, developed in the political and economic structure, in people's mentality and habits, in social consciousness, and in scientific dogmas.

Until now the conservative principle in the consciousness of surely every one of us has resisted the idea that we were not as perfect, not as irreproachable as it seemed to us for so long and was impressed on us. A longing for the old inner spiritual comfort has until now prevented some people from fully seeing the goals and scale of restructuring.

The development of a socialist society is not a simple or one-dimensional phenomenon. It is always multifarious and permits a multitude of specific developments, forms, and details within the framework of a single formation. We know that in the past this multifarious nature was rejected and could be punished, sometimes with the most dire consequences. Meanwhile, deformations occurred in Soviet society's development in the late twenties and early thirties—deformations which are now holding our progress back and fettering our thoughts and actions.

A most important theoretical and political question is often asked today: Is the product of restructuring really socialist? We shall try to examine this question because it is very important for an understanding of our development and for our unity.

Democracy, glasnost, the cooperative system, leasing, economic accountability, commodity-money relations, the socialist market, self-management, people's power, pluralism of opinions— all this has become a powerful part of our life, it disturbs life, sometimes it stops people sleeping or resting, and it fuels passions and sharp emotions, but it also creates new and real contradictions.

We talk about the formation of new economic relations, but they are bogged down in the old structural routine, the tenacious command system, and conservatism. Mismanagement is our scourge. Were we poorer, perhaps we would be better organized. Our wealth has made us poor, it has spoilt us, it generates laziness and irresponsibility. That is why nature must be treated rationally and thriftily, otherwise it will punish us severely.

We talk about political transformations, but how hard it is to break with the old power to which we have become accustomed. We still cannot see that true people's power will be far more durable, stable, and of course more responsible. We are still afraid of democracy, glasnost, and a diversity of opinions as though each of us always lives in harmony with himself and always thinks in convenient cliches. **Can someone really be called a man if he does not have his own opinion and does not feel his innate freedom of thought?** We are frightened of the cost of democracy, sometimes a very real cost. But does spring not purify the earth and, on the other hand, is the eternal truth vouchsafed to us alone?

We talk about spiritual rebirth and moral cleansing, but we are still highly suspicious of those spiritual battles which go on among young people and the intelligentsia, the working class and the peasantry. **Not all of us understand yet that socialism is a society of freedom and creativity, the flowering of science and culture, the exaltation of man, and the healing of the spirtually sick man and society by morality and culture.**

Of course, it is clear to every realistically minded person that society at the moment is still paying the debt for the past, and this has proved a most difficult matter.

Housing? It will take more than a year or two to turn basement apartments and shacks into palaces, and that is scant comfort to those in need of housing.

Food? The established principles of economic management on the land failed to resolve the food problem and have become obsolete. Thus it is necessary to change economic relations in the countryside and make fundamental adjustments to investment policy.

Goods? As long as the money supply exceeds the supply of goods, the shelves in the stores will remain empty. Therefore, it is necessary to use every means to increase the production of goods and services. . . .

The political reform also raises such problems as individual leadership. This point was raised at the 19th all-union party conference. Restructuring makes new demands on the individual, the qualities of the leader, and the procedure for selecting him. If the right to lead people is not acquired through rank or inheritance but is given to the leader by the people themselves, that is democracy, that is the prestige of power, the prestige of the party. Prestige that has been earned, furthermore. . . .

What is the meaning of the concept of common humanity today, in its purely concrete sense? It means: Preventing nuclear war. Halting the dangerous degradation of nature. Depriving reaction of such weapons as the ability to set peoples against one another. Feeding the hungry, healing the sick, teaching the uneducated. Preventing the shock waves of crises from which millions of ordinary people suffer. Ensuring socioeconomic development, eliminating backwardness, promoting the progress of science and culture and the exchange of real spiritual values, and protecting mankind's moral sphere from decay and poison.

That is the real meaning of common human interests today. Which of them is contrary to the ideals and goals of socialism?—not one! Which of them is contrary to the interests of the working class?—not one! Which of them is contrary to the interests of our country and world socialism?—again, not one!

On the contrary, the better, more fully and reliably each or all of these common human interests is ensured in the world today, the stronger our country's position is.

The sound, sober approach to the restructuring of economic and political relations and the solution of moral tasks, an approach based on life and people's needs—that is the key to turning hope into reality. The processes of improvement are complex, they may proceed unevenly, in leaps, and zigzags. But in creating the new relations we are also creating the basis for the healthy development of society.

DEMOCRATIC UNION

The Democratic Union (DS)
May 9, 1988

THE DEMOCRATIC UNION, founded in 1988, took Gorbachev's word about democratization of the Soviet Union at face value and from the outset promoted pluralism and a multi-party state. For its trouble it has often been harassed by the militia and other state security functionaries. The following is its platform, which owes a great deal to the American Federalist Papers and the Bill of Rights. It is somewhat brazen in its rejection of Leninism, "which constitutes the foundation of totalitarianism," but in so doing tests the limits of glasnost.

At the present time we define the content of our activity as *political opposition* to the existing social system . . . We declare our support to those forces in the CPSU which not in words but in deeds are striving to implement democratic reforms in the CPSU which not in words but in deeds are striving to implement democratic reforms by utilising their position as members of the ruling party . . .

The Programme of Principles, acknowledgement of which is a necessary condition of membership of the DS.

1. Condemnation of the system of political rule which arose in October 1917, the historical development of which consisted in the consistent formation of totalitarianism.

2. A denial of the ideology of Leninism which constitutes the foundation of totalitarianism.

3. An unequivocal denial of terrorist and violent methods of political struggle as incompatible with the ideals of freedom and democracy.

4. Activity, energetically directed towards the achievement of political, economic and spiritual pluralism, i.e. genuine modern democracy, the bases of which are:

- a multi-party system and parliamentarism;
- a legal, independent free press;
- the free activity of trade unions independent of state power;
- the existence of all sectors of the economy—state, co-operative, individual and private—on an equal footing and free competition between them;
- the division of powers: legislative, executive and judiciary; —the de-ideologisation of the state, i.e. equal rights for all ideologies apart from those appealing to violence or justifying it;—the unconditional guaranteeing of civil liberties: of expression, the press, gatherings, meetings, street processions and demonstrations which do not result in violence;— freedom of religion, religious and atheistic propaganda.

5. The recognition, not in words but in deeds, of the right of nations to self-determination.

6. The demand for the abrogation of the political articles of the Criminal Code, the freeing and rehabilitation (with compensation) of all political prisoners.

7. A declared repudiation of expansion as the cornerstone of foreign policy.

DOGS

Speak
by V. Klimovich, *Ogonyek*, January 1989

Having finished his dinner, the master picked his teeth with a silver toothpick, wiped his lips with a crisply starched napkin, and concentrated on his insides. He had no heartburn. Yet he drank a glass of mineral water, just in case, and walked onto the porch. Many dogs, lying around the yard, saw their master and stopped scratching, picking fleas, and licking themselves. Wagging their tails and whimpering quietly they surrounded the porch and stared loyally at their master. The barn door squeaked and opened and the manager of the estate walked out. Bowing constantly, he stole up to the porch and looking at the master as loyally as a dog, said:

"The dogs should really bark a bit. May they?"

"Well, I guess they may," the master answered benevolently.

The manager of the estate threw out his chest and shouted in a commanding voice.

"Speak!"

The frightened dogs with their tails between their legs began crawling away.

"Look at that. They are scared," the master noted as benevolently and then ordered gently: "Oh, go ahead."

The dogs stopped. The master's favorite barked quietly, yet hid under the porch, just in case. The master laughed. The dogs began barking timidly, then, gaining courage, continued in full voice. The dogs from the other yards began barking back to them. The whole village came to life with sounds: The sheep bleated, the cows mooed, the roosters crowed, and the hens clucked.

A stray dog, hearing the master's dogs, buried (just in case) a bone that he, after many pains, took away from another stray; lay down over it; lay his face on top of his front paws; and began waiting to see what would happen next.

ECONOMY

Why the Screen Burned Out: Once Again the Quality of Our Televisions
Interview with R. Varlamov, docent of the Moscow Technological Institute
by A. Yevgenyev, *Sotsialisticheskaya Industria*, March 12, 1989

Who could have thought that the small notice placed in our paper last May ("In the Center of GUM, at the Fountain, *Sotsialisticheskaya Industriya* No 106) would evoke such a long and resonant echo? At fault for all of this is a single phrase uttered by V. Sokolov, deputy director of the Moscow Television Scientific Research Institute [MNITI], who replied with restrained dignity to a journalist's request to assess the quality of our television sets that "they approach world standards."

And did it flare up! The editorship was literally flooded with a heated stream of readers' letters, casting serious doubt upon the existence of the announced proximity. The most amazing thing

(Sergei Tyunin, *Soviet News*)

is that this stream has not dried up to this day—the readership has proven to be people of sound memory. "I bought a Foton-Ts276 television made at the Simferopol factory," writes a reader from Yuzhno-Sakhalinsk by the same name as the MNITI deputy director V. Sokolov (he headed his letter in journalistic style, "V. Sokolov vs. V. Sokolov"). "Within the first year, while still under warranty, the set broke down four times. It broke for the fifth time exactly one month after the warranty expired. Including what it cost to get it to the repair shop, I invested 50 rubles in the repair. There was nothing but to sign a service contract. Now, over 10 years, I will pay the price of the television. Recently, the screen went blank for the sixth time, although hardly over eighteen months have passed since the date of its manufacture. I am enraged: what kind of world standards are these?"

So, who is right, the representative of the institute capable of seeing the general trend, beyond the anecdotal cases, or the unlucky purchasers, who know little about global trends and judge by their own real life cases? Our correspondent A. Yevgenyev met with R. Varlamov, candidate of technological sciences, a docent at the Moscow Technological Institute of the RSFSR Ministry of Domestic Services.

YEVGENYEV: Rem Gennadyevich, your institution of higher learning trains both designers of domestic radio electronic apparatus and specialists to service it. The problem, as they say, is both inside and out. What is your point of view?

VARLAMOV: Let us agree: any comparison must be correct. Today, Western industry offers buyers a broad range of consumer properties. Thus, the screen size ranges from 4 centimeters to 3.5 meters. Many sets have remote control. About three quarters of them have rectangular-shaped picture tubes, a flat surface, creating a cinematic effect. There are televisions using thick glass, up to two centimeters, with stereo or two-channel accompaniment, with add-ons for cable or satellite television, capable of receiving hundreds of channels. I can frankly say that for the time being, we can only dream about all that.

YEVGENYEV: You mean to say that our production and that of the television assembly plants of the West cannot be compared?

VARLAMOV: No, of course not. There are common and fairly objective criteria. For example, reliability can be characterized by maximum accrued operating time. For ours, it's 7,500 hours, while for the televisions of the foreign firms, it's 10,000–15,000 hours.

YEVGENYEV: As far as I know, just a few years ago, we were satisfied with only 6,000. So have we grown?

VARLAMOV: We are growing. But again, a note of caution here. We are really talking about different indicators. For accrued operating time, we think of the results of stationary trials, and they have in mind actual use, which is affected by a slew of supplementary factors—from the condition of the road you drive it home over to the consumer's inexperience. If we follow Japanese methodology, we should shorten our 7,500 hours by a factor of 1.5–2. Then we'll get quantities for comparison.

We can, however, comfort ourselves with the fact that a lesser share of TV sets with warranties wind up being repaired. According to the USSR Ministry of Trade, in 1987, 24 percent of black and white sets and 30 percent of color sets were under warranty, and in 1988, 20 and 22 percent respectively. However, even having figures like these at hand, I wouldn't exactly maintain that the quality of our television production is improving. . . .

YEVGENYEV: On what basis can we declare our televisions to be close to world standards?

VARLAMOV: What is at issue is by what indicators we are equating them. They have a lot by way of electronic radio apparatus. The weight of the television, its energy demand, you see, is not the last thing here, either. Until recently, we lagged behind here as well, but today, we are getting right up to foreign standards. But with televisions, the main thing is the picture quality. I already spoke about the rectangular picture tube. They give two to three times the brightness. Sunlight does not bother them at all, and their range of colors has been acknowledged to be ideal. In this sense, we have hopeless stagnation. Even worse, we are losing what we once had. **Our picture tubes lasted 2–3 times longer 5–8 years ago. And today, even with the best of our native color televisions, the Lvov "Elektron" and the Kaunas "Shnlayalis," the faces look pretty strange.**

YEVGENYEV: It is not hard to guess what they would tell us at the Ministry of Industrial Relations: "These weeds aren't in our garden. Picture tubes are the Ministry of the Electronics Industry's department.". . .

VARLAMOV: Of course. After all, what is happening now? The enterprises are starting to put out fourth-generation colors sets— improvements over the previous models. But the transfer is terribly slow and painful. The Ministry of Industrial Relations blames the electronics workers for this, that they held up the supply of the component base for the new model. That's all well and good, but as there's enough blame to go around, the development engineers should swallow their share as well. Overseas, as a rule, renovations are phased: one unit is changed, then a second and a third, and after some time, a qualitatively new set comes off the assembly line. We usually shake up the entire system from top to bottom. The designers don't think about what will happen to the accessories: that's their problem. In the end, the assimilation of the innovations is a monstrously prolonged process. An association of the development engineers, assembly workers and components suppliers could only be for the better. The role of the leading institute would change, and grounds for healthy competition would appear.

The Ruble Is Getting Dearer
by Andrei Muratov, *Moscow News*

But its price is rising not due to improvements in the economy. It is much simpler than that—as of January 1 this year, the Moscow administration of the USSR Zhilsotsbank ordered that the price of a ruble, as a product of the printing industry, be equal to 29 kopeks. A 10-ruble note costs now two rubles and a 100-ruble note 20 rubles. This is the price of spoiled banknotes.

In the past you could light cigarettes with banknotes. You light a cigarette, take care to get rid of the flames in time not to damage the numbers on the banknote and then exchange what's left of it for a new banknote in a bank. The operation was absolutely free of charge. Apparently this way of lighting cigarettes has become too expensive. Otherwise, it is impossible to explain such a resolute step by the bankers—for a damaged 10-ruble note you'll now get only eight new rubles.

I learned about the introduction of this educative measure first from a reader's letter and didn't believe it. Then I phoned the USSR Savings Bank where people also didn't believe it. "This cannot be," Vyacheslav Solovov, vice-chairman of its board, told me. "But you better phone the administration of bank issue-and-cashier operations. This is their responsibility. I'm sure they'll disprove this rumour." Sergei Ganichev, the chief of the administration, denied the rumour, saying there was probably a misunderstanding of the quite complex rules on the classification of the defects of banknotes. Here, it is true, there is a new law—if more than a quarter of an area of the banknote is lost then it is forbidden to exchange it. But there is no order to keep a part of its nominal cost.

I explained these fine points to the author of the letter to *MN*. But the next day I read with utter amazement another newspaper which quoted the people I spoke with yesterday, but from another central bank. They confirmed the deduction of 20 per cent of the banknote's value. But the vice-chairman of the board of the USSR Zhilsotsbank is responsible to the Moscow administration. Thus it is this administration which has effectively invented a new source of revenue for itself; however, it now doubts whether such "self-initiative" was legal and has spoken in favour of a serious analysis of the situation.

An analysis is quite possibly necessary. But we are aware that it takes a lot of time to abolish a law once enacted, even if its injustice is obvious without any special research. Elderly persons and pensioners, i.e., the least well-to-do people, will suffer the most from the state organization having raised the price of cut-paper, because it is hardest for them to see the quality of the banknote.

Zhilsotsbank justifies raising the price of the ruble by the transfer to cost accounting. I'd like to know how the state bankers and the USSR Ministry of Finance would react to such an action by some cooperative bank?

Viewpoint: Shares: New Rights or New Words?
by A. Vavilov, *Sotsialisticheskaya Industriya*, December 7, 1988

A. VAVILOV is a doctoral candidate in economic sciences.

Optimists may rejoice that there exists a new economic instrument, namely, shares. The Council of Ministers resolution "On the Issue of Securities by Enterprises and Organizations" has been published. It is all a bit unusual—machine tools, equipment, cast iron, and steel have always had value here—and suddenly pieces of paper become assets. But Finance Minister B. Gostev has openly stated that "shareholders are increasingly becoming masters of the workplace and have a direct vested interest in ensuring that state property at enterprises' disposal is well looked after."

I do not know about you, but I am troubled by a certain confusion here. Why will shareholders look after state property if, as the resolution points out, property relations are not changed? Let us try and see to what extent shareholders will really be in charge and what kind of property is involved.

The basic principles pertaining to the organization of joint-stock companies and shareholders' rights are roughly identical in different countries, although they can differ substantially in detail. To avoid getting enmeshed in the subtleties of international law, let us look at our state's civil code which operated in the twenties and regulated the activity of Soviet joint-stock companies.

A shareholder (together with other shareholders) was entitled during those years to establish a joint-stock company, to take part in elections to the board, to inspect the company's documents, to sell shares, and to receive an annual dividend. And, with majority agreement, wind the company up. Here the shareholder could lose his investment, for with a company being wound up only that money left over after all other commitments have been met is distributed to shareholders.

But what kind of rights does a shareholder have now? The right to set up, reorganize, and wind up a company remains, as the resolution makes clear, the monopoly of the state, or, to be precise, the state apparatus. An enterprise retains the right to utilize state property. A shareholder takes part in elections to the administration on an equal footing with a member of the labor collective—that is, he has no special rights here at all. There is no mention of inspecting documents here either.

A shareholder therefore has only one right, the right to receive a dividend, the size of which could, depending on the economic situation, amount to 30 percent but could also be zero. In practical terms our share is not a share but simply a loan from the population roughly the same as in a bank or savings account, save that a savings bank guarantees a minimum rate of interest and return on investment while the shareholder gets neither interest (dividend) nor the return of his share guaranteed. You may receive high interest but you can also lose the lot.

And, in my view, it is not at all fortuitous that the question of setting up joint-stock companies has been virtually unelaborated to date, yet it is they which really alter the attitude to property by involving workers en masse in management. In developed countries, Sweden, for example, considerable bundles of corporate shares belong to public organizations—public welfare funds, trade unions. This gives them a realistic basis for involvement in management. We for the time being, however, have only one paragraph in the interim provision "On the Procedure for the Issuing of Securities by Enterprises and Organizations Switched Over to Full Economic Accountability and Self-Financing" which speaks of the possibility of organizing joint-stock companies. I am certain that we cannot talk about them seriously until a law on joint-stock companies and societies has been enacted. No special inventions are required here, for the sections of our state's civil code from the twenties would be entirely suitable.

Usually the most serious objection to joint stock companies is the supposed nonlabor character of the dividends received from an investment. But permit me to ask: Does that mean that a man who risks his hard-earned savings by investing them in the development of the production of the goods that society needs is not entitled to some recompense for his risk? And the choice of investment, is that not a form of labor? A state functionary casts billions to the wind ("projects of the century" such as the diversion of the northern rivers cost that alone) and does not lose a single kopek, whereas a shareholder may lose everything. The shareholder does not rush off to the stores to spend his money on a fur coat or a video cassette recorder but instead offers financing to society to develop the production of those selfsame consumer goods—does he not deserve some reward for that? But even if one accepts for a moment that a proportion of the dividend is nonlabor income, there is still no logic in the actions of the state apparatus. The aforementioned resolution gives the right to receive dividends but does not give any rights to dispose of property. In other words, it seems to permit only the most "dubious" right of the shareholder while reserving all the rights of disposal and administration to the management of an enterprise and the administrative organs.

The redistribution of economic power from the state apparatus to enterprises and organizations is still making quite slow progress. The power of the ministerial "apparatus," based on the right to create, reorganize, or close down an enterprise and to influence the appointment of the administration, will be very great. This is whereas the broad distribution of the joint-stock form of organizing enterprises effectively breaks the monopoly position of the bureaucratic apparatus in the management of social ownership.

It must be recognized, however, that the opponents of the decentralization of power have won this round. You cannot trifle with economic laws, however, and we think that shareholders will gain their rights as a matter of course. But we must not delay. The socialist countries' experience has shown what is in store for us if we do not quickly create a developed financial structure for the management of the national economy with the capacity to rapidly transfer resources from a less efficient sector into a more efficient one. And that cannot be created without a joint-stock form of ownership—a democratic form of the people's participation in the management of the economy.

A Path Toward Prosperity
by Igor Lavrovskiy and Leonid Skoptsov,
   Sotsialisticheskaya Industria, April 9, 1989

No price reform will help without real money, without introducing a universal, that is, uniform, yardstick for measuring all values.

Given the convertible ruble, such reforms will not be necessary at all.

Therefore, the convertible ruble is the next logical step in restoring the health of the economy. Only the free circulation of world money in our country will let us partake in the abundance of the world table, and set real prices for both our goods and our working people.

Arguments against making the ruble a hard currency are simple: The economy is not competitive; this is why it must be protected from the external market. This is a typical example of the logic of monopolists who are sheltering themselves from competition. World experience suggests that only the economies sparing themselves honest competition are not competitive.

If we are going to wait until our tenderly cherished machine building becomes competitive then even our grandchildren will not see the hard ruble. Even now we export one car out of four, securing for them—what a shame—1 percent of total export proceeds. At the same time, the sale of one-fifth of the oil produced in our country yields four-fifths of the hard currency. What are we waiting for? We have billions on our hands. Even if we do not take into account dollar-denominated assets in Western banks (about 15 billion) the ruble may reliably rest on annual hard-currency proceeds of raw material exports which exceed $20 billion.

After all, the notion of convertibility amounts to nothing else but free purchases and sales of rubles for dollars and pounds, and of dollars and pounds for rubles.

What is the foundation for the lack of ruble convertibility today? That same monopolism of departments. Some earn hard currency, while others, using their proximity to the state trough, spend it without returning it to export production. The oilmen of Tyumen court heart attacks and make peanuts compared to their Arab or Canadian competitors. In turn, the black gold they extract gets rusty in the form of the ineptly used imported equipment and finances the collapse of agriculture.

For the ruble to become convertible again, the hard currency should be returned to those who earn it—the oilmen. This does not pose any danger for the country; after all, they are Soviet oilmen. However, those who want to spend the currency will have to purchase it from the oilmen, or earn it.

The ruble convertibility will open the world market not only to enterprises but to all of us. If rubles can be freely exchanged into hard currency the warehouses of foreign companies will finally open to us, and world standards will finally come closer to the consumer. The VAZ [Volga Automobile Plant] will have to compete with Montreal and Detroit which are already there rather than the Yelabuga [Plant] which is not. Will this bring about the collapse of the VAZ? Hardly, our native land is rich in talent. However, those whose work is shoddy will undoubtedly be tossed out into the street from collectives. It will become profitable to earn and spend rubles, and this will put an end to both inflation and the budget deficit. . . .

It seems to us that the bitter experience of our history proves that private, that is, isolated property, cannot be destroyed by expropriating the owners. After all, it is not the property that is getting collectivized in the process but the owner. Having convinced the people in his time that socialism is when nobody has property, Stalin simply became the only kulak-private owner in the country administering the entire national wealth privately.

Private property may only be "eliminated" economically, that is, by drawing it into **general** (including worldwide) circulation, the general world market. It cannot be socialized by a decree, even the most revolutionary one. This is not to say that decrees are unnecessary; it is important to understand that all they can do is transfer property from one owner to another.

So, we also need the most resolute and revolutionary decree which would remove property from the hands of the state apparatus and transfer it to those who produce themselves, or want and are able to. There is nothing "unsocialist" about it; **real socialism is not when there are no owners, but when everyone has property.** This is why every "cluster" of social property should get a live and specific master rather than an abstract one, such as the state.

In the masses of our country, the pauper's view of property as a ticket to the "beautiful life" still prevails. Meanwhile, in the economic sense, property merely amounts to an opportunity to make decisions and obtain (or fail to obtain) the results of economic operations, to take risks and shoulder economic responsibility.

Can a state official, if he is honest, take risks with property other than his own? No, he will do everything in order to preserve it, and thus nip in the bud the opportunity to enhance it. The owner answers for the correctness of the decisions he makes with property. A state official as a representative of the owner-state answers with his life. Therefore, why should we torment the people, largely those with integrity, and demand that they switch to economic methods of management for which economic risk is the basis?

"Dummy Issue" of New Business Magazine Produced
Moscow Television Service, December 2, 1988

[Summary] A dummy issue of the *Moskovskiy Biznes* magazine is out today. The aim is to give guidance to western business-men about the changes currently taking place in the Soviet economy. The first issue is due out in February 1989. A joint Soviet-Finnish limited liability company has been set up to produce the magazine. It is to be printed in Helsinki, based on Soviet data. The print run will be 5,000 copies and it will not go on general sale.

Lunar Landscape, or What Will Grow in Our Social Soil? Interview in Moscow with Academician L.I. Abalkin, director of the USSR Academy of Sciences Economic Institute
by Observer Aleksandr Afanasyev, *Komsomolskaya Pravda*, February 8, 1989

I made the acquaintance of this cultured man last summer, roughly 3 weeks before he became widely known. I recall his subdued checked suit, his rather toneless voice, his slicked-back dark brown hair, and his eyes peering over his glasses with attention and interest at his interlocutor. We got acquainted in Sweden, in the Haga government palace in a suburb of Stockholm. The green avenues were filled with the white northern sun.

"Leonid Ivanovich!" I hailed him. "Forgive me for starting up a conversation here. But as we are in the same delegation, I could not miss the opportunity. . . ." Ten steps forward along the avenue, 10 steps back: I sensed old-fashioned human nice-ness in his manner of speaking and his entire appearance. He does not evade questions. If he cannot answer, he gives you a long sad look straight in the eye, as if to say: The answer is so obvious that it is just not done to speak of this, young man, among a knowledgeable audience. . . . He is easy to get on with. A little later I realized why. He does not address the entire Soviet press in your person, as famous people usually do. He addresses you. He is interested in you—and your viewpoint, if you have one, of course. I rechecked my impression. I said: The man has simply not yet grown accustomed to the role of a popular academician and director of a key institute. But 6 months have passed since the party conference which Abalkin addressed—

and which he addressed, to put it mildly, in an unusual manner—dozens of interviews have been published, and his name has become a symbol of the economic reform, but he still looks you in the eye and seems to attach importance, real importance, to what a person thinks about a particular issue, regardless of post or rank. . . . Here is another detail from our first meetings. From when we had gotten to know and understand one another well: "I have never resorted to outside help. Now I feel I have exhausted all means. I will appeal to public opinion. . . ." A few weeks passed. And he addressed the All-Union Party Conference. You know the rest. . . .

He has had a difficult but successful year: In the age of glasnost criticism, too, gives rise to unplanned results. He has had a successful year, but a difficult one: The answers to many questions addressed to him depend, in the final analysis, not so much on him as on the state of the very productive forces and economic relations of which he spoke at the conference, and which cannot be renewed all together—even if you imagine the personal participation of Karl Marx in the processes taking place.

But he, Abalkin, has to answer. And he realizes this perfectly well.

I had hardly entered the office of the director of the USSR Academy of Sciences Economics Institute before Leonid Ivanovich said to me, without beating about the bush:

"Forgive me, but your idea of reflecting for the umpteenth time on the reform, price formation, and so forth, did not excite me. Let us do this. Write: When I arrived at 27 Krasikov Street, Abalkin refused to answer the editorial office's questions, after which he himself asked several questions. . . . Agreed? Are you ready to answer them together with me?" . . .

Leonid Ivanovich said, and I tried to picture, what is happening now. We are, as it were, holding before us a book in which useful socioeconomic prescriptions have been written over the millennia: What must be taken and in what proportions, and when must it be sown? **We take, sow, and water. But . . . it does not grow.** Or if it does grow, it does not do so as sturdily as the prescriptions state. The secret is simple: No prescriptions in the history of world civilization have provided for the dramatic moment when seeds have to be cast not onto soil but onto stones. The lunar landscape remaining after great and impressive cataclysms is beautiful, but it is, alas, not a beauty that can save the world. It is by no means life that such beauty promises. . . .

Social humus is the culture of labor, everyday life, and contacts accumulated over decades. It is knowledge carefully passed from generation to generation. It is the attitude to your own rapidly passing life, to everything that goes to make up life, as something of value. To people, known and unknown, to things, your own and other people's. To the implements and fruits of labor which you have to use in one way or another. . . . When this life-giving humus does not exist, dirt accumulates and turns to stone in its place. Drunkenness, long lines, loutishness everywhere—from buses to workplaces—slashed seats in suburban electric trains, humiliation and disparagement frequently seasoned almost with voluptuousness. . . . It is a still greater misfortune that we usually prove incapable of showing purgative indignation. Our displeasure blows over. We explode over trifles. We burst with irritation—at the past and at each other.

AFANASYEV: How many years will it take?

ABALKIN: Let us calculate. This is my first question. I recently visited a large radio manufacturing plant which once started from zero. The plant now has a backbone of high-class professionals. And it produces equipment of very decent quality. But it took 25 years to grow to this level.

AFANASYEV: Twenty-five years!

ABALKIN: That is if you start right from zero. But we must finally summon up the courage and say frankly: With our state of productive forces it is virtually impossible to attain world standards in 2–3 years.

AFANASYEV: Productive forces, Leonid Ivanovich. . . . Do you mean modern machines? But they can be bought.

ABALKIN: I mean people above all. And the machines which these people make. I mean the topsoil. The production, technological, scientific, everyday layer. It was scattered by the winds of "transformations." We struggled for too long against education (in all social spheres—from farmers to professors), against above-average abilities and skills, and against the "unhealthy" instincts which have always supported life. We reversed too persistently to be able in a matter of years to "leap" into the quality of life which our highly developed neighbors achieved over decades or even centuries.

AFANASYEV: ?!

ABALKIN: Yes, over centuries. An argument developed at a recent international symposium: How long is needed to prove the advantage of socialism? Some said: Ten years. Others: Twenty. Then someone said: One hundred! Stormy objections were raised. Then I stood up and said: Colleagues, is it really that important how long? It is more important, as you realize, just to prove the advantage! As for machines, they can be bought. But what are they without millions of skilled, caring hands. We will buy machines. You cannot "buy" the people.

AFANASYEV: It is difficult to argue with you, Leonid Ivanovich. But you are talking of some inconceivable times, when we are already accustomed to the assertion that we have been allotted very little time. . . .

ABALKIN: Why make wild guesses? It is a question of making substantial progress in our development. It will probably take the efforts of one or two generations. But how many years—17 or 25—who knows?

AFANASYEV: But there is no need for guesses here. Look what zigzags there have been in our history. The sharp turn from war communism to the new economic policy. From the new economic policy through 180 degrees to Stalinist kolkhozes. A certain deviation from them. Then dairy cattle were surrendered to the meat plan, oil was found, and the stagnation style was established. . . . What guarantee is there that there will not be a change of course when one generation succeeds another?

ABALKIN: That is the second question to you.

Only I would deepen the problem formulated today. Of course, we must be concerned about guarantees of irreversibility. But both ebbs and flows lie ahead. So it is more realistic to ensure that during the ebbs we do not completely lose what we are now accumulating with great difficulty.

AFANASYEV: Do you foresee ebbs. . . ?

ABALKIN: We must endeavor to be honest. Here is another episode. A foreign scientist said to me: The popularity of your restructuring is growing, but what will happen in 5–10 years? And I said to him: But surely any experience has limits? Even emotional limits, does it not? Therefore it is impractical to gamble on emotions, on an upsurge and explosion. . . . We have to have time to lay the groundwork for decades to come. When both I and even you are no longer here, this groundwork will only start working. And it will ensure another shift.

AFANASYEV: **Good Lord, how long is it possible to go on talking of a bright future?**

ABALKIN: Our trouble is that we talk a lot and build a lot (of ferroconcrete) but have relegated cultural building, this truly strategic potential of a power, to a third-rate task. . . . Turn to Japan, take a look at Sweden, which you and I have visited—any nation invests in the future, if only out of an instinct of self-preservation. And it scarcely dilates on this. . . . Superficially, this is like pouring into a bottomless pit. You will get a return neither today nor tomorrow. But there is continuity here! Someone in the thirties invested in the present-day Swedes. He is no longer alive, but they have a flourishing, high-quality nation that is full of strength.

AFANASYEV: In some 20 years' time we will probably realize that our ferroconcrete victories were nothing more than the excrement of civilization.

ABALKIN: Today's realization is already all the more bitter: No bricks and iron will patch the hole in national culture and intellect.

AFANASYEV: Last year, Leonid Ivanovich, two vice presidents of the U.S. Chrysler Company visited Viktor Bossert at the "RAF" association with regard to setting up a joint venture. They were most attracted, so they said, by the fact that they were dealing with the first elected Soviet director. And here they came out with a characteristic contradiction. Bossert, an energetic man, was in favor of installing equipment as soon as possible. The Americans were cautious: Let us first help you to "polish" the present technology and model. . . . Only then did I realize that this was not simple caution. It was something else. The Americans evidently understand too well that it is necessary first to "polish" the work force itself—otherwise the very modern, capricious equipment will simply be wrecked with hammers and sledgehammers: not with this intention, of course, but out of the very best intentions. This is what we are able to do. This is how we work at present.

ABALKIN: We have a certain mass misunderstanding of how strikingly different the industrial situation in the thirties is from the technological situation at the end of the eighties. It is possible to "catch up and pass" horizontally, by "crude" iron and riveting, without intellect, without virtuoso skill, by means of enthusiasm and physical strength. The gap now is a vertical one. A gap in education and culture—like a gap in epochs. You cannot cross this abyss through physical acceleration. Millions of quite different working people are needed!

AFANASYEV: I recently spoke on what way and to what extent our working person differs, let us say, from the Western working person. A very good producer proposed putting in an application [zayavka]. But at the same time he remarked: Would this not cause offense? For it would be like a slap in the face?

ABALKIN: Of course it would cause offense. But we probably need some kind of shock to make us at last take offense at ourselves! It's a shame, you know: Russia was renowned for its master craftsmen, and even now there are still master craftsmen and bosses, but there is no stratum of master craftsmen and bosses. There is no quality of the masses. . . . Here I mean managers, economists, and financiers. Our journalists boldly propose: The banks must be made the nerve centers of economic life. But will we find in our millions-strong country even 10 people who really understand bank policy? And leaders? For many of them are sincere when they turn the age-old peaceful grain-growing business into crippling battles for grain. . . . We must right now train a new generation of administrators, Soviet managers who are capable of directing without shouting, without banging their fist on the table, and who are able to see the distant prospects too. . . . And this again is a matter of more than one decade.

AFANASYEV: These battles, Leonid Ivanovich, these systematic expropriations expose with calendar precision wounds which will hardly cicatrize in a year. What buildup of social humus can there be if the "machine" set going during the times of war communism is still, with rare interruptions, equally efficiently mangling the managerial mentality?

ABALKIN: Only a machine can operate against a machine. This system, alas, is not only an apparatus. It is a tangle of relations which have grown into tens of millions of people: workers, kolkhoz members, agronomists, engineers, teachers, physicians, leaders. I specially put the leaders last. This is so. For without broad social support, without deep roots in the strong mass leveling psychology, conservatism would not long remain afloat.

AFANASYEV: Ideology has grown into psychology. . . .

ABA:LOM: Ideology has become psychology. Therefore I would support the action to implant the lease which you are implementing in Orel Oblast. I myself would willingly go there if I find the time during the next few months. It is necessary to create such socio-economic islets and experimental, preferential zones. There is the hope that a system of renewed socialism will grow up out of them.

AFANASYEV: But will it grow up? Will they let it . . . ? Although you refused to answer my questions about the "current moment," you cannot build a strategy without it. The editorial office receives hundreds of letters: The apparatus is putting increasingly strong pressure on enterprising directors and cooperative members. And now the Council of Ministers has adopted two new decisions, additional restrictions are being introduced. . . .

ABALKIN: I will tell you frankly that what worries me is not the restrictions: It is still possible to discuss and argue here over which kinds of cooperative activity should be encouraged, and which not. What is indisputable is something else: Enterprising people are being placed under the department's control. But the direct opposite was envisaged according to the concept on which the economic reform was based. By setting up in competition with the state sector, cooperative members were to promote the destruction of the departmental monopoly. The very monopoly that led to stagnation, to a loss of quality. . . . As a result of the latest measures this monopoly will only be strengthened, and the present state will be preserved. . . .

AFANASYEV: This question is now being discussed: From whom must land be leased? From the kolkhoz or from the Soviet power?

ABALKIN: From the Soviet power, of course. Otherwise it makes politicoeconomic nonsense! If it is a good kolkhoz, it will manage even without the lease crutch. And if the kolkhoz is ailing, what will we achieve with such subleasing? Will we close our eyes to the fact that a collapsed, unviable structure is essentially parasitizing on the living organism of the lease? What do we want: to discredit and stifle the present reform? To somehow justify "great changes" by sliding the results of real transformations under a dead skin? No? Thus the answer is unequivocal.

AFANASYEV: And yet the kolkhoz, viable or not, has received the land to use in perpetuity, has it not?

ABALKIN: In perpetuity means for life. And when the former owner dies, the land goes to his heirs.

AFANASYEV: I know, Leonid Ivanovich, that the institute which you head has drawn up an entire program for the liquidation of loss-making enterprises.

ABALKIN: Yes, and we propose making a saving of R20 billion out of this. This is real money to raise living standards right now. But I will make one correction: the liquidation of loss-making state enterprises. Cooperative members and lessees have suggested to us that they must be taken off the state balance and removed from the category of state enterprises, but if there are people wishing to lease an enterprise, why refuse them?

AFANASYEV: But what if there is no one wishing to do so? If no one wants its output? Or the ecological harm exceeds the economic benefit many times over?

ABALKIN: There are such enterprises. I spoke recently at the Council of Ministers. I was supported. A number of show closures must be carried out, in order to perfect the model of how to liquidate economic subdivisions which society and the state do not need, with the smallest social, economic, and political losses. The press could do a very great deal here. How about you? Will you undertake it?

AFANASYEV: Of course *Komsomolskaya Pravda* will, Leonid Ivanovich. But we have a counterproposal: Why not start with the Baykal Pulp and Paper Combine, which is causing colossal harm to Lake Baykal and has become a real symbol of the conservatives' confrontation with restructuring . . . ? The liquidation of the Baykal Pulp and Paper Combine would be a truly patriotic act. What do you think? Will the Council of Ministers support this? [Afanasyev ends]

Leonid Ivanovich smiled in reply:

"Let us first publish the proposal! And then we will see who supports it and who does not. My opinion is that we must urgently liquidate the Baykal Pulp and Paper Combine, without postponing it for years. In general, you know, there must be absolute values. We must not in principle calculate, as you said, whether the harm exceeds the good. If there is even 1 percent of harm, then there must be no question. Counting in such a case is not even pragmatism, but a primitive approach, mediocrity, a crime! It shows a lack of culture when, let us say, a trade union leader tries to convince you with figures that a plant needs a swimming pool and a sauna, and then the sickness rate will fall by so many percentage points. . . . It is high time to count not in terms of the machine tool, dear people, but in terms of health, of the genetic stock of the nation! I have noticed—the smaller a people, the more figures it has who think on a national scale. We are called a great people. But is the fate of a great people 'strapped' to production units? Thus, people who think on a grand scale must be consciously cultivated and educated. I cannot at once say how, specifically, to make the people's health, well-being, and culture into assets at the level of a patriotic absolute and a sacred object. This is a third question for me. But I am 100-percent sure that without this we will not survive as a great power. . . . I would like to appeal now to all thinking people who root for the country, to workers, peasants, and to the urban and rural intelligentsia. I appeal to patriots, citizens, and compatriots. We are now in a difficult situation such as our motherland has not experienced for a long time. Emergence from the stagnant past means liberation from steadfast mass illusions, and above all from the illusion that 'all is in order' here, and that we have only to tighten loose screws. Let us be honest with each other: All is not in order here. What is most alarming now is the fact that we have forgotten how to work. But, still worse, we are not fully aware of this. We have not become conscious of this as a public disaster. We have not realized that we will be able only by using our own hands to drag ourselves, pardon me, out of the 'hole' in which we found ourselves when we 'freed' millions both from proprietary rights and from civic responsibility.

"We must learn again to respect the master within ourselves, to value honest, good-quality work. . . .

"These are my questions, if you like. They cannot be answered by one person. But rivers, not just streams, are made up of single drops of common sense. We must gather up the people's experience, all who have something to say and something that they can share with the whole country: Write, speak, report. We have no other options. Otherwise we will not save and restore ourselves. . . ."

ELECTIONS

by Sergei Y. Andreyev, *Neva*, February 1989

Naturally, even raising the question of sharing power with the people causes apoplexy in many party workers, who have been taught for dozens of years that it is not the party that serves the people, but the people who serve the party.

Who'll Sit in the Kremlin?
by Vitaly Marsov, *Moscow News*, April 23–30, 1989

Filling the seats for the Congress of People's Deputies, the supreme organ of state power in the USSR, is continuing. The second round of elections, in the constituencies where none of the candidates received over 50 per cent, was held early in April. New elections will be held in some constituencies in May in the final stage of the elections. This time from 60 to 70 per cent of the voters came to the voting stations—the usual syndrome in second-round voting. However, the results of this voting, which became known just now, confirm the general trend for the elections—the people are voting for perestroika. The well-known

(V. Rozantsev, *Soviet News*)

journalist Yuri Chernichenko, historian Roy Medvedev and the young research associate Sergei Stankevich, nominated by unofficial organizations, all of whom have expressed themselves as adherents to perestroika, were elected people's deputies.

On April 10, the Presidium of the USSR Academy of Sciences approved 28 candidates to people's deputies for the 12 seats that the Academy had left unfilled after the elections in March. The candidates include Academicians G. Arbatov, R. Sagdeyev, A. Sakharov, and N. Shmelyov, D. Sc. (Economics). The final results of the additional elections in the USSR Academy of Sciences will be known on April 21.

Now, most of the 2,250 people's deputies of the USSR have been elected. Even though the ultimate results of the additional elections and re-elections will be known only by the end of May, it is possible to say that the forces of perestroika have scored a convincing victory at the elections.

The activeness of Soviet voters outdid the forecasts of the sceptics, who thought that the passivity of the people would slow down the rapid rate of the political reform. This didn't happen—some 90 per cent of the voters took part in the elections.

Juhan Aarne, a journalist and TV commentator from Estonia, is first in alphabetical order on the list of the USSR people's deputies. Journalists are one of the most active forces in perestroika. If in the past USSR Supreme Soviet there were only seven of them per 1,500 deputies (0.5 per cent), then today no less than 60 journalists, heads of media offices and writers who are active in periodicals (three per cent) are deputies. Their stand has a tangible influence on public opinion.

By the way, it is notable that the number of Party functionaries of the highest and middle rank decreased by about the same number as that of the journalists increased. About 40 of them were not elected by the voters. As for the number of Party members on the whole in the supreme legislative body of the USSR, it has increased.

As compared with the last elections, the share of workers among the deputies fell from 35.2 to 18.6 per cent; and of collective farmers—from 16.1 to 11.2 per cent. I don't see any cause for alarm in this. Most probably it reflects the real situation which has taken shape in the country, the essence of which is that perestroika has not as yet produced very many new workers' and farmers' leaders on a national scale. But, I think the time for this is in the offing.

The share of women among the deputies has also fallen considerably—from 32.8 per cent in the former Supreme Soviet to 17.1 per cent today. This fact, as I see it, shows only one thing—the women's situation in the country is so bad that the male majority of the deputies will have to take this matter up at once.

And who "compensated" for the losses of these groups of the population in the supreme legislative organ? Here we see two trends.

Firstly, the number of representatives of the intelligentsia, both technical and professional, has grown. It looks like the Soviet parliament may become one of the best educated in the world. And, secondly, by an increase in the Party, state and trade union functionaries on the Republican and regional level. They replaced the many ministers and chairmen of state committees, whom the present law forbids to be members of the highest legislative body.

However it may be, an optimistic and sober assessment may be as follows: Mikhail Gorbachev and other political leaders of perestroika got strong support for their policy. And even more important, the ordinary voters got perestroika supporters for deputies, people who are capable of uniting to circumvent the still blossoming bureaucratic patterns. This is an alliance of the leaders of renewal with the people.

Glasnost in Short Supply
by V. Noskov, *Sotsialisticheskaya Industriya*, January 10, 1989

Gorkiy—Nearly every day the local newspapers publish brief reports about who has been nominated for the post of people's deputy of the USSR. Unfortunately it is hard to understand from these notes how the discussion of candidacies takes place: smoothly and evenly or, on the contrary, heatedly and pointedly.

For instance, here is the story told when she came to the *Sotsialisticheskaya Industriya* correspondents' center by a worker from the "Krasnoye Sormovo" plant's number three ship hull shop, who asked us not to name her in the newspaper:

"Our party committee suggested nominating one specific candidate in the shop but at a meeting our collective opposed this and named its own candidate. Then party committee representatives went to neighboring shops and started trying to persuade the workers. But why?"

There is other talk in the city too. It is said that some candidates were nominated from organizations and institutions secretly, by a decision made by a narrow circle of leaders or the apparatus. In response to justified protests people are given vague explanations, being told not to worry, not all the candidates will be elected any way—considerably more candidates than there are seats are now nominated.

People do not know where to address their complaints. I tried last Sunday to find out the address of at least one Gorkiy agitation center. I telephoned to the palaces and centers of culture of the largest enterprises—in reply I heard that they had no agitation centers, there had not yet been any order to open them.

The party gorkom duty officer explained that answers to all these questions should be sought in the electoral commissions created under the party raykoms, but they do not work on Sundays.

Of course, it may be said that the election campaign is only beginning and everything still lies ahead. Yet it is important from the outset not to conduct it according to the old scheme but in a new way, in the spirit of restructuring.

Without a Parliament There Is No Real Democracy
Interview with F. Burlatskiy by N. Zyatkov,
Argumenty I Fakty, February 25–March 3, 1989

F. Burlatskiy, among other candidates, advanced along the line of the Soviet Peace Fund, the Soviet Committee for European

Security and Cooperation, and a number of other organizations. After meetings in Moscow, Leningrad, and other places with the aktivs of these organizations, our correspondent N. Zyatkov asked him to discuss the most crucial problems that are arising during the course of the pre-election struggle.

ZYATKOV: What role can be played by the principle of pluralism during the formation and in the work of the Soviet parliament? In general is pluralism possible under the conditions of a one-party system, or is this an illusion, as they think it is in the West?

BURLATSKIY: The USSR Supreme Soviet is called upon to become the central political institution where there is a convergence of all trends, opinions, and alternative programs that embody socialist pluralism. This is what explains the policy for elections to this agency—from the party, from the social organizations, and from the regions.

The USSR Supreme Soviet and the Congress of People's Deputies will have to accumulate new experience in real pluralism under the conditions of a one-party system, a multitude of opinions within the party itself, and integration of interests represented by various social, cultural, and national groups and trends. It will be necessary to develop a procedure which will give freedom of expression for all opinions and at the same time will not impede the adoption of decisions, will rely on the will of the majority and take into account the interests and positions of the minority, especially when it comes to numerically small nations.

It will be necessary to resolve one of the key issues of the procedure of parliamentary debates—making sure that they are polite and constructive in nature. **Glasnost has played a historic role; it has become a mirror of our society, its past, its achievements and problems, and its position in the modern world.** But there has also appeared an extremely dangerous tendency which, in my opinion, can become a throwback to the Stalinist spirit: impatience, malice, and the inability to listen to and understand the opponent. From here it is not far to accusing him of being an "enemy" and placing him up against the wall. . . .

"Socialist ideology never prescribed a one-party system. It just happened in our history. There are experiments that we are watching with considerable interest—in Hungary, for instance. However, what would happen, if we were to admit several parties now? At first, nationalist parties will be founded, with maybe 10 or 15 million members. What we need now is democratic parliamentarism and complete pluralism within the party. But the next step could already be in the direction of a multiparty system."

* * *

Burlatskiy says that such pluralism within the party also includes the reintroduction of the right to form groups, which was suspended in 1921: **"Although I do not know what to call it, there must be the right to form groups within the party."**

Answering a question from among the audience as to what would be left of the party's leadership role with all this pluralism, Burlatskiy says: **"I do not think that the party will retain its leading role. Such a thing just is not conceivable in a pluralist society."**

Agitation Without Agitation Stations. What Rights Are Given to Candidates and Their Constituents in the Election Campaign?
by V. Dolganov, *Izvestiya*, February 5, 1989

V. DOLGANOV INTERVIEWED Ye. M. Koveshnikov, chief of the Central Electoral Commission Juridical group. At the next stage of the election campaign, every candidate USSR people's deputy will have to face a keen political struggle for victory in the elections. What are the rules governing this struggle? What are the candidates and their supporters allowed and not allowed to do? How should someone campaign for a candidate or, say, for himself?

These were the topics of our correspondent's conversation with Candidate of Juridical Sciences Yevgeniy Mikhaylovich Koveshnikov, chief of the Central Electoral Commission Juridical Group.

DOLGANOV: In principle it is clear what a candidate's program ought to be. How about the means of campaigning against a candidate?

YE. KOVESHNIKOV: In both cases the requirements are identical. Neither a candidate's program nor any objections against him ought to contravene the USSR Constitution and Soviet laws. **I think that, when campaigning against a candidate, there must be no digging up of his personal life or exploitation of any intimate details.** It is, of course, totally impermissible to insult opponents. Generally speaking, the struggle must be waged within the framework of political debate, with each side bearing in mind the standards of such debate.

DOLGANOV: Suppose I have had photographs of my candidate printed, adding captions which present him in a favorable light. What do I do next? How and where can such material be distributed?

YE. KOVESHNIKOV: Anywhere you like. At a trolleybus stop, at the entrance to the subway or a store, at a plant or organization, on streets and in squares . . . Leaflets and slogans can be handed out in person, they can be posted in public places, and this can be accompanied by verbal agitation in favor of the candidate deputy. Any form of agitation can be used provided this does not obstruct traffic or pose a threat to the safety and health of others.

DOLGANOV: Nevertheless, a spontaneous rally may develop, a discussion of a candidate's merits and shortcomings. Cases like this are governed by the appropriate decree which makes provisions governing responsibility for unauthorized meetings, rallies, and demonstrations. What happens if permission from the local soviet has not been obtained in advance?

YE. KOVESHNIKOV: I want to emphasize in particular that the decree which you mentioned should not be applied in any circumstances in the election campaign, when it really is a question of preparation for elections. I am certain that no special permission is required. The law states bluntly: A candidate people's deputy can conduct meetings at rallies and in any other form convenient for the voters. In other words, a spontaneous rally can be held in a microrayon, near an apartment block, in a park or a small public garden. . . . You can argue, discuss, and campaign for your candidate in the way this is done in a civilized society. Just bear in mind the conditions we mentioned earlier: legality and safety.

I can understand how excited people are by the very opportunity to campaign in a new fashion. After all, we all are so fed up with the years and years of stereotype and almost always deserted agitation stations with their shimmering television sets, files of frayed newspapers, and agitators who are agitators in name alone. I personally am pleased that sociopolitical, debating, and other election campaign clubs are now coming into being. It is important to ensure that okrug electoral commissions, abandoning stereotypes, support their activity and create all necessary conditions for their work. It is probably more convenient to argue about nominated candidates and their programs in such clubs rather than in the street. They can show movie or videotape promotion clips, present original forms of visual agitation. . . .

DOLGANOV: People often ask us whether it is possible to campaign for candidacies which have yet to be examined at okrug election campaign meetings, selecting the best candidates to be listed on the future ballot papers.

YE. KOVESHNIKOV: Agitation is perfectly allowable even before okrug election campaign meeting. It can only be beneficial if people can meet potential candidates before the meeting and find out about their programs and themselves personally. Let us not forget: All of the election campaign work and struggle reflects our concern for the future USSR Congress of People's Deputies and the future permanently acting USSR Supreme Soviet. **The greater the number of different opinions expressed and the more diverse and more effective the election campaign programs, the more reliable will be the people who get elected to the organs of supreme power.** That means that they will elaborate more reliable decisions furthering restructuring and the interests of the whole people.

Prolonged Hesitation: Reflections on Some Lessons of the Elections in Leningrad
by N. Volynskiy and V. Loginov, *Pravda*, April 20, 1989

There are events that prompt an immediate response. But when a little time has passed, you realize: The event was assessed correctly enough in principle, but rather superficially, at an emotional level. At first we intended to give this article a different title. Sharper and more unequivocal, perhaps. But the more closely we studied the nature of what happened and the more different circumstances came to our attention, the clearer it became that unequivocal assessments are inapposite here. This is a measure of the unusual, novel nature of the situation on which we wish to reflect, without claiming to analyze the entire spectrum of problems it highlights.

It is now common knowledge that six party and soviet leaders in Leningrad and the oblast, among them CPSU oblast committee [obkom] first and second secretaries Yu. Solovyev and A. Fateyev and city committee [gorkom] first secretary A. Gerasimov, failed to win sufficient votes and did not obtain seats as USSR people's deputies. A few years ago no one could even have imagined such an outcome for elections. Now, though, it is a reality that cannot be hushed up, ignored, or disguised as some kind of chance phenomenon. What happened was clearly—given the situation that had developed in Leningrad over the years— what had to happen. Sooner or later. And it happened in spring 1989. . . .

The election campaign for the eventually unsuccessful candidates was launched by the party committees "by all the rules." Tasks associated with the preparation and holding of the elections were discussed at sessions of the obkom bureau, gorkoms, and rayon committees [raykoms] and conferences of primary party organization secretaries. A number of committees held "simulations" and training sessions with the ideological aktiv. . . .

The Leningrad leaders could not, of course, fail to give some thought to what to offer people, so to speak. There was a certain "capital." Considerable, they believed. For the first time in the country, a number of enterprises had been removed from the power of ministries, and independent concerns were set up. It was the first time that such huge resources had been channeled into the development of the social sphere and housing construction.

Since 1986 the obkom has markedly reduced "paper-shuffling." On the basis of the principle that "everyone should do his job," they tried to channel in the right direction—to their destination— the flood of telegrams and letters that was swamping the departments, containing requests to "get hold of some freightcars" and so forth. Then they set about revoking a series of their own former resolutions that run counter to present-day approaches in party work and political methods of leadership. After all, formerly the obkom had basically usurped the right to decide what to build and where, what enterprises Leningrad and the oblast needed, and with what structure. There were a great many decisions, sometimes concerning day-to-day matters, that the city soviet executive committee [gorispolkom] could not take without the consent of the party obkom secretariat.

The present concern is to restore full power to the soviets. And here there have not been very many energetic steps as yet. And the vast majority of the local soviets . . . are not taking power. We are not ready yet, they say. We are used to working "in harness." And today there are still workers in the soviets, their executive organs, and many departments, including central departments, who do not hesitate to shift the blame onto the party committees for purely economic blunders, for their own mistakes.

That was the basis of the election tactics that came to maturity in the Smolnyy, where the party obkom and gorkom are located. Restructuring is proceeding with difficulty, but it is proceeding, and there are already perceptible changes, there are marked successes, and as for the shortcomings, they will undoubtedly be dealt with eventually. The main thing is to make up our minds to prolonged, painstaking work to overcome the legacy of stagnation. . . . The stereotype—psychological and behavioral—suggested to the campaign organizers that the candidates will be sure of mass support if, in addition, they remind people about long-term programs, repeating slogans like these: "An individual apartment for every Leningrader by the year 2000!", "We will fill the stores with goods!", or—from an earlier arsenal—"We will fulfill the 'Intensification-90' program!"

A word about this last program, by the way. Hundreds of specialists and scientists worked on this multivolume program. Then an impressive exhibition appeared on the site of the youth leisure center, to which high-ranking guests were invariably brought. The guests examined the gleaming visual display screens and watched the antics of a one-armed robot. . . . The city was decked with appropriate banners, the word "Intensification" (with a capital "I") sprang out daily from newspapers and from authoritative platforms. And then the fuss began to die down and the banners quietly disappeared.

The program, which was nurtured on the old approaches and largely for show (according to obkom bureau member V. Smirnov, a worker at the optical mechanics association, it was not for nothing the people christened it "intensifiction"), proved, in essence, abortive. But let us be absolutely honest. In the prerestructuring times doubtless large numbers of obliging "theorists" could have been found to prove . . . the opposite. And how hard it is to abandon the habit of "making mountains out of molehills" when you are talking about successes, and vice versa. It is no accident that people in the Smolnyy offices today are most eager to talk about growth figures.

But what use are such promises to people when the counters in the food stores were becoming increasingly sparse and when, last year, one in every three Leningraders visiting other stores returned home empty-handed, because of shortages of goods, their poor quality, and ever longer waiting lines. The "Housing-2000" program is being implemented, but the waiting time for apartments has increased from 5 years to 10. There was a great deal of fuss when the "Health" program was born within

the walls of the Smolnyy—but there have been no changes for the better. . . .

Are we saying that the people in Smolnyy lacked information about the real state of affairs? No, they had information, exhaustive information, at that. To the credit of the leaders of Leningrad and the oblast, unlike their many opponents, who did not have that information and in some cases did not want to "know anything," they did not promise people a land of milk and honey "in exchange for support." But all the same, they counted on mutual understanding with the voters.

Did they anticipate meeting with alienation? They foresaw that it would not be easy to talk with the local people, but not as bad as that. . . . In a mere 3 or 4 years people had learned to break free from the mentality of indifferent and obedient citizens, and the hesitation that followed the slogans proclaimed before and during restructuring was too prolonged. Those party committees who were engaged—sluggishly, in the old way—in campaigning for the leaders who were candidates failed to take this into account. Even when some of the ultra-restructurers started openly describing the candidates as "knights of stagnation" (stronger things than that were said, too), they were not seriously worried. In any event, no significant amendments were made to the actions of the campaign collectives or the candidates themselves, who clearly had insufficient real, direct contact with the voters.

Two Worlds Meet at the Congress of Deputies
by Leonid Batkin, *Moscow News*, June 25, 1989

On June 1, Yuri Vlasov, stunned by the ovation the majority of deputies gave to General Rodionov, who supervised the massacre in Tbilisi, exclaimed: "After this ovation it is obvious to me: a split is practically inevitable, but . . . this is a matter of fundamentally different views about life."

Perhaps a still more formidable and staggering scene was played out on June 2, in the presence of the many people whom historical circumstances had willed to be this country's first parliament (after the Constitutional Assembly disbanded in 1918), and who so far had only a vague idea of what a parliament is.

A Komsomol functionary from Cherkassy who had lost both legs in Afghanistan came to the rostrum. It would be hard to find a more appropriate man to make a speech intended to charge Andrei Sakharov with tainting the image of the Soviet Army. In the same breath this deputy—Chervonopisky—charged the MPs of the Baltic Republics and Georgia, who had protested against the employment of troops to break up meetings and to kill civilians, with "political manoeuvring". He claimed further that popular fronts were training "stormtroopers". He managed to lump together psychologically and politically all that seemed alien, threatening, and hateful, and to get even with the pardoned Sakharov who continues to stir up trouble, with intellectuals who mutter something about democracy, with members of unofficial groups who now draw crowds of hundreds of thousands of people to meetings, and with the liberation upsurge of outlaying national areas. Increasingly rude and senseless insults were listened to by an unruffled Anatoly Lukyanov who chaired the session, and were leisurely applauded by members of the presiding panel who, by the way, were squandering in those sweet minutes the capital of "new thinking" earned during long months by the amiable and able Shevardnadze among the Western public. If there was a man to feel sorry for at this "moment of truth" at the Congress, it was Eduard Shevardnadze.

One shouldn't feel sorry for Sakhavrov. He has chosen his destiny himself. He has gone through much worse things in complete isolation and obscurity. Only yesterday he stood before the cameras. The country and the world watched with bated breath as Sakharov was slowly choosing plain words, but he spoke with his usual candour and firmness, and with an uncharacteristic passion prompted by the situation. He was not trying to defend himself and his reputation (the latter does not need this). He was out to uphold the truth and, with us glued to the screens, to uphold OUR reputation.

They tried to shout him down.

Sakharov said he did not mean to hurt the feelings of those soldiers who diligently and bravely obeyed orders in the Afghan hell. But he reminded the Congress that some of the orders were criminal.

"It was a disgrace and sin," Sakharov said. "Yes, nearly 15,000 Soviet soldiers died, and many became cripples in those nine years. In the name of what? Who is to blame? How can you say that you are sorry for 'Afghans', i.e. those who went through this undeclared colonial war, and in the same breath call them for some reason 'internationalists', and thus persist in repeating the vile Brezhnev propaganda lie? It would be better to recall some other statistics—six or seven million refugees, and about one million real Afghans killed. The direct blame for all this lies with top-ranking officials of the USSR, including that same Marshal Akhromeyev who registered his noble indignation on June 2. Indirectly, all of us are to blame who were afraid to speak out against the imperial Afghan adventure, and hence for saving from death and crippling (physical and moral) our young men, and for upholding the Soviet Army's reputation."

AND THE ONLY person among the audience and at the podium, and perhaps the only person in the whole land who is absolutely innocent of guilt before the Afghan victims, was precisely the one reviled by the people's (sic) deputies.

The Soviet people ought to ponder such things, in the context of the specific political contents of the "Sakharov" episode they witnessed at the Congress, since their importance transcends the Congress.

Well, the war did not teach charity but cruelty. It taught the lads to kill, not to rescue. We must know THE WHOLE sad truth about Afghanistan with the exclusion of the false romanticizing and heroization of those whose tragic lot was to fight there. More than that, it should avoid manipulating with the word "internationalist", which rivals the Stalin times for cynicism. We shall know the truth anyway. Upon this depend in no small degree the prospects of our sickly fledgling democracy. At the Congress the poet Olzhas Suleimenov compared democracy to an innocent little girl. He forgot to mention in our case, this innocent girl is the charge of our bureaucratic apparat "madame".

Excerpts from Speech to Congress of People's Deputies
by Yuri N. Afanaseyev, May 27, 1989

YURI N. AFANASEYEV is director of the Institute of Historical Archives.

I want to say that for a number of reasons the work of the Congress yesterday had a depressing effect on me . . . We have cranked up the usual machinery: a few moralistic speeches, including some by people I highly respect—Zalygin, Medvedev—after which comes a stupefying vote of the majority.

I have scrutinized the composition of our Supreme Soviet. I feel obliged to say [that] . . . if we compare the level of qualifications with the level of the tasks awaiting [it], if we consider the level of professionalism required under the current conditions, we have created a Stalinist-Brezhnevite Supreme Soviet.

The majority that has been formed here [is] so depressing that I wanted to address you. This—I would call it an aggressively obedient majority, which yesterday bottled up all the decisions the people expect from the Congress—I mean in the first place— Yes, I am finishing but I ask you to stop shouting and clapping, because this is what I took the podium for.

So, esteemed aggressively obedient majority, and you, Mikhail Sergeyevich who is listening attentively (I don't know whether listening attentively to this majority or skillfully influencing it), we can continue working like this, we can be obedient, foregoing lines here in front of the podium and sending up our notes neatly . . . but let us not for a single moment forget those who sent us here to this Congress. They did not send us here to be graceful but instead to radically transform the situation in the country.

Excerpts from Speech to Congress of People's Deputies by Gavril K. Popov

GAVRIL K. POPOV is an economist.

Democratic-minded deputies were inevitably fated to be in the minority. We operated on this assumption, we knew this would be the case. Nonetheless, we came to the Congress full of great enthusiasm. We had two options. The first was to play the role of the opposition. The second was to contribute to the constructive work of the Congress. We chose the second.

We realized that the country was in too grave a situation to be able to afford our playing the role of opposition, of entering into confrontation. We formed working groups and began preparing materials for the upcoming Congress because we received no materials from the party apparatus . . . But from the outset our work was met by serious mistrust and prejudice. The Presidium of the Supreme Soviet could not even find room for us or paper for our work. The materials we had prepared were not even duplicated or distributed.

Yesterday the machine of majority rule began in earnest. Delegates whose opinions differed from those of the majority ... were pushed aside, and the lists for the Supreme Soviet were compiled on this basis.

You have seen that we were trying to work in harmony. We resolutely supported the candidacy of Mikhail Sergeyevich [Gorbachev]. But it is becoming obvious to us that the apparatus is trying to take its revenge. Under such conditions it would be incomprehensible for us or for our constituents if we were to continue the option we chose at the beginning.

Why has this voting machine been set in motion? There can be only one answer: to form a Supreme Soviet obedient to the will of the apparatus and to keep up the pressure on the progressive wing in the leadership of the country.

Therefore we have no choice but to think of changing our position. First of all, a group of Moscow region deputies, from scientific organizations, from creative unions, finds it necessary to separate from the Moscow delegation. We propose to form an interregional independent group of deputies and invite all comrade deputies to join it.

In the election of the Supreme Soviet we see that the apparatus has undoubtedly won a victory, though it was not very difficult to win in this hall, as you can see. But who will defeat inflation in this country, who will defeat empty counters in the stores, who will defeat the incompetence of the leadership?

To tell you the truth, I am terrified. If the people here are unable to organize the work of one auditorium, what can they do to the country?

We can stand it for a while. We have been patient for dozens of years when we were ignored. We can limit ourselves to the role of opposition. But what I am concerned about is how long will the people tolerate all this?

Excerpts from Speech to Congress of People's Deputies
by Oleg M. Adamovich

OLEG M. ADAMOVICH is a writer from Byelorussia.

We must securely shield ourselves ... from the head of state himself, in case he starts dreaming the dreams of Stalin. Americans have an impeachment law to remove Presidents from power before their term of office expires. We cannot live without such a law, either ...

Shop window displays in the West are full of goods. In our shop windows we hang portraits of ministers: a portrait of the minister of agriculture in meat stores, of the minister of light industry in shoe stores.

They try to lullaby us with old songs. But we have no right to sleep, because when we wake up we may find ourselves in the embrace of a new dictator.

ENVIRONMENT

Acid Rain? What Happened in Chernovtsy?— This Question Was Put at a Press Conference in the USSR Health Ministry
by S. Blagodarov, *Sovetskaya Rossiya*, November 10, 1988

At the request of journalists a meeting was held at the USSR Health Ministry yesterday with Academician Ye. Chazov, USSR minister of health, the leaders of a number of the country's institutes, academicians, and professors. The extraordinary situation which has taken shape in the Ukrainian SSR's Chernovtsy Oblast was discussed at the meeting. At the end of August frightened parents began turning to the health care organs: **Certain children in that region had suddenly lost all their hair.**

The following pattern came to light: They were, as a rule, children of 2-4 years of age, when the organism has not yet grown strong and is not as resistant to various influences as in an adult. It was also noticed that it was mainly blond, blue-eyed children who were going bald. The hair fell out over 24-72 hours, following slight neuropsychic disturbances and hallucinations.

"So far 113 such children have come to light," Minister Ye. Chazov said. "Fifty-eight children are being investigated in Moscow, and the rest in Kiev."

What happened in Chernovtsy? At the end of August there

were isolated cases of alopecia among children. The peak, the minister pointed out, came roughly in the middle of September, but loss of hair is continuing (in 16 children over the past 10-12 days).

This question was put: "Why is the USSR Health Ministry commission working on the spot only 2 months later, although this happened at the end of August?"

"It is not such a simple matter," Ye. Chazov replied. "Such mass alopecia among children has happened nowhere before. We requested data not only from the USSR but also from other countries. At first, when there were isolated cases, local physicians might not have paid proper attention to this, although we were informed of this as early as the beginning of September. We swung into action when the phenomenon became more widespread. More than 20 institutes—not just of the Health Ministry but also the Kurchatov and Vernadskiy Institutes and institutes of mineralogy and biochemistry—were involved in studying the new phenomenon."

At first it was assumed that it might be some new virus. But after a careful study of all the factors the possibility of a viral infection was rejected.

After painstaking, multifaceted research, scientists reached a conclusion as to the most likely cause: acid rain and the effect of the chemical element thallium on the organism. Even an insignificant concentration of it is harmful to the organism. According to eyewitnesses, some strange rain fell in those places shortly before the children's alopecia.

It is interesting that no discharges containing thallium have been detected in Chernovtsy itself or the district, although an increased amount of it has shown up in the air there. These discharges (from chemical and other production facilities) have come from other places, perhaps from abroad (Chernovtsy is not far from the borders of several states). An excess of aluminum has also been detected in the atmosphere in the city. It affects the human organism, displacing zinc from it—which also causes hair to fall out. Plus there is an unfavorable geochemical background in Chernovtsy and a concentration of dust 4-5 times in excess of the norm. It was the combination of all these factors at once that led to this result.

So acid rain has begun to threaten not only forests abroad but also children in our country.

There was also a question as to whether the Chernobyl accident had been one of the causes of the Chernovtsy situation.

Specialists replied that there are no cause-and-effect links between them. No adverse consequences are expected in the future, either, with regard to the health of the alopecic children, medics believe. Specialists assume that all the children's hair is bound to grow back.

Mailman Vasilyev's "Bomb." When the Latest Commission Left Empty-Handed He Put the Documents in His Briefcase and Headed for Moscow
by S. Razin, *Komsomolskaya Pravda*, March 15, 1988

Kirishi, Leningrad Oblast—Now Volodya Vasilyev knows how to act. He had expressly taken me to the apartment so that I would fully understand why he had declared war on the ministry.

"After three nights of it I was worn out. They told me in the morning. On 29 April . . ." Vera Khitrina broke down and sobbed into her handkerchief, her shoulders shaking uncontrollably.

In the corner, behind an empty child's bed, stood a rolled-up home-made placard, the one her husband had taken on the May Day demonstration. A portrait of her son framed in black, and, beneath it, in shaky writing, in black ink: "This is your work, comrades from the biochemical plant!"

A staggering placard! The whole city saw it. . . .

Kirishi is a young city which has grown rapidly on the bank of the Volkhov, and now it is reminiscent of a coiled spring that could explode at any moment. Opposition—overt, fierce—to the departmental apparatus by 60,000 inhabitants has been going on here for nearly a year.

Mailman Vasilyev plays as big a part in the story as the leaders of the Ministry of the Medical and Microbiological Industry. As far as Volodya is concerned, perhaps, it all began when he, a 26-year-old correspondence course student, hardened by his hobby of winter sailing, had this strange cough which was getting worse and keeping him awake at night.

Having suffered night after night, he went to the hospital. And he was horrified to see the faces of the children in the corridor. Swollen eyes and red blotches, like burns, on cheeks, necks, and hands. What was going on? The intensive care department was chockablock, asthmatics everywhere were having attacks. . . .

Vasilyev wondered where the wind was coming from. He remembered very well when the people of Kirishi began to have trouble breathing—following the ahead-of-schedule startup of the protein-vitamin concentrates plant. Incidence of bronchial asthma increased by a factor of 35! But why? Why indeed was the second phase of the plant launched in 1982 and why was the ambulance service unable to keep up with all the calls?

Vasilyev did not keep the appointment with the doctor. He dashed off to the plant. That's it! The sharp, unpleasant smell hit him in the face. The purification equipment was clogged up and the scrubbers cleaning the exhaust system had been cut off with welding apparatus. The treacherous cloud had again descended on the city. . . .

Meanwhile, the then deputy minister of the Medical and Microbiological Industry, A. Sorokin, made a pronouncement in the local press. Shame on you, comrades, he said, the sickness rate in Kirishi is no higher than in other cities. A conference was held too, and a plan of additional measures was discussed and agreed on.

At that moment the city was like a coiled spring. There had been many empty promises before. But this ministerial reply amazed everyone by its savage indifference. At the very time there had been an accident at the plant: In two months or so another eight children had died, although, at first, they had been diagnosed as having "acute respiratory disease."

The spring exploded last May. The people of Kirishi poured into the Pioneer Center where, behind closed doors, they discussed the emergency situation in the city. "I am not indifferent to the fate of Kirishi! I got my party card here! I promise that there will not be a single molecule of protein in the air!" Minister V. Bykov almost shouted at the audience. "We don't believe you!" the people packing the gangways right up to the platform loudly declared. It was time for a rally. The action group which had formed around mailman Vasilyev set about organizing it. The action group also included engineers, doctors, and workers.

On 1 June, Child Protection Day, the rally was attended by 12,000 Kirishi locals. Without disguising their tears, people talked of their unhappiness, about how they used to go there to do all-union shock work, on Komsomol passes, and how they used to rejoice as the building progressed. Now they had all signed a petition against the poison plant.

The denouement seemed near. Under pressure from the public the minister shifted his stance three times in 10 days. After the rally the biochemical plant was halted, as was reported even in the central press. The local authorities insisted on a total reorientiation for the plant . . .

That was 10 months ago.

Mailman Vasilyev is now accused, along with his team, of whipping up mass hysteria by organizing rallies.

"By remaining silent we would be guilty of betrayal, of continuing to conceal our sores," Volodya retorted when they tried to silence him at the gorispolkom, having invited the prosecutor to come along to add authority.

It did not work. Vasilyev was invulnerable. They could not even pin the unofficial label on him. The action group he is in charge of has operated under an official umbrella from the start, having become the sixth section of the city nature conservation society.

The guys' first target was the plant reconstruction, because the shrewd economic managers were already starting their strange little dance. People were beavering away in the shops, but the reconstruction plan . . . did not exist. It appeared a few weeks before the allotted time ran out.

"Is that all?" the public experts said in surprise, having discovered, in conjunction with public health doctors, around 30 flaws in the plan. "Where are the guarantees that the harmful discharge will cease?" As before, there was no automatic monitoring. There was also something suspicious about the wastefree system. There was nothing like it anywhere in the world.

But a commission arrived at the plant in early August. The economic managers were ready with their "knight's move": The reconstruction, of course, is not complete, but we will be carrying out tests and we will stretch the new technology. The plant started operating at one-third capacity. The clouds began to gather again above the city.

"I've got it all on tape!" Vasilyev eagerly announced and switched on a four-hour recording made by someone at a scientific conference in Kirishi. Medical scientists from Angarsk, Ufa, Gorkiy, Leningrad, and Moscow spoke one after another, adding to the black picture of the protein-vitamin concentrates. Fungal infections, diseases of the lungs, bronchi, and skin, complications during pregnancy, and problems with the immune system—a whole bunch of serious diseases had been found in workers at the country's first biochemical plants.

Plant discharges had been damaging people's health for 12 years. A very powerful allergen had been hitting the city at the rate of 2 metric tons a day. How many Kirishi locals had suffered? And how much longer would they have to suffer?

"More than one generation, perhaps. The trouble is that the

weakened organism is now susceptible to other harmful factors, and we have more than enough of them too," V. Yesinovskiy, chief doctor at the Kirishi Rayon hospital, explained the situation. He had figures, facts, and tables. But this frankness would cost him dear.

How many invalids are there in the city as a result of the biochemical plant? Around 100, doctors claim. And another 4,000 or so are suffering from allergies which have a nasty tendency to get worse with time. Whether the statistics are complete no one knows. Local doctors have no specific means of diagnosis. It exists abroad. We do not produce it here. But without it, it is impossible to distinguish a mycogenic allergy caused by plant discharges from an ordinary one. Moreover, as Vasilyev found, medicines are also in horrifically short supply. . . .

He flabbergasted a director of a local enterprise, whom he knew, with the request: "We need help with foreign currency!" The director raised his eyebrows, but when he understood what the mailman was concerned about he promised every support. But why should a mailman have to attend to such an important problem? Why is the Ministry of the Medical and Microbiological Industry forging ahead with the establishment of a harmful production unit while, at the same time, it is obviously in no hurry to start up the industrial production of essential pharmaceuticals? Is it perhaps because it is afraid that the true scale of the Kirishi affair might come to light? And perhaps not just the Kirishi affair?

ESTONIA

The Soviet Election Carousel
by Tiit Made, *Svenska Dagbladet*, March 23, 1989

TIIT MADE is leader of the Estonian People's Front.

They are saying that for the first time in the history of the Soviet state, its citizens can now choose between several candidates. Gorbachev has set in motion a political reform. Part of this reform consists of the election of an independent body which is to represent the whole union and which is called the Congress of People's Deputies. From this congress 500 deputies will be sent to the Supreme Soviet, which will function as a parliament and meet in session for 7 to 8 months every year.

At the local level a predetermined number of deputies to the congress will be elected, but it remains to be seen which of them will have seats in the parliament. It is also difficult to select such people. Which of us has political experience?

Reformist leaders in Moscow hope that this complicated system will make it possible to have more decisionmakers who advocate perestroyka, or at least to reduce the numbers of perestroyka's opponents. Perhaps they are right. . . .

I am riding round on this carousel myself. It is difficult to say whether I really want to devote myself to the parliament in Moscow for 7 or 8 months, and besides, is there any real point? But anyway, I was nominated as a candidate in the Rakvere region, where problems of phosphorus and oil shale loom large, where the Soviet Air Force is polluting the environment, and where spring water glows in the dark. My name was put forward by 18 labor collectives. I have 4 rivals, including a political lieutenant colonel who has lived in Estonia for 18 months.

As has already been mentioned, the party does not approve of all candidates. Rakvere party boss Toomas Kork tried to persuade me to stand down as a candidate, because he—that is, the party—had his own candidate. But since I am an old sportsman, I wanted to compete, and so did not follow the party's advice.

In the Estonian press and radio there has recently been much talk to the effect that the party is stopping at nothing in trying to control the selection of candidates. This is like giving something with one hand and taking it away with the other. . . .

I have been asked time and time again if there is any point to sending Estonia's foremost talents to Moscow. Bearing in mind the additions to the draft constitution of 16 November 1988, it might seem that we decide our own affairs here in Estonia. There have also been calls to boycott the elections, since the existing electoral law really cannot be said to be democratic. If, however, we want to change our relationship with the central power base and make clear what we want, we cannot disregard this power base. It is unwise to make enemies and ignore central power. We know only too well the ambitions of the Kremlin leaders and their bureaucratic machine.

We have to win allies in Moscow, establish personal contacts

with the decisionmakers, and get them used to the idea that
Estonia wants to proceed more independently. . . .

We have to make the notion of self-determination and sovereignty attractive to other federal republics. That is why I believe
that it would be useful to do something for the benefit of the
Estonian people in Moscow, or at least to try to do so. . . .

EVIL EYES

Evil Eyes
by Mikhail Uspensky, *Ogonyek*, October 1988

A woman in Hospital #4 gave birth to a boy. His name was
Nikolai Afanasievich Permiakov. It is not difficult to figure out
that the woman was the boy's mother. When the creature was
first brought to its mother, it opened its eyes and looked at the
mother in such a way that all her milk disappeared. One elderly
woman from the medical staff explained to everyone that the
child has the evil eye.

"The child has the evil eye," she said.

From the first glance the eye looked just like any other eye.
The second eye looked like just any other eye, too. And even
though people say "evil eye," try to figure out whether it's the
left one or the right one.

From the time that the mother of Permiakov was in the hospital,
everything in the hospital went wrong: The radiator blew up and
a lot of other things. And the boy who was lying next to Nikolai
grew up to be a thief and a bandit, was put in prison, and shot.

Nor did things go well at the Permiakov home. The father,
Afanasy Permiakov, had a drink for the first time in honor of his
son's birth and still drinks today. The mother-in-law explains,
"He's just really thirsty." As for the mother-in-law, her house in
the city of Baranovichi, in the White Russian Republic, burned to
the ground. The mother remembered about the evil eye, and
took Nikolai to the eye doctor. The doctor, for a long time,
looked into the eye with his special instrument. He found nothing wrong with the eye, but suggested that Nikolai wear dark
glasses, or better yet, mirrored glasses.

And so he was, Nikolai Afanasievich, a little boy, wearing mirrored glasses, like a circus midget. As for the doctor, Vagrapet Arshakovich Movseian (that was his name), that day he did not come back home from work and until this day no one can find him, even though a countrywide search was declared. He should have known better than to look into the evil eye with his instrument. After all the instrument magnifies.

September came; time to go to school. Nikolai got his book bag and a bouquet of flowers.

"You can't come to school in mirrored glasses." His first teacher got upset. Her name was Aelita Stepanovna Borodun. "Only punks do that. Take them off immediately."

Nikolai took off his glasses as demanded. The teacher looked into his eyes. In one week, she was supposed to get married. Forget it! Her fiancé, Lekha, a town-famous taxi driver, suddenly fell out of love with her and fell in love with some pop-singer on tour. He drove her around town, since she was giving three to four concerts a night, left with her, and now follows her everywhere except abroad. They don't let him go abroad.

Finally everyone got used to the glasses in school. Nikolai himself both thought and said that his eyes ached. His mother would not take him to other eye doctors: she felt sorry for them.

He was drafted into the army, and obviously there was an eye doctor on the acceptance committee, a military doctor. He signed that Nikolai's eyes were just fine and that he had to serve. That evening the eye doctor went with his lady-friend to a restaurant, drank a bit, got really drunk, broke a window, and did a few other things. As a result he had to spend many days under guard, pay a lot of money, and face the military tribunal. In the old day he'd have to shoot himself out of shame, but nowadays, it wasn't too bad. He just lost a star.

Nikolai was brought to the army camp, and Ogurnoi, the ensign, took him and the rest of the newcomers to the showers. Permiakov went to the showers naked but in his glasses.

"Glasses, buddy, you leave with your clothes," said the ensign and took the glasses off him, then slipped on the slippery floor, fell down, and broke his arms and legs.

A soldier is not allowed to wear mirrored glasses. And so things started happening in his regiment. A soldier deserted, dysentery hit. In a year and a half, three commanders got dishonorable discharges. Only when Nikolai finally became an old-timer in the army did he go to the "Militgoods," an army store, and buy himself dark glasses and suspenders. The moment he put those glasses on, his regiment became #1.

Having finished the service, Nikolai did not come back home. He went to live in a large city. There he enrolled himself in the university. He still did not know about his eyes. He just thought that there was something wrong with them and the doctors who didn't believe him were just being stubborn. There was no old woman around to tell him: "Nikolai Afanasievich, you have the evil eye."

Only the gypsies, when he takes his glasses off to wipe them off, run from him as if from the militia man. After all, the gypsies know what's what.

The only time he takes off his glasses is before going to sleep or sometimes at work. And everyone knows where he works, since they see him every day or every other day; and without glasses. He has a very pleasant voice, which says: "Good day, comrades. This is the beginning of the program of the Central Television Station."

Now you can understand why your wife has left you, why your kid is growing up a bum, and why everything you do comes out all wrong.

FREUD

Jean Paul Sartre's "Sigmund Freud and the 'Compact with the Devil' "
by A. Belkin, *Literaturnaya Gazeta*, June 1, 1988.

A. BELKIN, M.D., is director of the all-union Psychoendocrinology Center at the Russian Republic Ministry of Public Health's Moscow Psychiatric Research Institute.

Today, one would have difficulty finding an educated person on the planet who has not heard of psychoanalysis. In the 1920s, the founder of that discipline, the Austrian psychiatrist and psychologist Sigmund Freud (1856-1939), was very popular in our country as well (all of his major works, edited by Prof. Ye. D. Yermakov, were published in Russian at the time). In a number of remarkable studies, well-known Soviet psychologists and psychiatrists developed many of Freud's ideas. For example, A. R. Luria, in reviewing psychoanalysis's "points of departure," showed its role as a progressive science of the "neuropsychic life of the personality." An integrated study of the personality, its components, its conscious and unconscious "complexes," he stressed, is the further development of ideas that were well known in Russia. These ideas were expressed vividly in the works of I. P. Pavlov, V. M. Bekhterev, A. F. Lazursky and K. N. Kornilov, among others.

The Freudian psychology of the unconscious—one of man's greatest intellectual achievements—would seem to have won a lasting place not only in medical practice and biology, but also in fields such as religion, literature, painting and the study of mythology. By the early 1930s psychoanalytical theories in one form or another had been incoporated into all the intellectual diciplines and had become an integral part of the thinking of broad circles of the Soviet intelligentsia of that time. Freud's insights illuminated in a most profound way such areas of the humanities as anthropology, philosophy, sociology and esthetics.

Western scholars, who considered Sigmund Freud an innovator and discoverer, compared him to Aristotle, Copernicus, Columbus, Newton and Darwin. Many writers and artists treated him with sincere respect. Among Freud's friends were such outstanding figures as Thomas Mann, Theodore Dreiser, Romain Rolland, Stefan Zweig, Herbert Wells, Albert Einstein and Rainer Maria Rilke.

Without exaggeration, one can say that Freud's teachings provided a stimulus for the development of various spheres of human knowledge and an inexhaustible source of scientific and cultural innovation. Freud's teachings were the stimulus for a new approach to many concrete problems in science (behavioral medicine, neurobiology, psychiatric endocrinology, ethnography, and the individual and society, among others). But his importance does not stop there. Frued's works provided a key to understanding the reasons for the tenacity of many stereotypes in people's thinking. Freud studied the processes of the socialization of the individual and such fundamental phenomena as humanism and freedom. In other words, for all its contradictions and errors, Freudianism provided the impetus for new areas of knowledge.

It is unlikely that anyone today has doubts about the importance of psychoanalysis, the role of man's subconscious sphere, the need to know oneself and others, the ability to depart from dogmas and cliches and be one's own person. . . .

How are we to explain the fact that, starting in 1931-1933, psychoanalysis began to be prohibited? How is it that in our country the publication of the works of Freud and other serious psychoanalysts was for all practical purposes stopped for many years for supposedly humane reasons—"to prevent the penetration of alien ideology?"

At that same time (May 1933) in another European country, at one of the book-burning ceremonies, when it came time to burn the works of Freud, Goebbels made the solemn pronouncement that he was committing these works to the flames "in the name of the nobility of the human spirit."

A huge segment of culture was expunged, a segment concerned with revealing the essence of Freud's psychoanalytical teachings and of his approach to studying the depths of the human personality; the hypothesis that reason triumphs over man's animal instincts was rejected, making it impossible to understand the origins of fear and man's situation of danger and psychological helplessness in the face of blind faith in the infallibility and wisdom of the powers that be. "Instinctive knowledge of external dangers apparently is not inherent in man from birth or is present from birth only on a very insignificant scale," Sigmund Freud wrote in his work entitled "Fear."

Only after the 20th Party Congress were the first timid steps taken to revive research on psychoanalysis. It turned out that our country was lagging behind in many areas concerned with the study of human psychology, that the understanding of the subconscious in the rest of the world had made great strides, and while we were engaged in criticizing Freud's works, the Western world had developed many of the rational aspects of his teachings. What's more, it became clear that the subconscious sphere is a huge source of reserves of the human psyche, and that by refusing to engage in serious and extensive study of this area, we not only denied medical care to hundreds and thousands of people, we also reduced the ability of whole generations of creative people to work in their fields.

I want to be understood correctly. I am not calling for the indiscriminate transfer to our soil of philosophical concepts developed in the West. I only want to stress that the negative treatment of Freud up until the mid-1950s, the partial revival of research, and then another 20-year period of stagnation seriously hindered the work of our scholars in this field. A conference on questions of the ideological struggle against contemporary Freudianism was held under the auspices of the Presidium of the USSR Academy of Medicine in 1958, after which many studies appeared in the Soviet literature—studies containing long-obsolete stereotypes accusing Freud of idealistic interpretations of the unconscious and attempting to prove the harm of using psychoanalysis in practice, although not a single author of these papers had himself conducted a single psychoanalytical session. But anyone who is familiar with the psychoanalytical method knows that one of the fundamental requirements of psychoanalysis is to "do no harm" and to draw out the truth, without worrying that it might not be to someone's liking.

The strength of Freudianism lies in the way that it "shakes up" thinking in its search for the truth, which is not something frozen and dogmatic. Now, when broad opportunities have opened up for the development of the science of man, our specialists in the field of individual psychology have kept silent for some reason.

It is always more difficult to recover than it is to get sick. However, the recovery of a society as a whole, like that of an individual, requires the overcoming of internal resistance, the mastery of fear, the acknowledgement of one's mistakes and an understanding of their origins—it requires that they be raised to the level of consciousness and, more than that, that their genesis be understood as well.

That is why it seems to me that Sigmund Freud's teachings are in need of new approaches today, from the standpoint of recent advances in biology, the natural sciences and the humanities.

FOREIGN AID

Under the Control of the People
Letter to the Editor of *Pravda*, April 16, 1989

There is much talk about democracy and glasnost at the moment. However, one aspect of our life remains closed. I am referring to our international policy. So far we live in accordance with the principle: Everything that is done is correct and right.

I believe that this is not always so. At one time our country was building stadiums in Indonesia and the Aswan Dam in Egypt. I do not know whether Egypt has paid for this project to this day. Or take another example. In 1961-1963 there were difficulties with grain in the country. At the same time our ships were carrying wheat to Algeria. Ageria paid for the wheat with wine that was sold at every corner at 20 kopeks a glass.

I do not feel any enthusiasm when I watch on television our wheat, sugar, dried milk and canned meat products being distributed among dushmans returning to Afghanistan. After all, dried milk and canned meat products are virtually unobtainable in Alma-Ata, not to mention other cities in the republic. Since 1984 we have been ferrying Ethiopians by helicopter from one part of the country to another in an effort to save them from starvation. In the first half of 1988 alone we have given Ethiopia 250,000 tonnes of wheat, despite the fact that we ourselves have to buy grain.

No doubt we are giving similiar assistance to Angola, Cambodia, Nicaragua, Cuba, Poland, and other countries, especially African countries. We are helping them not just with food, but also with medicines which are frequently not available in our pharmacies.

In order to eat properly and provide ourselves with clothes and footwear our per capita grain production should total 1 tonne. However, we are producing 211 million tonnes for 285 million people. In the United States where around 300 million tonnes of grain is produced per 246 million people, this is a different matter.

It seems to me that in the period of glasnost and democracy matters of foreign aid should be under the strict control of the USSR Supreme Soviet and the Soviet people.

—V. Maksimov, Alma-Ata

FUNERALS

The Way They Joked around in Odessa
by M. Zhvanetsky

A group of people with mournful faces and musical instruments, led by the leader-conductor. The doorbell rings. A tenant walks out. The leader takes off his hat in respect and says, "I am so sorry. I've been told of your grief."

The tenant: "What grief?"

The leader: "Aren't you burying someone?"

The tenant: "Burying?"

The leader: "This is Rizhelevskaya 6 apartment 7?"

The tenant: "Yes."

The leader: "So?"

The tenant: "What?"

The leader: "Shall we bury?"

The tenant: "Whom?"

The leader: "What do you mean whom? Who should know better, you or me? Stop fooling around. Carry him out.

The tenant: "Whom?"

The leader: "I brought people. An orchestra of fifteen people. They can kill anyone who will not carry the body out. Mania, go ahead."

Mania, a fat woman, wearing socks and man's shoes, hits the cymbals and looks at her watch.

The tenant: "Wait a minute, who sent you here?"

The leader: "How do I know? Maybe it was you? Am I supposed to remember everyone?"

A fierce trombone player pushes his way out of the group.

"Misha, will there be something here, or do we have to take this place apart?"

The leader: "Zhora, calm down. These people are grief-stricken and they need to bargain. Name your price and we'll discuss it like two rational people. After all, you haven't even heard us play."

The tenant: "I can imagine."

The leader: "Hold on a minute. If you hear us play you'll be willing to give us your last shirt. These people feel the grief of others like their own."

The tenant: "I can see it in their faces."

The leader: "Stand there and listen. It will be flowing from the heart. Mania, give the formation signal."

Mania, the fat woman, hits the cymbals and looks at her watch.

The leader looks over the group.

"Fedor Grigorievich Konstantin, button up, hide your horrible tattoo with those awful expressions. People keep reading your chest like a yard fence. You can't tear them away. Besides, you keep changing the signs. Erase them immediately. I know that you are a student of the conservatory. You might even be more cultured than we are, you know the notes. Nevertheless this T-shirt lowers your character."

The leader gives the sign and the orchestra plays a piece in which one can barely make out the funeral march. The tenant applauds:

"Thank you very much. That's enough. It's wonderful, but I think someone played a joke."

The leader: "That's not my problem. I got fifteen people from their jobs. I didn't give this young man a chance to finish the conservatory. Madam Zborovskaya left her household in the hands of her young punk, God bless him. And *you* are talking about jokes. Pay us and we will laugh together."

The fierce trombone player pushes his way out of the group.

"Misha, what's all the ceremony for? Hit him over the head and we can play. May it all go to hell."

The leader: "Zhora, calm down. You still did not serve the time for that last incident. Why worry now?"

The tenant: "How much is the burial?"

The leader: "The whole ceremony?"

The tenant: "Yes."

The leader: "Slowly?"

The tenant: "Yes."

The leader: "Five rubles a person."

The tenant: "And without the body?"

The leader: "In that case it's three but it's demeaning for the people."

"You have a deal. Play. Only sing 'In memory of Sigizmund Lazorevich and his sister from Kishinev.' "

The musicians, on a cue from Mania, begin playing and singing "How untimely is your death. Whom are you leaving us for? You go there and we remain. We remain and you go."

Backstage there is crying, tears and shouting. Someone is being carried. The leader becomes happy.

"There's the body."

The tenant: "No. It's my neighbor Sigizmund Lazorevich. It was his birthday today."

GLASNOST

Letter to the editor of *Nedelya*, February 15–21, 1988

It was with tremendous interest that I read *Nedelya's* article "Bukharin—Known and Unknown." Thank you very much for it. Its publication in the press was yet another manifestation of glasnost and the democratization of society.

I would like to voice certain thoughts and doubts in my letter. I am an ordinary worker (crane operator) with general secondary education, which, by the way, I gained by graduating from a young workers' school.

. . . The period of the late thirties is known among the people as the "Yezhov years." The expression "To be handled with Yezhov's gloves" has acquired a special meaning, a special overtone. People disappeared from life . . . Thousands of lives, thousands of human tragedies . . . The party embarked on a correct course by exposing, like a purulent abscess, the mistakes and excesses of the past.

Back in 1971 I was working in Priangarye in the Maritime Kray. Kezhma was a fairly large village and rayon center. Once I picked up in the library a bound volume of the journal *Yunost* and discovered several typewritten sheets of paper slipped in between its pages. The paper had yellowed with the passage of time, the typeface was almost illegible, some parts of the text were underlined, and there were exclamation and question marks in the margins.

"Stalin," I began reading, "you have outlawed me, in other words you have trampled on my rights, or rather stripped me of my rights . . ."

I read through these pages with bated breath.

The letter was signed by F. Raskolnikov, ambassador plenipotentiary in Bulgaria. It was dated 18 August 1938.

It emerged later that much of what was written was the truth. But I did not know this at the time. One point worried me more than anything else: Why was the author acting as advocate for Bukharin when even the dullest of schoolchildren knew that Kamenev, Zinovyev, Bukharin, and Rykov were all enemies of

[185]

the people? I was also perplexed by the claim that books were being burned on I.V. Stalin's orders. Especially books by him, by F. Raskolnikov.

A forgery, I thought at the time, a lampoon and a juggling of facts. I even had my doubts whether such an ambassador plenipotentiary—F. Raskolnikov—actually did exist. Later on, while in Sverdlovsk, I called at the university's Department of CPSU History and asked for an answer to a single question: Was F. Raskolnikov a real person?

"Young man," I was told, "either hide these papers or burn them. For your own piece of mind. As for Raskolnikov? No, I don't know of anyone by that name, I don't remember . . ."

But I did not leave it at that, I tried to explain and elucidate the question that was plaguing me, until a comrade of mine, without saying a word, tore up the letter before my very eyes and threw it in the fire. "Now you can be free," he said.

And it was only quite recently that I saw the name of F.F. Raskolnikov in an article describing him as a true Bolshevik and Leninist.

And now about my doubts.

M.S. Gorbachev has put forward the most correct program, a program that is most acceptable for the people: Restructuring, acceleration, glasnost, democratization. This program has touched the hearts and minds of many (I won't say all) people. But here is an interesting point. Now all our mistakes, all omissions and distortions are actively blamed on the period of stagnation. The word "stagnation" has gained currency. The period of stagnation— that says it all. A word used by way of both explanation and indulgence. As if it did not involve specific people and specific culprits.

I, like many others, agree with the course taken by the party. I would vote with both hands for it and am doing everything within my power to prevent any deviation from it. But on looking back, recalling the past, and comparing it with the present, one cannot help asking: How could *that* have happened? What must be done to ensure that *that* does not happen again?

Let us turn back to the "Yezhov years." Do you not think that this period is not only a lesson but also a warning?

So what is the point I am trying to make? Here is the point: I **think that it is necessary to guarantee that people who have wholeheartedly embraced restructuring will not be dubbed dissidents and that an even worse label will not be attached to them. There must be no retreat from glasnost and democratization.**

Yes, now we are on the correct path. But you feel somewhat uncomfortable when you recall the not so distant past. How one wishes that it would never return!

— Vitaliy Vladimirovich Kalmykov, crane operator, Miass

P.S. I have written this letter without beating about the bush, on the basis of my own views and my own confusions which—if they do exist—are also sincere.

Let Us Think: Review of Readers' Letters
by Yuri Orlik, *Izvestiya*, March 12, 1988

YURI ORLIK is deputy editor of *Izvestiya*.

Everything has gotten moving. Not surprisingly, some people are confused, they are looking around, saying: Is that where we are going? "For 50 years I thought the Trotskiyists and Bukharinists were traitors and their names filled me with loathing and contempt. What am I supposed to believe now?" T. Makhrochev from Zelenoborskiy settlement in Murmansk Oblast asks. One must try to understand the confusion. G. Radoman, a mine construction engineer from Karaganda, is also tormented by it. "Nevertheless the truth must be known," he believes.

But there have been letters which are striking not for their questions and doubts, but for their doctrinaire arguments, intolerance of other viewpoints, and claims to some higher truth. Some advise: "That's enough confession," and warn that "the past has yet to take vengeance on us," as if it had not had its revenge during the stagnation period, and even now. Others warn about the cost of democracy. Others smile sarcastically, claiming that a "harmonious combination of interests and ideals" is impossible. In all these letters one detects a nostalgia for the past, although they purport to be about other things—order, respect and authority, the unity of the people, loyalty to the principles of socialism.

For example, when I was preparing the previous review, I kept on coming across letters questioning whether under socialism cooperative and individual labor activity has an actual legal right to exist. N. Penin in Armavir considers that it is tantamount to "propaganda of the kulak philosophy." N. Sologub of Konotop writes that "using Lenin as a pretext, they intend to open private shops here." "A concession to capitalism, no less" is the opinion of N. Cherkashin of Ukyanovsk Oblast. Just look. The terms they use sound like political accusations. But is it so surprising: the teaching they have had . . . The paper also gets it in the neck for advocating—neither more nor less—"the birth of bankers" (I. Tyukavin of Leningrad). And they are suggesting that it be called to order, put in its place, for which purpose they should be writing to the authorities rather than the editorial office. Of course, the writer has the right to choose where to send his missive. But if we are really concerned about the truth, let us not wind up, but develop the debate and raise its political standard of it. But we have written about this before. . . .

Our tendency to idealize and canonize established forms of public and economic life is the subject of a letter from V. Kuzennyy, senior lecturer at the Kokchetav Pedagogical Institute: "We have become so accustomed to leveling that many people are still clinging to it, claiming that it is socialism. Nothing of the sort. People must get more, much more for innovative creative labor and a high end result."

Stereotype thinking leads to both moral and economic losses. This is what V. Krasnoborodkin of Nadymskiy Rayon, Tyumen Oblast, has to say about it: "How long have peasants here been squeezed on all sides. How much talk has there been: Do you give them a bigger plot or not? What if the harvest on the land is such that the peasants get rich? This is the attitude to the family contract now: Don't overdo it. It is a paradox for socialism. **They are scared lest people have a good living.** They have ordered people around so much that no one wants to keep livestock and there is no milk or meat in the countryside any more. The peasants go to the city for sausage and everything else. Young people go off wherever they like, wherever they can earn money. I used to be a peasant, now I am in the North."

There is another aspect to the problem.

The monolith has collapsed before our very eyes: We were rather surprised to discover how different we all are. Not only in the social and professional plane, according to questionnaire data, but in terms of interests, opinions, predilections. We have looked at life without rose-tinted spectacles and have seen that it is full of contradictions, conflicting interests, and conflicts, sometimes dramatic. All this must be interpreted and thought about. Not just by the "bosses," but by everyone. Everyone must have his own view of things.

"Throughout the stagnation period, not to mention the cult era, people were afraid to say anything that conflicted with the 'supreme' opinion, learning only one thing—to vote unanimously for anything," writes V. Matveyenko of Moscow. "We would take comfort from the fact that we were doing the same as everyone else. **We were only bold when it came to political anecdotes. . . . Now we are only just learning to speak the truth."**

It is naive to urge people to express views if one does not heed them, if one disregards them. But it still happens pretty often. However, a society cannot be run without taking its members' opinions into account. You can order people around. It is difficult to get out of the habit. It is hard switching from coercion to persuasion. But that is the task that faces us.

In the mail the idea is persistently put forward that in resolving the contradictions of modern life one must in no circumstances resort to methods borrowed from the past. "It is the easiest thing of all, in order to avoid a rally at which the 'wrong' pronouncements might be made, to dig up a square and send the city transport off on a detour," A. Zhemaytis writes from Riga. "It is harder to abandon the prejudices of the era of Stalinism, to amend the nationalities policy, and not to be afraid of the truth." And it is the easiest thing in the world to describe the conflict at the Yaroslavl engine plant as "alien to our system" (L. Zeverev, Taganrog).

Let us not be in a rush. Let us learn to think. Without stereotypes.

Let us agree that beliefs do not come with VUZ graduation diplomas. They are the result of an independent understanding of life and history. Only then are beliefs strong, only then are they not changed. Not quickly anyway, anathematizing today what was extolled yesterday. Only by learning, fully in accordance with Leninist behests, not to take anything on trust, to arrive at our own conclusions, and to have our own opinions, not second-hand ones, will we be spared the pain and ignominy of collectively recovering our sight.

"A cult of knowledge, common sense, and intellect—that is what is needed," writes G. Solomakha of Kerch, putting his finger right on the demand of the times. There is perhaps nothing our society needs more.

M. GORBACHEV

Not For Publication
Letters to the Editor of *Izvestiya*, March 31, 1988

Let's Make Haste!

I want to object to an idea expressed in the survey "Let's Have a Think" [*Izvestiya* No. 72]. "Let's not be hasty"—there's no need to urge anyone in that respect. **We have already spent decades not making haste.**

For 25 years we have been in no hurry to renounce half-truth and to finally debunk the Stalin personality cult. In so little hurry are we that we generate new cults and little cults. Khrushchev, who began well by attacking the cult, toward the end himself lapsed into it. Then Brezhnev believed in his own genius. How much sense will history have to teach us for us to learn to nip any eulogizing in the bud? I think that Lenin would not have been Lenin if, by virtue of his genius, he had not immediately understood the perniciousness of the cult addiction (that is my figurative expression for this phenomenon) and had not nipped it in the bud.

M.S. Gorbachev is acting in a Leninist manner. At the moment. As long as the press does not try to instill in him the idea of his exclusiveness. Any man, even the most talented, is suggestible. If he begins to believe in his own genius and allows people to trumpet his praises, he will come under the influence of the cult addiction which is no less perfidious than any other addiction. He must be safeguarded.

We are failing to make haste in every respect. We invent talented and brilliant things yet 20, 30, or 50 years later we buy them abroad from the people who do make haste. Now some people would like to extend restructuring almost to the end of the century, making appeals on television and in the press for people not to make haste!

Let's make haste! Not, of course, at breakneck speed, but by thinking. But we must not spend years thinking about our problems. With the aid not of semi-glasnost (which is what prevails so far) but of full glasnost we will be able to take error-free decisions in the minimum amount of time and introduce them into practice.

Let's make haste!

I know my letter will not be published. Even in your ". . . not for publication" section. But letters and opinions like mine are necessary not to the overthrown authorities but to the acting ones. When will we understand?

—G. Shilo, Slavyansk, Donetsk Oblast

TV Shows Kiev Conversations
Moscow Television Service, February 20, 1989

EXCERPTS: A convoy of motor vehicles arrived in Kiev from Borispol airport [video shows city scenes, big crowds, Lenin monument, Gorbachev and Shcherbitskiy, spouses behind them, laying flowers]. Mikhail Sergeyevich Gorbachev laid flowers at the Vladimir Ilyich Lenin monument in Kiev city center.

GORBACHEV: Do come nearer, one cannot hear.

Woman complains to Gorbachev that at her works no one, apart from the director, appears to be in charge.

GORBACHEV: Well, let me join in right at this juncture; you have had your say, now I will have mine. They say: Put things in order!

WOMAN: We say it ourselves!

GORBACHEV: That's just it, that's just it! But now if we do things in such a way that someone has to come and put the country in order, that someone has to come to the Ukraine, to Kiev, to the enterprises and the scientific institutes, to introduce order, then I'll tell you directly, we're going to remain exactly where we are. What, therefore, is today's leadership doing? Why are we going for this? The economy via reform, these are the new things: contracting, financial autonomy, the rights of the labor collective, elections of directors—if you don't like the director then have a meeting and decide; it's your business!

[Indistinct crowd voices]

GORBACHEV: You know what? Let the party body and the ministry and so on express a point of view; let the collective listen to everything. But the decision is the collective's. Now they say in the rayon that in the town they've got more savvy than we have! [laughter] So, let me say this to you: A session is convening and this is what we want to achieve—that the soviets ought to be like that, that they should decide what kind of people are needed; brainy people or brainless ones, you know; people who are ready and willing to meet you halfway or people who have no such desire. So, they should be brought to prominence via the soviets and this, all of this, we ought to get off the ground and, you see, this is already here—it is no longer the same society or country. Would a conversation such as this have taken place before? In 1985 I would not have been having a conversation such as this with you. . . .

So, how will we go about our cause, advancing it through restructuring? Well, despite the difficulties, hardships, painful problems, and teething problems, despite criticism and even abuse here and there, this cause did indeed get off the ground. Why is it that at times one does encounter criticism, painful problems, and all that? Because the issue of work has now been touched upon: Everyone has to work differently. This goes for us, you, and everyone, otherwise nothing will come out of this. Nothing will come out of this.

You can only divide what you have. Take the family: How does a family live? What and how do family members eat? Well, there you have it, the country is actually no different. There are 60 million pensioners in the country.

MAN: One has to feed them properly, what's there to think about, one has to work and to feed them properly.

GORBACHEV: Absolutely. Well, you will hear what I will have to say about it in March, to be brief. In March we will specially put forward major proposals concerning foodstuffs.

WOMAN: No point in beating about the bush; everyone from the countryside has left for the towns.

GORBACHEV: I believe that that's just about how we will go about things, emphasizing this. In the first place, we are restructuring these relations, so that if someone wants to do lease-contracting, then let him do it; if he wants to form a cooperative, then let him; if he wants to work individually, as a peasant family, then let him; if an individual peasant family wants to, then let's help them and let them—so all forms, so to speak, including firms, should be used in an enterprising way so that people are engaged in them. That's the first thing. The second is the social side of things. More has to be given to the countryside. The problem of fuel and supplies has to be removed.

MAN: The roads are very bad.

GORBACHEV: The roads, the roads, especially! And you haven't seen any really dreadful roads. I don't know, in the nonchernozem zone of the Ukraine, perhaps, but I have seen some dreadful roads. Roads, roads, roads. What else besides?

What we currently have is that we have both our data and not just our data. There is a direct way of calculating it: If we, today, preserved in full what we produce on the kolkhozes and sovkhozes, if we harvested it, preserved it, and processed it, then we would have a minimum of 20 percent more food.

MAN: What's going to happen to prices?

WOMAN: Is there going to be some increases in prices, because there's a lot of talk about prices going up.

MAN: That's why there's no soap, but a lot of talk.

GORBACHEV: You must remain calm about prices for this reason. If we do come to the conclusion that they have to be changed in some way—not just increased, not just increased, but changed in some way—then we will do that only when it has been discussed by the entire people, because if the people are opposed to it, prices mustn't be touched.

MAN: In general, the people are against it, (?I believe).

GORBACHEV: The market must be saturated, that's the main thing, production must be increased and made cheaper, that's what has to be done.

What did surprise me—and I want to tell you about it—this is what surprised me: the fact that there are these signals that reach us here. We will yet talk about and examine this together with Vladimir Vasilyevich [Shcherbitskiy]. **I mean things that are in abundant and plentiful supply—where are they? Why is it that they, too, turned out to be in short supply?** All of a sudden you get these holdups now with soap, now with washing powder, now with sugar. But, after all, all that is available. Something happened to disorganize this market as far as the goods which were and are in plentiful supply are concerned.

That is why, apart from everything else, and in order to improve the market, we embarked also on this path: we are creating a system of workers' control. We even want to pass a law on workers' control. . . .

One must participate. Well, take the Communists—the last time that the report-back and election campaign took place two-thirds were replaced, you know. I have to tell you this. And nonparty people took part; nonparty people took part! A very great change took place.

But you surely know this, too: People are often replaced, but still the restructuring life itself has failed to bring forward these most active people. In all likelihood time will form them yet.

Things cannot be done immediately. You might say let us propose this or that person, or let us change this or that. But what or who is to take their place?

WOMAN: But people are still afraid.

GORBACHEV: Well, let them rid themselves of it, because for as long as you do not. . . .

WOMAN: Mikhail Sergeyevich, what kind of thing is this, why is it, all the same, that construction of an atomic power station is underway in the Crimea? After all, it was proven there is great danger.

GORBACHEV: I heard this too. I heard that after you had heard this and began to raise this issue—Moscow got to hear about it, the government got to hear about it, yes they did. They did and they called for expert opinion on this project and asked the best specialists from the United States.

WOMAN: And why is no faith placed in ours?

GORBACHEV: Wait a moment. Our scientists will be involved, too. I mean here the specialists who built Japan's entire atomic power industry in 9 or 10 degrees of seismic conditions. Japan relies practically on atomic power alone. So, they have been called upon to give their expert views and this will require a certain amount of time.

The construction is proceeding. However, if expert finds are such that it is not feasible to hand this station over for use, to commission it there, it will then be turned into a station where cadres will be trained; it will be a training center and not an atomic power station.

So we will do what is necessary—this is not a game; it must not be a game where these issues are concerned, so to speak. So all this is in earnest. Just do not think that we wish to run rings round someone, because we can only get ourselves in a blind alley, so to speak. **Okay, comrades, keep the pressure up, only keep it up on the restructuring and not just on the bosses!** Press ahead, press ahead, comrades. We from above and you from below. Only in this way will restructuring take place. There is not other way. Just like the press, you know, from both sides; for if the pressure is onesided, things will be shifted to only one side.

The most difficult years are these, but we have been through far worse ordeals. When it was a matter of life and death, we coped. It is not a matter now of life and death, but of the fate of the state and the people. Fate can be in various forms. So that's what the question is.

HISTORY

"The Soviet Union is perhaps the only country in the world with an unpredictable past."

—**Anonymous**

Watching Old Newsreels . . .
by Tatyana Khloplyankina, *Moscow News*, March 8, 1989

Somebody had the happy idea of showing old newsreels in some of the city's cinemas during the recent Non-Feature Film Festival in Leningrad. Just imagine how it used to be. Walking along Nevsky Prospekt were girls and boys dressed in fashionable puffed up coats. Posters on the walls invited people to all sorts of charity functions and rock concerts. At a haberdashery people were buying toothpaste, now in short supply. In underground passages dark women were selling cosmetics and near a Metro station a young man was singing and playing a guitar. The weather was sunny and spring-like, despite the winter season on the calendar. In short, an ordinary day on Leningrad's Nevsky Prospekt.

You had only to step into an old cinema on the same Nevsky Prospekt, buy a ticket and take a seat in the packed hall to be transported into history.

The earliest newsreel featured the November 7, 1919 military parade on Red Square. It showed the troops marching through light snowfall, the wet snow covering people's hats and the streamers. Lenin, smiling, raises his hand to his cap in a gesture of a civilian unaccustomed to parades. Around him are his comrades-in-arms, also smiling. Looking at all this you caught yourself thinking how much time was left before . . . no, not before Lenin's death, but before, perhaps, an even more tragic moment when he realized that he had been betrayed by his associates, isolated and almost imprisoned.

Another newsreel took the audience to that day in December 1939 when Stalin was being elected to the Supreme Soviet. We saw a crowd of people heading towards a polling station even before dawn. Some of them had babies in their arms, wrapped up

[195]

in blankets. Others were carrying portraits of the country's leaders. A young man was playing the accordian, and not far away the cameraman had given a start to a group of jolly young skiers who were dashing right in the direction of the camera. (This little detail was probably meant to add more unexpected colour to the general atmosphere of festivity.) Inside the polling station there was, of course, a smiling girl who carefully drew the curtain of the polling booth behind everyone carrying a ballot paper. This was to indicate that all voters had the right to . . . to do what? To choose while having no choice? Or, perhaps, to pray to the leader just once more?

As far as I can remember, such booths were always a prominent feature at the polling stations, but nobody ever used them. People would hastily pass by these unnecessary structures, looking at them apprehensively, automatically dropping their ballot papers into the box. Sometimes they didn't even know the name of the person on the ballot paper. This was a streamlined ritual, the indignity of which gradually became obvious to many. But it seemed as unavoidable as rain, frost or any other natural phenomena.

People should definitely see these old newsreels. Then everyone will understand what brainwashing and what a mockery of democracy we are now trying to eliminate. And those films must be shown, not selectively, but in their entirety, for they are a terrible indictment against Stalinism.

There was a newsreel dated June 24, 1941, that is, two days after the beginning of the war. Byelorussia and the Ukraine were already in flames. We saw fire on the screen, too, but it was not real, front-line fire. The newsreel showed a practice alert on the *Chapayevets* launch, during which the young cadets extinguished the obedient fire with ease. "The war has not caught us unprepared!" we heard the narrator's almost triumphant voice. According to him, everyone was prepared for it, even the housewives from some small town near Moscow. "Here they are at the air-defence centre where they've come for training," he said. And we saw how, at a command, the pretty, smiling women in attractive summer dresses put their kerchiefs on, fixed their armbands and started marching off to the accompaniment of a lively tune.

At this point, an elderly woman sitting next to me began to cry silently. What did she recall? The horror of the Leningrad blockade? Or the girls who paid with their lives for the myth about our preparedness for war, the myth which Stalin's boastful propaganda machine went on building, through inertia, even after the outbreak of the war?

Then came a newsreel made in the late '40s. Indeed, a document is always a document. It can reveal a great deal, even when it is not meant to. Stalin's adherents are now claiming that, in the "wise leader's" time, people were well off and that there was no social stratification like that observed today. But just look at the postwar crowd. That particular newsreel also featured elections. A large group of people had been gathered outside a polling station long before 6 a.m., the hour when the voting was due to begin. (The press alleged at the time that people felt so agitated the night before the elections they simply couldn't sleep). Everybody was smiling in front of the camera, but one could see very tired faces in the background. People were shabbily dressed. Men were still wearing their worn-out wartime greatcoats and the women's coats were just as old and weather-beaten. And next to them were women garbed in beautiful fur coats: the elite had come to cast their vote—the military leaders with their wives, actors and academicians (who had, probably, already "gained the upper hand" over the geneticists and the cyberneticists). If only the camera would look into some other places, say, into the separate apartments of the very few and the grossly over-populated communal apartments in which the rest of the people lived (to say nothing of the prisons, the camps and the perishing postwar countryside).

So much for talk about the "absence" of social stratification in the past.

The next newsreel was about the gifts presented to Comrade Stalin on his 70th birth anniversary. The narrator informed us that Leningraders had presented the leader with a three-metre-high crystal vase weighing more than a ton. At the sight of this utterly tasteless object the audience, which had, until then, been watching the film in mournful silence, burst out laughing for the first time. The vase alone and the thought of all the effort and people's money that had gone into the absurd gifts are, perhaps, enough to shatter yet another myth—that of the leader's personal modesty. Yes, of course, Stalin did not take the gifts for himself—it would really have been quite impossible to put a one-ton vase to any good use. But can't other gifts, those easily put to use, be traced to that custom of marking the leader's jubilees with pomp as barbarous as it was lacking in taste? (Incidentally, the three-metre vase did prove to be of use, eventually: it was broken into thousands of very precious pieces of crystal and diamonds.)

But, I'd say the newsreels that shook me most were those produced in the '50s. People of my generation like to recall that period because so many hopes and initiatives were associated with it. However, when you watch those newsreels one after another, you begin to realize that the stagnation that followed was quite unavoidable. Nikita Khrushchev probably couldn't do anything in a country which was still oriented towards general jubilation and universal approval of every word uttered from a high rostrum. It was impossible to cast off Stalinism without first going through the anguish of repentance and without the spiritual renewal now under way in our society.

And here I'd like to make a little digression. When, several years ago, my family brought a new TV set, we didn't dispose of the old one, but put it in the kitchen. So, one evening, the whole of our family was dashing from the sitting room to the kitchen and back, trying to watch two TV programmes simultaneously. One, called "Public Opinion", was broadcast from Leningrad and the other, "View", was on the national channel. Both were a must. The people taking part in the heated discussion in Leningrad were literally snatching the mike from each other. The other programme showed a public rally. Pain and despair sometimes made it hard for the people to speak, and the sight of this hurt you at times just as much. But that pain and the divergence of opinion are a hundred times more precious than the uniform jubilation seen in the newsreels of the '50s. Our present awakening is a troubled one, for we see so many losses all around, but it is an awakening, nevertheless! As for the Khrushchev thaw, our society had stepped into it with the consciousness of a mass of people essentially still unawakened. And, again, it was done as if at a command. People no longer chanted, "Glory to Comrade Stalin!", they chanted, "Glory to the Communist Party!" but they did this with the same admiration in their eyes and, again, in chorus and at a command. The narrator in the newsreels of those years again tried to infuse us, as was the case in the newsreels from Stalin's time, with permanent enthusiasm as he described various developments in the country. A youth festival swept the entire city of Leningrad! The turbulent waters of the Angara River would soon be checked by concrete! The scale of industrial construction in Siberia was enormous! (And all the while we saw the maimed taiga on the screen.) Very happy and very cheerful people lived in Kiev, one of the country's oldest cities becoming ever more beautiful. (And this was said at a time when churches were being destroyed in Kiev like elsewhere in the country.) A new town, Sumgait, was coming into being in Azerbaijan, with new blocks of flats rising not far from the large industrial buildings. (And all we saw on the screen were rows of dreary box-like structures.) Soviet people, the narrator said, knew how to work and how to enjoy their leisure time. (At the same time the cinema next door was running B. Golovnya's film, "The Slumber of the Mind", which showed churches being turned into stables and storehouses, or simply reduced to ruins to be used by drunken couples as meeting places. The cameraman was not bold enough to reproduce the drawings and the words scribbled by those people on the walls.)

Today we are paying a terrible price for our chronic jubilation and credulity. Chernobyl is the price paid for the atomic power stations built ahead of schedule. Callousness is the price paid for the desecrated churches, and the Sumgait tragedy and the polluted Angarsk is what we are getting in return for our too long slumber of the mind. We didn't wake up from it even in the '50s, which we still remember nostalgically.

If we want to awaken fully from our slumbers, we must see the old newsreels. Let us stop our arguments for a while (they are already leading us up a blind alley) and just look at ourselves in the mirror. We have grown up and regained our sight, but there is still much we have to understand. So, let us see those newsreels, silently and seriously, as they were seen on that sunny day of our unusually warm winter, by an audience at a small cinema on Nevsky Prospekt.

HOMELESSNESS

The Soviet Homeless
by Gennady Vedernikov, *Moscow News*, February 8, 1989

He's known popularly as a "BICH" (pronounced "beech")—a Russian acronym which stands for "formerly cultured person"—but demographically he is hard to pin down: most biches have no permanent address.

. . . I met this man twice. He introduced himself as Lyovka the Fisherman. A smartly-dressed, well-built guy of about 30, he was travelling alone in a sleeping car compartment after a run on a fishing ship. "Did you have a good catch?" I asked. "Not bad," he said with a smirk and opened his attaché case for effect. It was packed full of money and bottles of brandy.

The next morning I saw him leaving the railway station in two taxis. One for himself, the other for his cap. Lyovka the Fisherman was enjoying himself.

A couple of months later I met him at the same railway station. All his smartness was gone. Not a piece of expensive foreign gear on him, but a swollen unshaved face and one black eye. His hands shook as he showed his crumpled passport to a militiaman . . .

Another bich had just been born. He would join the company of other homeless men and women gone to seed like him, clash with the militia and probably end up in jail . . .

Who is to blame for this young able-bodied man going down the drain? Has he chosen his fate? Or has destiny chosen him?

We asked research associate of the Khabarovsk Institute for Economic Studies of the Far Eastern Branch of the USSR Academy of Sciences Sergei Chernyshov, a social psychologist who has investigated this problem professionally.

CHERNYSHOV: To study this problem "from within" I decided to use back vacation time and mix in with the crowd in front of the recruiting office of one of the Far Eastern fishing fleets. Soon I was off on a many-month run on a trawler which operates around a floating fishing factory in the Pacific.

MN: Why did you start your research at the floating fishing factory? Why didn't you join the biches in front of the wine shop, for example?

CHERNYSHOV: The wine shop is the final stage in a bich's career. His prospects then are either jail or the cemetery. Incidentally, I visited a cemetery on the Kamchatka Peninsula where biches are buried. It's full of nameless graves . . .

For me it was more important to find out how a bich becomes a bich. I wanted to analyze the logic of his decline and fall. It was on the floating fish factories that I managed to do this. Similar situations could be observed in gold digging artels, geological expeditions, seasonal construction and lumbering teams, etc.

MN: What is a bich?

CHERNYSHOV: Biches are people expelled from normal social relations as the result of family or professional failure. They are former industrial workers, lawyers, doctors and journalists. At first, a person loses his housing (often as the result of divorce), then he loses his profession.

The Far East is the destination of many former convicts, alimony-evaders and just plain tramps. Seasonal work for them is a chance to make some quick money, improve their material situation and buy expensive things. Let me tell you straight away that the "easy" money made in the Far East does not make people happy. Less than one per cent of those I interviewed managed to make their dreams of buying a car or a cooperative flat come true.

Seasonal work does untold harm to normal people while finishing off the weak and the broken-down. We often say that work makes people better. But we don't specify what kind of work. Only the highly organized and creative kind. And what about hard unskilled labour, often a drudgery?

The work conditions on the floating fishing factories are almost inhuman. People work to exhaustion for 12 to 14 hours a day. They live in cramped, overcrowded quarters and have no chance for enlightenment. All of this has a destructive effect on human psychology.

Seasonal work which is so widespread in the Far East is profitable for local industries. They pay seasonal workers and offer them no social benefits like well-appointed housing, etc. The society leaves these people to their own devices, face to face with their problems.

Tragic is the lot of the young people who came to the Far East as Young Communist League volunteers. They gave their young years and strength to such projects as the Baikal-Amur railway and eventually found themselves no better off than when they started: no home, no family. Some of them have up to 50,000 roubles in their savings accounts, but feel disillusioned and hopeless. They have neither plans for the future, nor purpose in life.

Some of these people told me they don't know what to do with their lives. No one needs them. They are ashamed to go back home where they are remembered as cheerful lads. They have no roots in the East either.

A bich is a person who's lost all social ties. Nevertheless he craves appreciation and respect like any other. Once society cuts him off, he seeks to establish his own informal society, he joins other disaffected people with their own system of values and principles. Hence the wild "escapades" after hard work, a network of illegal hangouts, bloody fights, thefts and killings. Such inhuman working conditions inspire people to inhuman acts. It is within those seasonal communities that criminal bands spring up to provide aggressive anti-social elements for the underworld.

MN: How many biches are there in the Far East?

CHERNYSHOV: No census has ever been made. The city of Khabarovsk with a population of 600,000 has at least 10,000 biches, according to my estimate. This amounts to 2.5 per cent of the able-bodied population.

MAN: What can be done about the biches?

CHERNYSHOV: We need to do something not about the biches but about the social and economic conditions that keep producing them. Seasonal work must be drastically restricted and eventually banned altogether by appropriate legislation. No profit, however big, can be made at the expense of human lives. Local industries must employ people permanently, mechanize hard work and build housing. People must be protected by trade unions and the Labour Code, and enjoy every social guarantee.

Strange as it may seem, most biches are willing to break away from their habits and become "normal" citizens with homes, families and regular jobs. Alas, people with damaged reputations like theirs do not get regular jobs. Also, a resolute changeover to a settled way of life proves too difficult for some.

At present only the militia deal with this category of the population described as "persons without permanent residence or occupation". Militiamen pick them up at railway stations and illegal hangouts, find out their identity, issue papers and buy them tickets to their home towns. But even the militia fail to find jobs for them in most cases. Thus they become biches once again, working irregularly as stokers, seasonal builders, fishery workers, gold-diggers, etc.

We urgently need a special social service to help rehabilitate these people. It must be a Salvation Fund whose members would professionally and eagerly teach those social misfits to live in a community and form a desire for personal growth.

We need special shelters and bed-and-breakfast places for such people to go to in times of trouble. Apart from bed and board, such centres ought to provide care and advice.

There should be sociologists, psychologists and doctors working for the Salvation Fund to prepare misfits morally and physically for normal life and work.

The problem of biches must be studied and tackled because no one is going to solve it for us . . .

HOUSING

The Green Product
by M. Zoshchenko

The fall came. You could say that the construction season was coming to an end.

I don't know about other houses, but in ours they did do a little renovation. They painted the railing on the stairs.

Of course they did not do that at the expense of the tenants. The people that live here are not rich. They did this at the expense of one tenant. He, the son-of-a-bitch, won five hundred rubles. Got scared and coughed up five gold pieces for the renovation of the house. Later, when he came to his senses, he felt really bad. But it was too late. The railing was already painted.

They painted the railing with dark green paint. It turned out nice. Such a noble dark green color. You can even say that it had shades of red. Or was it the rust that was coming through the paint? No one knows. Only it came out really nice. In a word, not too ugly. You look at it and you don't get a gut reaction to turn your face away.

Everyone admired the railing. Even the chairman gave a short speech on account of the painted railing. Then, in three days, the tenants began getting mad, saying that the railing was not drying. They said that the kids get dirty and run around looking like zebras.

The chairman said thoughtfully, "Comrades, you can't place unrealistic expectations on this paint. Give it time, it'll dry, and maybe then it won't get you dirty."

The tenants began waiting patiently.

Two weeks had gone by, it just didn't dry.

They called a painter. He tasted the paint, turned white, and said, "Usually the paint is oil-based. I'll tell you why this one does not dry. It obviously has linseed oil instead of olive oil in it. Linseed oil ain't allowed to dry fast. But there is no need to lose your sleep over it. In a month, God willing, it'll not as much dry as evaporate. Only it's doubtful that the railing will remain green. It'll most likely become blue. And maybe even gray with streaks."

The chairman said, "You know, it's just as well. If it'll be with streaks, the dirt won't show."

And again the tenants began admiring the railing.

And so they admired it for a month or two, then it began to dry. Though to say honestly, there wasn't much left to dry. The house kids and inexperienced visitors took all the paint off.

But one must remain an optimist and find good sides in every sad situation. The paint, I say, did not really turn out to be that bad, and it was affordable for the not rich folk. It came off the suits. You did not even have to wash them. It just disappeared by itself.

Hell knows what it was made out of. Its creator, the bum, probably keeps his invention secret. I guess he's scared that someone will beat him up.

The Unforseen Situation
by M. Zoshchenko

You can congratulate me. I found me an apartment. A room and a kitchen. Needs a little fixing up.

That is really nothing, just the ceiling needs painting, otherwise you can see the beams, and the pieces with the upstairs neighbors fall down; everything else is fine.

So I painted the ceiling; fixed it and painted it. Then I notice, with such an incredible ceiling, the walls don't look too good. They're just too dirty and too shabby.

So I bought some cheap wallpaper. Put it up. It became kind of classy. One thing though, the floor let me down. With the bad walls it wasn't too noticeable. Now, it's scary to look at it; holes and pits. You walk on that floor like on a pavement, that's how uneven it is.

So I bought some reject tiles. Covered the floor. The room became pretty as a picture. Only the door is really awful. Hell knows what it is, but it's not a door.

I fixed the door. Put in a door handle, so it'd look nice. Made it look new with paint. Only I should've painted the door from one side only. Stupid me also painted it from the side of the kitchen. You just can't walk into the kitchen now. The door's nice and the rest is sheer crap. The walls make you want to scream. The stove stands there all broken up. The faucet is barely holding on. The floor is almost gone. The ceiling is nightmarish, it keeps falling on your head.

So I began fixing things up. Then gave up. I thought to myself that I won't have the stomach to finish all this. I figure I'll do the kitchen, but then the bathroom is shabby. There's no tank. The fourth wall's missing. Let's say I finish the bathroom, now you can't go into the hall. If I do the hall, the front door needs work. I do the front door, the stairs are crappy. There is no railing. If I do the stairs, the house needs fixing up. The house is in really bad shape.

You've got to understand, comrades. I can't fix the house. I only make forty-seven a month.

And so I live here as if on top of a volcano. I am not even thinking about renovating this place. This matter has to be approached carefully and thoughtfully.

HUMAN RIGHTS

Their Area Is Human Rights
by N. Sytezhev, *Pravda*, November 23, 1988

THIS INTERVIEW was conducted with Doctor of Juridical Sciences Professor B. Nazarov, Chief of the All-Union Juridical Institute's newly formed Human Rights Department.

Moscow—A human rights department has just been formed at the All-Union Juridical Institute. Doctor of Juridical Sciences Professor B. Nazarov has been appointed chief.

NAZAROV: We were faced with the task of writing a primer on human rights and compiling a program for the course "The History, Theory, and Practice of Human Rights." As of February 1989 we will begin to give lectures in this course to fourth-grade students. The department has tried to create an original course rather than duplicating things that are already well known. Specialists from our institute's other departments and scientists from the USSR Academy of Sciences Institute of State and Law helped in this work.

SYTEZHEV: How will the program be divided?

NAZAROV: Into five sections: Introduction to the theory of human rights, history of human rights, the main areas of the theory and practice of human rights in the 20th century, human rights guarantees, and international cooperation in this sphere.

SYTEZHEV: What do you see as the practical results of your department's activity?

NAZAROV: Above all the training and graduation of human rights specialists. More. The department is already working to defend the interests of individual citizens who have asked it for help. We hope that our experience will come in useful in the future when similar departments are opened in other institutes.

Supremacy of the Law: Academician Kudryavtsev Discusses Human Rights
by Yu. Feofanov, *Izvestiya*, January 26, 1989

IZVESTIYA OBSERVER Yu. Feofanov conducted this "dialogue" with V.N. Kudryavtsev, vice-president of the USSR Academy of Sciences and director of the State and Law Institute.

FEOFANOV: M.S. Gorbachev's UN speech said that all states, despite their ideological differences, must now "jointly seek a path toward the supremacy of the general human idea." In my opinion, we have started to talk for the first time about the primacy of general human norms of law, morality, and politics over class norms. This is a kind of personal revolution for me, who "took" historical materialism and dialectical materialism under Stalin. But how does science treat this whole turnaround? It would be interesting to hear opinions associated primarily with the law here. For this is also linked with the creation of the rule-of-law state and with the movement away from declarations to reality in guaranteeing citizens' rights.

KUDRYAVTSEV: The recognition of general human values is extremely important for legal science and practice in both its internal and international aspects. For it is these values that closely unite the law with morality and fully revive terms such as conscience, justice, honor, dignity, and compassion. And in relations with other countries and peoples they serve as necessary elements of mutual understanding and trust and as instruments in building world peace worthy of our civilization.

General democratic legal gains and humane moral ideas took shape long before socialism. Let's trace the views of progressive thinkers of the past on just one question—the punishment of criminals and mercy toward them. Democritus: "He who educates with the arguments of reason is better than he who employs coercion." Montesquieu: "A good legislator will try not so much to chastise as to improve morals." Radishchev: "The purpose of punishment is not revenge but correction." Marat: "It is not mildness of punishment but impunity of crimes that gives rise to the impotence of laws." V.I. Lenin: "It has long been said that the preventive effect of punishment depends not on its harshness but on its inexorability."

But what was our juridical reality like? Remember, for instance, the USSR Central Executive Committee resolution of 7 August 1932: theft punishable by execution; no amnesty. The resolution on cases of sabotage, arson, willful damage to machines, and other types of wrecking: The OGPU [United State Political Administration] must carry out repressions with particular severity. The resolution of 3 June 1934: Members of the family of a traitor to the motherland, even if unaware of the treachery, are to be deprived of their electoral rights and exiled to remote regions of Siberia. The resolution of 1 December 1934: Cases involving terrorist organizations are to be heard in their absence; no appeal against sentences or petitions for mercy allowed; sentence to be carried out immediately . . .

Those are examples from just 2 years alone! Yet similar practices continued for decades. The work to restore legality after the 20th party congress was not fully completed. Certainly even then ideas of humanism, mercy, and justice were considered alien to class-orientated politics. So they were not firmly established in the legal awareness of sufficiently broad strata of the population. This is graphically visible even now from certain letters that *Izvestiya* has received and that you have shown me. For instance, in connection with the discussion of the draft Fundamentals of Criminal Legislation. . . .

FEOFANOV: You referred to history and I remembered something. The two great revolutions of the late 18th century and the one of the early 20th century began with the proclamation of human rights, the rights of the citizen and of the people. I mean the American War of Independence, the great French Revolution, and our own. If we leave aside the social content of these revolutions, one can probably say that they are similar, if only on the basis of their adoption of declarations of rights. But in all three cases reality proved much grimmer than the slogans. What do you think, Vladimir Nikolayevich: Is there a pattern here?

KUDRYAVTSEV: You see, it is for historians to judge the reasons for such patterns. What I would like to say in this connection is this. Robespierre, that outstanding French revolutionary, said: "Revolution is the war of liberty against her enemies; constitution is the regime of victorious and peaceful liberty." The transition from revolutionary struggles to civil peace was very drawn out in our country. Even now we are still quite slow to free ourselves from the old dogmas. For the presumption of innocence was snubbed in the early eighties, just like the principles of the adversarial approach and the equality of the parties in a trial. The admission of the attorney to the preliminary investigation is being delayed. And, most inadmissibly of all, I think, the practice of "patching up holes" in the criminal code and other legislative acts on particular questions continues. At the same time clearly outmoded articles—for instance, on punishment for commercial mediation, which has long been part of daily economic activity—have not been repealed. Departmental lawmaking cannot be brought within reasonable bounds . . .

FEOFANOV: What is necessary for this?

KUDRYAVTSEV: In my opinion, the situation should change drastically after the election of the new Supreme Soviet, in which all legislative activity will be concentrated. Its Presidium will not publish decrees of a normative character. The creation of the Constitutional Oversight Committee, which is designed to keep an eye on observance of the country's fundamental law, is also important. Moreover, a statute is being prepared on departmental lawmaking procedure: All ministry and department normative acts are to be registered and checked by the Ministry of Justice from the viewpoint of their consonance with the law.

FEOFANOV: These are clearly essential elements in a rule-of-law state. But what I would like to hear about is this. **We emphasize that we are constructing a SOCIALIST rule-of-law state. At the same time we talk about the priority of general human values.** Isn't there a contradiction here? Doesn't the concept of a SOCIALIST rule-of-law state and SOCIALIST legality enshrine a class priority? Doesn't this mean that our "inalienable" civil rights will be different from the rights of people in parliamentary democracies?

KUDRYAVTSEV: A rule-of-law state is based precisely on general human values: supremacy of the law, mutual responsibility of the state and citizens, guaranteed rights of the individual, and others. The Universal Declaration of Human Rights adopted by the United Nations in 1948, international human rights pacts, and other conventions and agreements in this sphere are of a universal character. All these documents, which are recognized by states of different socioeconomic natures, graphically confirm the fact that the world is multifaceted yet at the same time united.

Of course, every country also has its specific features in the human rights sphere. Socialist countries, for instance, deny the possibility of exploitation and prosecute for nationalism, chauvinism, and racial discrimination. Capitalist countries don't guarantee the right to work; unemployment is used as an element in the economic mechanism. In proclaiming a socialist rule-of-law state, we see its task as being to maintain, establish, and protect by legal means not only people's political rights but also their social rights; to affirm democracy, citizens' equality before the law, social justice in the interests of working people, humanism, and peace between the peoples. We are endeavoring to renew socialism without rejecting its principles but while affirming and developing them—we are seeking to completely eliminate all the former deformations and relics of administrative-edict methods of management. Man, his rights and freedoms should be at the center of state and social life. Hence our insistent desire to democratize all social practice, consistently implement people's power, glasnost, and the responsibility of all decision-makers before citizens, develop independent principles in management, and boost the role of public organizations. **We aren't shutting ourselves off from the outside world or from other countries' legal experience, for instance, in the sphere of defending the rights and freedom of the individual.**

FEOFANOV: When people talk about human rights, especially in the Western interpretation of the term, the usual range of "freedoms" arises straightaway: freedom of speech, freedom to hold demonstrations and rallies, freedom to choose one's place of residence, freedom to leave the country, and so on. This is explicable: It is these freedoms that were suppressed in our country with particular zeal. In my opinion, a breakthrough has been made here for the first time. But dissatisfaction has arisen straightaway: The right to demonstrate is restricted; the right to live where you like is linked with residence permits, and so on. Couldn't you, Vladimir Nikolayevich, describe the process of implementing constitutional rights and the objective or bureaucratic obstacles that are impeding it? Aren't there collisions here

as a result of the contradictions between our domestic legislation and the universally recognized norms of international law?

KUDRYAVTSEV: In my opinion, we are still only starting to
create reliable legal mechanisms to implement and defend citizens' rights. We are acting primarily by the "trial and error"
method. Moreover, other countries have now begun to learn
from our experience. At any rate that was my thought when I
saw the Hungarian legislation on meetings and associations that
was adopted recently: It is much better thought-out than ours.

IDEOLOGY

We've All Come from Among the People . . .
by Yuri Solomonov, *Moscow News*, February, 1988

I don't remember now what kind of goods in short supply were
put on sale. What I do remember is how the queue attacked an
old man who showed the shop assistant his war invalid certificate. "Outrageous!", "We must have a look where you fought!"

Someone's attempts to help the veteran were unsuccessful.
The old man took his place at the end of the queue behind a
smiling young man who summed up the result: "The people,
father, are always right. You must take this into account . . ." I
don't know whether "father" took anything into account, but I
was struck by the cock-sure confidence with which the young
boy spoke about the people being eternally right.

But it is enough to ponder just a little to understand where
this "people are always right" comes from. This conviction is
fuelled by the old myth that everything bad, unpleasant, wicked,
false and criminal has no relation whatsoever with the people. The
real people are the guardians of lofty morals, high spiritual tenor,
great traditions and wisdom which cannot be found in any book.

This is regarding the question of whether or not a majority can
err. Experience has proved that it can. A mistake made by the
majority is further aggravated by the fact that the majority is
always stronger . . .

For too long we have been trained to believe in the powerful
righteousness of the majority, to believe that the people are

never wrong. But where was their powerful moral feeling when the trials of the "enemies of the people" thundered all over the country, when it was swept by reprisals?

One well-known writer recently put forward this contention: there is the people and there is the population. And the population, he claimed, has no relation to the real people. So what? To get the real people, should we exclude from the country's 1937 population all those who framed charges, wrote denunciations, spoke at meetings, stigmatizing all possible "enemies" and "deviationists", and still earlier carried out Stalin's collectivization? Who will then be on the other side, besides the innocent victims?

And today? Should those who last year "ensured" the recently published statistics on the state of crime in the country be included in the people or in the population? And the drug addicts, alcoholics and prostitutes? Bureaucrats and bribe-takers? Well, and what is to be done with those who left their villages and towns and thereby, in the opinion of some men of letters, lost their roots among the people? There are plenty of others on whom we can cast aspersions if we keep pronouncing the word "people" like a prayer.

The people are harmed, I believe, not only by their deification, but also by humiliating attitudes. And they are humiliated primarily by those who demonstrate profound concern over the moral health of the nation.

It is they who coined the sacramental: "The people will not understand".

With an invariable reference to the people, they try to make believe that they alone understand what articles journalists should write, so that the people should not fall into scepsis and frustration. When they begin to feel that glasnost is about to reach dimensions inconceivable and dangerous for them, they, with an invariable reference to workers or peasants, drop phrases about nationwide indignation and claim that the "people do not understand" what these intellectuals are calling for.

But is there anything more dangerous than to declare mass taste to be a peculiar yardstick of objectivity? Equally ruinous for the people are flattery, abuse and false concern. In these extremes our ultra-patriots join hands with our bureaucrats. We started an honest conversation about ourselves in April 1985, for the first time ever since Lenin's period in our history, corroborating Marx's thought: "The people must be taught to be terrified at itself in order to give it courage."

But what we must primarily be horrified by is the fact that, for decades, we have been in a state of undeclared civil war. The people have been at war with themselves, trying to find in their midst enemies, traitors, spies, "kosmopolits", "doctors-poisoners", "admirers of Western music", "stylish young people", "masons and zionists" . . . It is possible to write a history of the schism of a great, wise, humane and at the same time a very complex, contradictory and often erring people. A people whom history is now giving a chance to look at itself with the courage of a revolutionary, and to understand that megalomania and the inferiority complex are symptoms of one and the same disease.

Today there is no greater virtue than admitting the existence of different views, ideas, currents, virtues and vices, shortcomings and merits to unite for the sake of the main thing—to make a stride towards a genuinely civilized state.

Otherwise, "the people will not understand . . ."

FAZIL ISKANDER

If We Stop, We'll Be Thrown Back
An interview with Fazil Iskander
by Yelena Vesyolaya, *Moscow News*, 1989

FAZIL ISKANDER has always had many readers. But in the last three years we seem to have discovered him anew. He published manuscripts that had remained in his desk drawer for years, such as "Rabbits and Boa Constrictors" and "The Old House Beneath the Cypress". The Moskovsky Rabochy Publishers are about to put out the full text of his novel "Sandro from Cheghem" in three volumes, including the previously unpublished chapters. The writer says the publication of "Sandro" is the most important literary event for him, because the novel incorporates his major ideas, concerns and worries. "In general," Iskander said, "the time of publication has come."

Q: It is often said that our national tragedy has been talked about too much, with almost everyone trying to "kick" Stalin because that is in vogue and a sure way to get into print. As a result, the topic is getting stale and is no longer exciting, as psychologists have noticed.

A: That is partly true. But such talk also smacks of the familiar tendency to control the nation's mentality from above. There are objective market rules that cover literary works, too. Their market value is determined by what I would call the mystery of human interest. It is the market that will tell us when the Stalin theme ceases to be of interest to the reader.

I think, however, that it will never lose interest if every attempt at understanding that man's personality and historic role will bring us something new. At a certain point in time (which seems to have already arrived) mediocre and banal compositions on the subject might cease drawing the intelligent reader's attention. But we should go onwards rather than have someone on top switch on and off the flow of publications, thus returning to the old and ridiculous practice of controlling culture. Incidentally, those orders usually belong to people who in general disapprove of our literature's critical fervour.

It is no more than two or three years since works exposing Stalin, his entourage, and the many terrifying phenomena of our life have come to light, but there are already voices saying, "Enough, we are sick and tired of it!" What about those forty years that we spent reiterating praises and glorifying that luminary of all sciences? Didn't anyone feel like saying "Enough!" then?

I think many did want to say that, but nobody dared . . . Almost every book of poetry began with an ode to the Great Leader. Lots of novels ended happily in Stalin approving, Stalin nodding his assent, Stalin smiling, Stalin applauding, or Stalin rescuing a brilliant inventor from a dull bureaucrat. All this imperial rubbish was preached for years. It is natural, therefore, that many find the present changes not quite to their liking.

Q: It is a curious topic: Stalinism without Stalin.

A: For the "nomenklatura" in the broad sense of the word, it is a great temptation to try and consolidate Stalinism in our life, all the while knowing that they cannot disappear without trace at any moment, as happened under Stalin. Stalin gave his "apparat" every privilege except one: to sleep peacefully and plan their lives for years ahead. They wielded great power knowing that at any moment any one of them might vanish. Now they know they are safe and will not vanish, so they want to keep their power and authority in the bargain. Very convenient, isn't it?

For a certain psychological type that's a great temptation, too. Say, a shoemaker displays a portrait of Stalin on the wall of his shop. This man knows that Stalin was born very low and came to rule half the world. Stalin to him is the personification of his own cherished dream. His love and worship of Stalin is to him like the savings bond or lottery ticket he buys, knowing there is little chance of his winning an automobile. But it gives him pleasure simply to own the bond. For many, Stalin is such a bond, the psychological means of self-assertion. Why don't they display Lenin's or Marx' portraits, I wonder? Why only Stalin's? They sense psychological kinship there—the same suppressed desire to suppress others. This type occurs especially often among people whose profession is to wait on others. They hate having to constantly wait on others. . . .

Q: A lackey's complex.

A: Yes, and it is not all that easy to get rid of it.

Q: Do you imply that the cult is predetermined by a certain professional mentality? Yet there is an opinion that its origin lies in a national mentality . . .

A: Of course, after the 300-year Romanov dynasty fell, certain illusions and a popular belief in the tzar remained. But didn't Hitler come to power in Germany, Mussolini in Italy and Franco in Spain? I think all these phenomena have one thing in common: the emergence on the political arena of enormous masses of people who were barely literate, very ambitious and for the most part morally undeveloped.

This type was discovered and brilliantly exposed by Dostoyevsky. He called them "people from the underground". They created their own leaders, also a type. At that time the world objectively demanded change. Vast numbers of people in Russia and in the west sensed that something had come to an end. At a time like this, dictatorship and all sorts of imposture and deformations were possible. The emergence en masse on the political arena of highly ambitious and barely literate people certainly contributed to that.

Q: Do you think political involvement harmed those people, corrupted them?

A: The ethical type of behaviour evolves over time. Say, a peasant's—in rural surroundings, an urban craftsman's—in urban surroundings. When they were abused they revolted, went on strike, but never, not even in their wildest dreams, did they aspire to rule the country. The transition from their own age-long ethical stereotypes to the ethics of a cultured individual who has to make his own decisions independently rather than rely on a collective ethic proved very painful, especially for people inwardly unprepared to shoulder responsibility. The spreading of this semiculture among the broad masses paved the way for everything that happened.

One can imagine a situation where, say, Mozart is killed and Salieri takes his role, but another, a lesser "Salieri" will turn up to kill him. This is a kind of historical "dialectic".

Q: In retrospect, what do you make of Plekhanov's warning that the Russian proletariat was not socially mature enough to take power and ought not to have done so?

A: I don't think Plekhanov was far wrong when he predicted that the country would be ruled on behalf of the proletariat by somebody else. That is exactly what happened.

Lenin showed fantastic flexibility when he realized that, in the course of the Revolution, the introduction of NEP was an extremely bold step designed to give Russian society a chance to mature and ripen. Personally I think that, under the Party's control, it would have successfully done just that.

No doubt, the Party should have given up much of its power and retained control only over the most important issues. I believe this could have been worked out. But psychological factors, complex and difficult to explain, came into play at that very time. Just imagine the Bolsheviks who had been constantly persecuted and in hiding got suddenly all that power. They felt so euphoric that they seemed to forget what they had taken the power for.

When I think about the disputes of the 1920s, I find only Bukharin's slogan "Get rich!" noble and realistic. He said it was too early to begin collectivization. But he lacked firmness, and by then it was too late anyway. As is apparent from Lenin's "will", Stalin enjoyed unlimited power even before Lenin's death.

Q: A dangerous euphoria threatened us at the early stage of perestroika, too. Now it seems to have given way to greater realism in the assessment of events. For example, we now talk less of "acceleration".

A: By the way, I disapproved of that particular slogan from the very start. Acceleration has been the motto of the day since the 1920s. But in fact no one must be hurried—ever. I have always believed that socialist emulation discredited the state socially and economically. **The state must never take steps that can evoke an ironic attitude among its citizens.** Every state should strive to achieve authority through wisdom and an understanding of the nature of things. The slogans of socialist emulation can work at a crucial moment, for instance, after the war, when the people are called upon to make an all-out effort. But after a year or two life must go back to its normal pace. Workers must never be driven to show heroism every day, because this inevitably ends up in everyday drinking, depression and deception.

I prefer the words "renovation" or "revival". Our new revolutionary times, as we call them, must renew the human being, renew hopes.

Q: What do you pin your hopes on? What worries you?

A: I'm worried about the centrifugal forces that have emerged in our multinational state, and the irritation and impatience that accompany them. Perestroika began at a time when the nation was in a very bad moral condition, in a state of sheer nervous exhaustion. Things got out of control and the nationalities question grew out of all proportion, like a malignant tumour.

Nevertheless, I still hope that the future of the new democratic Russia lies in the union of all our nations. To achieve this, Moscow must become the centre from which the most interesting ideas and philosophical concepts emanate. In other words, it must become the spiritual and not merely the administrative centre of the country. It must not be just the source of primitive instructions, whose authority depends solely on administrative threats.

A vast multinational country like ours cannot rely on that. It can be held together by the power of ideas produced by the centre. Besides, the centre must show the whole country and all its nations the significance of law, its universality, on the one hand, and its absolute severity, on the other. Every citizen must see that the severity of the law is justified in every particular case. In other words, we must eventually come to a state committed to the rule of law, not of individuals, whether good or bad. We must understand that there's something more powerful than us. It's the law. **At present, millions of people do not believe in the law, they believe in their superiors.**

Strong, honest, principled thinkers—such as, say, Academicians Sakharov and Likhachev—must join in the country's leadership in the near future. People of that type are duty bound to be there. In the case of their disapproval of this or that government action, they must have the opportunity to address the people. This would help the leadership to avoid grave errors. Unfortunately, our history is full of errors, because there has never been any feedback, any consultation with the people, and the government did what seemed the most advantageous at the moment.

There is yet another problem that is much talked about. It is high time that all necessary means are found to provide the people with enough to eat—immediately. At any rate, a certain acceptable level must be achieved at all costs, even if we have to borrow the money. You cannot go on for 70 years giving nothing but promises.

Finally, we must not slow down the pace of glasnost. If we stop, the current will throw us back.

N. S. KHRUSHCHEV

Shelest Regrets Anti-Khrushchev "Coup"
Argumenti i Fakti, January 14-20, 1989

THIS INTERVIEW with P.Ye. Shelest, former first secretary of the Ukrainian Communist Party Central Committee and member of the CPSU Central Committee Politburo, was conducted by an unnamed correspondent under the rubric "Memoirs of a Participant in the Events About Difficult Moments in the Country's History: On Khrushchev, Brezhnev, and Others."

EXCERPTS: The articles about N.S. Khrushchev (*Argumenty i Fakty* Nos 25, 27, and 47 for 1988) provoked many readers' letters. There was a response, in particular, from P.Ye. Shelest, who was first secretary of the Ukrainian Communist Party Central Committee and a member of the CPSU Central Committee Politburo during those times. We publish below his interview with our correspondent.

CORRESPONDENT: On becoming first secretary of the Ukrainian Communist Party Central Committee [in 1962], you were in close contact with the country's top leadership, including N.S. Khrushchev. What is your opinion of his political activity?

SHELEST: He made many mistakes, but they must also be shared by the other leaders who worked alongside him. I agree with what Mikoyan said at that time. He declared at a Presidium session that Khrushchev's activity was the party's great political capital. Indeed, the debunking of Stalin's personality cult alone was worth something. Only someone with great courage and fidelity to socialism's ideals could have ventured to take such a step. In this connection N.S. Khrushchev's speech at the CPSU Central Committee Presidium session which decided his fate was characteristic. Apparently, I alone have preserved the record of it, since no shorthand report was made of that session. At that session—his last one—Khrushchev was crushed, isolated, and powerless to do anything, and yet he found within himself the strength and courage to say: "I am grateful that you have, nonetheless, said some positive things about my activity. I am pleased for the Presidium and, as a whole, for its maturity. There is a grain of my work in the shaping of this maturity.

"The party has educated us all, myself included. You and I have the same political and ideological basis, and I cannot struggle against you. I will leave and I will not fight. Once again I beg your pardon if I have offended anyone or been rude—anything might have happened in my work. However, I wish to say that I categorically reject a number of the charges made against me. I cannot remember and counter all the charges. My chief shortcoming and weakness is kindness and trustfulness. Perhaps also the fact that I myself did not notice my shortcomings. But none of you who are present here ever spoke to me openly and frankly about my shortcomings, and you always assented and supported me. You lacked principle and boldness. I am accused because I combined the posts of first secretary of the CPSU Central Committee and chairman of the USSR Council of Ministers. But I myself did not seek this, you know. This question was decided collectively, and some of you, including Brezhnev, even insisted on it. Perhaps my mistake was that I did not oppose that decision, but you all said it was being done in the interests of the cause.

"Yes, I was somewhat tactless with regard to scientific personnel, particularly toward the Academy of Sciences," Khrushchev continued. "But it is no secret that our science lags behind foreign science and technology on many issues. We are investing tremendous public funds in science and creating all the conditions for creativity and for the introduction of the results of science into the national economy."

Khrushchev went on to give a well-reasoned explanation of the measures taken earlier with regard to events in the Suez Canal, at the time of the Caribbean crisis, and in relations with the PRC. These questions, too, were decided collectively, he said. "I realize that this is my last political speech, my swan song, as it were. I will not address the plenum. But I would like to put a request to the plenum. . . ."

Before he had time to finish what he was saying, Brezhnev categorically replied: "That will not be." He was supported by Suslov.

After that Khrushchev said: "Obviously, things will now be as you consider necessary." At this tears welled up in his eyes. "Well, I am ready for anything. I myself thought that I had to go, because there are many problems, and it is difficult to cope with them at my age. We have to bring in the young people. One day history will have its weighty, truthful say about what is happening now.

"I now ask for my resignation request to be written, and I will sign it. I rely on you in this matter. If you require it, I will leave Moscow.". . .

CORRESPONDENT: What is your opinion of how this coup, as it were, was prepared?

SHELEST: I believe that R. Medvedev's article made Suslov the hero of the coup. His name is mentioned 18 times. I believe that that role is exaggerated. Under Khrushchev, Suslov was not considered the second man in the leadership, as he was under Brezhnev. Other comrades prepared the report which Suslov delivered. The idea was that Brezhnev or, in the last resort, Podgornyy should deliver it. Brezhnev simply funked it, and Podgornyy categorically refused. Then Suslov was entrusted with doing it. Whereas Shelepin, as Medvedev claims, had taken some part in preparing the materials for the plenum, Suslov had not known of the upcoming events until the last minute. When he was told about it, his lips turned blue and his mouth was distorted. He could barely utter: "What are you saying?! There will be civil war." In short, Suslov was made the hero. But he does not deserve it. The decisive role in Khrushchev's removal belonged to Brezhnev and Podgornyy from beginning to end. And to no one else.

CORRESPONDENT: Do you believe that Khrushchev's removal and Brezhnev's accession to power were objectively necessary?

SHELEST: No, there was no such need. That is my firm conviction, although I myself participated in what happened. I now criticize myself and I sincerely regret what happened.

I will also say this of Khrushchev. I knew him well: We traveled abroad and vacationed together. He described how Beria was disarmed. That was a courageous act. I regard his idea of creating national economic councils as useful. Khrushchev did a great deal to open up outer space and develop our missile troops. He called party workers and leaders of ministries strictly to account for affairs in that sphere. He was an honest man devoted to the core to the party. A real party worker with rich experience of life. He did not like gossips, he liked businesslike people.

CORRESPONDENT: You worked under L.I. Brezhnev for several years. What would you like to say about him? What do you remember?

SHELEST: I believe that as leader of the party and of the state, Brezhnev was a chance, transitional, temporary figure. If it had not been for Podgornyy, he would have been replaced after a year. Podgornyy supported Brezhnev. I do not know why.

Brezhnev was particularly afraid of those leaders who were younger than himself. So Semichastnyy, Shelepin, and Katushev were removed. Subsequently he made short work of everyone who had supported him initially—Voronov, Podgornyy, Kosygin. He sometimes did this jesuitically. Take, for example, the case of Semichastnyy, who was chairman of the KGB. A Politburo session was being held. Many questions were being decided. Toward the end Brezhnev took a paper from his breast pocket and said: "Now, Comrades, one more question, about Semichastnyy. Please call him." None of those present knew anything, and we had not talked with Semichastnyy himself. And then: "We have decided to reassign you." Where to? Why? The explanation was brief and unconvincing. Brezhnev at once proposed approving Yu.V. Andropov, with whom there had in fact been no prior discussion, as KGB chairman.

This was roughly how Brezhnev treated other people whom he disliked. He was altogether boorish with Kosygin, for example. The latter had already retired and was in the hospital following a heart attack. His party comrade Brezhnev visited him and asked: "When will you be giving up your dacha?"

Brezhev was a cowardly, mistrustful, and dull-witted man. He loved power and homage. Do you know how he got his second Hero's Star? By his 60th birthday he was already a Hero of Socialist Labor—a title conferred on him for work in the missile sphere. They decided to give him a second star for his birthday. I was in Kiev at the time. I was sent a petition from Moscow. I looked: Almost everyone had already signed it. So I signed, too. Podgornyy telephoned me 2-3 days later: "Petro, you know Lenya is insisting that he be given a Hero of the Soviet Union star." I said: "On what grounds?" The reply came: "Why do you ask! He has already persuaded everyone. You are the only one left." Just so. And he got his star.

I must particularly emphasize Brezhnev's general low cultural standing and his incompetence on many issues. This evidently accounts for the fact that he brought Suslov close to him. At every trifle: Get in touch with Mikhail Andreyevich. In my view, Suslov is a figure still to be exposed. He did the party more harm than good. We are still reaping the fruits of his activity, particularly in the historical, ideological, and nationalities questions. He strongly insisted on the speediest merging of nations and their languages and cultures. We see what that led to in the example of Nagorno-Karabakh. It is difficult even to describe him as a personality. He was divorced from life and very inward-looking.

We clashed repeatedly over questions of ideology and culture. Here is an example. Dovzhenko, who by then had died, had written a movie script about Taras Bulba. But there was no movie. Then Bondarchuk tackled the matter, and with great difficulty the movie was made. But the picture was not shown at once. Suslov banned it. I asked him why. He said: "Why revive nationalism, why alarm the Poles?" "But it is history," I replied, and went on: "Then let us do away with Gogol."

In short, I failed to convince him. He was of such a Stalinist stock. Here is an example. We were discussing what to publish in the newspaper in connection with Stalin's 90th anniversary. Everyone was silent. I advocated publishing the whole truth, taking the 20th party congress decisions as the basis.

"But how will the people take it?" Suslov asked.

In the end, there was an article, but in an abbreviated form—a great deal had been crossed out by Suslov.

Later, after I got to Moscow, Suslov organized an article in the journal *Kommunist Ukrainy* which criticized my book for extolling the Cossacks. Only I had not served in the Cossacks, but had used the archives. The book was withdrawn 1 month later. I went to Brezhnev and said: "What are you doing?" "I have not read the book," he said. "That was done on Suslov's orders."

The Secret Report on Stalin
Delivered by Nikita Khrushchev in the night of February 24-25, 1956, to the delegates to the 20th Party Congress was published in April 1989 by the *Izvestiya TsK KPSS* (News of the CPSU Central Committee)

THIRTY-THREE YEARS have elapsed since Khrushchev delivered his secret speech provoking a wide response both in the Soviet Union and abroad. However, for thirty-odd years the official text has been classified. Versions of the speech appeared in the West, but no one could tell for sure how authentic they were. That is the strange fate of a document of special political importance which had a decisive impact on the life of the party and the country as a whole, the communist and workers' movement the world over. It is clear why the speech has been made public today: it is the time of perestroika and glasnost. And yet the questions continue to surface. Anatoly Shlienkov, NT observer, Candidate of History, spoke to Colonel General Professor Dmitry Volkogonov, Ph.D., head of the Institute of Military History of the U.S.S.R. Ministry of Defence. On the table in front of them is the April issue of the *Izvestiya TsK KPSS*.

I remember how staggered people were to learn a mere three years after the death of the true disciple of Lenin, leader and teacher, outstanding military commander, etc., that in the actual fact everything was the other way round, there was the personality cult, grave violations of socialist legality, crimes and many other nightmarish things. These things were not discussed openly then, though, and some events were not mentioned at all. Let us return to the year of 1956 . . .

We must return to the past for our own benefit. Well . . . Khrushchev was on the rostrum. The First Secretary of the CPSU Central Committee was delivering his famous "secret" speech. Delegates in the presidium and the audience alike were looking at the man on the rostrum in a tense and melancholy silence, broken occasionally by cries of indignation and horror. As Khrushchev progressed with his report, the delegates visualized a ghost that kept appearing to the right and to the left of Khrushchev with increasing frequency. The characteristic accent of the First Secretary constructed before their eyes a radically new image of the "leader of the peoples." Soon the only thing that seemed to be left in the hall was the rostrum occupied by the duet: the party's new leader, one of the loyal comrades-in-arms of the dictator who had died three years before, and the mute ghost of the dictator himself, whom everyone present knew all too well. The dictator's image was changing with every passing minute in this truly historic arena, becoming bloody, tyrannical and sinister. These were rare hours of genuine historic importance.

That night Khrushchev performed an act of civic courage. Courage in thought, policy and action.

What preceded that night? It is hard to believe that Khrushchev, who could very well have ruled the country and the party without raising a world outcry over Stalin, decided on impulse to topple from the pedestal the Master himself with whom he had worked for so many years, to whom he must have been loyal, and in whom he must have believed.

Today we know that after Stalin's death latent processes had started within the party leadership towards breaking the fetters of Stalinism. These processes accelerated after Lavrenty Beria was arrested and shot. This dramatic action enabled the new leadership to realize what had actually been happening behind the scenes, though the leader's comrades-in-arms had been aware of what was happening earlier. After the date for the current 20th Congress of the CPSU, the first post-Stalin congress, had been established, Khrushchev addressed a Presidium sitting suggesting that a special committee be set up to investigate abuses of power.

You are right in saying that Khrushchev couldn't have acted on impulse, or in response to the "call of heart and conscience," as he himself claimed later. The fact is that immediately after the embalmed body of Stalin had been laid next to Lenin's in the Mausoleum, letters started pouring in to the Central Committee, the government and various government agencies. This flood of letters, increasing daily, came from those languishing behind the barbed wire of labour camps, isolated from their families, and those looking for their fathers, mothers, brothers and sisters. It was a spontaneous but at the same time natural wave of protest, hope, entreaty and faith in the restoration of shattered justice.

Khrushchev ordered that several memoranda be prepared for him on the basis of the letters, which together with the discredited "Leningrad affair" and the revision of a number of cases of individual prisoners who had managed to get a hearing in the Central Committee, proved quite convincingly that many charges were nothing but a criminal fraud. It transpired that a great number of prisoners sentenced on various points of Article 58 will have served their terms in the camps in a couple of years and that they would then have to be brought home. They would bring with them endless suffering, bewilderment and demands that the guilty be punished. Now that both Stalin and Beria were dead, there was no one who could take upon himself the terrible decision to leave these people to rot in the camps. In other words, Khrushchev felt that the party and the country were facing an extremely complex and crucial dilemma. The very proposal to set up the committee met with a bitter opposition on the part of Molotov, Kaganovich and Voroshilov. However, Bulganin, Mikoyan, Saburov, Pervukhin and the still vacillating Malenkov helped Khrushchev to win a majority. The committee was eventually set up. It was headed by Pospelov, who had been the long-standing Editor-in-Chief of *Pravda* and then the director of the Marx-Engels-Lenin-Stalin Institute. Khrushchev ordered that the committee be given access to MVD and MGB files. Pospelov worked hard, just as he had done several years before when compiling a concise biography of Stalin with Alexandrov, Galaktionov, Kruzhkov, Mitin and Mochalov. After Pospelov had reported the committee's findings to Khrushchev on the eve of the Congress, the First Secretary realized at once that the committee's report would either shatter the concrete shell of myths, legends and lies, or bury him, Khrushchev, under its weight.

The Pospelov committee's findings and conclusions hardly went down well with the Presidium, did they?

But of course. Khrushchev repeatedly returned to the question of the report, asking his colleagues what was to be done, and how the committee's findings were to be communicated to the delegates to the congress. Who would deliver the report? Pospelov? Molotov, Voroshilov, and Kaganovich put up stubborn, lengthy and sometimes bitter resistance. The heated dispute within the party's leadership was not recorded but, as Khrushchev and other people reminisced later, the opponents of the report had a set of "convincing" arguments: Why rake up the past? Perhaps we would do better to correct things on the quiet? Did Khrushchev himself realize what the report could lead to? And last but not least: weren't the members of the Presidium themselves involved in the arbitrariness of the past? Could we disregard all these fears? Khrushchev had his doubts as well. But he remembered the letters from prisoners, cast his memory back to the madness of the past and matured in his resolution: there was no way the results of the mass terror, lawlessness and grave abuses could be kept secret. Sooner or later the truth would out and it would not be long before it reached the people. He had to take the initiative in his own hands and tell the terrible truth to the party. However, he did not intend to tell it to the people.

When it was beginning to seem that the current 20th Party Congress would end without any trouble, like so many other empty and smooth-running congresses that the press dubbed "historic" the moment they were over, after the evening session of February 23, Khrushchev asked the members of the Presidium point-blank who was going to deliver the report "On the personality cult and its consequences." Perhaps Pospelov himself? After another clash with the Stalinist "dinosaurs," it was decided that it was up to the First Secretary himself to speak to the delegates. This was Khrushchev's hour of triumph. Once a loyal Stalinist, Khrushchev unexpectedly displayed civic courage and the ability to defy decades-old stereotypes. Later it transpired that this was not out of character on Khrushchev's part.

He was as resolute and impulsive as a politician as he had been shadowy as a member of Stalin's entourage. Besides the secret speech, and his domestic policies, Khrushchev's record includes such extraordinary moves as the visit to Canossa to see Tito, his attempts to blockade Berlin, his meeting with Eisenhower, the deployment of Soviet missiles in Cuba, his resolute involvement in the events of 1956 in Hungary, the establishment of friendly relations with Nasser, his irreconcilable attitude to Mao Zedong, his support for Vietnam, and other actions that testify to his complex and controversial personality. As is shown by these events, Khrushchev had enough courage and resolution and was not afraid to take responsibility. But at the same time it must be noted that he was often inconsistent and that he clearly overrated his intellectual and political capabilities. Sometimes his actions were badly thought out and shortsighted. Moreover, all this was complemented by the old ailment that afflicted not just Khrushchev but the entire Soviet system—the absolute role of the No. 1 figure. Post-Stalin political structures still lacked guarantees against Caesarism, and excessive emphasis on the role of the No. 1 figure, and these structures were no guarantee against a new cult. By his further actions

Khrushchev reinforced this failing inherent in a system that lacked genuine democratic attributes.

Do you think the secret speech reflects Khrushchev the human as well?

It may seem that I have departed from our story in trying to portray Khrushchev the politician. But without these digressions it is impossible to demonstrate the historic significance of that part of the congress that delivered the first crushing blow against Stalinism. It was the beginning of the historic defeat of the "victor" who had been building "Stalinist socialism" for thirty years. When I was finishing my book about Stalin and Stalinism, Khrushchev's speech had still not been published in this country though the rest of the world had learned its contents as early as June 1956. This very fact is an eloquent manifestation of the stagnant Stalinist system, the relics of which have survived until now. I am not going to relay the speech, the text of which has long been in my possession. I shall simply try to demonstrate its role in the process of destalinization it initiated and its profound impact on world developments.

. . . Khrushchev passed from section to section in the deafening silence of the large hall. Pospelov and his aides had prepared a report consisting of some 15 sections. Every section was a part of the whole, but it had separate meaning as well. As you see, its internal logic was weak. For instance, speaking on the general questions of the "personality cult and the Marxist classics," and "Lenin about Stalin," the report suddenly switched to the topic of the "enemies of the people" and then returned to more general problems such as "Lenin and party opposition," "collective leadership," etc. Some problems were raised several times: "responsibility for the terror," "genocide and terror," "terror." The speech "On the personality cult and its consequences" had also special subsections such as "Stalin in the war," "conflict with Yugoslavia," "Beria" and others.

As I see it, today when we know so much more about Stalin's crimes than Khrushchev mentioned in his speech, many people will be astonished by the tranquil and even idyllic beginning of the speech: "Stalin's services to the country were repeatedly described in numerous books, brochures and surveys during his lifetime. Stalin's role in preparing the socialist revolution, in the Civil War and in the struggle to build socialism in this country is generally recognized . . .

Yes. But later the continuation of the speech came like a bolt from the blue: "Now we will turn to a question of paramount importance to the party's present and future—the question of the emergence of the Stalin personality cult, which at a certain stage became the source of a number of grave and very painful violations of party principles, party democracy and revolutionary justice."

There were delegates in the hall who were learning of the political testament of Lenin for the first (!) time from Khrushchev's speech, as well as of Lenin's assessments of Stalin made as early as the 1920s. There were the revelations that enabled the truth to break out of captivity. Though blasting the "Trotsky-Zinovyev bloc" and the "Bukharinites," Khrushchev was the first to voice the "blasphemous" idea that under Lenin the struggle against the opposition was carried out by ideological means.

But it is not these ideas that were most important in Khrushchev's speech. The emphasis was on Stalinist lawlessness. In a number of cases, Khrushchev maintained, Stalin displayed his intolerance, cruelty and dedicated abuse of power. Instead of trying to prove the correctness of the line he pursued and mobilizing the masses, he resorted to repression and the physical elimination not only of actual enemies but also of people who had never committed any crime against the party or the Soviet government.

The audience was staggered by Khrushchev's detailed recital of frame-ups and the actual character of the "enemies of the people." This coinage rendered superfluous any evidence of the ideological errors of the person or a group of persons with whom one was debating. It gave the opportunity for the cruel repression, blatantly violating revolutionary justice, of any person who disagreed with Stalin, or was suspected of evil intentions or had simply been slandered.

In the course of the three to four hours it took to deliver the speech, Khrushchev managed to achieve the impossible. First of all, he denounced Stalin the leader. He capitalized on Stalin's incompetence: "He knew about the countryside and agriculture from films alone," disregarding the opinion of party cadres. The First Secretary, who was comparatively well acquainted with agriculture, was especially strident when condemning Stalin's agricultural policy. Khrushchev told delegates that in his later years Stalin had been nursing the idea of raising taxes on agriculture by 40 billion roubles and that "this plan was based not on a realistic assessment of the state of affairs, but on the fantastic delusions of a man who had lost touch with reality." Demonstrating the leader's incompetence and his speculative decisions, Khrushchev stripped Stalin of the mantle of infallibility and wisdom in which the latter had draped himself with the utmost care.

Though speaking at an official party forum, Khrushchev, as we see, resorted to emotionally coloured expressions ...

That's right. It was necessary for Khrushchev to portray Stalin as a butcher, a sadist, a person devoid of any human traits. Speaking of the fates of Kosior, Chubar, Postyshev, Kosarev, Eiche and other outstanding Bolsheviks, Khrushchev was eloquent enough to convince the delegates that Stalin had been the Chief Prosecutor in all these cases. He did not just give his consent to the arrests, but authorized arrests on his own initiative. As for the "confessions"—the main argument of the prosecution—it was not difficult to get it by the usual methods. "Contrary to all the legal norms of modern jurisprudence, the main and in fact only evidence of guilt was the 'confession' of the accused, which, as the investigation has revealed, was extracted by applying physical duress." Having cited a number of facts connected with the fates of delegates to the 17th Party Congress as well as with those of Kirov, Postyshev, Rudzutak, Voznesensky, Kuznetsov, Rodionov, Popkov, and the details of the Mengrel affair, Khrushchev succeeded in constructing a new image of the deceased leader: that of a bloody and ruthless dictator and tyrant.

Evidently, one of the most important questions raised by Khrushchev in his speech (which has not lost its relevance today) was on the style and methods of leadership?

Quite so. The First Secretary of the CPSU Central Committee especially underlined that the lack of collective leadership in the party's top echelons was the direct result of the abuses of personal power. For example, the speaker noted that no plenary meetings of the Central Committee took place in the war years. In fact, there was an attempt to convene a plenary meeting in October 1941, when all members of the Central Committee were called to Moscow from all over the country. They waited for two days for the meeting to start but in vain. Stalin didn't even want to see them or talk to them. Throughout his speech Khrushchev consistently maintained that while abusing his unlimited power, Stalin always invoked the Central Committee, without bothering to ask the opinion of the Politbureau, to say nothing of that of rank-and-file Central Committee members. He often chose to keep Politbureau members in the dark as regards decisions he took on his own on crucial party and national issues. The conflict with Yugoslavia was cited as one example of the baneful character of absolute power. Khrushchev was explicit in saying that Stalin's role in the conflict was "harmful." Khrushchev allowed himself to depart from the official text of the speech to recall a meeting with Stalin at which the latter had said: "I'd just have to move my little finger to eliminate Tito."

Thus, Khrushchev achieved several objectives in his speech: he demonstrated the false greatness of the leader who was neither competent, wise or incisive. The speaker was unequivocal when he said that Stalin was guilty of terror, crimes and abuses of power. He denounced the leader's absolute power which had resulted in many extremely grave consequences for the party and the people. It was an explosion of public awareness, a courageous and unexpected offensive against Caesarism, lawlessness and totalitarian rule.

What do you think were the consequences of the fact that this speech, a most important political document, has been classified until now?

Khrushchev himself was a product of his time, as we all are for that matter. It is not everyone who succeeds in breaking free of his time and living up to the future. I have mentioned Khrushchev's peasant wisdom. But the main thing—the civic courage of the man—remains beyond question. He did commit many mistakes, but they can be pardoned because of his speech at the congress. But Khrushchev and his entourage were products of the system. After the speech he sensed that further progress in tracing the causes and genesis of Stalinism was dangerous. And he was incapable of going further, or perhaps, he had not intended to.

Khrushchev's speech was an indictment rather than an analysis. Exposure is only the initial stage. The First Secretary again attacked Stalinism at the 22nd Party Congress. And what did all this boil down to? Just emotion. Neither Khrushchev nor his entourage were strong enough to carry out an in-depth theoretical analysis.

I believe we could have freed ourselves from Stalinism earlier. I firmly believe that had Khrushchev remained in office, had he not stopped, had he gone further, he would have been able to do it. But many of his entourage opposed—let us not be intimidated by the phrase—revolutionary changes. What was the situation like then? Stalinism could not be revived. That was simply impossible.

The personality cult was not exposed completely, primarily because bureaucracy, and dogmatism and violence—the pillars of the system Stalin had created—were too deeply rooted. Stalin could not do without dogmatism, and neither could the system. It was impossible to mummify Marxism without dogmatism. The people who were with Khrushchev were born of the Stalinist bureaucracy, too. They believed that the world would be ruined without moral, social and economic coercion. They wouldn't of course resort to such barbaric excesses as terror, atrocities, and concentration camps. But they cherished their system as they did their right hands. Eventually, Khrushchev had to retire "for reasons of health." Brezhnev and his team didn't give a fig for the struggle against Stalinism, since they too were born of that very system.

As for the consequences . . . I'll just attempt to give an outline of them, for today they are commonly known. Officially, we were trying to forget about both Stalin and Stalinism. The bureaucratic system again felt secure. We didn't have a single "drawback" in any sphere of life. We were always right. Nothing but pleasant words came from the rostra . . . The list is quite lengthy, but let us confine ourselves to a single lucid phrase: the Great Stagnation.

The action taken at the 20th Congress had no logical sequel. We know what came afterwards. Isn't this a lesson for all of us even in the time of perestroika?

We need a thorough and profound analysis of this phenomenon. You can't tell half the truth. We still ration the truth as if squeezing it out of a tube—a spoonful a day. We ration the truth as if we were scared of it. People must know the whole truth. No articles, no gossip will exorcise Stalin completely until we speak the whole truth, until we prove that we are capable of performing better, of living better, of doing away with crime, favouritism and corruption, that we can have a state subject to the rule of law. The main way of exorcising Stalinism is in practical action for the benefit of the people.

The truth can be classified for years or decades. But eventually it becomes known. Publishing the secret speech in the *Izvestiya TsK KPSS* is a very important step. True, this document has little new to tell us, because we have learned much in recent years, albeit after a long delay. I think this political step, very important in our times too, should have been taken thirty years ago. But still, it is good that it has been taken. It is a manifestation of renewal.

I, for one, believe that democracy can only realize its potential when it is accompanied by respect for law, order and discipline.

And—on the other hand—political and moral values. We still lack these concomitants of democracy. In a number of instances this lack is manifested quite simply in the distortion of the truth, the search for sensation, isolating negative (or positive) developments from the overall historical context. History does not admit of any blank pages. But we are only starting to learn to tell the whole truth. The publication of the secret speech is an important lesson in the school of democracy and glasnost. Let us hope that we will do our homework. We must remember that, in the final analysis, the truth is independent.

KULAKS

Peasant Archives: Expropriation
Letters to the editor of *Selskaya Zhizn*, February 16, 1989

"At present, our policy is to liquidate the kulaks as a class, a policy compared to which extraordinary measures against the kulaks are nothing—and nothing much has happened."

(I. Stalin, Closing Remarks at the 16th VKP(b) Congress, July 1930)

As early as 1928 the Peyve family was liquidated as kulaks and exiled. Voldemar Karlovich, the head of the household, was exiled to the Urals and perished somewhere. By the way, he is the father of two scientists—Academy members Yan Voldemarovich and Aleksandr Voldemarovich Peyve, who are now dead as well.

Three or four families of poor peasants from nearby villages moved into the Peyve house. They appropriated all property, cattle and land. I cannot say exactly what they called themselves—a collective farm or a commune. A fanatical, almost illiterate woman emigre from Latvia was their leader. Over 1 year of joint "work", they slaughtered and ate the cattle, and harvested nothing because they did not want to work and did not know how. After all, they had had their own parcels of land before which were neglected and abandoned. Having faced a situation with no way out, they made the following decision: they will live comfortably if they take over the property and cattle of other "kulaks . . ."

At the time, a lot depended on the local authorities, "the poor." They went around the homes as robbers and took away everything in sight. I remember very well how they descended on us at night, when the men were not home. They confiscated whatever they found appealing, loaded it on a cart and hauled it away. Soon all "kulaks" were moved into the houses of "the poor," and they were moved into our homes. Our exiled families were doomed to starve . . .

My father, my uncles or other inhabitants of Sementsevo were not and could not be kulaks. My uncles actively participated in the revolution and the civil war. One of them, Avgust Petrovich Berzin, took part in the Petrograd uprising, was for a while one of Lenin's bodyguard's, and then at the front until the end of the civil war. Another uncle, Adolf Petrovich Berzin, also fought at the front from the beginning to the end of the civil war. Two other uncles died in that war.

Before the revolution, my family of expatriates from Latvia, landless peasants, wandered with their children across Russia, worked as farm hands and had nothing. Having returned from the civil war and obtained land, my father and his two brothers built a house and acquired some property together. All seven families in the village of Sementsevo joined a cooperative which was called the TOZ [Association for Joint Cultivation of Land]. Five years later, all of them suddenly turned out to be "kulak" families! The riches of my father and uncles consisted of two horses, two cows and small cattle—among their three large families. Our clothes were exclusively home-spun. What kind of kulaks were we?
                —A. E. Berzin, Toropets Rayon, Kalinin Oblast

The Skorokhod family lived next to us. The father Aleksandr Skorokhod came back from the civil war having lost vision in both eyes. He had a parcel of land, 8 dessiatinas, a couple of horses . . . I remember three carts driving up to the Skorokhod place with a red banner on the first one. The banner said: "Liquidate the kulaks as a class." Within 3 hours, they took from the house and loaded on the carts bed linens, clothing, footwear, a pig, a cow, horses, grain in sacks. The blind Aleksandr Skorokhod was carried out on a piece of cloth and slammed hard against the road surface. Then the mistress of the house came out. She was leading by the hand their son Fedya, and in the other hand she carried a small bundle. She helped her husband up, beat the dust off him, the son took him by the hand, and then they set out toward the railway station.

They came to my father many times, threatening that he had supposedly been placed on the kulak list and that they would come to expropriate him the next day. However, all of them activists liked vodka very much. The father bent over backwards to offer them a treat, and—get this—he survived.
—I.P. Palamarchuk, Dobrovelichkovo Rayon, Kirovograd Oblast

A commissar from the oblast party committee, Andrushchenko, was sent to our village (we lived in Kiev Oblast). The rumor had it that this Andrushchenko was the son of a landowner who had stolen himself into the party and was operating under an assumed name. Andrushchenko would gather the village aktiv in the evening and would tell them: "I want the dogs to bark tonight, I want the roosters to crow, the windows to ring, and feathers to fly from the pillows. Ten, 12 or 15 kulak families should be tossed out of their homes, stoves should be broken and windows smashed." Teams of activists would go to their assigned areas, down and feathers would fly, and naked and barefoot people with small children would be thrown out into the winter cold and snow in whatever they had on.

Kulak expropriations were carried out as follows: fixed quotas are set—on a given date, 50, 80 or 100 poods of grain are to be delivered. A person delivers it, and thinks this is all. They set another quota for him, twice as large. The ones who were doing better would meet even two or three such quotas, they would buy grain and meet them. Those who would not were classified as kulaks.

I remember cases like this. A team of activists would drink moonshine and eat lard confiscated from the kulaks, and would summon [people] to the headquarters (every street had headquarters like that). **I remember how they made a 78-year-old man in canvas pants dance to their balalaika with a board 5 centimeters thick and 2 meters long on his outstretched hands. Also, they made him shout: "I malevolently failed to meet my grain quota!"** He danced until he fell down and fainted. Another case. A barefoot woman wearing only a blouse was taken out of the village in winter, given a whip and told: "Since you are not delivering grain, you will drive around the wind in the field." They would prevent the neighbors to take in those thrown into the street by threatening to toss the neighbors out, too.

In 1929, people were herded into comprehensive collectivization without applying [to join collective farms]. They confiscated horses and implements from every farm yard. Later, I do not remember which month it was, they announced that collective farms are to be disbanded as a result of Stalin's dizziness due to successes. People were lucky to take their cattle and implements to their own yard, but they again began forcing people to write applications. Many resisted joining the collective farm. They were also branded kulaks, and some of them kulak advocates. Their homes were destroyed, their land with crops on it was taken over by collective farms, and people began to die off to a man.

—T.M. Rikhtik, Sokuluz Rayon, Kirghiz SSR

As a member of the Komsomol, I was told to escort kulak Bochkarev. The militia could not do anything, could not send him off in any manner. The populace would turn out, stand in the way and say that he was not the kind of man to be exiled.

I came in the morning, around 8 o'clock. He and his farm hands were already up. I told him to take everything he needed, go to the city of Chistopol and live there. The man was not good-looking, but his wife and daughter were. He offered me to marry his daughter, and promised me mountains of gold. I told him that as a member of the Komsomol I was not allowed to marry the daughter of a kulak. He asked me to spend the night with her, but I did not agree.

Bochkarev sold the cattle overnight, smashed the machinery, and put 400 beehives out into the cold—the bees perished. He set out on 10 carts with his gear. Mounted militia men waited for him where the road forks and surrounded him. He wanted to turn toward the station of Nurlaty, and not toward Chistopol as the arrangement called for. They were arrested and sent to the Chistopol Prison. I did not know that this would be done to them . . .

—S. S. Ilyin, Yaroslavl

The farmers who were better off resisted collective farm construction, they always harmed collective farmers, set fire to their houses, poisoned their horses, smashed the implements and shot activists and party functionaries from sawed-off guns. In our hamlet, Litvinov, Dubynka and their sons committed particularly bad atrocities. Litvinov had his own mill, a lot of land and cattle. Dubynka also lived very affluently, and so they held sway. It came to the point when citizens of the hamlet asked to have them removed, because living in the hamlet had become unbearable. Along with them, there were also kulak advocates. This was the case not only in our hamlet of Malokorovka; affluent Cossacks were committing atrocities all over Kuban. I survived this horrible time, I saw collective farmers being killed for nothing or having dogs set on them, I saw their torched property. I recognize that it was a very proper decision by the government to exile them to Siberia and the Solovki [Islands].

At present, they say in the press that Stalin killed many innocent people. It seems to me that they who complain about Stalin were exiled for atrocities against the pioneers of collective farm construction. Now they are raising their voices. On top of everything, they are about to have a monument erected to their honor as Stalin's victims. Why doesn't somebody recall the people who were felled by the sawed-off guns of the kulaks? What kind of logic is that?

—I. I. Solovyev, Krasnodar Kray

After graduating from an agricultural vocational school I worked as an agronomist in Airtav Rayon, Karaganda Oblast. There was a lot of land in Northern Kazakhstan, and the parcels were large. Anybody who wanted to get rich could do it easily. Certainly, those who drank to excess and spent nights playing cards lived in poverty. There were not too many of them, but they made the most noise at village meetings. One could not notice class struggle in the political sense of the word. Something else was apparent—jealousy. They envied those who spent their nights in the field and lived comfortably. The poor called the wealthy filthy rich, and the wealthy called the poor beggars and card buffs. Party functionaries and even the GPU [Main Political Directorate] mistook such discord for class struggle.

I was a witness to the following: a meeting of the executive board of the rural soviet was underway in the village of Krivinka. The secretary of the Komsomol chapter left at the very beginning of the meeting. Toward the end of the meeting (about 11 o'clock, at night), he rushed into the hall shouting: "Kulaks have shot me!" There was blood on his cheek. Those in the hall immediately noticed that this was a simple cut rather than a gunshot wound. However, this sufficed for a call to the militia, and in the morning all persons deprived of legal rights were arrested and hauled away. About 5 years later, this communist youth organizer let on when drunk that he fired the sawed-off gun himself and scratched his cheek himself.

—A.A. Kolyada, settlement of Chertkovo, Rostov Oblast

*   *   *

I think that in our village it was possible not to put anybody through kulak expropriation because the seven farms which they did expropriate were the most diligent in the village. They did not use hired labor, and their own families were mostly large—between 6 and 11 persons. Their farms were well-managed, their houses were kept up well, their cattle and implements were in good condition, and their land was fertilized. In return for their hard, well-organized labor they got good harvests, milk and meat. They lived well, and this is why people were jealous.

I would say that slackers were the ones to decide who was to be expropriated. I remember that there were "farmers" at the time who only drank and played cards, and were not capable of getting hay for their cows or horses. They were given the right to rule on the fate of hard workers.

—A. A. Zashikhin, Vologda Oblast

My father was branded the enemy of the people just for saying: you are not leading us the way that Lenin mapped out.

From the day they took father away to this day we have not learned anything about him. Our mother as the wife of a traitor was also locked up in the basement, and the four of us were left, as they say, with nothing. The stove on which the four of us, underage children, were sitting was all raked up; they looked into our pots. In a mold, they found some cereal, and took even that away. I remember my mother crying and wringing her hands, asking them to spare the children. No chance, the order was not to give anybody an easy time. When they let mother out of the basement, they told her immediately: vacate the house, this is a kulak home and should be vacant in 24 hours. We were tossed out right into the street, into the cold. The neighbors took me, the youngest one, in, and then so did my uncle who brought me up. The older children started to beg in order not to starve.

At the time, they would not give mother any work. She went around and asked to be given something to do, because the children had to be fed. This is how we lived in other people's places until the year 1937, when things became somewhat normal and mother was hired by the collective farm as a pig-tender. She got commendations for outstanding work, and was even supposed to go to Moscow. However, she did not go to Moscow but instead passed a petition to, it seems to me, either Petrovskiy of Khatayevich asking that our house be returned. One day they called us to the village soviet and announced that they had a permission to return to us our yard. However, since schoolteachers lived there, they gave us instead an old open house where they kept sheep in the winter. I remember very well how much effort we had to invest into it. Nonetheless, we were very happy. We were going to have our own house!

—P. I. Yatsenko, Krivoy Rog

In 1930, our father was arrested, and a brigade cleaned our house of grain thoroughly. Four months later, a cart pulled up at night together with escorts, and we were told to get our gear quietly, taking along 20 kilograms of flour, an ax and a saw. My mother, myself, my brother Fedya, my sister and one other family were loaded up and taken to the station of Papelyukhi where they put us in freight cars. At night, they brought in our father as well. They closed the car, gave us a bucket for relieving ourselves, and put guards on the platform. The entire train of expropriated kulaks went God knows where. I would not know about other kulaks, but my father had on his farm a cow, two horses, five sheep, a hog, plus the seeding machine he bought. This is what he was expropriated for. . . .

They took as as far as Perm. There was a sea of humanity there, people like us—Ukrainians, Belorussians, Moldavians. . . . People shouted and wept as they were loaded onto barges and tow steamships and taken up the river Kama. I remember that those who died were tossed overboard. Our sister died, she was 2 years old. . . .

They took us to Komi-Permyak Okrug, and drove us 15 kilometers into the woods. We were told: that's your place, cut down the trees and build dugouts for yourselves. People, the old and the very young, began to get typhoid fever and die. We made mortars and crushed bark and hay in order to mix them into the flour. Many people died then, but there were guards around the place, and you could not run away. Carts drove through the settlement and collected the dead. They loaded 10 or 15 corpses, took them to the pit and dumped them whichever way they fell, worse than you would dogs. My mother and father also ended up in this pit. As far as I am concerned, I wandered a lot, survived the war, was wounded. At the time, the instruction was not to enlist children of kulaks in the army, but we did not admit that we were from an expropriated family. Many of us gave their lives for the Motherland.

—I. Ye. Karpenko, Kamenskoye Rayon, Moldavian SSR

* * *

In the course of kulak expropriation in 1930 through 1932 alone about 1 million farms were taken over, and their owners together with their families were exiled to Siberia, Kazakhstan, the North or the Urals or resettled within the confines of their krays and oblasts of residence. There are no data on the number of victims of the expropriation. According to some calculations, between 6 and 10 million people were subjected to repressions.

LAW

Pravda Round-Table Discussion in the USSR Academy of Sciences' Institute of State and Law: A state based on the rule of law—what should it be like?
by G. Ovcharenko, *Pravda*, August 31, 1988

EDITORS' NOTE.—The resolutions of the 19th All-Union Party Conference and the resolution of the recent plenary session of the CPSU Central Committee call the formation of a socialist state based on the rule of law a task of fundamental importance. Accomplishing this task means creating constitutional guarantees of the irreversibility of restructuring, establishing in our society the supremacy and triumph of law that expresses the people's will, strengthening the protection of the rights, interests and liberties of every person, and shifting the actions of state and Party agencies, public organizations and labor collectives to a strictly legal basis.

This was the subject of a *Pravda* round-table discussion in the USSR Academy of Sciences' Institute of State and Law. The following persons participated in the conversation: V. N. Kudryavtsev, member of the USSR Academy of Sciences; Prof. S. N. Bratus, Doctor of Jurisprudence (of the All-Union Soviet Legislation Research Institute); V. D. Zorkin (of the USSR Ministry of Internal Affairs' Academy); and V. Ye. Guliyev, V. P. Kazimirchuk, V. M. Savitsky and V. A. Tumanov (of the USSR Academy of Sciences' Institute of State and Law).

CORRESPONDENT: Many *Pravda* readers note that our Party has proclaimed the formation of a socialist state based on the rule of law as a practical task for the first time. In letters, some people even ask: Doesn't this mean that up to now we have lived in a state not based on the rule of law?

V. GULIYEV: To put the question that way would not be quite correct. We certainly have had laws. But there has also been lawlessness. Suffice it to recall the years of the personality cult and stagnation. And there are plenty of violations of the law in our time as well. . . .

CORRESPONDENT: To start off, let us try to define what a socialist state based on the rule of law is. . . .

V. KUDRYAVTSEV: In the final analysis, a state based on the rule of law can only be defined as a state characterized by mutual—I emphasize: mutual—responsibility on the part of the state and of all those (citizens and their organizations and associations) who enter into mutual relations that are regulated by law. In other words, whereas today it is basically administrative agencies that can bring claims against citizens and their organizations, in a state based on the rule of law each one of us, or our institute, enterprise or collective farm, may bring claims against the state and its administrative agencies if they do not fulfill their commitments. Incidentally, the Law on the State Enterprise provides for such a situation.

V. GUILYEV: Constructing such a state is no easy matter. We must not forget that the bourgeois "rule of law" (with all its pluses and minuses) was shaped over the centuries. History has not allotted us such a long time. We have to create a state based on the rule of law within the next few years, evidently.

Let's be frank: As yet, there is no firm legality, no stable law and order, in the country. . . .

V. TUMANOV: No, the situation is changing, and it has changed rapidly in the past three years. I disagree with those who say that we have nothing that is needed for a state based on the rule of law and that we must begin everything from scratch. The measures adopted following the 20th Party Congress marked a qualitative break with the lawlessness of Stalinism and played their role. The decisions of the 22nd Congress were also prepared on a wave of democratization, but that wave broke against the dike of stagnation. Stagnation struck a blow of enormous force against legality, in particular because the Party apparatus, and then the leaders of the administrative-managerial apparatus, proved to be outside any control, including legal control.

V. KAZIMIRCHUK: We often and customarily say that our laws reflect the will of the people. But what does this mean? Up to now, it has meant either departmental interests or interest groups, which in no way can be called the people. Even a number of recent laws that affect the interests of the people as a whole were not submitted for nationwide discussion but were adopted by the apparatus. As a result, an unprecedented incident took place at a session of the Supreme Soviet, one in which Deputies vigourously criticized certain provisions of the draft Law on Appealing to the Courts Illegal Actions by Officials. However— here's the inertia of stagnation for you!—it was adopted all the same, and later it was put into final form—once again, by the apparatus. Or take the Law on Individual Enterprise—it, too, is a mass of imperfections.

V. TUMANOV: It seems to me that this antidemocratic trend in drawing up and adopting laws is a consequence of a concept that is current in scholarly circles: A law must not be filled with details or turned into a set of official instructions. Life itself, it is argued, will fill in the details. But the details have been filled in not by life but by the departments, as they employ a multitude of legally binding acts to nullify the very idea of the law and make it inoperative. The upshot is that instructions are replacing the law. . . . Take the recently adopted Law on the State Enterprise. In a matter of months, the ministries and departments have so hedged it round with instructions that economic managers unanimously maintain: The law is not working! . . .

S. BRATUS: It is necessary to return legality to norm-setting activity. To this end, we must clearly define the jurisdiction of the higher-level bodies of power, so that they operate on the basis of the laws adopted by sessions of the Supreme Soviet. This is not the case at present. For example, a law is adopted, but the Council of Ministers promptly issues acts at variance with it.

V. GULIYEV: I sometimes get the impression that the Council of Ministers is a supralegal body altogether. For example, why has it arrogated to itself the right to move around holidays and nonworking days, which are established by law? In my view, an entire system of circumventing the law was worked out in our country in the past. It is expressed in the fact that the government delegates its norm-setting powers to the ministries and departments. . . .

CORRESPONDENT: So what, specifically, must be done to ensure that the laws that are adopted meet what might be called the highest standards, to erect a barrier to departmental instructions, and to democratize the very procedure of lawmaking?

V. SAVITSKY: First of all, the most important draft laws must be submitted for nationwide discussion and debated extensively at sessions of the Supreme Soviet, and we must not be afraid to set aside a draft law for further work.

V. KAZIMIRCHUK: It is necessary to organize a council of experts or a scholarly-consultation agency under the Presidium of the USSR Supreme Soviet, a body consisting of qualified legal experts. They would come up with conclusions on the suitability of a draft from a juridical viewpoint, reconcile it with other drafts, and so forth. After all, it sometimes happens that drafts contradict one another, as was the case with the laws on unearned income and on individual enterprise, and as a result citizens' rights and freedoms suffer.

CORRESPONDENT: The Party conference's resolutions cite, among the important tasks of restructuring, enhancing the role of the courts in the system of socialist democracy. What does this mean?

V. TUMANOV: Above all, in my view, it means expanding the sphere of the judicial protection of citizens' rights and legitimate interests. Take, for example, the setting of pensions. . . . If a citizen considers himself aggrieved and thinks his pension was set unfairly, he should have the right to go to court. After all, this is the only way such a situation can be appraised fairly. So far, alas, this right, as well as rights involving a great many other questions, is lacking in our country.

S. BRATUS: I agree. The courts should be the main instrument of exercising legality, not just in the sphere of property and personal relations but also in all other social and economic spheres. **Only a judicial decision based on the independence of the courts can ensure genuine legality in all relations. But for this to be the case, a radical reorganization of the courts is needed. . . .**

V. SAVITSKY: . . . The hallmark of a state based on the rule of law is its accountability to its citizens. Unfortunately, for a long time this principle has remained in oblivion, and it is still there. Here is one striking example. Virtually every Soviet citizen pays out of his own pocket a tax for the maintenance of the state apparatus, including the law-enforcement agencies, so that they can protect his person and his property from lawbreakers, especially criminals. Unfortunately, this is not always how it works out—the crime rate is still high. How should the state act with respect to a citizen whose safety it has been unable to ensure? In my view, it should first of all compensate this person for his property losses, and then look for the criminal and reimburse the treasury at his expense. At present, alas, this is done only with respect to those required to pay child support. Why not extend this principle to instances in which, let's say, an apartment has been burglarized or a car stolen? . . .

CORRESPONDENT: I would like to hear an answer to a question that, judging from the editors' mail, troubles many readers. How should the principle set forth in Party documents—everything not forbidden by law is permitted—be understood and applied in practice?

V. TUMANOV: In this formula, I would like to direct special attention to the word "law." It is absolutely necessary that in this context law be understood in the strictly constitutional meaning of the concept, that is, exclusively as an act adopted by the supreme body of state power. If, on the other hand—as frequently happens in everyday life and in the press—the word "law" is taken as meaning any normative act, then, as a result of the orgy of prohibitions that characterizes departmental and local norm-setting today, the formula you have cited will lose any real significance.

V. KUDRYAVTSEV: The trouble is that if this formula is extended to all administrative bodies, institutions and officials in general, the result would be high-handed behavior: Any of them would do whatever is "not forbidden" with respect to subordinates—for example, a ministry with respect to the enterprises under it. Strictly speaking, therefore, the formula should extend only to citizens and economic organizations in industry and agriculture. As far as administrative agencies and officials are concerned, they have their jurisdiction, the bounds of which they have no right to transcend.

CORRESPONDENT: In real life, however, we see that this legal principle governing the activity of administrative agencies, Party and Soviet agencies and officials is quite often violated. How can this be prevented?

V. SAVITSKY: A state based on the rule of law is founded on the principle of the precise separation of jurisdiction into the legislative, executive and judicial spheres. In our country, there are no clear-cut boundaries in this respect as yet. Often legislative authorities unceremoniously meddle in judicial activity. For example, when the USSR Prosecutor General asks the Presidium of the Supreme Soviet for authorization to extend the term for which an accused person may be held in custody (the law does not provide for this). As a rule, he receives permission. Apparently, the resolution of this question should fall within the jurisdiction of the courts. The principle of the separation of functions in a state based on the rule of law must be observed religiously; otherwise, any real possibility of protecting citizens' rights and interests will disappear. . . .

CORRESPONDENT: . . . The Party conference and the plenary session of the CPSU Central Committee posed the task of universal legal education. How is it being accomplished?

V. ZORKIN: This question is very important. **We must teach every citizen to fight for his rights. But how can we do this when there is not enough legal literature even for specialists?** There is a serious deficiency here. Obviously, the time has come—as has been said many times from various rostrums and in the press—to create a legal newspaper. The main thing here is that it should meet the interests not of the law-enforcement departments but of the people. . . .

V. GULIYEV: Universal legal education will become a reality if there is universal political education in the spirit of democracy. Specifically, everyone—and first of all the representatives of authority—must recognize that the Party, the state, the trade unions, etc., are no more than institutions subordinate to society and are in no way entities having command over it. Without this, "purely legal" universal education will be only a juridical apology for antidemocratism. . . .

V. Lenin

Political Leadership and the Struggle for Power Under Socialism
by Anatoliy Butenko, *Moscow News*, February 18, 1988

ANATOLIY BUTENKO is a professor at Moscow University.

Lenin passed away when the ruling Bolshevik Party, having encountered for the first time the problem of a change of a leader, and change of its leadership, had no mechanism for this:

the leading role of Lenin himself was ensured mainly thanks to his high prestige. Envisaging the dangers and risks due to the imperfection of structures, Lenin in the last month of his life did much and wrote a whole number of works aimed at extending the powers of the Party's Central Committee, strengthening its collective leadership, increasing control over the administrative-state apparatus and, the main thing, he wrote his famous letter-testament in which he proposed that the party consider the question of relieving Joseph Stalin from the post of general secretary.

Without Lenin

Lenin's death posed this question: would the ruling Bolshevik Party—the only party in the first country of socialism—be able to retain its role of collective leader, a recognized authoritative leader of the working people building socialism? Not everyone gave an identical answer to this question. Joseph Stalin and Lev Trotskiy were the main contenders for the top post. In the course of their vying for power there started well-concealed processes of modifying the role of state-party positions and the significance of various posts in the state and party apparatus, and also changing the entire atmosphere of personal relations in the nation's leadership. The Leninist spirit of comradely coopera-tion began to be ousted by the official-administrative and bu-reaucratic one, whereas Lenin's idea of separating the party from the state-administrative apparatus with a view to establishing control over it and retarding bureaucratization was pushed back by Stalin's new cadre policy aimed at creating a single party-state apparatus from among those who were personally devoted to him.

Lenin's letter-testament could have ruined Stalin's ambitious plans which were dangerous for the party. With some effort Stalin managed to prevent the letter being discussed at the congress. As a result of which the congress, I believe, committed a fundamental error: it did not heed Lenin's recommendation and kept the post of general secretary for Stalin.

History is yet to establish the price the party, Soviet power and the Soviet people had to pay for Stalin's realization of his ambitious scheme. Relying on the cadre selected by him and creating an administrative-bureaucratic pyramid, he secured un-questionable one-man rule. He began to seem to people, even to Communists, to be, if not a god, then at any rate the fourth classic of Marxism-Leninism.

Bureaucracy's Sinister Role

The anti-Leninist turn in the development of Soviet society's political system culminated in the assassination of Sergey Kirov. The 17th Congress counted on Kirov, against whom a mere three votes were cast, whereas a hundred times more votes were cast against Stalin. On Stalin's insistence the results of the voting were rigged, and the truth was concealed from the party. Kirov's assassination was used as a convenient pretext for launching veritable terror after the "Congress of Victors" (roughly a half of its delegates were subjected to repressive measures) and for unleashing the mass repressions of 1937-1938. These tragic developments marked not merely the completion of the affirmation of Stalin's personality cult, but a decisive victory for Stalin's party-state bureaucracy over Lenin's guard and its policy.

Those who were involved in the lawless practices were trying to depersonify responsibility, to shift it onto Soviet power and onto the working class said to be exercising its rule at the time. That can never be accepted. Responsibility for what happened devolves on those who pushed the working class aside and usurped its power. Nobody is going to pardon these Stalin-led usurpers for what they did. "We must never forgive or justify what happened in 1937 and 1938. Never. It is those who were in office at the time that are to blame for it," Mikhail Gorbachev has said.

The decisions of the 20th CPSU Congress were not someone's personal affair, but a line achieved by our party through much suffering. Therefore Soviet social scientists, especially the historians of the CPSU, are yet to make an in-depth study and give a scientific answer to the question: who shelved, if not reduced to nought, many of the changes directly proceeding from the resolutions of the 20th CPSU Congress and how, by what ways and means, by relying on what social forces, and for what purpose?

They are to sort out the role the bureaucracy played in the decades-long continuity of structures despite the changes of the leaders.

It is not accidental that perestroyka concentrates its efforts on the command-administrative principles in the life of the society. The bureaucracy must be inflicted a crushing defeat through glasnost and democracy and this success must be consolidated through the development of the working people's self-government.

Strictly According to Conscience. From the Discussion Mailbag: Addressed to the 19th All-Union Party Conference

Letter to the editor of *Pravda*, March 18, 1988

V.I. Lenin referred to the Central Control Commission (TsKK) as the party and proletarian conscience.

Young and not-so-young Communists today are either not aware or do not see a substantial difference between the former— that is, Lenin's TsKK—and the CPSU Central Committee Party Control Committee in its present form, regarding them as identical control organs. Meanwhile, they differ from each other very significantly.

The TsKK, just like the Central Committee, was the supreme organ of the party, but only with monitoring functions. **Just like the Central Committee, it was elected by congress and was accountable only to congress. In other words, in our party there was a separation of power between the Central Committee and the TsKK. The Central Committee had executive functions, while the TsKK was entrusted with monitoring functions.**

After V.I. Lenin's death, the TsKK did not survive long. It was abolished on a proposal from I.V. Stalin. To begin with, at the 17th party congress in 1934, it was transformed into the Party Control Commission under the All-Union Communist Party (Bolsheviks) Central Committee, and from the next, the 18th congress, it was no longer elected by the congress but organized by the Central Committee. Did any of the delegates at the time understand Stalin's design and the tragic consequences this decision was to have? Our present political experience gives us every justification to claim that this was a fatal political mistake which cost the party, the state, and the people dear. The Stalin cult in its ugliest and most criminal form—the totally unfounded repressions— began precisely with the abolition of the TsKK which, according to Lenin's concept, was to ensure "irrespective of personalities" that no one's authority, be he the gensek or any other member of the Central Committee, could stand in the way of . . . unconditional access to information and ensure that everything was strictly aboveboard. To ensure that no one could stand in the way—but the TsKK stood in Stalin's way, and very much so. It was the most serious obstacle in the path of the establishment of unlimited personal power. So Stalin thought up a monitoring organ for the party which would not monitor him but be subordinate to the Central Committee, and thus to him himself as gensek.

Many violations of the Leninist norms of state and party life date back to the abolition of the TsKK.

What most concerns the party and nonparty masses at present is ensuring that restructuring becomes irreversible. People have not quite forgotten the brief "thaws" of the fifties and sixties. And they expect guarantees. Glasnost, democracy, and the people's activeness are such guarantees, of course. However, glasnost and democracy, restructuring and the activeness of the masses themselves need guarantees.

But what kind of new organizational structure of party democracy will have to be invented in order to guarantee the irreversibility of the present revolutionary transformations? There is no need to invent anything. The organ which would guarantee this existed under Lenin and Leninism. It is the TsKK. It is as if Ilich had forseen our difficulties and troubles in their future concrete form. Not just Lenin's thoughts, even his words on this theme are most topical. Here they are: ". . . under such conditions, we have the best possible guarantee that has been conceived to date, a guarantee that the party will create a small central collegium which will be able to counter effectively all local influences and all other bureaucracy and establish a truly uniform application of the rule of law throughout the republic and throughout the whole federation".

Some 15 years ago, in the presence of a learned man, I somehow expressed aloud my dreams about the restoration of the TsKK. To be honest, I wanted to talk to him about my dreams since he lectured on party building. But what he told me was not in the least what I had expected to hear:

"That is absolutely impossible. It would mean a dyarchy in the party. . . ."

I then reminded him of Lenin's words uttered in a similar context in his article "How We Sould Reorganize the Rabkrin [Workers' and Peasants' Inspectorate]": "I foresee one objection coming directly or indirectly from those circles which make our apparatus old. . . . The objection consists of the claim that the transformation I am proposing will lead to complete chaos. Members of the TsKK will tour various establishments . . . , introducing disorganization everywhere. . . . I believe that the malicious origin of this objection is so obvious that it does not even require an answer."

Lenin's remark that the party represents the intelligence, the honor, and the conscience of our age is well known. In this aphoristic "psychological" portrait of the party, there is one interesting detail. It appears that Ilich attributed the most moral aspect of the party's qualities—its conscience—to the TsKK. In the Politburo draft resolution on the need to publish "a very detailed and solemn" statement in the press about the establishment of the Control Commission, he said outright that he deems it essential "to turn it into a true organ of party and proletarian conscience." Precisely an organ of conscience!

The hope V.I. Lenin was pinning on the TsKK was brilliantly simple. The most able and honest leaders of the party are not insured against falling prey to "purely personal or fortuitous circumstances." The existence of a "party and proletarian conscience" in the shape of the TsKK was to "provide the maximum safeguard" against possible mistakes and abuse of power.

With the abolition of the TsKK, Lenin's definition of the party was deprived of its last word which expresses the most moral of its qualities. The thought keeps coming back that precisely the abolition of the "party and proletarian conscience" led to the beginning of the personality cult, the unjustified repressions, and the numerous distortions of recent decades. Yet we, party members, asked each other sometimes when the moral need for this arises: "Do you have a party conscience, comrade?"

In short, I believe that what we need is the TsKK. I believe that it is necessary in the interests of the cause.

However, it cannot be revived without introducing the corresponding changes in the CPSU Statutes. Waiting for the next 28th CPSU Congress in . . . 1991 is a luxury we cannot afford! History has not allowed us time to drag our feet. In this situation I see only one solution, namely to discuss this important question.

—I. Sokolov, CPSU member since 1946, Novosibirsk

Excerpts from Speeches at Soviet Communist Party Meeting April 28, 1989 (Moscow)

Ratmir S. Bobovikov

Party chief of the Vladimir region; candidate member of the Central Committee

The atmosphere of democratization and glasnost, freedom of expression of one's will, is used by some people to undermine from inside the positive processes that are going on in the country and to impose controversial points of view.

* * *

Sometimes we come across irresponsibility in the choice of topics to be discussed on TV. . . . It also caused me great indignation when, on the birthday of Lenin, Mark Aleksandrovich Zakharov suddenly talked about removing Lenin from the mausoleum and whether or not to inter him in the earth, as if this were a private enterprise and not a state-run television. Lingering over such issues is simply immoral. Literally in the morning people were phoning party committees and asking in bewilderment how it was possible to understand this?

Whose opinion is this? They also asked us why, for example, responsible officials, secretaries of the Central Committee, in particular comrades Yakovlev and Medvedev, who in the Politburo are responsible for ideology, do not personally participate in open discussions at rallies and don't rebuff our ideological foes? And they would not have to go far. Everyone knows that in Moscow, there's no shortage of rallies.

The elated tone of the articles in our press about how bourgeois leaders praise perestroika also causes natural questions in people. Because they remember well Lenin's testament: think carefully any time your class enemy praises you.

Valery T. Saikin

Mayor of Moscow, member of the Central Committee

It is strange, but many have accepted democratization as all-permissiveness, as a delegated right to ignore our legal and moral norms.

Strange, but pluralism of opinion has been taken by many as a legal and open opportunity for wholesale disparaging of all socialist values, all achievements of socialism, of everything associated with the Communist Party. It should be said that a massive attack at the hearts and souls of people has been launched in this direction.

Strange, but under the guise of the priority of the universal values, mindless imitation is taking place—imitating on our socialist ground, in our socialist reality, everything that is considered novel, for the single reason that this novelty is borrowed from across our western or eastern borders.

Strange, but today when we are are building a law-ruled state, we are more concerned about humane treatment of criminals. . . .

Aleksei P. Myasnikov

Miner from Irkutsk, Central Committee member

The time has come to thoroughly analyze and assess the informal organizations that have political tones. Sometimes the activity of their leaders takes the form of attacks on soviet power and the party. Unbridled criticism aimed at discrediting the party and state bodies and social demagogy sponging on the healthy processes of democratization and glasnost damage the cause of perestroika. . . .

Our democracy, which is gaining force, needs reliable legal protection, protection from both open and hidden enemies of perestroika, from different anti-Soviet and anti-socialist elements.

The decree on state crimes might have a positive effect in this regard, though it was adopted belatedly. It is time to define our position on such new phenomena in our social experience as strikes. In many cases they take place as a result of administration ignoring the just demands of the workers, arbitrary rule by management. However, sometimes they are used as a means of pressure on administration to reach selfish group goals.

*   *   *

Comrades, a lot has been heard under current democracy and pluralism, but what was said on "Vzglyad" about the most sacred thing—about Lenin—is worse than incomprehensible. I do not and do not want to understand such pluralism. And I would like to ask those who speak about this: don't you live on the same soil where Soviet power was gained by the blood of our fathers and grandfathers?

LITHUANIA

Lithuanian Democratic Party Members Interviewed
by Virgilijus Liauska, January 26, 1989

VILNIUS RADIO COMMENTATOR Virgilijus Liauska conducted this interview with Lithuanian Democratic Party representatives Petras Vaitekunas and Saulius Peciliunas.

LIAUSKA: At the end of last year a working group of the Lithuanian Democratic Party announced its existence. Here in our radio studio I am talking to (Petras Vaitiekunas) and (Saulius Peciliunas), representatives of the working group of the Democratic Party.

Today when we have the Lithuanian Reform Movement, Sajudis, is it necessary to have a party in Lithuania? What do you think? What are your motives, P. Vaitiekunas?

VAITIEKUNAS: Sajudis emerged as a national liberation movement that practically engulfed all the citizens and social strata in Lithuania, begining with the clergy and ending with the Communists. Such a broad movement is strongly atomized, representation of personal views is strongly felt in the Sajudis; it is the representation of one's self. Such decomposition, or I call it, atomization, in a critical situation will prevent it from adopting one definite decision. There are as many opinions as there are people. The Sajudis, it seems to me, should play the role more of a political parliament and the Lithuanian political forces should be represented in the Sajudis.

Socialization, reflecting the social structure of the republic, would be the first step toward making the Sajudis a political movement. The first steps in this direction are being made, but they are very slow, and perhaps inadequately coordinated. I have in mind the forthcoming Congress of Farmers. This will be the reflection of the working group in the Sajudis in the council, in real terms. The congress will inspire the emergence of numerous groups in Lithuania, as it was before the Sajudis congress.

[251]

At that time, groups emerged mainly in schools, cultural offices, institutes, and of course, in the factories, although these were not numerous.

LIAUSKA: The position is more or less clear. Perhaps you could say some words about your platform statements?

VAITIEKUNAS: You mean party platform statements?

LIAUSKA: Yes, yes, about your party platform.

VAITIEKUNAS: **Our main objective is sovereignty and freedom for Lithuania.** We strive for freedom by democratic means. We do not declare what the ideology is and what, according to our point of view, the state system should be. We simply maintain that the state system should be democratic and that the authorities should be elected democratically. These are the two main principles. If it is going to be socialism or capitalism, or some other -ism, all these principally may turn out to be defective because we set ourselves an objective for some theoretical-ideological concepts without bothering if these are possible to achieve, as the Communists did. They simply pave their way with millions of victims.

LIAUSKA: A question for (Saulius Peciliunas). What is your point of view on the Lithuanian Communist Party?

PECILIUNAS: **In our point of view, a Lithuanian Communist Party, as such, is nonexistent in Lithuania at the moment.**

In practical terms, it is a department of the CPSU in Lithuania, or you may call it a subunit. This means that this is not a self-governing Lithuanian Communist Party. We can say that nevertheless it is dependent on the center. Of course, we would welcome it if an independent Lithuanian Communist Party emerged because only when several independent political trends exist does political struggle become possible, in common struggle it is possible to reach a sensible decision.

LIAUSKA: Struggle, and perhaps, normal political life is necessary?

PECILIUNAS: Yes, perhaps we should not interpret the word struggle as shaking fists. There should be a normal discussion in an attempt to clarify positions on both sides and only by way of argument discover which of the sides is more right and which side proposes the most correct way.

LIAUSKA: What are your short-term plans?

PECILIUNAS: Well, the short-term plans are already being implemented. First of all, comes the press. We must first explain many of our issues to the public by means of the press. We must explain our main principle, what we aspire to and how we want to achieve it, so that the public has no uncertainties in the future.

At present there are many people willing to join the party, but we are not rushing this. First, we want to make up our main documents, our statutes, and make them public so that people will have a full understanding of what they are joining. We remember when the Sajudis was being organized. There also were many questions. What is it? What is it for? Members were admitted to the Sajudis practically without any selection. After a certain amount of time many people left the Sajudis. I have in mind those party members who found this or that idea promoted by the Sajudis unacceptable. Other organizations emerged, like the Jednosz [Russian- and Polish-speaking population of Lithuania].

LIAUSKA: So, to put it in a nutshell, you do not want that to happen?

PECILIUNAS: No, we would not like to have that happen. We should like for people to know what kind of party this is, what it wants, and what means it will employ to achieve its aims, so that later there will be no cause for unnecessary theoretical discussions merely because of ignorance.

VAITIEKUNAS: I would like to make an addition concerning the relation of the future Democratic Party with the Lithuanian League of Liberty. First of all, I would like to stress that the league has declared that it is not a party, it is an organization that declares the truth as an expression of the moral fight, the conscience of the nation.

The Lithuanian Democratic Party is a party in the full sense of the word. We want to set up an opposition to the Communists in power. We pledge to carry out our activities [words indistinct] within the framework of occupation laws.

The Sajudis: Why is the Sajudis not enough? The Sajudis does not name the main obstacle hampering our setting up a society governed by law and order and by democracy. This is the Communist Party, and in more general terms, the one-party system, which has frozen in its structure the social structure of our society. . . .

LIAUSKA: Thank you for the talk.

MAPS

Accurate Maps Reveal Former "Secrets"
by G. Alimov, *Pravitelstvennyy Vestnik*, March 1989

The ball started rolling: It appears that the Main Administration of Geodesy and Cartography of the Council of Ministers of the USSR has begun to release secrets divulging what it considered inconceivable as recently as a year ago. Highly accurate maps were not available. Extremely simplified and emasculated versions of many of them were produced for public consumption. In the age of space and satellites, this looked at the very least funny.

However, the practice of making accurate maps secret and consciously distorting maps available to the general public—dating back to the late thirties—was continued. Some points were not shown at all, others were indicated at a misplaced location. Rivers and highways were "moved." Even the most experienced tourists easily lost their bearings in the field when using such guides. Not all the streets were indicated on city maps. For example, only 50 percent of streets are indicated on the existing map of Moscow available to the general public.

As the chief of the Main Administration of Geodesy and Cartography V. Yashchenko admits, such "work" was no less labor-intensive than making accurate maps. At times, in order to simplify them, a map of a 1:250,000,000 (25 kilometers to 1 centimeter) scale was taken as a base, enlarged and printed. However, changes had to be made even on such maps. All of this ran counter to common sense and claimed a lot of resources and personnel.

V. Yashchenko said: "Beginning last year, we have finally begun to get rid of the chronic complexes of spy mania and to get freed from the heavy burden which we had to carry since the Higher Directorate of Cartography came at one point to report to the NKVD [People's Commissariat of Internal Affairs]. This is where it all began. . . ."

However, times are changing. Fifty years were needed in order for this truth to become apparent: Why conceal from ourselves something that is no secret for others? So, work on declassification began. It appears that the world has not been profoundly surprised. . . .

In March or April, a map of Moscow will be released. As V. Yashchenko says, all streets and lanes of the capital city have never been shown on a map available to the general public so diligently. Similar detailed maps of densely populated areas of our country, oblasts, and regions are close to completion. This great endeavor will most likely be completed as soon as the next year.

"Broad circles of the public have never seen such maps before. Believe me, they can rely on them completely," noted V. Yashchenko.

R. MEDVEDEV

A Tragic Statistic
Interview of Soviet historian R. Medvedev, *Argumenty i Fakty*, February 4–10, 1989

WE HAVE GLASNOST. We are learning a lot. And now, as I prepare material on the repressions of Stalin's times, I encounter figures on enormous numbers of victims. I ask myself: "Is this true?" Would AiF name the precise number of persons repressed under Stalin? (I. Romanova, Archangel)

"This is a difficult question, and no precise answer can be given," we were told by well-known Soviet historian R. Medvedev, whom we asked to respond to our reader.

Stalinism concealed its crimes. No one made a precise count of those shot, resettled or who died of hunger.

Red Army burial teams went from village to village in the southern Ukraine in spring 1933, unable even to learn the names of the peasants who were covered forever by the soil of fraternal graves. Why do we only count the factory directors or brigade commanders shot in 1937 among the victims of Stalinism? And what about the families who lost a father, husband or son, and were thrown out into the street from the departmental house?

From 1927 through 1929 inclusively, "only" about a million people ended up in prisons, exile or political isolation. These were recent party members from the opposition parties, and "bourgeois" specialists, who, as a rule, had worked conscientiously in soviet establishments, but who, after the "Shakhtinsk Affair," were declared "wreckers." Arrests took place in all the republics of "nationalists" and "NEP men," who did not want to surrender to the state profits lawfully obtained in the 1920s. In rural areas, veterans, agricultural technicians, and members of cooperatives, who were declared members of the mythical "Labor Peasants Party," were arrested.

In 1930–1932 the fearsome blow of the punitive organs befell virtually all the rich peasants. Their homes and property were transferred to hastily created kolkhozes, and the entire family of a "kulak," prosperous "middle peasant" or poor "kulak follower" was forcibly resettled to Siberia, the Urals or the North— Archangel Oblast, the Kola Peninsula, or the Komi ASSR. Official figures on the expropriated kulaks were changed many times, and there is no faith in them. Statistics of 1926–1927 counted 5 percent of peasant houses, or approximately 1.2 million, as "kulak."

We can find roughly the same figure in the TsIK [Central Executive Committee] figures on the elimination of kulak households. According to accounts of eyewitnesses, only a few of the rich peasants, who had sold their property ahead of time, fled to the city. Given an average peasant family size of 6–7 people, this was 6–7 million new victims of Stalinism. We would hardly err if we added to this another 3–4 million "kulak followers."

No fewer than a million peasants were also exiled in 1933. The hope that the hastily and forcibly created kolkhozes would quickly give the country needed bread and other products turned out to be an illusion. Grain production declined, and the production of animal husbandry products fell even more noticeably.

In almost all the country's grain producing regions, a famine started in fall 1932, which in the winter and spring of 1933 reached the scale of a national calamity. Various authors now give varying figures on the peasants who died of starvation— from 3 to 10 million. From indirect data of the censuses of 1926, 1937 and 1939, the figure of 6–7 million persons who died of starvation in 1932–1933 can be accepted as the most reliable.

Probably no fewer than another 1.5–2 million peasants, mainly from among the poor, were arrested "by the ears," on the basis of new and extremely harsh laws, which contradicted the principles of kolkhoz-cooperative property.

In 1935 a massive new repressive campaign began—the expulsion of "class alien" elements from Leningrad, Moscow, and certain other cities. The families of former noblemen, merchants, capitalists and functionaries were expelled to remote provincial cities. Without great error, the number of expelled can be placed at 1 million.

In 1937–1938, i e., in the years of the Yezhov purges or the "great terror," from 5–7 million people, by my calculations, became victims of the mass repressions. Of this number, almost 1 million were party members. Almost 80 percent of pre-revolution party members, and the bulk of the party-state and economic *aktiv*, military leaders, and representatives of the intelligentsia who had been promoted during the Soviet period, were arrested. Of those arrested in 1937–1938, almost 1 million were sentenced to be shot, and the rest were sent to the camps. However, few of them lived long enough to be rehabilitated.

In 1939 mass repressions took place in the western Ukraine and western Belorussia, and in 1940–1941 in the Baltic region, Bessarabia and northern Bukovina. A large portion of these victims of Stalinism were rehabilitated only in 1987–1988, at the decision of republic authorities. The number of those rehabilitated is nearing 1 million.

The war did not stop the punitive policy of the NKVD. Already at the start of the war, trains with the country's German population, who were deprived of all rights and expelled, dragged on to the east. Overall, up to 2 million Soviet Germans were expelled, including more than 500,000 from the Volga German autonomous republic. Forcible expulsion to the east of the peoples of the north Caucasus and Crimea—Kalmyks, Chechens, Ingush, Karachayevs, Crimean Tatars and others—was carried out in 1943–1944 at the decision of the GKO [State Defense Committee]. The overall number of Muslims expelled was approximately 3 million. According to estimates by representatives of these "punished" peoples, during the expulsion up to 1 million children, women, old men and sick people died.

Beginning in 1940, several more extremely harsh laws were introduced in the country, based on which, for being more than 20 minutes late to work three times, or having one unauthorized absence, workers and employees were tried, and could be sentenced even to 3–5 years in the camps. It is not yet possible to establish how many people became victims of this legislation (in the camps they were called "ukazniki" and ukaznitsy" [persons sentenced for infringing labor discipline], and among them were many young people of 16–17 years of age). I think that this also involved 2–3 million people.

The NKVD organs were given a tremendous amount of work of "filtering" not only the surviving former prisoners of war or young people who had been marched off to work in Germany, and large masses of "resettled" persons, but also residents of the German-occupied territories, on which more than 60 million people lived. In order not to die of starvation, many of these people had had to work in enterprises and establishments created by the fascists.

It is true that the majority of these people were not punished, for otherwise it would not have been possible to restore the economy in the western oblasts. But, all those people who had been in the occupied territories were limited in their rights, and a considerable number of them were sent to camps nonetheless, in order to supplement the ranks of prisoners, which had thinned during the war years. It is difficult to count the number of people repressed without sufficient cause during the war years. But, I think that a figure of 10–12 million would more likely be low than high.

In the postwar years our country experienced a considerable number of new repressive campaigns—the "Leningrad Matter," the "struggle against Cosmopolitans," the "Doctors Plot," "destruction of the "Morganites-Veysmanites," etc. I think that about 1–1.5 million people were arrested in 1946–1953 for political reasons. Thus, the overall number of victims of Stalinism reaches, by my calculations, approximately 40 million people.

The number of victims of the war, begun so incapably, also requires a special calculation. Even today we do not know the precise number of soldiers who fell on the battlefield, or were missing, captured, or died of starvation. But this is another topic, requiring a special discussion.

"MEMORIAL"

Yevtushenko Solicits Help for Memorial
by Yevgeniy Yevtushenko, *Literaturnaya Gazeta*,
  November 9, 1988

What happened over the 2 days of 29–30 October in Moscow's
Central House of Cinematography Workers was in itself yet
another incontrovertible proof of the changes—in deed and not
just in words—that are now under way in the country's social
life. We recall—and it seems only a short while ago—how signatures were collected in streets and squares in support of the idea
of creating a memorial perpetuating the memory of the victims
of Stalin's repressions.

[Memorial,] the movement to erect a monument [to Stalin's
victims] gained support at the 19th party conference. Account
No 700454 was opened, and it immediately started receiving
voluntary donations from citizens, institutions, and organizations.

The "Memorial" Public Council was formed, and Academician A. Sakharov was elected its honorary chairman. The action
group was joined by the Public Council and the founder members of the new All-Union Voluntary Historical Education
Society—the creative unions of cinematography workers, architects, theater workers, artists, and designers, *Literaturnaya Gazeta*,
and *Ogonyek*—and they embarked on the implementation of this
noble idea. Meanwhile preparatory work was being done to organize a competition for the concept and plan of the future memorial complex, and also to collect documents and memoirs. And
now a meeting has been held to prepare for the constituent
conference of the "Memorial" Society.

What should "Memorial" be like? What sort of memorial
complex should be erected? How to provide swifter and more
effective assistance to former prisoners and their relatives, who
need it so urgently? These and many other questions were discussed at the meeting. Its participants took a firm stance against
attempts by some individuals connected with the notorious "Democratic Union" to take advantage of the sacred cause of "Memorial" in pursuit of their own unseemly goals.

Almost every family in our country had at least one of its members killed or wounded during the war against the fascists. Almost every family in our country had at least one of its members killed, arrested, exiled, or wounded through all sorts of humiliations during the war waged against our own people by those who spoke in the name of the people.

And even if there are some families unaffected by either of these two wars, surely our multinational people are a united family, and surely our memory should mourn our shared family losses? To mourn the victims of just one of these accursed wars would be as criminally unnatural as it would be to allow compassion to be felt by just one-half of one's heart while forcibly clamping the artery feeding the other half.

Our people's war against the fascists lasted 4 years and, according to official data, we lost 20 million lives, the unofficial figure being even higher.

The war waged against the people by those who spoke in the name of the people lasted for decades, and nobody has yet accurately calculated how many millions of lives we lost.

There is a theory that the repressions were supposedly a harsh necessity and that otherwise we would not have withstood the clash with fascism. But this theory is based either on historical ignorance or on historical cynicism. How can anyone perceive the prewar destruction of the people as preparation to protect the people from destruction?

Here are figures from Lieutenant General Todorskiy about the bloodletting among Red Army command cadres before the war: The repressions accounted for 3 out of 5 marshals, 3 out of 5 army commanders first rank, all 10 army commanders second rank, 50 out of 57 corps commanders, 154 out of 186 division commanders, all 16 army commissars first and second rank, 25 out of 28 corps commissars, 58 out of 64 division commissars, and 401 out of 456 colonels.

There were also lieutenants and privates who were interned first in Hitler's concentration camps, and then in Stalin's. Even when they escaped from Hitler's concentration camps and fought against facism with the Italian or French partisans, this did not prevent them from being classed as "traitors." We are awkwardly and haltingly learning the basic truths of historical memory, leaving bleeding open wounds where we have torn off the brain-constraining camelskin belts of mankurty [allusion to people in Aytmatov novel who are deprived of their memory by invaders who tie belts around their heads]. We are beginning to

honor the memory of outstanding revolutionaries, military leaders, scientists, and writers who perished in prison cellars or
behind barbed wire. Names that were famous in the past and
were only whispered for so many years, can again be heard
aloud. But the people's conscience and the people's talent are
not the exclusive privilege of the famous. It is our duty to honor
the memory of the dead innocent grain growers, workers, engineers, physicians, teachers, and people of all professions, nationalities, and religions, each of whom represents a fragment of the
assassinated people's conscience and people's talent.

In all corners of the country there are flickering eternal flames
which were lit in memory of those who died in the war against
fascism. . . .

There can be no restructuring without the restructuring of
memory.

Therefore help "Memorial"!

To this day, children on the banks of Kolyma River sometimes
carry berries inside human skulls they have found, and smile in
their innocent ignorance.

How are we now to decipher the code signs "B-13," "V-41,"
and "Ya-178" on the nameless rickety pegs and small boards in
the tayga? How are we to make out the sign written in indelible
pencil on some plywood tag tied to an emaciated bare foot when
the tundra's permafrost yields one more of its terrible secrets in
springtime?

**Belorussian peasants in Kuropaty look in terror at the ditch
filled with human skeletons as witnesses for the prosecution in
the trial of history.**

Muscovites shudder on learning that the Kalitnikovskoye Cemetery in the very heart of Moscow has its own terrible secret
ditch, Moscow's Babiy Yar, where naked bodies were brought in
carts in the middle of the night during the thirties, with rags
stopping the two bullet holes in their heads.

Our moral law—"Nobody has been forgotten and nothing has
been forgotten"—must apply to both of these terrible wars, the
Great Patriotic War and the war against our own people.

The memory we possess today accommodates neither the tears,
not the blood, nor the hopes. Not being armed with the knowledge of history, we may find ourselves disarmed when we face
up to history.

History cannot be escaped by means of monuments, not even
the most beautiful ones. The best monument is memory. We
take the term "Memorial" to include the air of historical memory

around the monuments themselves. The memorials are conceived by us not only as architectural complexes but also as spiritual complexes, as libraries of facts and tribunes of public thought.

The "Memorial" Society must become the organizer of the restructuring of memory, a cause of the whole people, a universal cause. The recreation of the people's memory is impossible without the people's help.

Therefore help "Memorial"!

The rusty barbed wire of the former camps, lying in wait in the brushwood, is a viper that can still cause a deadly bite. The poison contained in the barbs of the camp wire has contaminated those who perceive the path into the future as leading not through democracy but through forcible subordination, not through pluralism but through conveyer-belt uniformity. This camp wire entangled so many talented sons and daughters of all nationalities in our motherland—peasants, proletarians, members of the intelligentsia, party members, nonparty people, clerics, and simple believers. Who knows, had they remained alive maybe democracy and glasnost would have developed naturally as far back as the twenties, and then there would not have been so many crimes, the war against fascism would have been won much earlier—and maybe the fascists would not have been able to capture power by reference to worldwide "Red terror," and the entire political atmosphere in the world could have been different. Our future was stolen for several decades. We must know how this happened so that our future can never again be stolen. The study of the past is the salvation of the future, the guarantee of the future. The task of "Memorial" is to study the past not for the sake of accurate records but for the sake of accuracy in mapping our future prospects, for the sake of ensuring that the tragedy that befell our recent forebears does not recur to befall our immediate or distant off-spring.

Therefore help "Memorial"!

Following the tragic years when conscience, justice, and truth were locked behind bars, it is necessary to morally sentence Stalinism to life imprisonment as an antipeople phenomenon. This is not so much a matter of Stalin's actual personality or his close associates, it is a matter of Stalinism. Its result has been paradoxically tragic—the state and man, class interests and universal interests have all suffered through it. An analysis of the trampling of democracy in the past means ensuring the protection of democracy in the future. The memorial in Moscow must be an all-union lecture and research center where the morality of the present is elaborated as the foundation of the future on the basis of verified facts of the past. Research activity must not follow the biased line of bringing only negative facts to light and deliberately sensationalizing the horrors. We must make public not only the crimes and betrayals but also the courage of resistance, the feat of mercy, and the spiritual hygiene of nonparticipation. It was in those terrible years that many great books were written and many remarkable technical ideas were put forward. But at the same time we must not use the talented and honest work of many people in those years to justify the self-genocide that was being simultaneously conducted.

The tasks of the "Memorial" Society lack all vengefulness. We are not advocating the physical persecution of those who were in some way or another involved in Stalinism's bloody crimes. We deem it profoundly immoral to groundlessly accuse people who are still alive or are already dead. But if there is irrefutable evidence of guilt before the trial of history, then let the social punishment take the form of publishing the truth about specific crimes committed by specific people, accomplices in the war waged against our own people. The coverup of the truth about crimes contains a potential danger that they might recur.

The "Memorial" Society must become one of the centers for most active assistance to restructuring, glasnost, new thinking, and democracy. The "Memorial" Society will strengthen interethnic ties between our country's fraternal peoples, because nothing bonds as firmly as shared suffering. The "Memorial" Society hopes that it will receive international support because our society's democratization and complete de-Stalinization offer one of the main historical arguments for the sake of nuclear disarmament and mutual trust between peoples.

Therefore help "Memorial"!

The "Memorial" Society gratefully accepts donations for the erection of a memorial complex to the victims of repressions (Account No 700454).

The "Memorial" Society awaits any documentary material and suggestions from you, addressed to: 125319 Moscow, No 2 Chernyakhovskiy Street.

Remembrance—Not Just a Monument . . .
Letter to the editor of *Pravda*, April 19, 1989

There has been a lot of talk lately about setting up a memorial to the victims of the personality cult. My father was also illegally repressed, so I care about what kind of monument it will be. Forgive me for my bluntness, but I think that erecting yet another bronze or stone idol would be to sweep aside the memory of innocent people who were killed. A monument would be erected, huge amounts of money would be spent on it, and people would be content thinking they had paid their respects.

But if you look closer you can see that there are still so many "living monuments"—people who themselves need people to remember them. Would it not be better to use the funds collected to set up a hospital or hotel for victims of the personality cult who are still alive? For instance, in Poland a "Mothers' Hospital" was built instead of a monument to mothers. And it is of use to everyone!

I also disagree to some extent with the concept of "victims of the personality cult." Take such well-known figures as Yagoda, Yezhov, and others. Should they be listed as victims or butchers? All the more so since their families and friends were not guilty. How many similar cases—victims or butchers—are to be found among People's Commissariat for Internal Affairs workers who were killed in their turn. Who are they, where should they be listed?

I would like to say something about people such as Bukharin, Rykov, and others. Should they now be turned into heroes-cum-martyrs? After all, before collectivization they occupied high state office. They enjoyed prestige among the people and the party. Some of them led leading press organs. Why did they not defend the starving, dying Ukraine and Volga regions? After all, back then, before collectivization, Stalin did not have the same power and authority that he wielded in 1937–1939. What were they afraid of? Or were personal power and prosperity more important to them than the lives of millions of people? Nowadays everything is being boiled down to a "common denominator." It is simpler and more convenient to say that there were guilty men and victims. The truth seems to have triumphed. But has it?

—I. Starostenko, Vasilyevka Village, Dobrushskiy Rayon, Gomel Oblast

MILITARY

The Military Lesson: A Civilian's Polemical Notes on Restructuring in the Army
by Albert Plutnik, *Izvestiya*, March 21, 1989

. . . It was announced that we are cutting our military budget by 14.2 percent. The degree of accuracy—down to tenths of a percent—is striking. Down to the last kopek, so to speak. Yet none of us can name an accurate figure for our military expenditure, and consequently no one really knows that these percentage points mean in financial terms. Although, because we are well aware that our military department is not hard up, we can safely assume that it is a question of a very substantial sum. And some of our readers are now worried: Are we not weakening our military might, are we not giving way, so to speak, in the face of world imperialism?

Incidentally, this anxiety appears not unfounded if you bear in mind certain striking facts that are cited in the press. Former Afghaners, after being discharged into the reserves, repay from their own pockets damage that was done during the years of service, by no means maliciously. Yet for our illustrious paratroopers it is by no means a simple matter to obtain new boots to replace worn ones. And if the military department stoops so low as to seek a financial settlement from those who, only yesterday, gave their lives in fulfilling their international duty, if its funds are so low that it cannot issue a soldier with a spare pair of boots, then evidently its affairs are in very poor shape. Rather than cutting the budget, it is time to increase it. . . .

Only it is clear to everyone that even if the military budget were halved, problems like the above should not happen—they arise not from poverty, but from disorder.

Speaking at a meeting with USSR Armed Forces General Staff Communists, Army General M.A. Moiseyev, candidate USSR people's deputy, recently appointed chief of General Staff, observed that the reduction of the military budget is justified both politically and strategically. "At the same time," he stated, "this makes it incumbent on us, on the one hand, to learn to count our money better and be thriftier in our use of the material resources allocated for the training and development of the Armed Forces, and, on the other hand, to more actively seek ways of maintaining defense at a level of reasonable sufficiency within the framework of a reduced budget."

I suppose everyone realizes that in seeking ways to do this we must bear in mind that reforming ideas earn the right to exist only when their implementation does not weaken defense. In reducing personnel we do not expect lower manning levels to mean that the Army becomes a weaker force. Is this utopian? It all depends on the extent to which the Army, for all its different characteristics, can profit from the experience of those civilian areas of production that have fewer people, but are more useful. This is only possible when the optimum form of organization can be found.

Where we go depends largely on where we start from and what we leave behind.

We are becoming an increasingly open society. We are no longer afraid to wash our dirty linen in public, even the Army's linen. What we say about ourselves is no longer confined to things that have long been secrets. Only recently, when we watched television reports from the West showing how thousands of people protest outside the gates of military bases and near nuclear testing ranges against, for instance, the siting of lethal weapons on the territory of their country, district, or state, for some reason we did not even register the fact that people apparently know where the base or range is located. (And they could hardly fail to know, when there are even road signs saying "military base.") When at the same time we ourselves, the true masters of the country, so to speak, did not have a clue about anything of the kind—in our own country, republic, or oblast. But glasnost and democratization are doing their work. We now know about the missile complex in Udmurtia, in the city of Votkinsk. True, we heard about it when American specialists arrived there—to verify the end of production of a certain class of missiles. We now know something about the military facility at Shikhany, which is on the territory of Saratov Oblast. Alas, only yesterday there were as many military secrets held from our own people as from the "foreign military."

It is not society, not the people, but the departments that have the greatest interest in mysteries and secrecy. In many cases secrets are not merely an insult to society, they are both economically and politically disadvantageous. Remember how agitated the local inhabitants became when they learned that near Chapayevsk, in Kuybyshev Oblast, an enterprise was under construction for the destruction of chemical weapons. When people are informed about the "secrets" that exist in the neighborhood of their homes, the departments should naturally be prepared for an open discussion. Events at Chapayevsk showed that there is no need to hide from the eyes of outsiders if you have everything in good order behind you. A kind of monitoring organ even sprang up there, including both military men and civilians— representatives of the public. It need hardly be said that now the military men themselves will also be more exacting with regard to the quality of the "facility" under construction, and indeed its operation. The department itself is no longer both the defendant and the judge.

There is no denying that military secrets exist that should remain so while military confrontation persists. And no one is calling for every secret to be revealed forthwith. I am talking about something different: Society should monitor more widely and effectively the decisions of the military department, because these decisions have a marked effect on many things that concern all of us.

The military superdepartment has for too long lived a life that is isolated, so to speak, from society. In effect it informed society only to the extent that it deemed it necessary to do so. We are all learning to live in a world of new realities, we are learning the new thinking, while sometimes unconsciously gravitating toward the old patterns. I read an article by a prominent military specialist. He writes: The regular U.S. Armed Forces have a strength of 2.13 million men. Some 1.16 million serve in the National Guard and the reserve. In all, about 3.3 million men. You wait: Now he will tell us about our Army. Equally clearly and specifically. And he does indeed tell us, but seemingly in a different language: We are reducing the Armed Forces by 12 percent of their strength. In percentage terms, not absolute terms. Yet we all know that this 12 percent is in fact 500,000 servicemen who are being discharged into the reserve. So even a backward fifth-grade student can soon calculate what 100 percent equals, that is, the numerical strength of our Army.

Today, representatives of military circles still have the right to say, in reply to all our questions: We are under no obligation to give an account of ourselves to you. Indeed, they are under no such obligation. To us. But to the Supreme Soviet? I cannot call to mind any hearings being held there at which, on the model of the U.S. Congress, questions connected with financing particular military programs are examined comprehensively and openly every year. Should we perhaps look more carefully at some aspects of "their way of life"? Over there, the Defense Department's budget is published in the press. And also there is the defense secretary's annual report to Congress, which covers in some detail all defense matters and the main provisions of military policy. Naturally, the Americans by no means talk openly about everything, but it is noteworthy that at present the U.S. public is raising increasingly persistently the matter of the extent of the need for keeping secret even the top secret "black" programs.

Could it be, perhaps, that in our country it is nothing more than a tradition—to allow the Defense Ministry to keep its programs in absolute secrecy? And is it the only such ministry, anyway? What do we know about the activities of other ministries, whose very names are vague and unclear—the Ministry of Medium Machine Building, the Ministry of General Machine Building? If these departments themselves exist more or less in secret, what about the vast complexes that are subordinate to them? No one is supposed to know where they are, they are never mentioned in the newspapers, there are no signs on the buildings, they are not usually discussed aloud. Unless, perhaps, a bus driver, off his guard, suddenly announces: "Next stop—the secret plant."

We grew up and were raised in the conviction that what is good for the Army is good for society, for the people. The people and the Army are one. The Army always wants and strives for what the people want and strive for. And thus everything should give way to its interests. The examples from the times of the Great Patriotic War, which arose in extraordinary circumstances, became established as the norm—for all time. You remember: The fatherland is in danger. The dire necessity of the war years: Everything for the front, everything for victory. That is how it was. All of industry—on a war footing. All the people—reservists. Elderly workers, shortsighted musicians, and unworldly scientists joined the people's militia. Essential! A sacred cause! So the whole people became the Army. And conquered. But then what happened was what should happen in peacetime—the Army became the Army, a small part of the people. And the people's cause was no longer only the military cause. But all "other matters" were, so to speak, subordinate to the military. A kind of hierarchy grew up, military matters were the generals, while other matters held lower ranks—from colonel to private. There was, among other things, a "barely perceptible" substitution of concepts—whereas formerly people used to speak of the total fusion of interests of the Army and people, now it appeared that the Defense Ministry, which is intended to represent the Army's interests, seemingly represents the interests of the whole people.

Tell me, whose idea was it to draft students into the Army? And when? Not in the fateful forties—but in the stagnant seventies. Teaching a student with a break for Army service is like interrupting him in mid-word and expecting him to finish the sentence 2 years later. What kind of people are the VUZ's [higher educational institutions] producing as a result, when even before, without a "break in studies," the quality of training was not particularly good. And this at a time when it is vitally important to us to overcome in the shortest possible time our laggardness in relation to the developed countries, when we cannot do without a major leap forward in the sphere of scientific and technical progress if we want to avoid sinking to the level of a third-rate power.

I would have no hesitation in blaming departmental egotism for ignoring common interests, if the Defense Ministry had sole responsibility for determining the procedure for military service. . . . They left the rear unprotected, thinking that they were thereby strengthening the country's defense capability. But who can say where the front is and where the rear is, in peacetime? In wartime, where the Army is, is the front, that is where the key events happen, and therefore you send more resources—human and material—there. But in peacetime, perhaps the rear and the front should change places. Peaceful constructive work is the front line, military building is the rear. Yes, the rear should always be strong, but all the same, the front is the front. The rear should work for the front, rather than the front for the rear. Does not economic and scientific progress strengthen defense capability? Is not the molding of a good specialist a contribution to our defense capability?

And by the way, how many generals do we have? And how many do we need? . . . What are their salaries, privileges, duties? Various, I understand. A general who commands an army is one thing. A general who commands a song and dance troupe or a sports club is another. Incidentally, the Army illustrates clearly how sometimes a department, creating its own laws, begins to structure its life according to those laws. Army sportsmen, as everyone knows, are given military titles—lieutenant, captain.

Naturally, the trainer has to have a higher rank, or how can he command his subordinates? So he is a major, or even a colonel. That being so, a sports club must necessarily be run by a general. One thing leads to another, but there is no kind of logic in it.

It is, of course, a bad thing that "their" soldier receives more than our general. But why is it that in this "accounting" in their favor, our own private soldier has somehow disappeared from view entirely? It would be useful to bear his income in mind, too. On a recent trip to Hungary, more than once I came across soldiers in a familiar uniform at the roadside, cautiously "flagging down" passing cars—in order to ask for a smoke. My Hungarian driver explained that this is a common phenomenon. "They get paid very little," he said sympathetically. One can easily, from habit, blame the soldiers themselves for everything: They are belittling the dignity of the Soviet serviceman, we say. But perhaps it is time we thought about why they have to belittle themselves.

It was with regret that I read the following sentence in an article by V. Serebryannikov, Lieutenant General of Aviation: "The proposal on, for instance, the introduction of alternative civilian service for those who are unwilling (!) to fulfill their military duty is patently demagogic. . . ." And I assessed it as a sign of being out of training in public debates—it is a long time since all our military men took part in open disputes concerning not particular, but fundamental problems of military building. The word "demagogic" as applied to someone else's opinion is patently not in the spirit of the times. And why not talk about the substance of alternative service, why not talk about it in more concrete terms? It is a serious matter, and not a new one.

Let me quote an extract from the Soviet of People's Commissars decree on exemption from military service on religious grounds, signed by V.I. Lenin: "Persons who are unable, by virtue of their religious convictions, to participate in military service are granted the right, by decision of the people's court, to replace such service, for the specified period for which their age group is drafted, with medical service primarily in hospitals for infectious diseases or other appropriate socially useful work of the draftee's own choice." The decree was adopted on 4 January 1919, not the most tranquil of times, you realize. But if it was permitted then. . . .

I am a civilian. And it goes without saying that I do not have the competence of a military specialist in formulating my conclusions. In my view, if there is to be an open discussion of what form our Army should take, that discussion should be calm and concrete. Fastidiously brushing aside the opinions of "outsiders" is a typical departmental stance. What can "they" understand about "our" problems, people say. At the same time the brief history of democratization to date has already provided a number of instructive examples on this score. Who doubted that the Ministry of Land Reclamation and Water Resources was and is staffed by people who are very knowledgeable in their field? Nonetheless, they were the originators of projects that the whole public rose against. Rose against, and showed that the public understands these matters.

We all inherited a sad legacy from past times. The command, bureaucratic style of leadership did not bypass a single ministry or department, a single organization, high or low. We were in a position that is absolutely inconceivable in the context of the triumph of a normal economy and common sense. Factories were producing footwear that no one needed, publishing houses were printing books that no one was buying. In short, the departments existed only for their own benefit. We lived a long time in this antiworld. It is not so very easy to come to one's senses and return to normal. All of us, both military and civilian, are now making considerable efforts to do this. And there is no need to offend one another in the process. Ultimately we share the same true strategic interest—let our native land live, and let it live in such a way that everyone feels confident and calm, that everyone has a normal, prosperous life.

Despite our age-old inclination to seek the enemy within, we have only now realized that the main enemy within is the low living standard. This enemy cannot be stopped with a rocket launcher or annihilated with machine gun rounds. The Army by other means can make a very weighty contribution to peaceful transformations. That is what is needed now.

"NOMENKLATURA"

Moscow Restricts Officials' Vehicular Privileges
Moscow Domestic Service in Russian, March 15, 1989

The Moscow city soviet ispolkom has decided to reduce to the absolute minimum the number of official cars allowed to travel at high speeds on city streets. Naturally, this decision in no way extends to such services as ambulances, the fire department, the militia, and various emergency departments. Instead, this is a matter of depriving officials working for party and local soviet bodies, ministries, and various institutions and departments who use such transport for their own personal use of advantages on Moscow's streets.

It is precisely in these organizations that the number of vehicles fitted with various signalling devices or number plates with a special combination of figures and letters has grown from year to year. Then it became fashionable not to have a number plate on the front bumper, but to attach a special headlight on the front which did not so much light the way as clear the way. How could you tell whether the vehicle was taking the rider on an urgent official matter or whether is was racing along on his personal business?

But all this is not justified in any way. This speeding is taking place in a huge city where on each of the main thoroughfares there are as many as 10,000 cars moving along in the rush hour. The state of the roads is far from being satisfactory. This is why it was decided to introduce some order into Moscow's transport arteries. The staff of the capital's state traffic inspectorate have prepared themselves for difficulties in carrying out the decision of the Moscow ispolkom. They have a realistic idea of the pressure they will have to withstand by some leaders who have become accustomed to privileges they did not deserve. However, things are under way.

NUCLEAR POWER

Last Command Given: Armenian Nuclear Power
  Station Stops Work
by Armenpress special correspondent S. Babadzhanyan,
  Kommunist, March 19, 1989

**Something unprecedented in the history of the power industry
has happened. The Armenian Nuclear Power Station has stopped
work forever.** This is the first instance of the effective elimination of an operational nuclear power station that is technically
in perfect working order. This step reflects the great concern of
the Communist Party and the state for Armenia's working people, and moreover the decision was adopted under conditions in
which the Transcaucasus is experiencing an urgent need for
energy capacity.

Under a USSR Council of Ministers resolution the nuclear
power station's first unit was stopped 3 weeks ago—on 25
February—and the second and last power unit last Saturday—18
March.

Thus the republican working people's wish was fulfilled: The
nuclear power station, which gave its first current in December
1976, was stopped. Since that time the power giant has generated 48.5 billion kilowatt-hours of electricity, playing a major
role in the development of the republic's national economy and
its power-labor ratio.

Naturally, the closing down of the nuclear power station com-
plicates power supplies both in Armenia and in other regions of
the Transcaucasus. To safeguard the work of industry, agriculture, and transport and provide for domestic needs in the republic, a number of measures are being implemented and a struggle
is under way to ensure economical utilization of electricity. At
the same time work is under way to make up for the shortage
and replenish the energy system with new capacities in the near
future. Specialists will soon begin work on the formulation of
technical and economic documentation for redesigning the nuclear station as a thermal station. After the closing down of the
power unit, S.G. Arutyunyan, first secretary of the Armenian

Communist Party Central Committee, and N.D. Lukonin, USSR minister of the nuclear power industry, talked with workers and employees at the station on questions of concern to them, inquired about the problem of finding jobs for the collective's members, and announced that after the closure of the nuclear power station work will be provided for its workers on the spot. Measures will be carried out to provide amenities for the settlement of Metsamor and develop it, and it is planned to build a large number of social facilities and a considerable quantity of housing. Metsamor will remain and will develop as a city of power workers. Its inhabitants will become workers at the future thermal power station.

When the Fog Lifted
Letter to the editor of *Literaturnaya Gazeta*,
  November 2, 1988

Over the last few years, Belorussia's residents have been perturbed with persistent regularity by news that an AES will be sited first in one part of the republic, then in another.

The power station has been shifted all over the place—first near Minsk, then near Tolochin. . . . It was kicked out of everywhere. Why? Because the departments are playing a dishonest game on a dark pitch, in the semidarkness of secrecy and without consulting public opinion. The silence of the republican press and mass media is also perplexing.

The fog of uncertainty was lifted only when the weekly *Literatura I Mastatstva* published in a recent issue the article "Mezha" by Vitebsk journalist S. Naumchik. The republic's public is alarmed: This time the technocrats have set their sights on the Vitebsk region. And even though local authority organs deem it inexpedient to site the AES in the oblast's territory, surveying work is going on at full speed.

The planners' arguments? It appears that Lake Mezha was created by the Lord for the sole purpose of planting a nuclear giant on its shore, since the surrounding area is distinguished by "insignificant population density."

This is true, alas. During the last war, the Hitlerites burned alive 32 residents of Mezha Village, and dozens of villagers did not come back from the front. One in four of the republic's residents died. The numbers in Vitebsk Oblast were one in three. Prior to that, there was dekulakization and exile, famine

and Stalin's bloody terror. The war was followed by famine
once more and then, for many years, by functionaries' ill-starred
economic management. Just go there and see for yourselves the
moss-covered peasant huts with dilapidated roofs and boarded-up
windows. . . .

Powerful equipment arrives as soon as the last hut in a village
is abandoned: it brings down the house, plows up the yard, and
even takes in the cemetery to avoid having to come back sometime in the future. This is how what was once a densely populated region acquired the "insignificant density" so desired by
the power industry. Incidentally, there have been 38 major industrial enterprises built in the oblast over the last 20 years, and
this has resulted in a sharp decline in the size of the working
population in villages. Right now there is a 25-percent shortage
of cadres on the oblast's farms. There can be no question that
the erection of an AES and a power industry workers' city for
50,000 residents will render the work force problem virtually
insoluble.

The planners have thought up yet another argument—apparently
Gorodokskiy Rayon is perfectly suited to supply water for the
AES's operations. True enough, on condition that "appropriate
engineering work for an additional annual supply of up to 300
million cubic meters from the Western Dvina River during the
spring and fall" is organized and implemented. Long-suffering
Western Dvina River! Some 18 months ago (28 January 1987),
Literaturnaya Gazeta wrote about the building of the Daugavpils
AES, which threatened to flood 150 population centers in
Belorussia and Latvia and to destroy thousands of hectares of
fields and meadows. The public succeeded in halting the implementation of this foolish (and secret!) project. And now we are
facing a diametrically opposite threat—shoaling. Has the power
industry department thought of the possible ecological consequences? Or the unique natural reserves located near Lake Mezha?

In giving its consent to the construction of the Belorussian
AES, the republic leadership did not take into account the consequences of the Chernobyl tragedy. Ignoring these consequences
and derisively dubbing them "radiophobia" means nothing but
perceiving the Belorussian land as an ordinary construction site,
and unscrupulously exploiting the Belorussian people's supposedly obliging nature.

Oh, this famous Belorussian "obliging nature" of ours, which,
not without the bureaucrats' help, has been elevated to the
status of almost a national virtue! Readiness to put up with

absolutely everything: We put up with salinated Soligorsk, smoke-engulfed Mogilev, gas-smothered Novopolotsk, poisoned Svetlo-gorsk. . . . We put up with the terrible pain of Chernobyl. . . . Pain and patience are interdependent in the people's life. And the pain is steadily growing.
— Rygor Borodulin, Yanka Bryl, Vasil Bykov, Aleksey Dudarev, Sergey Zakonnikov, Viktor Kozko, Vladimir Orlov, Pimen Panchenko

'My Word of Honour, No More Explosions!'
by Ales Adamovich, *Moscow News*, November 29, 1988

———————————

MORE THAN TWO YEARS have elapsed since the nuclear accident at Chernobyl, but the problems engendered by it continue to be of universal concern. Like in the rest of the world, when danger has to be encountered, the alarmed voice of public opinion is also heard in the USSR, including in public statements by scientists and cultural workers. From the rostrum of the recent 19th All-Union Party Conference Boris Oleinik, a Ukrainian writer, demanded that planners who had miscalculated in substantiating the construction of nuclear power plants near Rovno and in the Crimea should be made answerable for their gross blunders. Ales Adamovich, Byelorussian writer, whose talk with an "MN" correspondent is published below, wrote an alarmed article to the "Novy Mir" magazine about the social consequences of Chernobyl.

———————————

Among those who took part in the operation to seal the failed reactor was Academician Valery Legasov, Member of the Presidium of the USSR Academy of Sciences. Two years later he took his own life at the age of 51. The date he chose was April 27, 1988. The day after the second anniversary of Chernobyl.

As the closest aide to the then President Alexandrov of the Soviet Academy of Sciences, Valery Legasov was involved in the designing and siting of nuclear power stations.

He was at the scene of the disaster from the very first day. He went to the most dangerous area and received high doses of radiation. I was struck by his frankness. We talked for a long time, and he told me a Chernobyl-size disaster could strike again. It just could not be ruled out because 14 Chernobyl-type reactors are operating in this country. I was overwhelmed. Can I quote you? I asked.

"You can put it on record. I am convinced, unfortunately. The most important contributing factors to the Chernobyl accident have not been and cannot be removed. They include faults from poor construction and the lack of reliable emergency systems for similar plants, and the impossibility of constructing any concrete 'cones' to seal them at this stage."

Like many others in the spring and summer of 1986, Ales Adamovich, who lived in Byelorussia then, tried to do something to help. He says:

I had gone to the Central Committee of the Communist Party of Byelorussia in Minsk to meet a man. Possibly because he, the frontline soldier, remembered how many misfortunes had been brought upon us by the habit to fear superiors' displeasure more than enemy attacks. A group of sleek, well-fed men entered the room, chatting. Byelorussia's former Minister of Health stood in the middle. Those huddled around him were discussing how to deal with "irresponsible" mothers who had arrived from the affected areas.

"They have come uninvited with their children. OK, if they came with their kids, they should leave them here but then they should go because we are not supposed to provide bed and board for them, too. But they don't want to leave. They're creating panic, saying that the situation is very bad not just in the three areas we told Moscow about, but in dozens of areas. . . . That's OK, we'll try to persuade them."

The Minister was damned nervous. He knew his Ministry had been trying to save face while ignoring the public interest. **His staff were not ashamed of telling the women and children fleeing from Chernobyl that there is no science without victims.**

I think the most shameful thing revealed by the Chernobyl blast was the behaviour of one or two of our doctors. Many doctors behaved honourably at the disaster site, in the hospitals and in the affected areas. But it is also a fact that a doctor, a member of that Government Commission, said he wouldn't clear Pripyat residents for evacuation. Maybe, he wanted the wind to start blowing from the side of Chernobyl and radiation reached the level specified in the evacuation instructions! The ministers of public health in the Ukraine and Byelorussia lied to concerned citizens: to hear them talk, radiation wasn't radiation but manna.

An honest doctor in the Mogilyov Region, where radiation has failed to reach the normal level, tried to do what seemed the right thing—to monitor not only the servicemen doing decontamination but also tractor and combine-harvester drivers who worked in the dust.

This angered the local medical boss, who told a gathering of medics: "What a preposterous idea! I'll cut him down to size!"

The main concern of people like this is to conceal rather than reveal problems. They are well aware of the dangers because on field trips they refuse to eat anything except the food they have brought with them.

Bureaucrats don't change their ways even if other people's lives are at stake. They always give priority to their own interests.

Agroprom (Agro-Industrial Committee) directly profits from the heartless practices prevailing in the contaminated areas of Byelorussia. Radiation has been found to boost the growth of certain cereals. Some areas reported unusually big grain harvests. So Agroprom harvests these crops, meets production targets and then worries about what to do with the grain. Byelorussia has repeatedly urged Agroprom to exclude all contaminated land from its plans and to destroy the thousands of tons of irradiated meat in the refrigerators in the Mogilyov and Gomel regions. The response so far is bureaucratic fog.

And we also read in the reply from Agroprom: "How very good it would be to pool the efforts of scientists and writers in the direction of implementing the recommendations for lessening the supply of radioactive fission products into objects of agricultural production—that would be tangible aid." And even: "Your hand, comrade!" This would make a miraculous emblem: three hands firmly holding one another—Glavatom, Agroprom and Medicine. Add to this the hand of the Writers Union, and what you get is total departmental idyll.

Nothing of the kind.

The departmental interests do not tally with those of the state, let alone with humane principles—there's a glaring contradiction.

The veil of secrecy should be lifted off the area affected by the Chernobyl blast. Byelorussia needs **its own centre** in the Gomel or the Mogilyov Region to monitor the long-range effects of the accident, as well as for medical services which are independent of the nuclear engineering authorities. There should not be secrecy on things essential for the making of correct decisions.

People are leaving the areas anyway, but they are mostly young girls, future mothers. They don't go for the incentive where your wages are supplemented at the rate of one rouble for every day you spend in the danger areas. People call this "coffin money." The medical department cares more about keeping its secrets and projecting a "good image." It goes out of its way to play down the scale of the disaster. Its main goal is to save face and its programme, which is to build more nuclear plants.

Some enthusiasts are already claiming that it is perfectly safe for those who lived in the 30-kilometre zone to return there. Others are talking about non-Chernobyl-type reactors which, though nuclear, are water-cooled and so wonderfully safe. True, they don't say they're "fit to be installed in Red Square", something they used to say about the Chernobyl reactors.

Some people say: "But there are plenty of nuclear plants in other countries, and they generate a substantial amount of their electricity."

They love to remind us how many there are abroad, saying that we have less, so let's build more. We have to build up our power engineering industry. Not to worry. But wouldn't it make more sense to look at the changes, the dynamics?

Since the 1979 Three-Mile Island disaster the Americans have not built a single new nuclear plant. They have dismantled or mothballed even those which were 70 or 80 per cent complete. Since 1981 not a single order has been filled for a nuclear plant project in the FRG, England, Sweden, Spain, Switzerland, Canada or Belgium. In the meantime we have built another dozen. The European part of the Soviet Union is stuffed with them: Armenia, Lithuania, Leningrad, Kursk, Smolensk, Rovno, Zaporozhye, Feodosia, etc.

Today's nuclear engineering is everybody's concern, as is the prospect of nuclear war. After Chernobyl the peaceful and military uses of the atom very closely identify in our minds and in reality with the same danger.

Many serious commentators have repeatedly warned, that if there is a nuclear blast, it won't be because of human error or military actions but because of terrorists. There are already reports about stolen fission materials. What if terrorists blow up a nuclear plant?

This would be a global disaster because the cumulative long-term effect of the radiation from a fully destroyed reactor of the Chernobyl type would be the same as that of a ten-megaton bomb.

Other professionals of the calibre of Sakharov say that if more nuclear plants are to be built, they should be built underground, one hundred metres or so down.

Could Chernobyl and its terrible aftermath have happened had opponents in the scientific community had the right to openly criticize the trends that flourished under former Chairman Andranik Petrosyants of the State Committee for Nuclear Power and other optimistic enthusiasts? Of course not! This means it's high time to ensure that dominant trends in science can be criticized by those whose ideas are not in fashion.

Chernobyl and the station in Byelorussia have motivated me to do something I never considered before. This happens to many people these days and I'm prepared to absorb all the torrent of abuse directed at laymen who poke their noses into other people's affairs. But I cannot keep my nose out of it.

I happened to hear a nuclear-plant builder arguing with a geologist. When the builder had exhausted all his ammunition in support of a broad-based programme for the construction of nuclear plants he pressed his hands to his chest and pleaded: "My word of honour, no more explosions!"

A shattering argument, I'm sure!

Scientists not involved in the departmental gambles fully agree—we cannot build nuclear plants in the densely populated European part of the Soviet Union. Rather than build new stations here, the existing ones should be shut down.

Let's come to our senses before it's too late!

BORIS PASTERNAK

Doctor Zhivago Shown for First Time in USSR
by V. Malukhin, *Izvestiya*, February 15, 1989

For 2 days readings of Pasternak's works organized by the commission on the poet's literary legacy, headed by A. Voznesenskiy, have been given in the Central House of Writers.

Scientists, writers, public figures, and poetry lovers took part in the readings. There was a soiree in memory of Boris Pasternak where for the first time a Soviet audience was shown the movie *Doctor Zhivago* supplied by the U.S. Embassy in Moscow.

The present Pasternak readings are the second so far, which means that it is already possible to speak of the birth of a tradition giving every indication of becoming a significant event in our cultural life. This name, a magical one to the reader yet so long deprived of public recognition, has finally taken its place among the galaxy of brilliant poets whose names are remembered on special days each year.

The shameful decision to expel Boris Pasternak from the USSR Writers' Union was marked today, his ill-fated novel has been published, and, as Yu. Lyubimov stated at the soiree at the Central House of Writers, the staging of *Doctor Zhivago* at the Taganka Theater is already in preparation. . . . But like a piece of bad news from the past, like a bitter reminder and unforgettable lesson to us, the minutes of that Moscow writers' meeting which mercilessly attacked Pasternak 30 years ago were appended to the program of the readings distributed to those taking part. However, the poet had a different notion of time, art, and himself: "I have made the whole world weep over the beauty of my land. . . ."

PERESTROIKA

Perestroika—Debate
Letters to the editor of *Izvestiya*, March 9, 1989

"The 'revolutionary' transformations (American style) have merely introduced discord and confusion into the normal rhythm of life and created an explosive situation in many regions," writes T. Chabanyuk from Pervomaysk in Nikolayev Oblast, addressing his remarks "to the very top."

These are typical admissions. In many people's minds there is confusion and apprehension. But these are not the only letters reflecting social moods.

"I am an ardent champion of the great cause launched in our country, and the 27th CPSU Congress was my congress although I am not a Communist," writes M. Kurganskiy, a teacher from Ladozhskaya village in Ust-Labinskiy Rayon, Krasnodar Kray. "I and my comrades have always believed that the time of truth will come. A time when the country's leaders will not cover up its problems and when people will not have to hide their convictions. When people who do not share the official viewpoint will no longer be entered in the files as turncoats, dissidents, and so forth. The absence of threats, of violence being done to people's minds, and of the persecution of dissenters must become a norm of our life."

The coexistence of cautious, wait-and-see attitudes with the readiness to participate "in the great cause which has been launched" is a characteristic feature of any transitional period, including ours. Its dramatic nature is due to the clash with the powerful inertia of the past. "After all, restructuring is affecting the social structures and economic relations themselves, which automatically kept reproducing the former order and called for precisely that kind of talentless leader and executive who did not care about anything," G. Sanaya, an engineer from Kutaisi, writes. "This is why both these categories of people are playing an active part in hampering restructuring."

Restructuring is being blamed for allegedly "having brought anarchy rather than democracy to the country" (S. Kolosov, Irkutsk). "Today's heroes are strikers, informals, homosexuals, and Riga market bingo players," notes L. Savkina from Lyubertsy, Moscow Oblast, with irritation. "Both Stalin and the 'Voprosy Leninisma' ["Questions of Leninism"; a Stalin work published in 1926] are being rejected, as is everything that has been built up over the past 70 years. . . . Let's see where 'mixed capitalism' will get you,"—this is a quote from a letter by V. Shatalov from Donetsk. "There is nothing sacred to you," N. Shumilin from Krivoy Rog declares.

When you read letters like these you inevitably think: Are their authors not exaggerating by claiming that virtually all the foundations have been destroyed, that continuity has been disrupted?

Let us clarify what kind of foundations and what kind of continuity are at issue here. It is true that the foundations of the administrative-edict system are being destroyed today, that the fetters of the dogmas which constrained our life are being shattered, and that false authorities are being debunked. It is true that we are trying to cast off the burdensome legacy of Stalinism, that we are trying to put an end to the mortifying spirit of stagnation with which Brezhnev "enriched" us, and to rid ourselves of some other "values." Is it worth mourning these losses? In general, has the time not come to stop manifesting only vigilance and a protective zeal whenever we encounter anything new?

(I. Novikov, *Soviet News*)

This is what I. Osadchiy from Krasnodar writes, for instance:
"The slogan 'More Democracy!' is not a call for liberalization,
total license, or anarchic dissipation. Democracy means people's
power, rule by the people. In conditions of revolutionary restructuring it must not become eroded, grow soft, or take on a vis-
cous state." It is impossible to disagree with the author of the
letter thus far. But then . . . Having advised the authorities to be
"firmer, tougher, and stricter," I. Osadchiy declares that "at the
current stage of the development of our society there are quite a
few places where revolutionary violence could be applied in the
interests of strengthening democracy and socialism, in the interests of cleansing the socialist society of all kind of antisocialist
filth." He proceeds to mention these places—"the multifarious,
multifaceted informal associations."

**"What is needed is the big stick of Peter the Great," writes V.
Shevchenko from Leningrad, shifting the discussion from the**

theoretical to the practical sphere. "Stalin issued orders only once. There was never a second time," Muscovite A. Mikhaylov adds. "Restructuring needs to get tougher. . . ."

Restructuring has brought about an unleashing of social energy. Powerful popular movements in support of restructuring have emerged, informal associations, civic initiatives, alliances, and clubs have stepped up their activities. "Political life has emerged from the underground," writes Candidate of Sciences I. Shamshurin from Leningrad. "The party has gained new helpers and critics as a result of its revolutionary transforming activities. Yes, it has gained critics. And it stands to gain from this in the process of mastering the methods of political leadership and political struggle after the long years of issuing commands on the one hand and of unconditional subordination on the other. . . ." "It would be politically naive to assume," I. Shamshurin goes on, "that in conditions of radical change and the polarization of social forces no extremist, adventurist groups will spring up and try to seize the initiative and establish their influence. . . . However, it is impermissible to condemn all social initiatives for this reason, or to clip their wings."

Reading the letters one is able to see, alas, how tenacious the philosophy of lack of freedom still is. Many people are afraid of change; they would prefer to live in ignorance as in the past. "Is it not time to put an end to all this glasnost?!"—V. Sokolov from Izhevsk exclaims. We seem to be unable to rid ourselves of suspiciousness. V. Trutnev from Odessa, frightened by events in certain national republics, claims that "hidden enemies of Soviet power have begun to surface." Yu. Pokryshkin from Chelyabinsk proposes that a law on strikes be adopted and that their organizers be "tried like criminals since they have been bribed by foreign intelligence." "The time has come for arrests," N. Kobychenko from Baku advises—without bothering to specify who should be arrested.

Today we are reaping the fruits of yesterday. We are able to see this for ourselves at every step. "The country," A. Badadin from Feodosiya writes, "has gained freedom! **Do you know what this means? So much indignation, pain, humiliation, and protest has been stored up in people's hearts that unless the process of dispelling it all is controlled and kept within reasonable bounds, disaster is not far away."**

This is particularly true of interethnic relations. It must be noted that the events connected with the exacerbation of interethnic relations are perceived by readers as evidence of weakness on the part of the authorities, as a manifestation of the selfsame anarchy which "we have arrived at." V. Korotyshka writes from Semipalatinsk: "Not a single question is resolved quickly in our country. Everything drags on and on. Take, for instance, the same old Nagorno-Karabakh. . . ."

What can be said in this context? By no means can the old, tight historical knots always be cut through with one swing of the sword, as the mythological hero did. We must take care not to damage the living fabric of society, not to inflict new wounds on society. The heated atmosphere cannot be cooled by means of administrative zeal alone. "Tanks and commandant's offices (if this stage has already been reached) do not resolve the question," V. Bovkun from Kiliy in Odessa Oblast notes very aptly in reference to the events in Azerbaijan and Armenia.

Tension in ethnic relations is more often than not the result of unsolved, neglected social problems and regional contradictions pertaining to economic and social development. Here is a very characteristic letter: **Ye. Tarasova from Liyepaya describes how she was prevented from sending a box of candy to Siberian friends to mark their name day.** The post office refused to accept the parcel, alluding to a local regulation according to which the dispatch of goods in high demand is temporarily banned. These kinds of excesses stem from an economy beset by shortages. "A society plagued by shortages and unsatisfied essential needs is itself fraught with conflict," L. Karskiy from Tashkent notes in this context.

Writing about the fact that social life has grown more complex and strained and has spilled into the streets and squares, readers note that the voice of party leaders simply cannot be heard in the ballyhoo. G. Alekseyeva, an engineer from Leningrad, writes that "this is particularly important in situations which are difficult to control—of which there are quite a few today." "If the secretary for ideology is unable to persuade people whose attitude is by no means hostile but who simply cannot tolerate lies, is he in the right job?"—V. Morozov from Chelyabinsk asks with good reason.

Street democracy and rally-mania is, of course, not the best way of resolving questions and ascertaining public opinion. People's power must not be confused with mob power. "Are the noisy speeches and strikes likely to improve our life?"— T. Golubovich from Gomel asks. "This way we will be standing in line for another 100 years telling each other about the good life abroad."

Today we are only just learning the knack of living a democratic life. **We are learning to understand what freedom means—we are learning that it is not just the presentation of ultimatums but also the achievement of sensible compromises.** We are learning that political or national passions are not to be gambled with. We are learning to resolve conflicts in a civilized fashion. We are learning democracy without anarchy.

Beware: A Hoax
by Leonid Treyer, *Moscow News*, 1989

Oh, that All Fools' Day—the day of universal merrymaking. From Murmansk to Odessa everyone makes a fool of everyone else, and no one gets hurt. You can phone a friend and congratulate him on being promoted (the papers, you assure him, have already been signed). Or you can warn an acquaintance that tomorrow the price of eggs and margarine will go up and that he or she should start hoarding. True, there is practically no chance of anyone swallowing this bait, everyone is on the alert. Since childhood we remember "not to believe anyone on the first day of April".

But the saddest thing of all is that we have learned to disbelieve the whole year round. The bitter experience of mammoth-scale practical jokes has not been wasted. Let us remember the gloomy befuddling when millions of "enemies of the people" were dying in prison camps while the remaining millions were singing sincerely: "I know of no other country where man can breathe so freely." Let us recall a later practical joke when a precise deadline for building paradise on earth was given. It turned into another long drawn-out construction project to be "mothballed" in the first stages.

When they pulled the trick about developed socialism the masses were more sceptical. Then our society reached a state of stone-deaf disbelief. The sick king, wearing nothing but medals, muttered something inarticulately, but we smiled mockingly and shouted: "Viva!", not to breach the rules of the game laid down by the wise tale-teller. Of course, there were boys who stubbornly kept repeating that the king was wearing nothing, but they were publicly flogged for their nonsense.

A salient feature of the black humour of stagnation times was that the befuddling proceeded both from top to bottom and from bottom to top. The waves of "overfulfilled plan targets", "com-

(V. Kazanevsky, *Soviet News*)

missionings ahead of schedule" and "labour records" rolled towards the top of the pyramid, and from the top there came awards, prizes, titles and other earthly joys . . .

There is no hiding the fact that, in April 1985, we thought we were witnessing another hoax. We read, listened, wondered, but didn't believe that *this* was in earnest and long-term. Let's be frank—even today, many doubt. But society is being given oxygen, and people are gradually recovering from the anabiosis of past years, because there is stronger faith that the game is being played in a fair way. I'd like to end on this optimistic note, but the facts do not allow me.

Now and again jokers from among our nomenclature tend to undermine our faith in perestroika. They suddenly impose a limit on subscriptions to newspapers and magazines referring to various technical difficulties. Then, equally suddenly, all the means become available to print enough copies for everyone, though, of course, an effort is made to look for them.

Then they suddenly ban an already sanctioned meeting and then wonder why passions flare.

How many hopes have production workers pinned on the Law on State Enterprise. It will, we said, rid us of diktat by the ministries and ensure independence. Not on your life, boys, you want too much! There is a law, but no independence. Because administrative bodies without real power are the same as generals without an army. There is no need to make references to the law. For every law we have devised a powerful set of "sublaws", restrictions, explanations and instructions. If you try to get round them you'll be punished somehow.

Here's another hoax. A rather attractive Law on Cooperatives was adopted, inviting business-minded and enterprising people to act and display their mettle. Long live healthy competition! Hardly had the business-minded and enterprising responded to the call when restrictions came down in showers. This you can't, this you mustn't, and this—under no circumstances! And, so that these people should not grow rich, a Decree on Taxes appeared out of the blue like lightning—finally putting the cooperative movement into the hands of local authorities. Congratulations on the first day of April, dear cooperative members!

It is sad to note that, when given this gift, cooperative members immediately understood that they could be crushed any moment in exactly the same way as the nepmen once were. They were therefore hardly ready to risk undertaking serious and long-term projects requiring massive outlays. In the final analysis, it is not cooperative members that we pity—they will not die. We pity our economy, stuck in the quagmire of monopolism.

All these regular hoaxes are staged for us by one and the same command system, long condemned and athematized. It's alive, citizens, it's alive. It sits in numerous offices, sings hallelujah to perestroika and is not going to leave us. Because it has nowhere to go. That is why it keeps throwing up surprise after surprise, in the hope of provoking a feeling of profound disillusionment. So let us be vigilant! Let's allow ourselves only to be cheated on the first day of April!

POLICE

Caller Claims To Plant Bomb on Airliner
TASS, January 12, 1989

Leningrad January 12 *Tass*—A man who refused to name himself called to the traffic controls of Leningrad's Pulkovo Airport to say that a bomb was planted in an airliner that was to make a flight to a Caucasian resort yesterday evening.

All the services of the airport were immediately alerted and the airliner and its luggage compartment were most thoroughly checked. The search for the anonymous caller was conducted at the same time. **On the basis of a tape recording, militia personnel managed to identify the caller. He was detained. His name has become known today.** He is Aidulaziz Abdullayev, a 24-year-old cooperator.

It was established that the telephone call was made to the airport to amuse a drinking party. In such cases Soviet law envisages criminal responsibility and a restoration by a culprit of material damage to the injured party, the Soviet Aeroflot airline in this case. Preliminary estimates show that this will be a quite considerable sum.

"You Give Us the Man, We Will Find the Clause"— Why Can This Cynical "Principle" Still Be Applied By Internal Affairs Bodies?
by A. Ikonnikov, *Izvestiya*, March 31, 1989

A. Ikonnikov is department editor with the newspaper *Leninskaya Smena*.

Alma-Ata Oblast—The papers in question are not marked "Secret" or "For Official Use" and bear neither seal nor signature. These papers are only documents by virtue of the handwritten inscriptions of those who decided to make them available for publication. T. Seksenbayev and R. Giulayev, divisional inspectors of the Chilikskiy Rayon Internal Affairs Department, Alma-Ata Oblast, and their former colleague A. Amurlayev, supplemented their statements with these typewritten lines, frayed at the edges from being carried around for so long in pockets and map-cases:

"Minimum:
"1. LTP (Occupational therapy units)—8 persons. For divisional inspectors in Chilik—10 persons. Those who failed to meet the target in 1987—8 persons plus the shortfall of the previous year.
"2. Article 202.1—1 person per month; 6—in the first 6 months; 6—in the second 6 months.
"3. Administrative surveillance—2 persons.
"4. Three petty thefts per month; 36 in the year as a whole.
"5. One firearms charge per month; 11 in the year as a whole.
"6. Fourteen breaches of passport regulations per month; 156 in the year as a whole.
"7. Five DL (fiduciary) cases. . . .
[Numbering as published]
"13. The use of transport for mercenary purposes—1 per 2 months; Article 140—6 in the year as a whole.
"14. Breach of fire safety regulations—2 in the year as a whole; 1 in the first 6 months, 1 in the second 6 months.
"15. Breach of motor transport garaging regulations (Article 141)—4 per quarter.
"16. Breach of PDD (traffic) regulations—1 per quarter; 4 in the year as a whole. . . ."

So what is this document we see before us? An aide memoire, instructions, or what? It is a plan. A plan of work for a divisional inspector for the year. In this case, for 1988. For example, point one: He must commit no fewer than eight people for compulsory treatment against alcohol abuse. Divisional inspectors at the rayon center must each commit 10 people. And those who "failed" the plan for the previous year must make up the shortfall in addition to the set figure. . . . Point two: Each divisional inspector must arrest one person per month under Article 201.1 of the Kazakh Soviet Socialist Republic (SSR) Criminal Code (for parasitism), but in such a way that he arrests a total of six parasites in the first half of the year and the same number in the second half. And so on and so forth—the list contains 22 points in all, but we have cited only the most typical. As far as the abbreviations are concerned—"LTP" stands for occupational therapy unit; "PDD" stands for traffic regulations; and "DL" means fiduciary. And these figures are the "minimum."

The maximum, as we see, is not stipulated.

I showed these papers to two different people who do not know each other. Here are their comments.

P. Lushkov, who used to be a member of the criminal investigations department, but left the militia for personal reasons and at his own request: "There is no doubt that these 'minimum requirements' are an unofficial order to establish the quantitative work norm for members of the rayon internal affairs department. Unofficial, without any signature, seal, or other 'identification marks,' because it is illegal. After all, a 'plan for people' obviously gives rise to inevitable distortions, and militia workers quite often have to resort to blatant breaches of regulations in order to achieve their set targets. During my time in internal affairs bodies, as a member of the criminal investigation department, I was not set such targets, but I did hear more than once of their existence in one form or another—from divisional inspectors, for example. What is more, as a rule, those who fulfill their set 'quota' on all counts are considered the best divisional inspectors. This system is convenient for the leadership—it means that there is always something specific on which to call an associate to account. It is believed that these methods provide reliable incentives for work."

Candidate of Juridical Sciences, Militia Colonel A. Ginzburg: "Unfortunately, I fully admit that the chief of a rayon department could issue such 'work programs' to his subordinates. This depraved practice, inherited from sadly remembered times, has certainly not been eradicated everywhere and is still making itself felt. What is more, this kind of thing is sometimes done 'with the best of intentions'—to galvanize personnel and mobilize them to a more effective struggle to guard law and order and so forth. It is impossible in this connection not to recall the quota system of Stalin's time. . . ."

Now to how these "minimum requirements" are met in practice!

On 1 May, Marat Dzhangozin met his divisional inspector in the street. He said hello to him. The other did not reply but sat him in his car, drove off, and locked him up. He released him the next morning. But a week later, Marat suddenly received draft papers from the military commissariat.

"To Citizen Marat Dzhangozin, 9, Gagarin Street, Kuram. Under the 'Law on General Military Duty' you are liable for conscription for active military service. I order you to present yourself on 5 May 1988 at 0900 hours at the conscription section at the following address: Rayon Military Commissariat, 2d Department, Chilik. Rayon military commissar (the signature is illegible)."

Marat Dzhangozin completed his active service 17 years ago. But he answered the summons. In the 2d Department they asked to see his papers, shut them in a safe, and let him go home.

"The next day, 7 May, I was taken from my place of work in the morning by the divisional inspector," Dzhangozin said. " 'Where are your papers?' he asked me. 'At the military commissariat,' I replied. 'Let's go!' And again I was locked up in a cell. He got hold of my papers the same day and immediately registered the matter with the courts. It turned out to be one big fraud—and the military commissariat was in league with them."

Marat assured us that he was in the court no longer than 5 minutes: Quickly leafing through his papers, the judge silently pointed a finger at him. This signified 1 year of compulsory treatment against alcohol abuse. The court's records say that Dzhangozin's mother allegedly could not cope with her drunkard son. In reality, however, no one even spoke to Natalya Petrovna and she was not invited to attend the hearing. At first, she just thought that her son had been drafted for some sort of military training—until, by some miracle, he managed to contact her just before he left for the occupational therapy unit. For 4 months she pestered various authorities and only in September were her efforts finally successful.

"Following an appeal from the oblast public prosecutor, the presidium of the Alma-Ata Oblast Court passed a valid resolution to release Marat Dzhangozin, of the 'Kuramskiy' State Farm [Sovkhoz], from compulsory treatment in an occupational therapy unit," I was drily informed by B. Dzhumadilov, chairman of the Chilikskiy Rayon People's Court. He also told me that a similar decision had been taken in relation to M. Dusekeyev from the Kabylov Sovkhov.

It was only thanks to the tireless efforts of his old mother that Marat Dzhangozin found himself home again. Otherwise he would have been "treated" in the occupational therapy unit for a whole year. And then? Let us take another look at the "minimum requirements": Divisional Inspector Shukelov could perfectly well have arrested him for some other transgression; reasons can always be found, in view of the compulsory "norm." You give us the man, we will find the clause, as they say. . . .

Lawlessness, once elevated to the rank of an order (even an "unofficial" order) gives rise to a deprivation of rights. Instead of protection for citizens, which law enforcement bodies are supposed to guarantee, people sometimes find themselves completely unprotected in the face of these bodies' arbitrary rule. But people work in these bodies. And people are not all the same. Far from everyone obediently submits to the bosses' will, expressed in an impersonal list of "minimum requirements." Here is one example.

Anuar Amurlayev is 27 years old. He, a divisional inspector, was dismissed from internal affairs on 2 June 1988 on instructions from the chief of the Alma-Ata Oblast Internal Affairs Administration "for reasons of incompatibility with official requirements." He has been without work since then.

"It is not only to do with me," A. Amurlayev said. "It is to do with the actual organization of work in our rayon internal affairs department and the atmosphere that has been created there. It is like this: If someone 'does not make a good showing,' he seems to automatically become a candidate for dismissal. The 'minimum requirements' must be met—at any price. That is the demand made of personnel. Our rayon internal affairs department chief, Berdybayev, stopped me at every briefing and asked: 'How many people have you sent to occupational therapy units? How many have you arrested under administrative surveillance?' I told the comrade lieutenant colonel that there were no habitual drunkards in my sector and that everyone released from places of confinement was behaving well and not breaking the rules of the community. His usual response was obscenities and insults. But on 20 May there was a total uproar. Berdybayev said to me at a briefing meeting: 'You should commit your own wife to an occupational therapy unit if you think that there are no alcoholics in your sector!' I could not restrain myself and replied: 'In that case, you should commit your own wife as well and we will fulfill the plan together.' I was dismissed a few days later—on Berdybayev's representation."

He complained for several months, writing letters to the oblast party committee and the Kazakh Communist Party Central Committee. So far, no verification measure had brought complete clarity. So he decided to turn to a journalist. Later he was joined by two divisional inspectors from the Chilikskiy Rayon Internal Affairs Department—Militia Lieutenant T. Seksenbayev and Militia Lieutenant R. Giulayev. It was they who brought the "minimum requirements" for various years, certified with their own signatures.

. . . All that remains to report is that, according to members of the Chilikskiy Rayon Internal Affairs Department, they have not been issued with any "minimum requirements" this year. The instructions are: Use the old ones. . . .

From the editor: On receiving the manuscript of this article from the author, together with the necessary documents to back it up (originals of the "minimum requirements," written statements by the divisional inspectors, recorded conversations, and dictaphone cassettes), the editorial office instructed its correspondent in Alma-Ata to try to find an answer to the question: Who is responsible for initiating such instructions, and how typical is this work practice of internal affairs bodies in Alma-Ata Oblast?

Setting a typewritten copy of the "minimum requirements" for 1988 cited at the beginning in front of T. Berdybayev, chief of the Chilikskiy Rayon Internal Affairs Department, I asked him to explain the origin and point of this document. Turgan Chinadilovich showed no particular surprise. He even shrugged his shoulders rather gaily:

"We have not issued any such papers in this rayon department or given them to any divisional inspectors. Nor does the administration plan our work in any way. There is no plan in the militia, nor could there be! Only Amurlayev could invent such a thing. . . ."

I had to explain to him that, in addition to Amurlayev, another two associates had handed such documents to a journalist. T. Berdybayev looked away:

"If you told me who, I would be able to explain. . . ." His voice trailed away, but then, not waiting for my reply, he suddenly burst out indignantly: "But what right, tell me that, did Amurlayev or anyone else have to give secret documents to anyone?!"

THE PRESS

Gerasimov Criticizes Delayed Reportage
from the "International Panorama" program presented
  by Gennadiy Gerasimov, Moscow Television Service,
  April 16, 1989

GERASIMOV: In light of the imminent information forum to be held in London, an offshoot of the Vienna CSCE meeting, I visited the Moscow office of *Time* magazine to see how journalists function in Moscow and to talk about the kind of news they are sending home. I spoke to Nancy Trevor about the worldwide circulation of the magazine and went on to discuss the benefits of glasnost in enabling foreign journalists to provide wider coverage of Soviet affairs.

[BEGIN TREVOR RECORDING] . . . We intend to continue recounting what is happening in your country. This week, for example, the main event for us has been the situation in Georgia. The nationalities issue, of course, interests us. We would like to go there and to produce a report, but Georgia—Tbilisi—is closed to us. So, unfortunately, we have been forced to give up this idea. We have had to use just the telephone in the hope of getting information from local residents. We reckon, however, that there will nonetheless be more glasnost. Were we allowed to go there, that would be full glasnost. But we hope that Georgia will soon be opened up to us. [end recording]

GERASIMOV: You have heard the complaint. In this particular case there is a reason for not allowing them in. It is difficult for the foreign correspondent to get through to objective observers amid the sea of emotions; he could be dragged into things. However, to discuss this generally, it should be recognized that our media starts to cover up as soon as anything unforseen crops up. And most often, this is not out of consideration for the interests of the state, but for secondary considerations such as: What will they say abroad? Or: Why worry people? These arguments are first and foremost a cover for concern for official honor. Hence, the paucity of information at a critical moment.

In the past few days the papers have been writing in detail

[295]

about the coverage of the sailors as their submarine perished, but why is it that the world found out about this very misfortune exactly 24 hours after it had happened, to the minute? Moreover, by that time the world itself already knew all about it. Of course, this is not several days' silence like that following Chernobyl, but the disease of holding back unpleasant news, as if it were going to disappear of its own accord, this disease has not yet been cured, and manifests itself every time an irregular situation arises.

What Kind of Law on the Press Do We Need?
Moscow News

MIKHAIL FEDOTOV: We decided to hold this round-table discussion to try and define in advance just what we're expecting from this Law. Otherwise, when the draft has officially been submitted for discussion, we'll find ourselves bound by a text that has already been prepared. And then any, even the most sensible, proposal will only be considered if it fits into the framework of the given version.

ALEXANDER BORIN *(Literary Gazette)*: Getting information is the key issue. The Law must, first of all, state clearly that a journalist is entitled to get any kind of information. The information that cannot be provided must be clearly listed in the Law. We have the well-known principle: everything is allowed that is not prohibited. This must apply to the press, too.

But, what is to be done if information is not provided anyway? In such a case, a newspaper or a journalist should be given the right to take the matter to court.

A few words about responsibility for mistakes and the right to cover criminal cases while investigation is still in progress. In my opinion, we should not give pretrial reports. Some people argue: "But in the West they do give such reports". Yes, they do. But, first, in the West a newspaper's opinion does not influence the court the way it does in our country. And, second, should a Western journalist call someone a criminal and the person proves to be innocent, that person may literally make him a pauper, because in the West one is held materially responsible for causing moral damage. I think our Law on the Press should also provide for such responsibility.

And something else. Is cost accounting necessary in journalism? I think it is. At present the circulation of newspapers is going up by the million. As a result, the treasury gets millions of rubles. But does a journalist stand to gain from this, materially? Not at all. The Law must change this.

You sometimes hear that the press only reluctantly gives the floor to those wishing to put its publications to debate. The Law on the Press, it is said, should oblige newspapers to carry different points of view. No doubt, opponents must be given the floor. But what is to be done if the opponent's reply to your publication, while being courteous and civil, is absolutely incoherent and confused? At present, a newspaper is free not to publish such material. And this is correct. I think that the Law is in no position to interfere with relations of this kind.

VLADIMIR ENTIN (USSR Academy of Sciences' Institute of State and Law): World jurisprudence has some experience in tackling this problem. Take French legislation, for example. Among other things, it provides for the "right of reply", which can be used by a private person or an organization whose interests have been infringed upon in a press publication. They can come up with a statement in the pages of the same publication. As a rule, the reply can be of the same size as the newspaper's article in question, but should not exceed 200 lines. A special body sees to it that similar rules are observed on radio and television.

As for the question of access to information, I agree with you that this is going to be one of the main issues during the democratization process. The Law must, first, set rigid and early deadlines for the provision of information, otherwise it loses its value. Second, each government department must have a person responsible for providing information. And this person must bear double responsibility, administrative-disciplinary and financial.

YURI BATURIN (USSR Academy of Sciences' Institute of State and Law): Over the past twenty years, there have been several draft laws on the press. Vladimir Entin and I took part in preparing the latest version. We had a chance to see what had become of our proposals after they had been sent to "higher instances". The article on the provision of information remained: "Press organs and other mass media are entitled to get information. . . ." But what we had written as our next proposal had disappeared, namely: "Information can be denied only if it contains data which constitute a state or military secret. The refusal should be handed in to the representative of press organs and other mass media in a written form, within three days. It must indicate the name of the official, the organ or organization that denies the information, the date, and the reason why the requested information cannot be singled out from the data containing state or military secrets. A refusal to provide information and failure to observe the stipulations of the given article can be appealed against within a month, through administrative or legal means. The official who signs the refusal to provide information to press organs and other mass media should pay a fine of 50 to 100 rubles or meet the expenses of a lawsuit, or do both if the court finds the refusal ungrounded."

The same happened to the other articles of the draft law. Such an attitude to drawing up laws worries me greatly.

ALEXANDER ARONOV (*Moskovsky Komsomolets* newspaper): **While talking about the law on journalism and printed matter, we somehow leave out the question of protecting journalists.** In the present conditions of openness we have all become very bold. But this reminds me of an animated cartoon about a ballerina who dances on the deck of a ship. Whirling and leaping, she edges towards the bow, and all but flies off the deck. One of three things may happen to her under the circumstances: either the ship moves fast enough to be there for her to land on the deck, or she manages to make a turn and leap back, or she flops into the water. I am afraid we are close to the latter. **We boldly leap ahead while there is no solid ground under our feet, as yet.** And the one on whose toes we step can do whatever he pleases to us. I would like to see this situation changed and a "dual power" established, that is, I would like power to be exercised not only "vertically", by all kinds of superiors, but also "horizontally", by our journalistic workshop. The court of brother-journalists, based on a code of professional honour, must be able to both censure and protect a journalist. Of course, this does not apply to anything coming under the Criminal Code.

YURI BORIN (*Krokodil* magazine): From what Yuri Baturin has said here I come to the conclusion that the Law on the Press is being prepared with some apprehension, they fear journalists may become a nuisance for the various departments and win the right to demand something from them. I think the Law on the Press should have a section on the efficiency of the press. Respective organizations **must be obliged** to react to press publications. **I, for example, am sick and tired of writing about the content of nitrates in food products. I have already written eight times about it. And no response.**

MIKHAIL FEDOTOV: This does not mean, of course, that the ministries should stand to attention for newspapers. **But the Law** must oblige official bodies to react to criticism every time, and the press must carry their answers or refutations.

VLADIMIR KRYAZHKOV (Sverdlovsk Law Institute): I agree that the right to information is the core of the Law on the Press. It is necessary to provide for a definite system of obtaining information in different spheres, including archives and state and public organizations.

ALLA VERKHOVSKAYA (Moscow University's Department of Journalism): Today people often write critically about "directives by telephone" to courts. But what about similar "rights" used in relation to editorial boards, for example, the right to confiscate or hold up an issue, to take material out of an issue, a refusal to OK or to visa a material? One of the laboratories at our Department of Journalism has conducted a sociological survey in the Tomsk Region. The local journalists least of all complained about the difficulties connected with obtaining information from the local authorities. But they had a serious problem of a different nature—the command approach used in directing the press.

VLADIMIR DEREVITSKY (*Zhurnalist* magazine): **Alexander Borin said that one cannot guarantee every opponent the right to reply to a press publication, since this would mean publishing even "indigestible" material. We know, however, that such a pretext is often used to turn down quite "coherent" articles which happen to be too much to the point.**

Can I Have the Floor?
A Noose Around the News
by Alexander Bovin, Vladimir Pozner, and Vladimir Tsvetov, *Moscow News*, April 9–16, 1989

Will an athlete run faster with a weight attached to his foot? Will a ballerina dance better in toe-shoes one size too small? Judging by the decision to introduce passes for correspondents covering emergency situations, athletes do run faster with ankle weights and ballerinas do dance better in too tight toe-shoes. The idea is that journalists will work more efficiently when their activity is restricted.

The new regulation, instituted by the Union of Soviet Journalists and the USSR Ministry of Internal Affairs, outlines the procedure for admission of journalists to the site of a fire, earthquake or meeting. To cover these events, a journalist must now have a special pass in addition to his official identity card.

Along with other anomalies from the stagnation period, our society is getting rid of everything dubbed "special": special commodity supplies, special depositories, special cemeteries. But the bureaucrats cannot exist without something being "special". Perhaps this is why it occurred to them to regard natural disasters as "special fires" or "special accidents", and public meetings as "special meetings" which only "special journalists" with "special passes" may cover.

Henceforth, these "special" correspondents, showing the special pass marked "Press" registered well in advance, will be able to go wherever they like without having first to coordinate and make numerous telephone calls. But aren't the identity cards issued by a paper, a magazine or television—legal organizations formed in conformity with Party and state resolutions—sufficient to give one ready access to the scene of a fire "without having to coordinate or call"? Of course, at the site of a fire the identity card won't protect a journalist from danger. But will a "special pass"?

We were told that these passes were prompted by "concern" for the life and health of journalists. But in reality the authors of this novel regulation are concerned about something entirely different: first to restrict access to places where natural disasters have occurred or public movements are occurring, then to restrict the amount of information about these events ... What this leads to we all know well enough from recent history.

Maybe we've had enough of bureaucrats' "special amateurishness" which runs counter to perestroika and glasnost?

Can I Have the Floor?
Vague Wording May Hurt Journalists
by Yuri Chernichenko and Mikhail Poltoranin, *Moscow News*, April 23–30, 1989

The just published Decree of the Presidium of the USSR Supreme Soviet amending the USSR Law on Crimes Against the State and other Soviet legislation is too serious a document to be ignored. As journalists, we are especially concerned over the following lines in the Decree:

"Public insults or discreditation of supreme bodies of the USSR state power and government; of other state bodies set up or elected by the Congress of People's Deputies of the USSR or the USSR Supreme Soviet, of officials appointed, elected or endorsed by the Congress of People's Deputies of the USSR or the USSR Supreme Soviet; or of public organizations and their all-Union bodies set up according to the legal procedures of and operating in line with the Constitution of the USSR shall be punished . . ."

If only public insults were included here we would not qualify it except to say that this law should cover public insults not just of officials appointed, elected or endorsed by supreme bodies of legislative power, but of all USSR citizens. But the word "discreditation", which is not defined in the Decree, is a cause for very great concern. This concern results from the fact that Article 49 of the Soviet Constitution guarantees all citizens of the USSR the right to criticize. As journalists, we feel it is our duty to criticize specific persons, organizations and state bodies mentioned in this Decree.

Does this mean that now all criticism in the press is to be regarded as "public discreditation", subjecting the authors to punishment under the law? Shall we now, with the help of legal aides, do independent investigations, in addition to those of authorized bodies whose job it is to check on the observance of Constitutional norms by the persons or organizations? Since it appears that such judgements can only be passed by juridical bodies and, in the final analysis, by courts of justice, are we obliged, before we attempt a criticism in the media, to first sue the person or organization we are criticizing and only after the court charges them with unconstitutional actions voice our criticisms publicly?

These questions about the Decree should be answered promptly and competently because their vagueness undermines the very foundations of Soviet professional journalism in general and in the age of perestroika whose objective is to resolutely put an end to the numerous bureaucratic abuses in the operation of our state bodies, public organizations and officials in particular.

Reader Urges End to Publication of Greetings
Letter to the Editor of *Izvestiya*, November 18, 1988

Leninabad—Our press now contains far fewer eulogies, high-flown publications, and so forth. The majority of published items are to the point. Perhaps the only exception is the telegrams of congratulations sent by the heads of foreign states on our holidays. It would be possible simply to list briefly who has sent congratulations and no more. And use the newspaper area to publish topical articles and sharp letters from readers.

I don't know, perhaps these telegrams must be published in accordance with some written or unwritten procedure? But after all, we have recently abandoned many obsolete customs. Perhaps we can also do without the full text of these telegrams?

—F. Bagautdibov

PROSTITUTION

The Ministry of "Easy" Behavior
by Mikhail Uspensky, *Ogonyek*, October 1988

Pavel Karpovich Pilipchuk has led his life well, and all in high positions. Having ruined agriculture, furniture manufacture, and exact machinery manufacture, he was, through a unanimous decision, sent into a newly formed ministry.

The ministry was established when finally, with heavy heart, it was accepted that the ugly a condition called by common folk prostitution is a fact in our society. There were, however, great minds who had decided that since such a condition exists, it should be directed to serving the highest interests.

"We'll appoint Pavel Pilipchuk to this!" said his friends in very high places. "It is true that he has made a few mistakes but this after all is not that difficult a thing. Every fool can do this. After all it's such a commonplace thing."

They had to start from scratch. Drubetskoi-zade, a consultant, brought to Pilipchuk's office the works of Kuprin, Maupassant, Remarque, and other shameful literature. The new minister looked at the colorful book covers for a long time but could not bring himself to open a single one of the books. "I've read all of these when I was still walking to work!" he told the consultant. "This is not for us. Big deal—Remarque! It's time to stop looking to foreign technology."

A twenty-five-story building of a rather symbolic shape was built for the ministry. Pavel Karpovich went to the Intourist hotel to gather information. "Cough up the cash," the first beauty he met said to him, and named her price in hard currency. Pilipchuk sighed in excitement, became very happy, and not wasting any time spent all the dollars given to him by the ministry. At the same time, he never stopped oohing, whistling, and using his personal computer, which really annoyed the beauty. Finally, the figure that appeared on the screen was so high, that Pavel Karpovich phoned it in to the high authorities, without leaving the beauty.

The authorities had the same reaction as he did and allotted a sum that would be enough to build one aircraft carrier, two theaters, and a wax museum for half a million statues. "I will bring this flow of money into the state pocket!" Pilipchuk announced publicly, and assigned himself a salary in Swiss francs, in an amount never before heard by anyone. "At least I'll live normally," he thought to himself.

All over the country, disregarding regional and nationalistic peculiarities, the foundation was laid for two thousand five hundred . . . For a long time they tried to decide what to call the establishment. The old name was not appropriate. "Public house" in English simply means a bar and that might disorient the foreigners. Besides, many libraries are called "public," which in no way implies that their employees are ready to share their flame with any reader. Drubetskoi-zade dug into the history and after a little while pulled out the word "bordello." Everyone got busy on the sites of "Main Bordello Construction," "East Siberian Bordello Construction," "Far East Bordello Construction," but that did not last long since no one knew what a bordello is supposed to look like: a hospital, a disco or an area for feeding young herds.

The construction stopped dead in its tracks. Pavel Karpovich ran to consult the beauty. "I rent a place on Kutuzovsky Street," she said with pride. Pilipchuk raised the required sum and convinced the ministry to allot the sum for the building of new apartment houses. But financial committees were formed asking: How will you control what's going on? Who knows what your employees will be doing behind closed doors? Is this how you take care of the state capital? Pavel Karpovich ordered all the doors broken down so that everything would be in full view and under control, and ordered that a booth be put up for the guard in the middle of each floor.

Finally, everything was finished: Light bulbs were screwed in, drapes were hung, even the plumbing worked once in a while. The first inspection committee, however, noted the lack of visual aids. So Pavel Karpovich, instead of putting up the pictures from his favorite *Playboy*, ordered the posting of lists of regulations and obligations, plans, graphics, health bulletins, and the

Best Worker of the Week board. And so the plans began to take root.

Only three months after the official opening, with TV coverage and a performance by Alla Pugacheva, the first employees, still blushing, stepped over the threshold of the first establishment. Having put in the first week from eight to five, and not seeing a single client, the Russian joy girls renewed their former business on their own time. Actually, a few intoxicated persons attempted to pay a visit to the bordello, but the guard on duty quickly put them in their place and sent them to the detox center. Then matters became even worse with the high officials. The specialists from the capital sent to them were immediately given assignments, while the small-town girls could not overcome burning provincial shame. Organized recruitment was the only thing left to try. Additional benefits were offered: free meals, and outfits composed of black army coats, black orphan hats, and black thigh-high-boots at three rubles a pair. This attracted many train station regulars, but as far as their clients, those were their old friends who entered through the window, and brought no profit. The reason that they came through the window was that in order to enter a bordello, one needed to submit a passport, an autobiography, a questionnaire consisting of ninety-six points, a certificate from your place of residence, and a certificate about the health of your wife; and the "old friends" had never even seen such things.

The experimental bordello for youth, "Zoriushka," was at first quite popular, since for entertainment it had a famous rock group, Bliakha-Mukha. One day, however, a few young people who had previously served in Afghanistan demolished the bordello in a matter of minutes, and beat the hell out of the rockers. For a long time after that, the ruins of the bordello carried a bad name.

Pavel Karpovich still continued throwing the magic number into the faces of the leaders, though they were already looking at him with obvious displeasure. For the third time, Pilipchuk ran to the beauty. "All right, you nut!" said she, taking pity on him, and called her partners. Demanding for themselves a number of benefits and getting rid of bureaucratic catches, the capital's joy girls organized an examplary bordello, which if you are looking for comparisons, was like comparing "Beryozka" to a small-town convenience store. In the visitors' book, the very excited reaction of the 120 year-old american billionaire was registered; he had now become an even better friend to our country. There was even a satellite experience exchange set up with colleagues in San Francisco, which showed that our ladies were very strong on ideology. Yet even if the joy girls, partiotically motivated by hard currency, could work twenty-four hours a day, it would still not be enough to cover all the expenses.

Also, some famous lady journalist, after a short change in occupation, raised hell in the *Literaturnaya Gazetta.* In the article, she as a woman, a mother, a wife, and a lover pleasantly pointed out that bordellos work during hours that are inconvenient for the working class, employees steal the imported contraceptives, alcohol is sold in the buffet at highway-robbery prices, sheets, like those on trains, are constantly damp, health hazards are all over the place, and in one word what's going on there is nothing but debauchery. "Imagine," she wrote, "some of these men and women see each other for the first time!" Everything was of course blamed on the schools, the komsomol, and bourgeois ideology.

The fact of AIDS decided the fate of the ministry for good.

Only the faithful beauty took pity on poor Pavel Karpovich Pilipchuk. "Oh well, I'll take care of you, you sorry man," she said. And she is still taking care of him today.

REHABILITATION

Questions of Democracy
Moscow News

I drive into the yard of my theatre. Then I get out of the car and do something as automatic as wiping one's feet before going inside. Damn that passerby who caught me in the act and grinned. I wish you'd seen that grin: it was a mixture of irony, pity, bitterness and scorn. For me? For me too, perhaps. Not only for me, I get the impression, but for my whole way of life. Amazing that such a trifle should have triggered so many questions in my mind, not necessarily connected, but they kept piling up and then burst to the surface.

Here's one of the things that's puzzling me. How it is possible that a power-crazy official—not just anytime, but after April

1985—ruins the life of a fighter for the truth and then is only "strictly reprimanded" instead of being thrown out of office? And then what kind of a punishment is a "strict reprimand"? What does it sound like? Something like: "Tut, tut"?

I'm also puzzled by this: how are we to learn democracy without textbooks, manuals or even visual aids? Can we (for the time being!) borrow them from those who have already learned democracy? On a visit to Amsterdam ten years ago I read about a traffic cop stopping a car, sniffing alcohol on the driver's breath and fining him 200 guilders (a fabulous sum compared to the per diem allowance of a Soviet on business abroad). The poor devil accepted the fine with a childish smile.

"What are you so happy about?" the somewhat taken aback pillar of the law asked gallantly.

"I'm the Minister of the Interior. . . ."

And another question. How can one reinstate someone in the Party posthumously? In the first place, not all the dead would necessarily welcome their reinstatement in the Party which failed to protect them in the fateful hour. Second, if posthumous reinstatement is possible, why is posthumous expulsion not possible? Playing such games with the **other world** isn't a good idea, I think. It's even blasphemous.

Why is it that the colour of a car bespeaks the rank of the person in it and grants him certain freedoms on the road not written into the traffic rules? Why not, before appointing someone to a high office, ask him: "Is your driving licence in order?" Otherwise we have to hire and feed burly drivers for them.

Can society be socialist if those who most need help—children, old people, and the disabled—are not properly cared for? Which one of us wouldn't agree to a more modest lifestyle if we were sure that all of the best things were being given to them? Not the other folks? . . .

Remembering the TV report about the Pamyat society suing a Moscow newspaper, I wonder why I can't sue the procurator who failed to bring an action against the frenzied type prancing before the camera showing off his T-shirt covered with chauvinist slogans? There are articles in the Constitution and the Criminal Code that punish this! So can I sue a district procurator or even an all-Union one? They also saw Pamyat's display on their TVs! Maybe I'm going too far mentioning the USSR procurator? But he, like myself, remembers how elated we were when there, in the United States, the president was forced to step down because of the Watergate break in. . . .

Now that we are really nominating candidates to the main body of power, for the first time ever, why is it that officials caught cheating in the campaign aren't instantly barred from this clean and conscientious affair but only reproached in the press and on TV?

If we call perestroika a revolution, why do we indulgently call those who oppose this revolution anti-perestroika forces instead of counterrevolutionaries? Not many people mind being called "anti-perestroika", but they wouldn't dare let themselves be called counterrevolutionaries.

REMORSE

I Hope! Seriousness from a Humorist
by Alexander Ivanov, *Moscow News*, 1989

It has become so thrillingly interesting to live!

Hopes, fears. Everybody is deeply worried about the future. The opponents of perestroika can't sleep. Who'll beat whom? We should beat them. But if they beat us? Doubts, arguments, discussions. We are not too good at all this yet. But then, how could we have acquired this ability? Many people think that pluralism means simply "to spit at", don't worry, we'll soon learn to argue. But why am I feeling ever more powerless, sad and worried? What is the source of my pain? At long last I understand—my soul is in pain and my conscience is ill at ease. I frequently recall the words of Academician Dmitry Likhachev about the need for universal repentance. This ancient concept, reborn in the great film by Tenghiz Abuladze, is discussed nowadays more and more often. Some say we should repent, others declare there's no need for us to do so, and still others—that some ought to repent, but not everybody. Why am I thinking about this all the time?

On the day I was born there were 22 days left until 1937. I was 16 the day Stalin died, a teen-ager. It is hard to make anyone of such an age responsible for the last crime of Stalinism—the "Doctors case". And after that? Well, I became an adult and if adults regard themselves as human beings then they're responsible for quite a lot, if not for everything that's going on around us.

You know which is the most tormenting question for me, one which I hear over and over again? "And where were you before?" asked either maliciously or gloatingly.

Asked this question I feel awful. Of course, it is possible not to answer it, or to joke or lie. But if I'm to answer in earnest—where was I in fact?

I was already quite a mature man when the revolting, shameful baiting of Pasternak started.

At the time I didn't read *Doctor Zhivago* but I understood perfectly the injustice of what was happening. And what did the senior-course student do? Nothing.

At a time when dangerous clouds started hovering over *Novy Mir* and Alexander Tvardovsky, I was already a professional man of letters. True, I wasn't yet a member of the Writers Union. I remember well the "letter of the 11". One of those who signed it declared recently that he has nothing to repent. That's understandable. If you don't have a conscience, there's no use calling on it. But what did I do? Why, nothing at all.

How many things happened after that! I was already a "real" writer, with a "writer's card". I saw everything, and I understood everything. And yet Veniamin Kaverin, not so young and in poor health, signed, I think, all the letters of protest that were sent at the time to the most supreme instances. He was taking a risk, of course. But he couldn't just sit and watch.

And I didn't sign anything. But then I wasn't offered anything to sign—I wasn't that widely known, mine was not the required name—in general, what could you get from a humorist? But I am not trying to justify myself. I could have said something on my own but I didn't.

But there were people. And there still are.

Academician Andrei Sakharov, he spoke out. Without the faintest hope of winning in his lifetime, as far as he was aware. He sacrificed everything and got nothing in return—except the right to live eternally in the memory of his descendants. He is alive and in good health, thank God, and much of what is going on now coincides with his appeals and recommendations. What a happy man he is! And I? And I am nothing. I preferred my tiny cosiness and calm. The usual contention of the little man—"What could I do alone?"—doesn't work when you ask yourself.

And where was I when, in Leningrad, Iosif Brodsky was being humiliated, persecuted and charged with being an idler, finally to be forced to get out of our country? I think I was in Leningrad. Taking advantage of this moment, I'd at least like to congratulate the major poet on winning the Nobel Prize for literature, even though I am not personally acquainted with him.

But I was acquainted with Alexander Galich! Not very closely, but I was. Once, when we met, Galich told me that he liked what I was doing. I'll brag that I was proud then and I'm proud now. I always admired Galich's songs, but at the time . . . oh, how monotonously and without any imagination did the ousters act—and I was away. I was goodness knows where! I was probably arranging my own affairs, and now there is no one left for me to repent to or ask pardon from. But can you ask pardon for *this*?

And now something very recent. The discussion by the Secretariat of the Union of Soviet Writers of Leonid Brezhnev's trilogy *Little Land*, *Rebirth* and *Virgin Land* was published. I still remember the torment of shame that I felt when reading the report in the paper. The gulping tone of admiration and the lauding almost like ecstatic prayers! This can only be the result of a complete loss of human dignity. No one forced them to react like that, they could very well have kept silent, without losing anything. Well, and me? Of course, I wasn't there, but if millions of people like me hadn't kept silent, would this gamut of triumphing, grovelling good-for-nothings have been possible? Maybe not. And our culture would not have suffered such a loss.

So where was I, what was I doing? I kept myself to myself, insultingly. I was an orator, but only in my kitchen, and I spoke sincerely only to my closest friends—and quietly, too, without raising my voice. Anecdotes, ironic commentaries—nothing serious. You can persuade many people, but not yourself if, of course, there is inside you that untouchable something which would not be discovered even in a postmortem.

But such things are impossible now, today!

Oh, here we go . . . Publications of forces opposed to perestroika surface here and there like poisonous bubbles, under different pretexts. They are rebuffed, but it is usually an apologizing, simpering or reconciliatory rebuff: some of our compatriots don't seem to understand, but let's excuse these confused co-citizens. Maybe they'll realize and repent. . . . All the advocates of renewal, me included, are to blame for such connivance.

When will we realize that a mortal threat looms over our barely-started perestroika? We would do well to remember more often that a revolution that can defend itself is worth something. And it is *defended* by its advocates—by all and each one separately. And everything depends on what each one of us is.

Returning to my own soul, how important it is to realize how

far a man can go and still call himself a man. Then, overcoming
fear and indifference, man says—that's the limit, I can't continue
like this!

Can it be that I'm incorrigible and hopeless?

If I at least feel ashamed and wish to repent, doesn't that mean
there's hope?

How is one to live without hope?

REVENGE

Our Armor Is Strong
by M. Zhvanetsky, *Ogonyek*, December 1988

I'd like to do this the way it was done during the war; to buy a
tank and use it for myself for some time. It is probably a nice
feeling to show up at the building committee and request that
they change the floor in the kitchen, without getting out of the
tank. It will also probably be nice to stop by the market and ask
through the hole "how much?!" "For a kilo or for the whole
sack?!" It's also nice to have a friend with a helicopter who'd fly
ahead, and a few friends with machine guns who'd run in the
back. This way, you can go from city to city, sleep whenever you
want. It's great when you hear someone screaming, a saleslady
for example, who is screaming so loudly that you can hear her in
the tank. You can just ride up to the stand, ride up on the
sidewalk, wait until the smoke clears, and ask, "What seems to
be the problem here?" "Why can't we all live in peace and
quiet?" And when she screams "Who's the wiseguy here?" to
answer, "Me." And then to ride up closer to the stand, asking,
"What seems to be the reason for complaints? Service? Are you
weighing off the wrong amount? Why don't you weigh me something? And put it right here into the hole. And now smile, right
here into the hole; and keep smiling while I'm reweighing it."

Or you can ask, "Why are you not building houses on schedule?" and take the guy in charge to the wall where they have
time schedules. Let him explain them to us. Let them also
explain whether the drugs that are prescribed should be the ones
that are available or the ones that actually help, and what is the

difference between the two. Having such a piece of machinery, it should not at all be difficult to invite the entire creative union over, to talk about the acceptance of this monologue. And if someone is against it, you can always ask while sitting on the tank, "For what reason, exactly?" We can even go onto the stage together, one of us will be reading the monologue, while the other one will be explaining right there why it should not be read. Then we'll see who will draw a larger crowd . . .

REVOLUTION

The Fate of the World Revolution
Interview with Prof. I. Krivoguz, doctor of historical science,
by I. Solganik, *Argumenty i Fakty*, April 8–14, 1989

THE VICTORY OF socialist revolutions in all countries of the world was predicted by Marx, Engels, and Lenin. The first 20 years of the existence of the Soviet state have been marked by the world socialist revolution—people have waited for it and tried to bring it closer.

Why a world revolution has not and could not have transpired is discussed by our correspondent I. Solganik with Prof I. Krivoguz, doctor of economic sciences.

SOLGANIK: Igor Mikhaylovich, it is known that the concept of the world socialist revolution was developed by V. I. Lenin. As early as the 1920's he proposed the concept of peaceful coexistence of the Soviet state with capitalist countries. How are these two concepts, which are largely mutually exclusive, linked, and how did Lenin's views evolve?

KRIVOGUZ: As early as 1908 Lenin declared the need for a world revolution of the proletariat. When analyzing imperialism Lenin attached decisive significance to its negative tendencies and contradictions and the readiness of the objective prerequisites for socialism, and on this basis he estimated that imperialism was on the eve of a revolution. Taking into account the irregularity of social development, Lenin thought that the socialist revolution would triumph initially in one or several countries and that "socialism would be realized through the combined actions of the proletariat not of all but of a minority of countries that had reached the stage of development of advanced capitalism."

Having been victorious in even one country, Lenin wrote in 1915, its proletariat would rise "against the rest of the capitalist world, attracting the oppressed masses of other countries, inciting them to rebel against the capitalists, and if necessary even acting as a military force against the exploiting classes and their states." Although Russia was not one of the leading capitalist countries, Lenin, having analyzed the alignment of forces in the world after the February revolution, decided that the Russian workers could lay the foundation for the world socialist revolution. "We ... have begun our work," wrote Lenin about the October Revolution, "counting exclusively on a world revolution." Its victory was perceived at that time as the creation of the World Federative Republic of Soviets.

Revolutionary socialists of all countries regarded the victory of October as the beginning of the world socialist revolution. "The Russian proletariat," declared the revolutionary socialists of Germany, "is perceived only as the vanguard of the world proletariat."

From October 1917 until the summer of 1920 Lenin imagined that the proletarian revolutions in the more developed countries would win out "either immediately or very soon," that the revolutionary forces were "close to a world proletarian revolution." In the summer of 1919 he expressed his confidence "next July we shall see the victory of the international Soviet republic ..."

Lenin thought that Russia was only temporarily the vanguard of the world socialist revolution and that the last decisive battle would flare up when the socialist revolutions burst out in the most developed countries—they were awaited as the basic part of the world revolution. In 1920 after the disappointment of hopes for a revolution in Europe resulting from the Red Army campaign against Warsaw, which appeared to be a revolutionary liberation campaign, Lenin finally arrived at the idea that the world socialist revolution "will ... continue for many years and will require much work."

In politics Lenin was a great realist and was very sensitive to all the changes in world development. He always thought that if the facts did not fit into the theory it was necessary to change the theory. Lenin's flexibility and sensitivity to the new made it possible for him to be the first to see that the rates of the revolutionary movement were slowing down and the world revolution was being delayed.

Having been convinced that fate had doomed us to remain alone in capitalist surroundings—and Lenin saw this before others did—he managed to arrange for peaceful coexistence with capitalist countries.

The deep meaning of this Leninist concept, which corresponded to the new economic policy developed by Lenin, was that it directed our country toward cooperation and business relations with capitalist countries, the creation of joint enterprises, the granting of concessions, and so forth. If the proletariat of Western Europe had not yet won out, Lenin thought, it was necessary to enlist capital and have it serve to restore the country's economy.

As concerns the world revolution, at the 4th Komintern Congress and in January 1923 Lenin describes it already as in the historical perspective and not as a "developing revolution" (1919). Illness and then his death kept Lenin from revising his unjustified hopes for a world revolution.

SOLGANIK: After Lenin's death was there disagreement among the Bolshevik party leadership regarding the question of world revolution?

KRIVOGUZ: The forces were grouped as follows. On one side were Trotskiy and Sinovyev who thought it was impossible to build socialism in Russia without assistance from a victorious proletariat of Western Europe because of our country's backwardness.

Stalin objected to this very convincingly: If socialism could not be constructed in the country, what were Russia's prospects? Since the party demanded that the future be clear, the success of Stalin and Bukharin, who supported him, was predetermined in spite of all of Trotskiy's eloquence and the logic of Zinovyev's arguments.

These differences became especially acute because of the struggle for power and ultimately led to a schism and then to Stalin's destruction of his opponents—first political and then physical.

SOLGANIK: From the Bolshevik viewpoint what explained the fact that the world revolution had not taken place?

KRIVOGUZ: When explaining this circumstance Lenin very frequently blamed the treachery of the Social Democrats and opportunists. But the opportunists could not be traitors because they had never been in favor of a world revolution—as we know, one can be betrayed only by one's own and they were always in the opposite camp regarding this issue.

Let us recall Marx's statement: "No social formation will perish before the dissolution of all productive forces for which it provides adequate space. . . ." I see in this the main reason why the world revolution did not and could not take place—capitalism had by no means exhausted its possibilities; it was very strong and still is strong both economically and politically. To such an extent that we are still unable to catch up in spite of the objective advantages of socialism.

SOLGANIK: Could you give us some examples of how our orientation toward a world revolution influenced our foreign policy?

KRIVOGUZ: Not everyone could master the great art of keeping separate the USSR state policy and the policy of the Komintern, the organization created for leading the world revolution. And certain eminent diplomats—Chicherin, Krasin, Rakovskiy—frequently protested against the fact that the Komintern was interfering in their negotiations with capitalist countries.

The statements of the Komintern in the spirit of damning all imperialists and their underlings, the Social Democrats, hampered very much the realization of Lenin's concept of peaceful coexistence.

For instance in 1924 Kh. Rakovskiy was in London conducting negotiations with the MacDonald government, and this government itself considered it its task to normalize relations with the USSR. In this situation very negative consequences were felt from the statement of Zinovyev, who was the head of the Komintern at the time, in which he called MacDonald an imperalist stooge.

Later, when the Komintern began to implement Stalin's policy, it was more and more difficult to distinguish where the Komintern left off and where Soviet diplomacy began.

SOLGANIK: Could you give us a general idea of how the personality cult of Stalin affected the world Communist movement? What was the Stalinist concept of world development and how was it actually different from the one which up until recently has been present in party documents?

KRIVOGUZ: Several generations of communists not only in our country but throughout the world have learned Leninism at the hand of Stalin in his interpretation. And since in the second half of the 1970's we found that certain Communist parties in Western Europe spoke of the inadequacy and narrowness of Leninism, we should be aware that they were speaking against Leninism in Stalin's interpretation.

Apparently in the 1930's Stalin became very skeptical about the world revolution, although there is no precise information to this effect. Stalin always emphasized the Soviet Union's leading role in the world revolutionary process, and at the 7th Komintern Congress it was stated that the successes achieved in the USSR were a new stage in the world socialist movement. The fact that after the defeat of the republicans in Spain and the disintegration of the Popular Front in France all the hopes of Communists were linked only to the USSR contributed to the complete subordination of the Komintern to the Stalinist leadership. On Stalin's initiative, as we know, the Komintern disbanded the Communist Party of Poland because of false accusations. Hundreds of leaders of Communist parties of foreign countries were subjected to repressive measures in the USSR.

After World War II Stalin interpreted the concept of world development as the concept of a struggle between two camps—the democratic camp headed by the USSR and the imperialist camp. Stalin proposed defeating imperialism under the slogans of peace, democracy, and national independence. At the 19th party congress Stalin directly announced that the task of Communists is to raise the banner of the struggle for national independence and democratic freedoms, and the bourgeoisie, he declared, had thrown this banner overboard. This was a great underestimation of the bourgeoisie which made it difficult for the Communist Party to have a correct orientation, especially in the zone of the national liberation movement.

The concept of the struggle between two camps was schematic, and it ignored many changes that had taken place in the world. In particular, up until the middle of the 1950's we underestimated the significance of the victor of the national liberation and other revolutions in India, Indonesia, and other countries of Southeast Asia and the Near East. Nehru was regarded as a henchman of British imperialism and not as the leader of the liberation movement in India. Only in the second half of the 1950's did we revise these schematic ideas about world progress so as to return, it would seem, to the primary sources—to the idea of the world socialist revolution.

At the international conferences of representatives of Communist and workers' parties in Moscow in 1957 and 1960 they proposed the concept of a unified world revolutionary process and indicated its main motive forces. It was asserted that these forces merge into a single flow which will bury imperialism. This concept did not withstand the test of time and turned out to be inadequate for reflecting all the complexity and diversity of world development. Therefore, a new concept of world progress is now being developed as a basis for the new political thinking.

The revolutionary processes in the world are diverse. On the one hand there is a transition to socialism both from capitalism and from the precapitalist formations, but even more widespread is another process—the transition from precapitalist formations to capitalism. There is no justification for equating these two processes.

I think that it is necessary to revise our ideas about the general crisis of capitalism and evaluate capitalism realistically. Obviously, we cannot see in world socialism the main springboard for social progress in any country and reduce the essence of any regional conflicts to an antagonism between the two systems.

SOLGANIK: Finally, the last question. I have heard it said that the spread of fascism in Europe was a kind of defensive reaction to our attempts to spread communism.

KRIVOGUZ: Fascism gambled a great deal on this. But one can probably not assert seriously that our widespread propaganda of world revolution led to the appearance of fascism.

Fascism was the response of German imperialism to its defeat in 1918 and to the labor movement which was threatening its existence. But the labor movement in Germany had deep roots in its own country and existed independently of whether or not there was a Komintern or whether or not there was a Soviet Union.

The bugbear of world communism was very opportune for the fascists. One must say that up until now our concept of a world revolutionary process has been a kind of bugbear for those who do not wish to improve relations with the USSR. Usually they refer to articles of our Constitution where it says that we shall help any liberation movement, and on this basis they draw the conclusion that the USSR, under the guise of talking about peace, is ready at any moment to intervene in the internal affairs of other countries.

But the main reason why we should reject the concept of the world revolutionary process is that this concept is unrealistic and does not adequately reflect the processes taking place in the world.

M. ROSTROPOVICH

M. Rostropovich: My Dignity Means a Great Deal to Me
by Yu. Kovalenko, *Izvestiya*, January 24, 1989

The enchanting strains of Tchaikovsky's music filled the expanse of the Grand Opera, and after the last sound died away, the entire audience gave a standing ovation: ministers, writers, ambassadors, industrialists, musicians and singers all applauded. Wild "bravos" were screamed from the balconies and orchestra. Touched, Rostropovich bowed, clasped his hands to his heart, thanked the conductor and orchestra and went backstage, but returned to the stage at his public's demand.

This was his third concert to aid the Armenian earthquake victims. "Dear friends," I read in the program notes Rostropovich's hand-written appeal to the public, "people with generous hearts have always united in misfortune, when help is needed for sisters and brothers who have endured tragedy. This help must come quickly. Thank you for your kindness!"

... In order to give a concert to aid Armenia, he flew from India to France for two days, and the next morning already set out for guest appearances in the USA. In the West, Rostropovich is considered an outstanding performer, and the famous artist's life consists of concerts, rehearsals, flights and hotels. Rostropovich comes to Paris infrequently, although he has an apartment here, near the *Izvestiya* press room. I have visited Mstislav Leopoldovich, conversed with him several times on the phone and read the letter of the West German professor published in *Nedelya*: "Why is it that Rostropovich is still not played on Soviet radio? Could it be that his interpretation is considered anti-Soviet?"

Of course I discussed perestroyka and glasnost with Mstislav Leopoldovich. He spoke with enthusiasm, clearly and graphically, of occurrences in the Homeland, but declined to be interviewed, and did not wish that our conversation be published in the Soviet press.

"I don't consider myself guilty of anything in anyone's eyes," he emphasized, "but to meet with fellow nationals while having the rank of an enemy of the people, a man without citizenship, is not what I want. For my human dignity means a great deal to me. Why do they talk only about how Brezhnev destroyed the economy, and they don't mention that he wreaked havoc with performers, the artistic intelligentsia? The time has come to explain this. The decree which stripped Galina Vishnevskaya and me of Soviet citizenship was signed by Brezhnev, and we have remained in this state ever since."

Let's go back to 1976. Before leaving for prolonged guest appearances abroad, with the permission of the Soviet Government, M. Rostropovich and G. Vishnevskaya sent a letter to P. I. Demichev, the USSR Minister of Culture in those years. In it they wrote, in addition to words of gratitude for attempting to assist them, "We have only one creative life; we consider it unnecessary and impossible to waste it on a humiliating struggle with fools and scoundrels, who, we are certain, are intentionally creating our unbearable situation."

They intended to return home, supposing that the "passions" had cooled, and that with time, the attitude would change as far as the bureaucrats from Culture were concerned. But, alas, nothing had changed. On 16 February 1978, Rostropovich and Vishnevskaya applied at the Soviet Embassy in the USA, a request directed to Brezhnev himself, to extend their passports for three years. They had signed new contracts for this period.

A month latter, in Paris, on 15 March, they learned from the television news that they had been stripped of their Soviet citizenship. On 18 March, two employees of the USSR Consulate in Paris requested that they give up their Soviet passports. The musician declared that he considered deprivation of citizenship "a lawless act."

The next day, Rostropovich and Vishnevskaya wrote a letter to Chairman of the Presidium of the USSR Supreme Soviet L. Brezhnev: "You have deprived us of the opportunity to live and die in our native land, the land in which we were born and to which we gave almost 50 years of our lives, dedicating our work and talent to our people." They wrote that regardless of any accusations, they had never participated in any anti-Soviet organizations, and that their only guilt was that they had given A. Solzhenitsyn comfort in their home, bringing persecution down on themselves. Concerts were canceled, guest appearances prohibited, there was a press boycott by the mass media. While still in the Soviet Union, Rostropovich appealed to Brezhenev for help. Unsuccessfully. **"It is within your power to force us to change our residence,"** their letter said, **"but you are powerless to** change our hearts, and wherever we are, for the sake of the Russian people, and with love toward them, we will continue to promote our art with pride."

No one deigned to respond to this epistle, a "cri de coeur," although articles appeared to the effect that, while living abroad, Rostropovich and Vishnevskaya conducted "anti-Soviet activity," "defamed the Soviet system" and "systematically aided subversive anti-Soviet centers," and they were pasted with the label of "ideological turncoats."

In attempting to justify the decision to revoke citizenship, the newspaper *Voice of the Homeland* did not mince words: "the shifty guest stars," "unscrupulous, self-centered types who were not squeamish about anything that had to do with money-grubbing. . . ." The newspaper's special rage was provoked by the cellist's solo concert in San Francisco to benefit a committee for Russian invalids of the First World War, a group of "monarchists and the White Guardists."

This was how, 10 years ago, we were "emancipated" from two People's Artists of the USSR. It seemed that the door had slammed behind them forever. They were both deprived of their titles; broadcasts of their concerts were prohibited, records withdrawn, their names expunged from the encyclopedia. And we were deprived of the opportunity to hear the playing of Rostropovich and the singing of Vishnevskaya, winner of the 1977 "World's Best Opera Singer" prize.

From foreign "Voices" we learned of Rostropovich's regular conferral of awards, prizes and titles. He was appointed to the French Academy of Fine Arts. In accepting his congratulations, he said. **"Mankind is my family's name. My home is the world."**

Rostropovich's younger daughter Yelena travelled to Moscow recently. "For a whole week we discussed what is happening in Moscow," Rostropovich said in one interview. "She got together with friends, and saw that everything was in a state of motion. I subscribe to Soviet newspapers and magazines, and as I read them, I also see that everything is in motion. Much is changing in the Soviet Union. **Gorbachev is acting like a doctor who has made the correct diagnosis ... I hope that the economic and moral health of our country will be restored ... Gorbachev wants to change psychology. The is very important and very difficult ..."**

Interviews, endless interviews, and the journalists' obligatory questions about what is happening in the Soviet Union, what restructuring's chances are. "It takes time to get results. The

West must assist in this transformation." This is not the response of an impassive man. In the musician's words was the pain of the past, and profound, sincere joy over the beginning of the great processes of renewal and democratization. "I am a soldier of restructuring on the Western front," the musician once said.

. . . For the majority of Russian people in emigration, the question of returning home arises sooner or later. For some, it arises with the onset of old age; for others, it tortures them their whole life long. Perhaps creative people sense this more keenly.

The return of Soviet citizenship to Vishnevskaya and Rostropovich signifies the restoration of justice. Can it be that we have abased ourselves by publishing the works of Zamyatin, Nabokov and Khodasyevich, printing Brodskiy's poems, showing Tarkovskiy's films, Chagall's paintings, Goncharova's and Larionov's? Our national pride only increased. Attempts to divide Russian culture with a soundproof wall have done serious damage.

A. RYBAKOV

Anatoly Rybakov: You Must Part with Your Past with Dignity
by Olga Martynenko, *Moscow News*, November 29, 1988

"MN" OBSERVER Olga Martynenko interviews the author about his new novel.

It is August 1936 and Stalin is on his way to Moscow from his dacha. As his car sweeps along the deserted road, he muses on the fact that people in ancient times prostrated themselves at the sight of their lord and master. It was not to show their obedience but because the act excluded chances of an attempted assassination. A raised head was chopped off instantly!

These thoughts come to him following the first show trial of those implicated in the NKVD "Trotskyite conspiracy"—including

Kamenev, Zinovyev, Bakayev, Yevdokimov (16 in all)—which unleashed the terror that carried off millions of lives.

This is one of the notable scenes in Anatoly Rybakov's latest novel *1935 and Other Years*. It will appear in the literary magazine *Druzhba Narodov* this autumn and excerpts will be published in *Ogonyek*.

The novel concerns itself with the preparations for and the machinery of this trial and is the sequel to the author's immensely popular *Children of the Arbat*.

Children has had a print of 1,200,000 and that number will be doubled before the year's out. But the demand still outstrips the print run. Twenty-four companies, including amateur ones, have based stage productions on the book, which is being published in 26 countries. While the author is naturally pleased with this success, he worries that it will lead readers to expect too much from the sequel.

Rybakov lives in the writers' village of Peredelkino near Moscow. The bird song and summer greenery were somehow out of keeping with what we discussed.

Some people wonder why the past should be raked up to bring back the blood-smeared shadows. They would rather forget it all and make believe it never even happened.

"Are you suggesting all these be dropped?" The author casts an almost hostile glance at me as he walks over to the shelf packed with thick folders labelled "Stalin and the War", "Tukhachevsky", "Varya", "Sharok", "Statistics"—files of his characters, sketches for his future novels.

His factual material comes mainly from newspapers of the 1930s and the letters of people who lived through those times.

He showed me one such letter, a dozen or so typewritten pages, each signed as if it were an official record. It comes from a former high official in the procurator's office and he writes: "I will soon appear before God, but before that I would like to appear before you. . . ."

Letters

Rybakov is getting such letters by thousands and they bring him invaluable information, are a sort of a readers' referendum. They show 85 per cent support for Rybakov; 15 per cent are against his book.

Says the author: "Those against are not so much indignant at myself as at the authorities who they think should punish the writer and ban the book. The extreme example of this style is a xeroxed anonymous letter, as usual full of grammatical mistakes, urging me to repent by a specified date or else face physical destruction. The date has already expired."

Rybakov does not react to threats. He went through exile and the war, and says that the feeling of fear is biologically alien to him.

Another curious document is a letter from Nina Andreyeva. In her article in *Sovetskaya Rossiya* she had alleged in passing that Rybakov had frankly admitted borrowing some ideas for *Children of the Arbat* from emigre publications. He immediately demanded that the newspaper answer where, when and to whom he had "admitted" that. Which ideas and from which sources had he borrowed? Nina Andreyeva's reply came after a two-month delay and it is really worthwhile citing at least this part of it: "A participant in one of last autumn's TV programmes, discussing books devoted to our recent historical past, said that you had not denied during your meeting with Moscow readers that you had used some foreign sources."

"The rest of her arguments are much of the same kind," laughs Rybakov. "I may add that I believe everyone is free to use any sources, including emigre sources, like the memoirs of Denikin, Vrangel or Kerensky, as long as the facts are straight."

What is the author's reaction to criticisms which range from reproaches for the denigration of Stalin to blame for idealizing him?

"I accept all criticism if it does not contradict the truth. It's dishonest to blame some dark forces and their machinations and conspiracies for the abuses of our history.

"Nor can I accept Valentin Rasputin's advice which appeared in the press that I write about, for example, Stalin's henchman Kaganovich, rather than Stalin. By the same token I could suggest that Rasputin go ahead and write, say, about the tsarist politician Purishkevich."

"Cadre Revolution"

But let's go back to the novel. The deep wound in our history, which Rybakov has touched, is still festering. **People continue to ask: how could lofty ideals and goals degenerate so ominously, how could a man for whom terror was an ordinary tool of government reach the very heights of power?**

The author traces back the evolution of reasoning by Stalin

who finally arrives at conviction in his own absolutism. Stalin reasons that everything potentially harmful to his power should be destroyed. Hence his "cadre revolution", the systematic replacement of those close to him, using the medieval methods of the Inquisition. His principle is—everything that promotes the interests of the Party and the state is ethical. The Party and the state is HIMSELF.

In practical terms the meaning of ethics is demonstrated by this story in the novel: the NKVD investigator Sharok asks a higher-ranking officer what kind of questions he has prepared for the coming grilling. **"Questions?" the officer returns. "Here are my questions—this rubber truncheon."**

"What should we make of our past?" I ask Rybakov.

"Unfortunately, history is unpredictable," Rybakov says.

"On my recent lecturing tour in the US they constantly asked me about the Stalin phenomenon. I replied: despite your Bill of Rights, the most democratic constitution at that time, signed in 1786, you tolerated slavery till 1865. There are some zigzags in the past of every country and every nation. I'm convinced that Stalin is but a tragic chance, that we had all preconditions for taking a different path. Helped on by the New Economic Policy (NEP), the country quickly overcame economic ruin and matched prewar standards—all without repressions and dispossessions of the kulaks (rich farmers).

"Stalin's scheming, perfidy and cruelty were helped by the absence in the country in those years of democratic experience in relations between Party members. The people in key positions had been through the Civil War and preferred commands to persuasion. For many of them NEP was an unacceptable tragedy, and they withdrew from the Party and shot themselves. When Stalin sent NEP to hell, many liked it.

"This is only one of many reasons, but as a novelist I am primarily interested in Stalin's personality, his views, deeds, the mystery of his power over people. His phenomenon needs an in-depth historical analysis. That is why I think it imperative to publish Roy Medvedev's fundamental book **Let History Judge**, a remarkably honest and sober piece of research into the origins of Stalinism and its consequences."

Were the People Silent?

What category in his opinion did the people's attitude to the leader belong to—cause or effect? People in his novel were far from being silent: they shouted, applauded and urged for the execution of "enemies of the people". He shows how yesterday's accusers and executioners themselves became victims the next day. People forgot all sympathy because they were in the grip of a great, all-absorbing fear. To blame the crimes on everybody, to make everybody blind to the facts—is also part of Stalin's insidious strategy. But why is it people so willingly refused to see?

"Yes, Stalin is our shared guilt and common misfortune. Admittedly, we shouted, applauded, there was a mass-scale psychosis, a hypnotic trance. Even after nothing threatened our lives, we voted to condemn or to expel other people. I think the greatest harm done by Stalinism to our society is of an ethical nature: we have unlearned to reason and feel.

"We must have the courage to face our past squarely, it lives on in us, good or bad. Good? The 19-year-old soldier lads fighting in the last war, their mothers who had to till the land, those who died in the war or who were tortured to death in the camps. The memory of them helped us survive to this day."

As a pioneer of books about Stalin in recent times, what does he think about the growing number of publications denouncing Stalin's personality cult?

"Most of them are serious and deep. But I see some written by people whose life has been quite all right yet who try to portray themselves as victims of the cult. You can't sensationalize the national tragedy, turn it into a fashionable subject or cash in on it. You must part with your past with dignity.

"I quite frequently hear calls for unmasking, condemnations and trials. Of whom? I'm not calling for forgiving and forgetting everyone and everything, but feelings of revenge and hatred are counterproductive. Those with a scrap of courage in them can come forward and repent publicly; those who are too afraid, let them repent in their heart, for we can't advance without moral cleansing."

But besides moral cleansing and repentance, doesn't he think that guarantees must exist, too? Civil courage must be protected by law. He's given a very good description of arbitrariness, but the first novel ends in January 1937.

"The number of facts is not as important as understanding them. The message of those dark years, of the innocent blood is that people living now and those who will live after us should know that arbitrariness under whatever pretext leads to degeneration."

A. SAKHAROV

For Peace and Progress
Interview with Academician Andrey Sakharov, *Moscow News*,
February 5, 1989

Academician Andrey Sakharov has been nominated as a candidate for the people's deputies in the Moscow City National-Territorial Precinct.

Our reporter Gennadiy Zhavoronkov interviewed him.

Q: People at large see the life of a nuclear physicist as romantic, secret and secluded. When did you start your public activities?

A: My public activities started more than 30 years ago. I was fortunate to have taken part in the conclusion of the Moscow treaty banning nuclear tests on land, at sea, and in the atmosphere. The views reflected in my electoral programme took shape over many years and were openly published starting in 1969. At the time my views clashed with the official position and this resulted in the 70s and 80s in the persecution of myself and my family.

Q: Could you describe briefly the objectives of your election programme?

A: The objective of my programme is to deepen and further perestroyka, democratization, pluralism, the building of a law-abiding state, social and national justice, an efficient and ecologically safe economy, peace and progress. Hesitation and controversy in carrying out a political, economic and national constitutional perestroyka should not be allowed to lead the country deeper into crisis.

Q: Which points in your programme reflect your latest conclusions?

A: I formed some of my conclusions long ago. Some were formulated in my book "My Country and the World". But what is happening today has led me to make the following important changes in my programme.

1. The scrapping of the administrative-command system to be replaced by a pluralistic system based on competition and the market. The ministries and other government agencies should

be stripped of their monopoly power. There must be more independence for state-run enterprises. We must allow free market for labour, the means of production, raw materials and intermediate products. We must expand production based on leasing, cooperatives and joint-stock capital. Inefficient collective and state farms must be dissolved immediately and their land leased on favourable terms, as well as the buildings and equipment. It is our duty to feed the country. In addition, unprofitable industries should be either leased out or sold to shareholders. Large enterprises should be broken up into smaller units in order to encourage competition and to eliminate monopoly pricing. Independent commissions of ecologists and economists should be set up to evaluate major projects and plans for national development. We must abandon the extensive development of the national economy, stop the needless processing of raw materials and the growth of industrial production which doesn't result in higher quality. There must be sharp reduction in industrial capital construction. There must be an immediate stop of financing the Ministry of Water Conservation (either disband it or make it pay its own way). Nuclear power engineering is essential to mankind, but it must be made safe (account should be taken of the danger of earthquakes, terrorism and conventional war). No construction of nuclear power or thermal power stations should be allowed whose reactors are above ground level; they should be built underground so as to prevent radioactive fallout. Public ecological groups should be legalized and encouraged. All data on the ecological situation throughout the country should be made public. All hydroelectric and other construction projects that endanger the ecology must be halted. Each person should be paid according to his work. All restrictions on the size of one's earning should be removed and a progressive tax instituted. All privileges unrelated to the performance of one's duty must be eliminated. The foundations should publish annual financial accounts, including the pay scale, expense accounts, and travel expenses. All public organizations should cut their staffs to the minimum. A realistic exchange rate for the rouble should be established before making the rouble convertible.

2. Social and national justice. The protection of the rights of the individual. Openness of society. Freedom of political beliefs. Freedom of choice of one's country of residence and place of residence inside that country. Freedom of association and freedom to demonstration. Public control over important decision making. The revision of the law on elections and the 1988

amendments to the Constitution. Direct elections of the Supreme Soviet deputies and its President. A democratic system of nomination of candidates and their registration without interference from the apparatus and the screening of candidates. Everyone should have only one vote, and at least two candidates should run for each seat. There should be a return to Lenin's concept of the USSR as a union of equal states. There should be no restrictions of smaller nations by bigger nations. Small national regions should enjoy the rights of union republics. The absence of foreign borders should not be a pretext for restricting their rights. We should establish a federative system based on agreements between member states. Support the principles which form the base of the programme of the national fronts of the Baltic Republics. There should be cost accounting for each republic and region. We must adopt a law for the press based on freedom from ideological control and all forms of restriction, while banning propaganda advocating war, violence, national strife, pornography and the divulging of state secrets. There must be fewer secrets in an open society. Private and cooperative ventures should be allowed to run information services abiding by the above bans.

The residence passport system should be phased out. Pensions and other fixed incomes must be adjusted in line with the rate of inflation based on 1960 prices. NO price increases on food and essential goods should be made without a thorough analysis of the possible consequences. Unnecessary offices could be converted to housing and all forms of housing and all forms of housing construction encouraged. There should be more funds for public education and medical care. Changes in legislation and the social structure to ease the position of working mothers should be made, as well as monetary incentives to women who stay at home to care for preschool children.

3. The eradication of the consequences of Stalinism. The archives of the NKVD-MGB must be opened and all information concerning the crimes of Stalinism and all unjustified repressions be published. We must establish commissions of the Supreme Soviet to monitor the activities of the Ministry of Internal Affairs, the KGB and the Ministry of Defence. The opportunity to appeal to court decisions and actions of individual officials and government and party organs must be provided for. There should be a right to trial by jury, and a lawyer be made available at the start of an investigation. Sentences should be rescinded if there are violations of legal procedures or illegal investigation

methods, and the violators punished. We must humanize prisons and abolish the death sentence. We must free and rehabilitate prisoners of conscience, including members of the Karabakh Committee and the Krunk.

4. The reorganization of science. There should be a much greater role for scientists teaching in higher schools, broader international contacts for Soviet scientists, especially young scientists and those in the provinces who were rarely included in this process in the past. We must undertake the financing of and material support for scientific research projects put forward by initiative groups. The role of the Academy of Sciences in basic research and its responsibility for the results of ecological and economic investigations must be enhanced.

5. Support for the policy of disarmament and the solution of regional conflicts. Data on the USSR's policy and actions in regional conflicts (including Afghanistan and the Middle East) should be published. The length of armed service and the Army personnel should be cut in half, and all forms of weapons cut proportionally. The number of officers should be cut with an eye to a gradual transition to a professional Army. Chemical and bacteriological weapons should be banned and nuclear weapons be deployed only defensively. We should switch over completely to a defensive military strategy doctrine.

6. Convergence of the socialist and capitalist systems recognizing the need for decentralized decision making in the economy, social sphere, culture and ideology. This is the only way to completely eliminate the threat of the destruction of humanity in the event of a nuclear or ecological disaster.

Q: *Moscow News* wishes you success in your electoral campaign.
A: Thank you.

I Tried To Be on the Level of My Destiny. . . .
Interview with Academician Andrey Sakharov and his wife Yelena Georgiyevna Bonner by special correspondent Mark Levin,
Molodezh Estonii, October 11, 1988

CONCLUSION OF THE publication of materials prepared by *Molodezh Estonii* special correspondent during the 38th conference of the participants in the Pugwash Movement.

For some time the name of this person has thundered throughout the world. He is quoted everywhere and looked upon as a standard of civil courage and spiritual firmness. Whereas in our country. . . . Obviously we are not all that able to protect our geniuses if we dared to deprive Academician Sakharov of his three stars of Hero of Socialist Labor by an "arbitrary decision," and send him into exile without a trial and an investigation. . . . Now, however, when the age of the triumph of conservatism, dogmatism and vulgarity appears to become part of the past, the name of Academician Andrey Sakharov is beginning to return in our country as well as though from nonexistence.

Okudzhava is right: Anything can happen! At the 38th conference of the participants in The Pugwash Movement in Dagomys, A.D. Sakharov read a paper; the U.S. ambassador to the USSR presented him with a certificate of honorary membership in the American Academy of Fine Arts and Literature. . . . The only prize that he has is the Nobel. . . .

During the proceedings of the 38th Pugwash conference, Academician Sakharov kindly agreed to be interviewed by *Molodezh Estonii*. His wife, Yelena Georgiyevna Bonner, participated in our conversation.

Q: Some speak of the "age of Brezhnev;" others speak of the "age of Sakharov." Who is right, Andrey Demitriyevich?

A: I think that it is excessive to name ages after specific people. For that reason, it seems to me that neither name should be used. A precise name has already been found for our age: "the age of stagnation." Let us keep calling it such. As to the way individuals act during that age, that is a different matter.

Q: If the state is a machinery of violence, under such circumstances a person may not feel too comfortable. You experienced this personally. . . . Therefore, from your viewpoint, is it possible to find ways to harmonize relations between the individual and the state, between the person and society?

A: An ideal harmony will always remain inaccessible, being ideal by definition. However, the more democratic the state is, and the more punctiliously it observes human rights, the more it is a state of law, i.e., the stricter both individuals and the state must obey the law (regardless of the position of that individual in society), the closer we come to the state of harmony. Naturally, the laws as well must be democratic.

Q: Since we are speaking of harmony, it may be pertinent to recall Dostoyevskiy's formula: "Beauty will save the world."

What could save the world today? What could also save man in the world?

A: On the individual level, I think that what matters here is a certain moral code and the individual qualities and features which are manifested through the action of the people and their active morality. As to the global situation, I believe that the world is threatened for a number of reasons. All of them, however, become drastically aggravated as a result of the division of the world into two competing (or confrontational, which is worse and more dangerous) systems. A rapprochement between these sociopolitical systems (the capitalist and the socialist) and their convergence are the necessary prerequisites for eliminating the danger which threatens mankind.

Q: You just mentioned "active morality." What meaning do you invest in this concept?

A: Active concern for those around us and, if possible, active concern for those who are far from us. The first condition, however, is mandatory.

YE. BONNER: Kaysyn Kuliyev wrote the following: "It is easy to love all mankind, learn how to love your neighbor!" I am saying this as an extension of Andrey Dmitriyevich's thought. . . .

A. SAKHAROV: In our life together, Yelena Georgiyevna has frequently quoted those words to me and today I believe that it is precisely under her influence that this thought has become closer to me than in the past, when I was, let us say, somewhat dealing with the abstract.

Q: Nonetheless you, Andrey Dmitriyevich, have always been a very active personality, whether in science or social practice. . . . You also developed the atomic and hydrogen bombs, this too is a universally known fact. Have you ever regretted that you became involved with this terrible weapon? Although what weapon is not terrible. . . .

A: Let me begin with a factual reference. I was recruited to do secret work in 1948, to work on the creation of a thermonuclear weapon (and not simply atomic, for technically there is a difference between the two). This weapon was even more terrible than the one which was used on Hiroshima and Nagasaki. . . . So, we (and here I must speak not only in my behalf, for in such cases moral principles are formulated as though collectively-psychologically) believed that our work was absolutely necessary as a means of achieving a balance in the world. Lack of balance is very dangerous: The side which feels itself to be stronger could be encouraged to make the fastest possible use of its own temporary advantage, while the weaker side may be pushed into taking adventuristic, desperate steps to gain time while the advantage enjoyed by the opponent is not too great. I still think so. In the final account, the work which we did was justified as was the work which was done by our colleagues on the opposite side. Nonetheless, we can say that the world was able to stop sliding toward its doom, toward the horror of Hiroshima and Nagasaki, and has been holding out for more than 40 years now. However, it is always wrong for a person to retain the same position or to assess it outside the dynamics, the changes of the times. You, Yelena, recently quoted Thomas Mann. . . .

YE. BONNER: He said that the stubborn defense by a person of any one of his viewpoints or doctrines, regardless of changes in social and historical conditions, can be described only as historical stupidity.

A. SAKHAROV: It seems to me that in the course of my life I have tried to avoid this "historical stupidity." The word "historical" seems somehow pompous. However, my destiny has been, in a certain sense, exceptional. Let me remark, not because of false modesty but the desire to be accurate, that my fate turned out to be greater than my personality. I merely tried to be on the level of my own destiny, while avoiding the temptation of such a "historical stupidity."

Q: In general, do you believe in fate?

A: I believe in virtually nothing other than a kind of social sensation of the inner meaning of the course of events, events occurring not only in the life of mankind but, in general, in the universe. I do not believe in fate as such. I believe that the future is unpredictable and undefined. It is created by all of us, step by step, in the course of our endless complex interaction.

Q: If I understood you correctly, you believe that everything is not "in God's hands" but "in the hands of mankind?"

A: Here we have an interaction between both forces but the freedom of choice remains man's. That is what makes great the role of the person positioned by fate at some key points in history. Parts of a personal destiny may be predetermined and parts may not. For example, I was asked on several occasions to participate in work on nuclear weapons. . . .

YE. BONNER: Voluntarily to participate! He was offered scientific freedom, comforts, material goods. . . .

A. SAKHAROV: Yes, to participate voluntarily. . . . Each time, however, I refused. My fate, however, caught up with me. . . . and when I was recruited for such work (and we, I repeat, considered it important and necessary), at that point I began to work not because of fear but of conscience, with a great deal of initiative. Although I cannot conceal another aspect of the matter: I found the work very interesting. This is not what Fermi described as an "interest in physics." The interest here was caused by the grandiose nature of the problems, the possibility to prove what one can do, above all to oneself. That is what makes a scientist. Let me add that all of this developed against a background which was influenced by the still fresh memory of the terrible war which had just ended. I had not participated in that war, and now that was my own war. As though a war. . . .

YE. BONNER: Should work at the defense plant where you were while the fighting was going on be ignored?

A. SAKHAROV: Nonetheless, this was on a different level. Now I found myself on the front line itself. Later I even joked that if we were awarded a gold star, it should be not as a Hero of Socialist Labor but as a Hero of the Soviet Union, for we had to assume great responsibility for technical and political decisions of tremendous importance. This demanded courage. . . .

Q: Therefore, already then you realized that the political significance of your research and experimentation and tests was not transient? That your bomb could change the political and psychological climate on earth?

A: Not entirely. The fullness of this understanding came later, sometime in the mid-1950s, during the time of the second thermonuclear test. But let me say more about our psychological motivation.

Naturally, it changed both in me and in Igor Yevgenyevich Tamm (USSR Academy of Sciences academician, Hero of Socialist Labor, Nobel Prize laureate—M.L.).

Although he was much older than me, we were close. At that time we were working in a closed city and maintained close contacts and, I believe, easily understood one another.

Q: What kind of life did you have there?

A: We went to work in the morning and at breakfast, lunch and dinner talked about all kinds of subjects and after the working day I visited Igor Yevgenyevich in his cottage where we had heart-to-heart discussions. This lasted 3 years, after which he was allowed to go back to science. This was proper, for he was best suited for that. I remained behind and very dramatic events in the development of our goods were ahead. I did not go to Moscow frequently but on each such occasion I visited Igor

Yevgenyevich and our relationship remained close. Although in the course of time, as I continued to change. . . .

YE. BONNER: Igor Yevgenyevich was much older and eventually the effect of his age was telling. He was of the generations of the "fathers" in terms of Andrey Dmitriyevich, and like all elders, he could change only up to a point. . . .

A. SAKHAROV: True. However, he continued to respect me. I believe that he simply loved me.

YE. BONNER: You know, when Igor Yevgenyevich was awarded the Lomonosov Prize he was already gravely ill, he could no longer move. . . . However, among the many of his students it was precisely Andrey that he instructed to represent him at the award presentation ceremony. . . .

A. SAKHAROV: Not because I have a beautiful voice which, precisely, is not beautiful. . . .

YE. BONNER: And not because Sakharov was a recipient of the Hero Star. No, Igor Yevgenyevich's choice was based on an inner closeness, this could be sensed.

A. SAKHAROV: I feel it to this day. But shall we return to the motivation? On one occasion I admitted to Igor Yevgenyevich how hard and painful it was for me to be aware of the horrible work we were nonetheless doing. He accepted my words quite responsibly, although he found them unexpected, for we were gripped by the feeling of the scale, the grandiose nature of the project we were dealing with. I recalled Eichmann's words on his ecstasy when finding out that it was "precisely he, a simple offspring of the German countryside, who would carry out such a major act. . . . Such a stir and pride in the scale are, clearly, inherent in people, although I hope that the parallel with Eichmann is very, very remote. . . .

Q: And after this conversation with your teacher, you, Andrey Dmitriyevich, began to conceive of your work differently?

A: Rather, I began to conceive of it more comprehensively. The very witnessing of the tests led to this. The impressions from the tests were of a dual nature. On the one hand, let me repeat, there was a sensation of the tremendous scope of the project. On the other, when you see all of this yourself, something in you changes. When you see the burned birds who are writhing on the scorched steppe, when you see how the shock wave blows away buildings like houses of cards, when you feel the reek of splintered bricks, when you sense melted glass, you immediately thinks of times of war. . . . The very moment of the explosion, the shock wave which moves along the field and which crushes the grass and flings itself at the earth. . . . All of this triggers an irrational yet very strong emotional impact. How not to start thinking of one's responsibility at this point?

Q: Previously I imagined this entire horror only speculatively: It is unpleasant to think that somewhere someone may press a button and such an object would drop on one's head from the sky and everything would end. . . . I can see this now much more tangibly. Yet, there were many people there. . . .

A: In our city, all construction work until 1953 had been done by prisoners. All of us, naturally, realized that a terrible cruelty was being perpetrated, an unfairness to many of them. . . . It is true that we did not issue orders but we communicated with those who commanded these people This fact as well had a dual significance, strange though this might seem. On the one hand, if such sacrifices are being made, we should justify them with the results of our work. We could not forget those who were working at the uranium mines, those who, at dawn, were moving under our windows in columns, guarded by shepherds. . . . **On the other hand, one had to think: What are you personally doing, are you not participating in this terrible crime yourself? Therefore, one had to make oneself feel that one's occupation was not criminal.**

Q: Here is what I thought, Andrey Dmitriyevich. Our state became stronger with the bomb. However, it also became stricter toward man. . . . I do not wish to say that it became more merciless, for it had never been distinguished for its particular mercy. However, the simple people immediately felt on themselves this strictness . . .

A: This new strictness is not entirely simple. When someone is pushed into a corner and finds himself in a hopeless situation, he becomes the most aggressive and adventuristic. Therefore, to a certain extent the existence of nuclear weapons in the Soviet Union led not to a greater strictness but, conversely, to greater tolerance. Remember that after Stalin's death the USSR softened its policies. It was this that was the main factor and whether this would have occurred without the thermonuclear weapon is hard to claim. This process was not simple (recall the Cuban crisis). Nonetheless, we do not know the way events would have developed had the Soviet Union not armed itself properly. . . . I am not certain that our domestic and foreign policy would have turned out to be any softer on this level. I will even say that I am virtually convinced that no, it would not have. Although we cannot make such experiments with the past: One cannot replay history. However, what is more important is to think of the future, of how our present will develop.

Q: Are you referring to restructuring?

A: I believe that in the past few years major changes have taken place in our country, described as restructuring. These changes were prepared by the preceding periods, including the views of people who already then claimed that one could no longer develop in the same way, that in many ways the country was in an impasse. Today this is entirely clear to anyone other than the extreme-right leaders who, unfortunately, still have a great deal of power in our country. If we speak of the present, I think that the implementaiton of the ideas of restructuring means the salvation not only of the land of the soviets but of all mankind.

Q: However, as the saying goes, it is not all that simple to mature to an understanding of this concept. In our country not everyone has grown up to it and you, personally, had to pay a high price for it. . . . However, you were able not to give in, and "not to lose face" as a simple person, not as an academician or winner of all conceivable and inconceivable prizes. For it is a simple man, in that case, who remains on a one-to-one situation with the governmental machinery, with its organized apparatus. . . .

A: Let me begin by saying something about myself and my wife. Despite all regalia, a great deal fell on our lot. The regalia rather postponed that which was to fall on us without eliminating it. Furthermore, the following happened: The main blow, the center of pressure was deflected and aimed not only at me but at my wife and, indirectly, at her children. This was a very clever tactic which put me in a very difficult psychological situation and which was extremely different for Yelena Georgiyevna. She had to muster absolutely exceptional willpower. It seems to me that she displayed it and, furthermore, helped me to remain the person I was. Therefore, our situation was rather complex. As far as normal people are concerned, "nonacademicians," we know that their lot is indeed quite difficult. Nonetheless, many of them are holding out and the power of resistance of the individual is inordinately high. The very concept of "normal man" is meaningless. The people have the broadest possible range of features, from infinite baseness to infinite self-sacrifice. We saw this, for even during the darkest of times people are able to preserve their dignity. However, this demands of them sacrifice.

Q: It would be so desirable for any further preservation of one's dignity not to require paying such heavy dues.

A: A phrase from Brecht's play about Galileo comes to mind now. The student notes the following: "How unhappy must be a country in which there are no heroes." And Galileo replies: "No! Unhappy is the country which needs heroes."

Q: And our country. . . .

A: Has always needed heroes. However, in addition to heroes it has also needed people who would simply preserve their dignity, who know how to follow a dignified line of behavior at work, and in specifically helping others. Such a stance is almost always possible. Naturally, in our country as well there has quite frequently appeared a situation in which a person had to choose whether to become a hero or a scoundrel. . . . Nonetheless, we have always found worthy people in our country. I personally have frequently seen this and so has Yelena Georgiyevna as she has described, based on her own practical experience. . . .

YE. BONNER: I am a pediatrician by profession and have spent many years teaching in medical school. I knew in Moscow a woman, an inspector in the militia's children's room, where the very small children, children who were still nursing, would be brought in. They had either been abandoned or forgotten by their parents. The little ones were frozen and hungry and, sometimes, dying. . . . This woman was ready to give her entire heart to these children. One could have become callous in such work yet she never stopped giving of her soul. She was not a hero but simply a person working with dignity.

Q: But where does one find the strength to preserve this dignity?

A. SAKHAROV: Within oneself.

YE. BONNER: Within oneself. However, the family should not be taken out of consideration. Everything that is essential, valuable in life—spiritual and social—everything starts in the family.

A. SAKHAROV: Hence, incidentally, the conservative nature of the moral type of society: It is slow in changing. I would put it even more sharply: It changes for the better slowly. It could change quite quickly for the worse. This trend toward the worse is difficult to surmount. When our youngest fellow citizens are directed toward a career at any cost, so to say, this in itself is an alarm signal. It is an alarm siren! That is why readiness to pay any price means, actually, profound indifference, indifference toward others, toward anyone other than oneself. This trend, unfortunately, is quite widespread in our country and it can be eliminated only slowly. The main danger is that it may not be eliminated at all.

Q: In that case what, from your viewpoint, is the strongest corrupting factor? For today we are speaking a great deal, achingly, about moral corruption in society. . . .

A: The most dangerous thing to the young is lies, social hypocrisy. When everyone lies—social and youth leaders and parents. . . . This was a factor which operated for a long time in our country, for which reason one could say that to a certain extent the society is sick, it has been poisoned with lies.

YE. BONNER: I may be wrong, but it seems to me that most young people in our country today are internally rejecting lies and turning away from adult society. They reject it on both the social and family levels. . . . However, this is not to say that such boys are bad. I believe that if society were to change for the better, they too would change.

Q: Do you have anything to substantiate these hopes, Yelena Georgiyevna?

YE. BONNER: I have extensive experience in work with adolescents. In our medical school most students were girls from low-income families, minors. . . . At first it is not all that easy to speak with them about lofty things, about spiritual values. Nonetheless. . . . If one tries to teach them to love something, it is out of this "I love something" that a human being develops. . . . In the school, we taught the children poetry, and music or, in a word, everything all at once. Essentially, these were students who were scheduled to be expelled for a variety of reasons. They smoked in the lavatory and drank under the staircase. We had to work a great deal before becoming the best collective for amateur artistic activities in the medical-hygiene labor system of Moscow Oblast. We traveled around the country giving big shows and even staged Shvarts' "King Without Clothes." We learned how to communicate with one another about everything and were no logner indifferent toward one another or toward anything which was happening around us. Such relations will remain with them a lifetime. However, I was not afraid to invite them in my own home or take them to the homes of our friends. . . . In short, it is always important to have at least one adult who would identify what is bright in the child, something one could hold onto. What specifically is not important, whether it is passion for rock or abstract art. It is equally unimportant whether you personally like rock music or prefer "Francesca di Rimini." . . . We have quite a lot of people who are not indifferent and who can understand the young.

Q: Therefore, you do not fear today's youth?

A. SAKHAROV: Today's youth, no. I am horrified by the generation which preceded it, the generation in its 30s. That generation saw but did not reject the lie and accepted the falsehood. . . . It is exceptionally important for hypocrisy no longer to triumph in our country. This would be a catastrophe, a psychological tragedy from which it would be extremely difficult to come out. . . . Today, however, many people can be found who care for honesty.

YE. BONNER: Andrey Dmitriyevich and I have attended several meetings or gatherings on Pushkin Square in Moscow. There everything is done by young people and those attending were also young, with long hair and unbelievable T-shirts. . . .

A. SAKHAROV: I even noticed some young men wearing earrings. . . . All of this, however, is tawdry. . . .

YE. BONNER: There were good boys! Remember Drunina's verses; "We too passed for twits once but then the time came and we became soldiers?" In my view, these boys are entirely ready to become the soldiers of restructuring, of the new life. Like the young from the Leningrad charitable society, like the Estonian "Greens". . . .

A. SAKHAROV: This creates a feeling of hope which is all the more necessary because there is in society another sensation, one of instability. So far, reality has changed little. This means that the old machinery which, for long decades, was in power, is frustrating changes and not surrendering its power. Furthermore, it is trying to mount a counterattack. Is an unreasonable tax on the earnings of members of cooperatives, which literally removes the ground from under their feet, not a counterattack? Some of it has been revised but only partially. . . . The state order is strangling the state enterprise. This is another form of counterattack. . . . I fear greatly that the party conference was attended by all too many people who were opposed to glasnost, to whom it goes against the grain. This too is entirely reactionary. That is why I keep having this sense of insecurity as far as the planned changes are concerned; I still fear that there will be some compromises which will prove to be fatal to restructuring. In this sense the Karabakh drama is no exception. There the resolutions of the oblast soviet proved to be insubstantial and the subsequent discussion of that question at the meeting of the USSR Supreme Soviet Presidium disappointed me profoundly.

Q: Obviously, in this case the practical implementation of the principle of federalism could have helped?

A: Only federalism! The true union among republics, big and small, but equal. It is only then that what is behind the facade of big words about friendship among the peoples will have a real meaning, will be real and democratic. As to solving the Karabakh problem, let us recall the familiar Marxist stipulation according to which one nation which keeps another nation in a state of subordination can itself not remain free. We see today two potentially progressive detachments of restructuring—Armenia and Estonia—and that which is happening in Estonia, I think, is in the interest of the entire country and not only that republic alone, although here as well things must be strictly weighed and considered. . . .

Q: Sakharov's prestige is probably a substantial argument in favor of this approach. However, forgive the next question if it seems tactless to you. Sakharov the "academician" is not only a person but, in our social consciousness, he is also a concept. How do you feel about it yourself? Is it easy for you to be "ACADEMICIAN SAKHAROV?"

A: Is it easy for me to be a concept? Naturally, this is an internally false concept. Pasternak said that "to be famous is ugly." He was right, it is indeed quite ugly. I am doing everything possible to remove from myself the psychological poison related to it. I do not know whether I shall be able to accomplish this. In all likelihood I shall, partially, for I do have certain immunity.

Q: Your fame, and the "curses," which were spewed out by the mouthpieces of the recent semi-official authorities, how did you withstand both?

A: The "curses" fell mostly on my wife. It was she who experienced the monstrous load of dirt and lies. . . .

YE. BONNER: Well, this gave me a new opportunity to be proud of my husband: He was able to slap in the face the offender (this gesture, which has become nearly forgotten in our unchivalrous times, was preceded by floods of disgusting insinuations toward Yelena Georgiyevna. When one of the authors of these base fabrications impudently showed up in the premises where the people he had insulted lived, Andrey Dmitriyevich demanded that he apologize to Ye.G. Bonner. The uninvited guest was amazed at the need to apologize for past "trifles," at which point her husband slapped him in the face—M.L.).

A. SAKHAROV: I too am very proud of this slap in the face. Although someone close to us did not approve of it, believing that one should have acted with words. I am confident, however, that in that case words would have been to no avail.

Q: Dignity must be defended but how difficult it is sometimes to defend it.... There are Pushkin's bitter words: "The devil shrewdly made me to be born in Russia with a soul and talent!" To you, Andrey Dmitriyevich, does this thought seem groundless today? What if we were to project it to your own destiny....

A: I somehow cannot imagine such a mental experiment as my being born in another country and another time. When I read the *Time Machine*, I feel great pity for a person who finds himself in an alien world and in an alien time. This could no longer be called life.... As to moving to another country, this too would be moving to another time, forward or backward, depending on the country in which I find myself, whether in the United States or Ethiopia....

Q: Therefore, although it has been repeatedly suggested to you (to trust various "voices") you have never hesitated with your answer?

A: No one has ever offered me this, although the "voices" have mentioned it. Actually, I have never had to face such a problem.

YE. BONNER: Andrey Dmitriyevich has never been abroad in his life alone and I do not know whether he would ever be allowed to look at the world. But I can add to Andrey Dmitriyevich's answer as though looking from the side (if a wife can look at her husband from the side): He is quite cosmopolitan, in the good, in the loftiest sense of this word.

A. SAKHAROV: Pushkin as well was cosmopolitan. I think, however, that his bitter words should not be overestimated: He could not conceive of himself outside Russia and, at that time, outside the Russia of the language which he himself shaped. To go back to your question, I believe that Pushkin wrote this phrase emotionally, for essentially he felt himself to be in his proper place, in his historical place, which was organic to him. As to myself, I can say the same. Understandably, I do not compare myself to Aleksandr Sergeyevich, this would be unseemly. However, a certain analogy does exist. I fit where I was born.

Q: Erenburg states this in stricter terms: "Like a mother, a homeland is not chosen and one does not reject it like an inconvenient apartment." Do you agree with this?

A: There are many facets to such things. When Pushkin thought that "the devil had the shrewdly...," he may have been entirely sincere. However, I now recall a sentence which was written by the Yugoslav journalist Mikhaylov: "Homeland is not a geographic concept. Homeland means freedom." I learned this during our hunger strike before the departure of my daughter-in-law and later wrote it to her in the parting telegram, when she was forced to leave. . . . The thought that "I fit where I was born" is accurate but somewhat jingoist and should not be absolutized, like the facet which Mikhaylov has expressed so sharply. Both are true. In this case one must not be dogmatic: Both sides could be morally justified.

YE. BONNER: Today there is a great deal of discussion about migrations. But then everything has already been said in the "Universal Declaration . . ." and the "Pact on Rights," which asserts the freedom of choosing one's country and place of residence. . . .

A. SAKHAROV: That right is on the same level as the right to the freedom of convictions, as one of the most important and inalienable human rights. Without it, how can one feel free?

We held this discussion on the balcony of the hotel where Bonner and Sakharov stayed during the Pugwash Conference. These two already elderly people, who have truly developed through bitter experience "the precise knowledge about evil and good" discuss life. Were their own lives not spent in repelling the evil? I once again recall Okudzhava's lines:

> All those unyielding strings,
> and with every passing minute it becomes more
> difficult
> to see in the smile of fortune
> one's hope smile.

These are sad lines. But it is not for nothing that they are known as "living, arise. . . ." Well, we shall rise. It is time. Dagomys-Tallinn.

Sakharov, Bonner on Gorbachev, Restructuring
Interview with Andrey Sakharov, Soviet nuclear physicist and human rights activist, and Yelena Bonner, his wife, by French journalist Jean-Pierre Barou in Moscow, *Sueddeutsche Zeitung*, January 26, 1989

BAROU: According to the new election law, a Congress of People's Deputies consisting of 2,250 members will be created in March. Two-thirds of the deputies will be elected in general elections. The other third will be appointed from political or social groups. . . .

SAKHAROV: Let me interrupt you. What you just said represents only an extremely small part of a very complex mechanism containing a large number of traps and hidden aspects that do not make it very democratic. In my view, this new election system has two main faults: The candidates who are proposed for appointment from among the groups are selected in a way that is not democratic or based on formal criteria. On which basis are they selected? I do not know anything about that. I can only point out that the same thing happened last June when delegates were sent to the party conference. We saw that people opposed to progressive ideas such as glasnost were favored and appeared at the party conference. The most important thing, however, is the fact that the elections are taking place on several levels.

BAROU: Are you talking about the Supreme Soviet?

SAKHAROV: Indeed. Its 400 members, all of whom will come from the Congress of People's deputies, will elect the president, but we do not know what criteria will be used for electing them. We have now been told that they will be replaced—1/5 of them annually—but we do not know what the criteria are.

BONNER: There is another important point. These 400 apparachiks, whom nobody knows, can remove the president without consulting with the people. The only real weapon the head of state has is direct elections. What was Gorbachev afraid of? We would have voted for him. Our country has no other leader. He has deprived himself of the defense by the people. I personally believe that he will be overthrown soon, together with all those in the country who have believed in perestroyka. I would not stake R100 on Gorbachev.

SAKHAROV: They will overthrow him, or they will dictate which views he should hold. I have been saying this ever since I returned from the West. Gorbachev is annoyed by the fact that I ever condemned the election system. People told me so. However, I do not at all understand the logic of his criticism. He was seized by a kind of rage that I find totally incomprehensible.

BAROU: Are the people—and I mean not only the intellectuals—interested in this debate?

SAKHAROV: Yes, but they are demonstrating wisdom. We cannot foresee material success for perestroyka.

BAROU: People talk a lot about that. . . .

SAKHAROV: However, the people are not just interested in material goods. They want the lies to stop, but the lies still exist. During this period of transition, we are trying to find a way to move up, but we will have to wait and see.

BAROU: Do you believe that military or diplomatic secrets could be less important? Could there be an opening in this respect within the framework of glasnost?

SAKHAROV: I think that there are only a few true secrets. In my view, the fewer secrets there are, the better it will be for world-wide stability. Therefore, I think that spy satellites are a factor promoting peace and confidence. If we know other countries and our potential enemies better, the world will be more secure. The term military or diplomatic secret should be abolished.

BAROU: Could you be considered to be the leader of the democratic opposition in the Soviet Union today?

SAKHAROV: I do not think that I could ever have been characterized as a leader. I have never tried to represent anyone other than myself. My position changes in response to changes in conditions.

BAROU: How do you assess perestroyka at the present stage?

SAKHAROV: I think that it is absolutely necessary, that we have no other solution. However, this does not include having to unconditionally support Gorbachev, even if the whole process has been started at his initiative. By the way, it would not be fair to link perestroyka 100 percent with his name. Gorbachev can be subject to pressure, he can have other ideas. Restructuring must be supported in general—without fear of insulting any particular person. It is important for everyone to understand that cooperation with the West is only possible on the basis of a progressive development of perestroyka. This is what is being announced officially, but the question is becoming increasingly complex and contradictory. In my view setbacks have already occurred. I do not agree either with the electoral law or with the law on the dispersion of assemblies and rallies. I do not agree with the arrest of members of the Karabakh Committee and the detention of Pulatov, an activist from Azerbaijan—even if I do not like him because he has advocated violence.

BAROU: You recently visited Armenia together with your wife and the vice president of the Academy of Sciences. What were the circumstances?

SAKHAROV: When I returned from the United States, I was very concerned about the fate of the Armenians. I paid a visit to Aleksandr Yakovlev, who must have told Gorbachev about my visit. They suggested to me that I tour the region. There is no doubt that they thought I would arrive at a more positive assessment on the spot. In Armenia we made a tour with a helicopter. What I saw there was far worse than I had expected. First, there were the massacres in Sumgait in November; everybody was shocked about the local mafia, which diverts R10 million to the underground economy every year. There is no doubt that it also has links with the police and the KGB. Sumgait—to cite just one example—is only 20 minutes away form Baku, the capital of Azerbaijan. If the authorities really wanted to, they could control this area. This is what makes me angry. A pregnant woman was raped there and burned alive; her belly was slit open and the fetus was thrown into the middle of the street. An Armenian family was besieged for 3 days, and then one of its members was also burned alive. Crowds chanted in Baku: "Aliyev, thank you for the weapons (Geydar Aliyev was removed from his post in 21 October 1987. He was a member of the Politburo and head of the KGB in Azerbaijan—the editors). In any case, developments had reached a point where the mafia controlled everything. I saw a young girl in Baku who had pinned a portrait of Khomeyni on her scarf. Religious fanaticism also played a role. In Armenia, however, it was of little importance. If a mafia exists there, it is certainly less important. A rather democratic movement exists there.

BAROU: Did you suffer setbacks as a member of the "Memorial" movement, which is concerned with the rehabilitation of the victims of Stalinism?

SAKHAROV: "Memorial's" goal is to establish a documentation and research center which is devoted to the victims of Stalinism, and which is also intended as a public library. We have opened an account with the Gosbank for donations from the public. When the members of the "Memorial" movement went to the bank they were told on the orders of Yudin, who is responsible for cultural matters, that they no longer have access to the account. He had also given orders that the money be used for the erection of a monument for the victims of Stalinism, he pointed out. "Is this not what you want?" we were asked by the Central Committee. I was summoned to the Central Committee, and there I recognized a militant activist of the nationalist "Pamyat" movement. However, we will certainly continue our activities.

BAROU: Let us talk about the current problem of Jews in the USSR . . .

Andrey Sakharov turns to Yelena Bonner (his wife is of Jewish origin): "Yelena, are refuseniks still being arrested? Are they still being dismissed from their jobs without prior notice?

BONNER: Not according to my knowledge.

BAROU: But are there still not many refuseniks who are not permitted to leave the USSR?

SAKHAROV: I believe that the number has considerably decreased. However, there are still some, and the legislation has not been changed yet. It is important for the standard to be the same as in Western legislation. If this is achieved, the refusenik issue will lose importance. By the way, in order to emigrate several of them are trying to find secret ways to withdraw from professional life; many of them are living on their savings and from the help of others.

BONNER: In general, one may leave the country today. Psychologically, in this respect, the situation has changed. The authorities do not have such a negative attitude toward the refuseniks or all the others who want to emigrate. Rather, it is the Western world that is the problem. Except for the United States, developed countries do not have a real asylum policy. The Americans have to support it all. At the moment, a large number of emigrants is stuck in Italy—the United States cannot grant the refugee status to everyone. It cannot be reproached with insisting on a contingent of immigrants. At the Vienna (CSCE) conference people are talking about nothing but the absence of the right to emigration in our country. The other developed countries should first do their homework! Not even a dissident as famous as Yuriy Orlov, who is living in France at present, can get French citizenship! In the West, brains work the wrong way. For example, nobody thinks of saying to Mikhail Gorbachev: "Destroy the Berlin Wall!"

BAROU: You have been saying and writing for a long time that an individual's freedom of movement and freedom of choice in residence is the cornerstone of human rights.

SAKHAROV: Thus, the situation has developed, priorities are no longer the same. I concede that the freedom of assembly is ranking first now. All groups that have been unofficial so far and whose membership is increasing must be able to find their place in our society. Today, the question of collective rights is more topical for the individual than that of personal rights.

BARU: Would you call the concept of the rule of law the magic term in new Soviet thinking?

SAKHAROV: The establishment of the rule of law is justified by our history in which man has been the victim of dictatorship by the state. However, the law has to protect man from the excesses of the state, the crowd, the masses, and the mass media and give preference to a pluralist society. And if a society is pluralist—in other words, not totalitarian—it will watch over moral principles.

BAROU: In the Soviet Union, much tribute has been paid to Lenin lately.

SAKHAROV: Gorbachev talks about it a lot. He says that we are renewing the ideas of Lenin's epoch. In reality, we are establishing something completely different because we are not returning to Lenin's epoch. Impossible. When there is an interesting development today, one can predict a mind set which reminds me of "Solaris," a science fiction novel by Stanislav Lem where the images in people's brains are bathed in a terrible orange color. I mention this to express the idea that I am not very happy about the situation. However, I repeat: Perestroyka is our only choice, and nobody knows what lies in store for us.

BONNER: However, one does not talk much about Khrushchev to whom we owe everything that we now have: fair pay for the kolkhoz peasants' work; a housing policy; our pension system; the first actual reduction of troop strength in the history of the USSR.

SAKHAROV: When Khrushchev reduced the importance of the Army he was taking a great risk. This is why he was overthrown. However, thanks to him we have made a giant leap forward compared to 1953.

BAROU: Something else that needs to be pointed out: The West does not always have a clear idea of the political prisoners.

SAKHAROV: To my knowledge there are no more prisoners of conscience according to Articles 70 and 190 of criminal law, which refer to deeds that are regarded as anti-Soviet. However, the imprisonment of members of the Karabakh Committee has to be regarded as a setback. The problem of people being sent to psychiatric institutions has not been fully solved yet. There are also reports of arrests where certain articles of the criminal law were applied that concern criminal acts that had nothing to do with that specific case.

BAROU: It seems that you are not too enthusiastic about holding a human rights conference in Moscow in 1991?

SAKHAROV: The west has to continue exerting pressure on the USSR, at least until the international human rights conference in Moscow to prevent if from taking place if the situation in the USSR is not really satisfactory.

"SAMIZDAT"

Social Portrait of a Phenomenon: "Samizdat"
by A. Malysheva, *Komsomolskaya Pravda*, February 9, 1989

Initial print run—four copies. How many outstanding Russian writers' works suffered this fate? Platonov, Pasternak, Akhmatova, Bulgakov . . . One could go on. The list would be enormous.

An "Erika" [East German typewriter] does four copies.

"That is all, and that is enough," the poet Aleksandr Galich, whose unpublished poetry was widely available "in copies" and whose songs circulated in the form of tape recordings, wrote in the early seventies.

Some 25-30 years ago (not to mention times 40-50 years past) four copies on a typewriter—another four from each and so on— was an entire publishing process. How many typewriters are there in the country? And who decided what kind of edition the unpublished book would come out in?

But look more closely at the names. Behind them lies an era that is in no way conducive to freedom of thought and original ideas. Because, whatever the era, free thinking, civic consciousness, and incorruptible talent remain deep within society.

It is not only article 190 (1) [article banning works that "discredit the state and social system . . ."] that links "Woe From Wit" and, for example, "By Right of Memory," Pushkin's "The Village," and, for instance, Platonov's "Chevengur."

The thread that links these works through the ages is far stronger. There is a continuity here, a dual continuity, what is more. Continuity not only of the Russian intelligentsia, which has always had an innate acute moral sense, an ability to think independently, and a responsibility for the people's destiny; but also a continuity of nonacceptance of heterodoxy.

And it was this explosive mixture of "inconvenient" verse and those banning it that gave rise to "samizdat."

To be fair, not all "samizdat" works are masterpieces. There have been weak and profascist and downright bad books. But they were more the exception that proves the rule. The worth of a book was a kind of guarantee of its quality—a bad book might be read and discussed, but it was unusual to spend nights copying it and then risk keeping it at home.

It is hard to imagine, for example, someone who has only samizdat books in his home library or only reads such books. Someone who has not read A.F. Abramov, V. Tendryakov, and N. Dumbadze simply because their books have been published.

"Not one of us," "enemies," "ideological sabotage"—each of the numerous labels attached to heterodox writers hinted very clearly at the alienation of these people from society, from "all of us." Is that not why forcible exile of cultural figures abroad became so popular: It was easier to portray a voice "from over there" as hostile . . .

"We lost a whole stratum of our culture," Daniil Granin wrote. "We can remember the inconvenient, the intractable, the refractory being driven out of the country . . ."

You can deprive people of their homeland, and you can deprive them of their freedom.

Times, ways, views change, the faces of the enemy and the hero change. . . . But the penal articles of the Criminal Code remain. And since the articles exist, do the crimes exist too?

Article 58 (10) (now repealed), which made a bad name for itself in the repression years, was formal grounds in the thirties and forties for dispatching hundreds of thousands of people to camps. Times, thank goodness, have changed radically for the better, but the wording of the "successor" article—70—has changed for the worse. According to article 58 (10) of "that" code, a person could be held criminally liable for agitation and propaganda "containing a call to overthrow, undermine, or weaken Soviet power." Article 70 is not satisfied with calls, but with the mere intention to undermine power, that is, a highly ephemeral, vague, and subjective concept: "agitation and propaganda carried out for subversive purposes . . ."

One might object, saying: leave it be, the wording, since the particular article has not really been used in recent years. But my reply would be: So why do we need it? After all, the Criminal Code is not a lady's album—there is nothing *frivolous* in it.

As long as article 70 is no more than a gun hanging idly on the wall, but. . . .

I risk bringing down on me the wrath of those who have given their all to the fight against heterodoxy, against unsanctioned criticism of our life, but . . . "samizdat" is of their making. It is what people were forced to resort to in conditions of unwarranted bans by the censor and editorial instructions.

They did not "manufacture," they did not "disseminate," of course; on the contrary, they strove might and main to destroy the spontaneous editions, and there was no winner in this struggle.

But victims there were. . . .

In 1985 the "black book gang"—so called by an *Ulyanovskaya Pravda* journalist—was exposed in Ulyanovsk. They were showing an "unhealthy interest" in "garbage that distorts Soviet history . . . in individuals who were cast onto the garbage heap of history long ago."

Our own correspondent in Ulyanovsk, Igor Virabov, obtained the details of this recent incident. . . . apparently, a worker, a cook, an engineer, a colonel, and even a Komsomol obkom worker had been engaged in "subversive activity." Igor Romanov, deputy chairman of the "Sputnik" International Youth Tourism Bureau, had a book by Stalin's daughter—S. Alliluyeva. How this became known is not known. But Igor handed the book over to the authorities when tactfully requested to do so. Let us emphasize that no steps were taken against him. But Igor's bosses reacted. . . . After a while there came an urgent recommendation that Romanov resign, in order "not to compromise the obkom apparatus." The "unreliable" crew also included a whole group of people who were little known to him or were total strangers: All those who had acquired and read samizdat "Diaries." Before removing Romanov from the party register the Komsomol obkom called an emergency party meeting of the apparatus.

Excerpt from record No 5 of 12 February:

Chairman: the primary party organization has received information about a display of political naivete by Comrade I.G. Romanov. . . .

Question to I. Romanov: How were you able to obtain literature that is not published here, in the Soviet Union, because it is ideologically damaging?

From the speeches: Strictly speaking he has betrayed the motherland! While the party struggles against alien ideology, he brings it into his home. In fact, he should be expelled from the party.

At the party raykom Igor made the aquaintance of some of his "accomplices." They compared notes. Romanov received a reprimand plus endorsement. Eduard Grigoryevich Fomin, officer, was expelled and demoted. Ilyushiun, the cook, was expelled, and then reinstated with a severe reprimand. . . .

Our society, as is known, is only now learning democracy, and unless this is being done in order to "learn and then forget," then, obviously, the Criminal Code will have to be amended and some of its articles sacrificed in the name of future democracy. Especially as in the past 6 months I cannot really recall any instances of literary "samizdat." Times have changed.

Since we are having a go at two entire articles of the Criminal Code, one of which relates to "particularly dangerous state crimes," we have to have on the subject the view of those who, on the one hand, are the guardians of citizens' interests and, on the other hand, are authorized representatives of the law.

Here is the view of Vladimir Leonidovich Golubev, Moscow assistant prosecutor:

"Of course, article 70 of the RSFSR Criminal Code and the corresponding articles of the union republics' criminal codes require major editorial amendments and changes in the formal definitions of crimes.

"The wording of the article must be very specific, revealing the significance and nature of the crime. Such criminal law norms are necessary and they must perform the function of protecting the interests of the state against criminal encroachments connected with any kind of call for a forcible change in the constitutional setup and political system. But this punishment must not apply to citizens' artistic work and personal views! It is absolutely self-evident that every citizen has every right to express his disagreement with state policy, as long as he does not carry out specific actions aimed at undermining it, and the state has no right to take any steps of a criminal law nature against him. Juridical practice of past years shows, when cases in this category are being examined, the wording of article 70 as it stands at the moment has contributed in some cases to an incorrect assessment of the actions of individuals who have been called to account."

So, people might ask, anything goes?

"By no means. Our constitution and laws stipulate punishment for propagandizing war, for fueling ethnic strife, and for pornography! And in our discussion of the principles of new criminal legislation we must bring them into line with the Constitution." But the producers of samizdat now have far more urgent problems than Criminal Code articles which have a low profile at the moment.

In a period when samizdat periodicals have become more active, under the stern and disapproving gaze of the bosses, when the Moscow University weekly *Demokraticheskiy Universitet*, the interschool paper *Barrikada*, The Tambov journalists' press bulletin *Sodeystviye,* and many other amateur journals and papers have been published, the vast majority of which, incidentally, are pursuing the aim of promoting restructuring and the democratization of society, a USSR Council of Ministers resolution comes out, restricting cooperative publishing activity, among other things.

But they are publishing. The journal *Kommunist* too, in the edition that is an anthology of the best political articles of the year, prints materials from the interschool samizdat paper. . . .

Yes, we have gotten used to doing nearly everything ourselves. There is a shortage of good-quality vegetables, so people resort to subsidiary plots. There is no fine, beautiful clothing, so everyone sews, knits, and spins. There is a lack of authentic information and variety of opinion in books and newspapers, so other books and other papers appear, homemade again.

When we have plenty of everything, when the book-publishing process is geared to readers' interests and needs, when our press starts responding more swiftly and becomes more consistent than the amateur, people's press, there will be no need for "samizdat."

And despite my deep respect for "samizdat," I would not want to live to see its next renaissance. Because it would mean . . . But let us not be morbid.

SATIRE

by M. Zhvanetsky

I was once asked:
—Do you think that satire is a weapon of defense or offense?
—For me it is of course defense. After all, I sit home, then I go to the store, someone punches me in the face. I go home and write an answer.

SHORTAGES

Thoughts While Waiting in Line
Letter to the editor of *Izvestiya*, February 3, 1989

We are patient people, that is well known. But is it really necessary to test our patience so stubbornly and for so long? Could there be another option?

What prompted me to write was my distress at what I heard while waiting in line at the Barnaul Central Department Store. The thing is that since August soap, laundry detergent, toothpaste, and many other things have not been on sale in Barnaul's Stores. The same is true, I have heard, in other cities, but does that make it any easier for us?

On 24 November I stood in a line from 1600 to 1800 hours—there was not enough toothpaste, so I had to wait again from 1500 to 1740 the next day. I bought three tubes of toothpaste and three bars of soap. However, my good fortune was overshadowed. In the time I spent waiting in line, I heard a great many unflattering things from the purchasers about our economic policy. What upset me was that they were mainly berating restructuring. As if it was to blame for everything! I tried to change their minds, but they told me: The lack of goods is created by the trade workers: The "flea market" sells soap, toothpaste, shampoo, and so forth at three times the price, and the people waiting in this enormous line are not going to sell things at the "flea market," it all comes from the stores and from the people who fail to control them properly.

I could not rest for what I had heard. It is upsetting to hear people blaming everything on restructuring. No doubt difficulties are inevitable at the start of anything complex and new. But how much can you take? And why is it all at our expense, at the expense of people who live very modestly?

I went to the "Merkuriy" cooperative. Not long ago the "Svezhest" store used to be there, where they always sold many different kinds of soap, laundry detergent, and so forth. Now it is all different at "Merkuriy." It is nicer and . . . more expensive. There, they were selling cotton panty hose at R13. I bought

(I. Smirnov, *Soviet News*)

exactly the same panty hose in Moscow in July at a store on Gorkiy Street for R2. When I asked who makes the panty hose, the girl dropped her eyes and answered: "A cooperative".... They also sell ordinary boots there for R167. In Moscow they are R70–80.

It is no better at the "flea market." Here there really is everything, but the prices ... Shampoo at R5–8, rabbit-fur hats—R50, boots—T100–200, lipstick—R5–10, and so forth.

After all I had seen, I wondered: What is going on?

I have been living in Barnaul since 1963. I have never once seen either rabbit-fur hats or felt boots on sale in the stores, but the "flea market" is always full of them.

So it has nothing to do with restructuring. We expect it to resolve rapidly problems that have been accumulating for years. No doubt it is necessary to step up monitoring of the trade in shortage goods and to take a close look at the cooperatives. But we also need more substantial, purely economic measures that would enable ordinary people to draw breath, so to speak, and provide their families with essentials. Otherwise people will get angry in the end, and no talk about restructuring, no bright prospects will make any impression on them. Some people might regard this as a consumerist approach. But is that all that concern for consumers is?

—S. Kalmykova, Barnaul

News Conference in USSR MVD
by V. Shcherban, *Selskaya Zhizn*, February 2, 1989

Meat and meat products transported in refrigerated units are being stolen on a large scale. There is a simple and efficient way which will make it possible to minimize thefts on the way. In the opinion of the transportation militia leadership, it is not the consigner who should seal up the refrigerated units with the meat, as happens now, but the teams accompanying them. It is they who will be entirely responsible for the loads' safety. But the Ministry of Railways' leadership will not do this, believing this to be inefficient.

Up to 40 percent of motor vehicle and agricultural equipment is also misappropriated. So-called "electronic guards" could also assist in this situation. But the militia only recently found a common language with the administration of enterprises which have already started to produce the mechanical means to protect socialist property. And while the hearing is in progress, large-scale embezzlement on the railroad is continuing unabated. The Odessa, Moscow, October, and North Caucasus Railroads are unfortunately preeminent here.

Recently we have often been perturbed by aviation accidents. How do matters stand here? In the past year there were 36 accidents. Some 228 people were victims and of these 119 died. During airport inspections more than 250 firearms, 86,117 edged weapons, and 411 kg of explosives were confiscated. A few words about the new criminal epidemic—anonymous calls with warnings about alleged imminent explosions on aircraft. There were 53 such calls last year. This year there have already been 12. Proposals have been submitted for the introduction of more severe punishments for "pranks" of this type.

The figures are not very pleasant . . . But only if we know

about all the serious shortcomings and problems can we unite our efforts more quickly in a matter which is vitally important for each of us—finally putting transport in order.

That will make things calmer for all of us.

Humiliation
by Alexander Kabakov, *Moscow News*, No. 11, 1989

Queueing up for everything from sausages to razor blades has long been part and parcel of Soviet life. It is a humiliation for citizens of a country that builds nuclear power stations and space shuttles to have to stand in line even for a bar of soap. But we do stand for it . . .

The government in the last twenty-five years has passed at least 25 decisions to end queues. All for naught! There is no change. What changes though, is the name of the goods people queue for. According to statistics, we spend at least one hour a day in lines for food, and between two and three hours for clothes, washing powder, tissue paper . . . We spend days, months, years in a queue as long as a lifetime.

Why Sales Clerks So Don't Like Shoppers:

The first, a comparatively short line, is for transistor batteries. There are nearly fifty people in it and each buys twenty or thirty batteries—for friends and relations. The man behind the counter shouts: "I'm opening the last box, don't join the queue!"

In a sports goods section the line is a hundred or so people long. On sale are gym shoes made in Czechoslovakia. The line is growing by the second . . . .

Stanislav Sorokin, GUM's director: "As the old joke goes, goods in short supply begin with the letter 'A'—all. I'm convinced, the way out is in imported goods. Instead of cutting down on imports, as has been the case in recent years, they should be expanded until our own industry picks up in the new economic conditions. The growing customers' demands should be met within the next few years, otherwise the shadow cast by these queues will fall on perestroika. The appalling conditions of trade is another reason for queues. The staff of GUM's main building is 5,000 and we sell goods worth 700 million roubles each year. The building is an architectural landmark and it is crumbling. It was built in just three years in the 19th century and it is ten years now that we've been promised reconstruction. Going to work places to sell our goods cannot be a way out either. This corrupts the working people: they buy things in short supply they don't really want and then resell them at a profit. Think of what we are paid! I get 230 roubles per month. An ordinary shop assistant gets a bit more than a hundred. And there are dozens of opportunities of enrichment, because he or she sells items in short supply. This is why those behind the counter are popularly reputed to be swindlers. Is a shop assistant interested in working faster or asking his mates to give him a hand when the pressure is on? Not in the least. He doesn't care either about the customer or the store's profits. His only concern is to see that the goods he is responsible for are not stolen. We will not be able to work well unless profit becomes the sole motivation in training."

In GUM's food section people are queueing practically at every counter. The rules in the line are strict: "I grabbed the place next to this young man and only went off for a minute!" "We don't know, we didn't see it. Don't let her jump the line!" This is a tea line. The line of 80 people for cheese (of the one and only brand—no one seems to mind). Another queue is for cakes . . . Aware of the general situation with meat, I head for the meat section anticipating the longest line. But there is no line for meat, as there are no lines for sausage or chickens, for the simple reason that the section is closed. Because there is nothing to sell?

Queueing as a Way of Life

Winding through a narrow gallery on the first floor is a line of nearly 300 for nighties of snythetic silk of doubtful taste and quality, made in Hungary and costing an impressive 70 roubles— a third of the average monthly pay.Those in the line are nearly all from places other than Moscow, many from the southern republics. Nighties are on sale at four different counters, with 200–300 shoppers in each line.

People in the line act as if they are being examined by a doctor: on the one hand they are ready with their emotions and complaints, on the other with the wish to remain anonymous. No one wishes to give their names and they answer questions on the run as they hurry to make new purchases.

Zinaida L., a woman of 62, came from the city of Ordzhonikidze. She has just spent more than one and a half hour queueing for two of those nighties—one a garish red and the other blue. "The red one is for my daughter, the second . . . well, I don't want it, old as I am! My daughter has a friend. If the girl doesn't like it, our next door neighbours would, perhaps. I'm retired on pension, so I am here to do some shopping. Where I live, the shops are empty."

Yet another line is for men's boots made in Romania and priced at 47 roubles. The line is 150 people long. There is no room to try on the boots, so people walk a bit aside and start swapping to get right colours or size. The place is littered with empty boxes.

Nina and Alexander G., a young couple from Nikopol. They use their vacations specially to shop in Moscow. They've just bought three pairs of boots. "They aren't quite snug and the colour is not perfect, but what can you do? A pair of boots like these would cost you 150 bucks or so on the black market in Nikopol."

Mikhail Yegorov: a militia colonel (Ministry of Internal Affairs): "Queues also breed profiteering and cheating by the sales staff. To a considerable extent queues result from the deliberate actions of some sales clerks. Suffice it to say that goods worth 16 million roubles were found stacked under the counters in shops around the country in a recent militia operation. There are 15,000 criminal cases a year involving the hoarding of goods in shops. Hence the shortages. In addition to this is the operation of the mafia, which brings together those who have access to goods in short supply and those who sell them on the black market. In our recent operation we intercepted 4 tons of butter, 2 tons of sweets, 146,000 packs of Yava cigarettes, and 27,000 bottles of imported beer trucked from Moscow to Azerbaijan. Queues are also the consequences of uneven distribution: all goods in short supply are mainly sold in Moscow, hence the longest queues and the big elbow room for profiteers. It is they who benefit from turning Moscow into a 'showcase for foreigners'. There are 130 'hotbeds' of profiteering around Moscow. One of them is the Jadran shop where one can see queues of up to one thousand.

"One step to combat organized profiteering would be a change in legislation. Stiffer fines and mandatory seizure of the items of profiteering should make the trade unprofitable on purely economic grounds."

The longest line of nearly 500 people is for men's polar fox caps at 190 roubles each, or nearly the average monthly pay. The people are queueing inside a channel formed by militia barriers and metal goods containers. They are prepared to spend at least three hours to buy a big shaggy cap which has long become a status symbol ... "Are you sure you need it?" I turn to a guy of twenty who squeezed his way out of the crush. He mistakes my question: "It's all yours for 230, OK?"

"Just" Prices or Just Earnings?

Forty or so people are queueing up for the world famous denim that goes to make jeans. A man of 25 or so has bought 8 metres of this fabric at 18 roubles a metre. "My girlfriend will make jackets for herself and me. This is cheaper than buying one from a coop for 250–300 roubles ... This is the genuine stuff, from Cyprus. By the by, I can't see any coop people in the line, what with all this talk about them buying up all kinds of fabric ..."

Tatyana Korvagina, Professor and D. Sc. (Economics): "I wouldn't point to a 'conspiracy' of the decelerating forces as being at the root of today's queues. Hiding the goods and thus starting rumours that coop people have cleaned out shops is an effective tactic for sabotaging perestroika. But this isn't the most important thing. The old joke goes: "A queue is a socialist approach to the counter." There is much truth in it. A surefire formula against queues is to encourage a market economy, to go over to market prices that respond to demand, rather than fixed prices. The prospect draws vehement protests: "Price hikes are socially unjust." As for me, the real social injustice is the present prices at which only the nomenklautura and trade elites can afford to freely buy things in short supply.The rest of us have to pay two or three times the retail price to profiteers. Wage-levelling should be ended, as should all economic privileges in favour of differentiated wages. High pay for efficient workers would benefit the entire society, as has been practically shown by the industrialized countries. To minimize the advantage this would give those who have grown rich operating on the black market, there should be a money reform. Money should necessarily be exchanged at work places in accordance with officially earned incomes. This should have been done in 1984. But it is not too late to do it now, as long as it is carefully planned."

GUM is a favourite haunt for tourists. There I see a group of Italians taking pictures of what baffles them: a line formed in an empty space. But any experienced Soviet would know right off: an ice-cream girl will come on the scene any minute now.

Muscovites and visitors enjoy ice cream even in winter. Are they frosty? Or is it because of a lack of other opportunities to get fast food? The queue is patiently waiting. Is it there perhaps because of an ingrained patience?

We Are Having To Pay for Our Mistakes; Why There Have Been Delays with Wage Payments in Donbass Cities
by V. Tolstov, *Izvestiya*, March 3, 1988

Torez, Donetsk Oblast—At 4 o'clock on a winter's morning, when the night had not even begun to think about receding, several people appeared at the doors of Cash Office No 3225/018 in the city of Torez. Their collars turned up against the wind, they waited patiently. Nearer to daybreak more people arrived and, when more than 100 had gathered, they had a roll call. Everyone had memorized their number or written it on the palm of their hand. Several days later I found a battered notebook with a list inside on the windowsill of the cash office. Judging by the entries, 254 people had stood freezing in the line that morning.

It was a line for wages. . . .

"We had something in the area of 600 people waiting here in December," senior cashier Nadezhda Gurnyak explained. "We have 20 enterprises registered with us for wages distribution. It is absolute bedlam on payday. Windows get broken. The noise, the shouting! The names they call us! As if it is our fault that there is not any money." . . .

Yes, it really is a crisis, because passions in Torez and in other mining towns in the Donbass region are running quite high and emergency measures have had to be taken. I had occasion to witness a conversation at a savings bank between some Torez people and gorispolkom workers. It is not easy to calm people driven to distraction by the lack of meat products in the stores and the meager choice of clothing, footwear, children's goods, and other items. On top of all that, having to jostle in queues in the freezing cold to get your wages or money out of your own savings account!

We were surrounded by a dense ring of people and showered with questions. Why is there no special children's food or baby food in the stores which are supposed to sell these items? Why is there no candy on sale, despite the fact that there is a candy factory in town? Why are people's homes poorly heated and

without hot water, for which payment is regularly taken? There were many, many more "whys" like this, which painted a picture of serious neglect of the social sphere in the Donbass region.

So, the time has come to pay for the mistakes of past decades, when production and its needs were given priority while concern for ordinary people was always put off until another day and substituted by empty rhetoric. "Temporary difficulties" in the development of the social sphere have become firmly entrenched economic and moral losses. . . .

In the line leading to the window of cash office No 3225/018 a young man with traces of coal dust beneath his eyes exclaims in exasperation, totally justified if you consider that he has already had to wait several hours for his wages: "This is restructuring?!"

Yes, this is restructuring. In the years of stagnation cash plan problems were solved very simply: The sale of alcohol and the export of oil and other national resources for the foreign market were increased. Only timeservers can act in this way, as they feel no concern for the country's future, but this path does not lead anywhere. The main thing, however, is that measures like these simply conceal the illness, thereby delaying the cure and making it more difficult.

Soviet Report

"Even the transfer of individual organizations from one department to another, as the practice of recent years has shown, does not increase the quantity of vegetables and fruit."

A. SOLZHENITSYN

Let's Not Live by a Lie!
by Alexander Solzhenitsyn, epilogue by Igor Vinogradov, *XX Century and Peace*, February 1989

There was a time when we didn't even dare to speak in a whisper. Now we write or read Samizdat, and complain to one another to our heart's content, even in the smoking rooms of research institutes: "They're messing us about!" The unnecessary bragging about outer space when the country is ruined and poor; the strengthening of distant wild regimes; the stirring up of civil wars. They recklessly supported Mao Zedong (with our money), but it will be us who will be sent against him, and we'll have to go, there'll be no escaping it. They take legal action against anyone they like, and healthy people are driven to lunatic asylums—always "they" while we are helpless.

We already reached a limit, general spiritual ruin is threatening all of us and physical destruction is about to burn us and our children, but we go on smiling cowardly like before and babbling inarticulately:

"How can we prevent this? We have no strength."

We have become so hopelessly dehumanized that for a bit of food we're ready to sacrifice all our principles, our soul, all the efforts of our ancestors, all opportunities for our descendants, just so long as no one disturbs our frail existence. We have no more firmness left, no pride or fervour. We don't even fear universal nuclear death, World War III (maybe we shall hide in some hole), we are only afraid of taking steps of civic courage! If only we could not stray from the herd, not take a step on our own—and suddenly find ourselves without a long white loaf, without gas and without a registration of residence in Moscow.

In political study groups, they kept repeating the same thing to us, so often that it became deep rooted in us,—to live comfortably and well all our lives in the social conditions which cannot be overstepped. Being determines consciousness, but what have we to do with all this? We cannot do anything.

But in fact, we can do everything! We are cheating ourselves in order to be calm. It is not "they" who are guilty but us, only us!

Objections may be raised: Really there is nothing we can think of! We have been gagged, nobody listens to us or asks us anything. How can we make them listen?

To make them change their minds—but it is impossible.

It would be more natural to re-elect them! But usually there are no re-elections in our country.

In the West people know about strikes, demonstrations of protest but we are too downtrodden, we are afraid of them: How is it possible, all of a sudden, to give up work and go into the street.

But still, the other fatal roads, tested over the past century of bitter Russian history, are not for us either. We have had enough!

Now that all the axes have done their work, and that all that was sown has sprouted, we can see how misled and dazed were those young and conceited people who thought they could make the country a just and happy one through terror, bloody uprising and a civil war. No, thanks, fathers of enlightenment! Now we know for sure that foul methods are bred in foul results. May our hands be clean!

So, the circle has been closed? And there is really no way out of it? And it only remains for us to wait: Something might suddenly happen of its own accord.

But it will never come off all by itself if we continue to recognize, glorify and strengthen it without departing from its most sensitive point.

From the lie.

When violence bursts into people's peaceful lives, its face is glowing from over-confidence, flying the flag and crying; "I am violence. Disperse, make way or I'll crush you!" But violence quickly grows old, a few years and it is no longer sure of itself and in order to hold ground, to look decent, it has to adopt Lie as an ally. This is because violence has nothing to use as a cover except Lie, which may hold its ground only by means of violence. And not daily, not by laying its heavy paw on each shoulder—it demands from us only submission to the Lie, and daily participation in the Lie: herein is its loyalty.

And here lies the simplest and most accessible key to our liberation, ignored by us: personal non-participation in a lie! Let the lie cover everything, let the lie possess everything but let's resist in very way: Let it possess but not through me!

And this is the slit in the imaginary ring of our inaction!—the easiest for us and the most destructive for the lie. People flinch from the lie and it simply ceases to exist. Like an infection, it can exist only on people.

We do not succumb to a call, we have not matured enough to march to the square and speak the truth out loudly, to speak aloud what we think—don't do that. That is too frightening but let's, at least, refuse to say what we do not think!

This is precisely our road, the easiest and the most accessible with all our deep-rooted organic cowardice, much easier (it is terrible to pronounce) than Gandhi-style civic disobedience.

Our road is: not to back the lie consciously; having realized where its foundry is (different for everyone) to give up this gangrenous boundary; not to paste the dead bones and scales of Ideology; not to stretch rotten rags and we will be surprised how quickly and helpless the lie drops off. What is naked, let it appear naked in the world.

So let each one of us choose: to remain a conscious servant of the lie (oh, of course, not because we like it, but in order to feed the family and bring up the children in the spirit of the lie!) or, to shake it off and become an honest person worthy of respect, both of our children and contemporaries.

From this day on he:
—will not write, sign or print a single phrase that distorts the truth;
—won't pronounce such a phrase either in private conversation or before a crowd, neither in the role of agitator, teacher or educator, nor in a theatrical role;
—neither through a painting, a sculpture, a photograph, technical means or music, won't transmit any false thought, or a single distortion of the truth;
—won't give, either orally or in writing, any "guiding" quotation to please, or to provide a safety measure for the success of his work if he doesn't share fully the quoted thought.
—won't let himself be forced into a demonstration or meeting if it is against his desire and will; he won't take or raise a streamer, a slogan which he doesn't share fully;
—will immediately leave the session, meeting, lecture, play, or film as soon as he hears a lie, ideological nonsense or brazen propaganda;
—won't sign or buy from a newsstand a newspaper or magazine in which information is being distorted and the facts of paramount importance are being keep back.

We have not enumerated all possible and essential deviations from a lie. But the person who starts purifying himself—will easily discern other cases, too.

Indeed, at first it won't come equally for all. One person will temporarily lose his job. For young people who wish to live by the truth this will complicate their life in the initial period: After all, the lessons being answered are also stuffed with a lie, and they have to choose. But no loophole is left for anyone who wants to be honest: Never will any of us, even in the safest technical sciences, trample down at least one of the above-mentioned steps—either towards the truth or towards a lie; towards spiritual independence or spiritual servility. And the person who lacks courage even to defend his soul, let him not be proud of his advanced views, not boast of being an academician or a people's artist, honoured worker or a general. So, let him tell himself: I am a commoner and a coward, but am well-fed and warm.

Even this road—the most moderate of all roads of resistance—won't be easy for those who have been in this state too long. But it is much easier than self-immolation or even starvation: The flame won't envelop your body, the eyes won't burst from heat and black bread with pure water will always be found for your family.

The great people of Europe—the Czecholovak people, betrayed and cheated by us—haven't they really shown us that an unprotected person can stand even against tanks if a worthy heart throbs in their chest?

It won't be an easy road, but will be the easiest available. A difficult choice for the body but the only one for the soul. A difficult road, but there are people in our country too, even dozens of them, who stood for years for all these paragraphs and who live by the truth.

So, let's not be the first to embark upon this road, let's join it! Then this road will become easier and shorter for all of us, with the more concerted ranks which embark upon it! If there are thousands of us, they won't be able to cope with any of us. If there are tens of thousands of us, we won't recognize our country!

But if we get the jitters, then no excuse, we are our own enemies! We shall bow our heads, wait a little longer and our brothers-biologists will help bring closer the reading of our thoughts and the alteration of our genes.

If we get the jitters even in this, then we are worthless, hopeless, and Pushkin's contempt is meant for us:

Why do herds need the gifts of freedom?

Their inheritance is passed from family to family.

A yoke with rattles and lashes.

February 12, 1974

Epilogue

This appeal of Alexander Solzhenitsyn to the intelligentsia, to the youth and all his countrymen was written shortly before his arrest and deportation in February 1974. Immediately after this disgraceful action it was passed on in dozens, hundreds and thousands of Samizdat copies. Those were difficult years—years when the Lie, the Evil and the Violence, which stepped back only half a pace during the so-called "Khrushchev thaw", came down again with all its weight upon the country, making it bow its head, strangling and dragging it into the abyss of inevitable rotting and disintegration. And there are no more hopes, like those which had begun sprouting in 1956, for renovation, for the success of any civic opposition to the triumphant carrion. But Solzhenitsyn didn't call for this—he appealed to each of us, to our conscience and to our sense of human dignity with a passionate reminder that if we do not take care of our soul, nobody else will. The liberation of the social organism from evil may and must begin only from our own purification and liberation— from our firm resolve never to back the lie and violence, personally, by our own will and consciously.

Was this appeal heeded? Did it produce any results? Weren't the skeptics right, even those pierced by the irresistible strength of Solzhenitsyn's appeal for whom the writer's hopes seemed Utopian? His personal example of the highest spiritual and civic courage—wasn't it only for individual heroes?

Let's ask ourselves: Would the changes started in our country three years ago have been possible at all if the general contempt and aversion for those who personified the reigning evil and violence, and also for their wretched yesmen who flooded the country with demagogy and lies had not matured during these years in all strata of society? And wasn't the role played by a few people really great? And haven't quite a number of them, especially among the youth, encouraged by Alexander Solzhenitsyn's appeal to radically change their lives, embarked upon the road of resolute and firm personal non-participation in the orgy of the official Lie? Even those who managed only by a pace or half a pace to depart from this disgraceful line of moral degradation.

That is why it was a great pity that Solzhenitsyn's appeal was not and could not be heard in those years by all, by the entire country and all the people. That is why it is so encouraging that, today, many more people will be able to hear it than in the 1970s. Even today, it has preserved its whole lively moral meaning, and it still remains the unconditional formula of that initial moral imperative, by following which we can firmly guarantee our civic renovation.

—Igor Vinogradov, man of letters

SPIES

Anonymous

An American spy decided to give himself up. He came to the government office, walked up to the receptionist, and said: "I am an American spy. I came to give myself up.—Hold it, the receptionist said. We only take British spies here. You have to go to the third floor, room 308. They will take care of you there.

The spy went to the third floor, to 308, and said:

—I am an American spy. I came to give myself up. I parachuted down . . .

—Hold it, said the man he was talking to. We only take the spies that came in by submarine. You have to go up to the fifth floor, room 511. They'll take care of you there.

The spy went up to the proper room and said to the receptionist:

—I am an American spy. I parachuted down with the assignment to take pictures of high-security establishments

—Hold it, the receptionist told him. We only take the American spies whose assignment it is to sabotage military plans. You have to go the building across the street, top floor, and talk to the man in office 2001.

So the spy went across the street, discovered that the elevator was out of order. He barely made it to the top floor, dragged himself into the office, and said to the man sitting at the desk:

—I am an American spy. I parachuted down with the assignment to take pictures of high-security establishments.

The man raised his head from the pile of papers on his table, looked at the spy in disgust, and said:

—So what do you want from me? You were given an assignment. Go carry it out.

—Current joke

STALINISM

Lawyer Recommends Putting Stalinism on Trial
From the "View" program, Moscow Television Service, November 11, 1988

THE FOLLOWING TRANSCRIPT documents a studio interview with Valeriy Mikhaylovich Savitskiy, departmental head at the Institute of the State and Law.

PRESENTER: The theme of Stalinism is back on our screen again. Right up until now we have very often told you stories about the dramatic fates of ordinary people who were victims during this period, ordinary unimportant people. Now, voices can be heard ever more frequently about the fact that it is at last necessary to hold some sort of a trial, or even a regular trial, of Stalin and Stalinism. Valeriy Mikhaylovich, are there any personal motives for this? What is generally your own attitude to this idea—a trial of Stalin?

SAVITSKIY: As to personal motives . . . generally I support this idea. I have no personal motives, because in my family, thank God, there were no victims. [passage omitted] It is not, however, a matter of personal motives, I repeat. It is a matter of Stalin having caused grief to the people as a whole, the people as a whole. I think that he must be brought to trial, but not a legal one. For we have laws which we must not violate even for the sake of Stalin. We must not follow the path that we followed before, under him, violating our laws. Our law does not allow a criminal case to be instituted against a dead man. It is a matter of human values. Only for the purpose of rehabilitating him, a dead man, may a criminal trial be instituted. As to Stalin, of course [word indistinct]. . . .

PRESENTER: It is impossible to reverse things.

SAVITSKIY: Yes, it is impossible to reverse things. It is not necessary to change the law for his sake. As to having a public

[367]

trial, I think this would be a very useful measure. Of course, it is definitely necessary for the public judges to be very well known people in the country, those on the side of restructuring, people with a great deal of civic spirit. Naturally, there have got to be public prosecutors. Public defenders will also probably turn up. We know that some people do not like what is being said about Stalin. This public trial should have the right to question witnesses, victims, and experts. It must have the right, it seems to me, to have access to archive material. It must not last very long. Otherwise, hearings which will only traumatize the people could be endless.

PRESENTER: When do you think it could start?

SAVITSKIY: Well, it is necessary to carry out some preparation work. I think that, perhaps, in 2 to 3 months it would be possible to start this work. And I think that a public verdict which would brand Stalin—I would say—as the most malevolent enemy of the Soviet state should be passed at the end of it. For no code of law, of course, can account for what he has done and what we know now. This is my view.

Medvedev Comments on 1930's Repressions
Argumenty I Fakty, March 18–24, 1989

After the publication of the material "Tragic Statistics" (*Argumenty I Fakty* No 5), and R. Medvedev's appearance on television on 5 March of this year, quite a few letters arrived at the editorial offices whose authors ask that certain statements be clarified.

We present R. Medvedev's answer to a question from our correspondent.

Q: Roy Aleksandrovich, you are a candidate for deputy of the Voroshilov electoral okrug in the city of Moscow. On Sunday, 5 March, during a television debate on the "Good Evening, Moscow!" program, in answer to the question "Do You believe that the Communist Party as a whole is also responsible for the mass terrors of the 1930's?" you said that you believe that not only was Stalin responsible for this terror, but those around him as well, the leadership of the party, but not the party as a whole. You added that the party itself became a victim of this terror. However, on the very same program on the following day in television debates of candidates for deputy from the Gagarin

(I. Smirnov, *Soviet News*)

electoral okrug, G. K. Ashin, professor of the philosophy department of MGIMO [Moscow State University of International
Relations] answered to the same question that the entire party
also is responsible for the repression of the 1930's, and A. Ye.
Beylinson, a physician, agreeing with Ashin, even made reference to your books about Stalinism. Could you clarify your
position in more detail?

MEDVEDEV: I do not know in what works of mine A. Ye.
Beylinson was able to read an assertion about the responsibility
of the entire party as a whole. In the book *K sudu istorii* ["In
the Court of History"] there is a special section on the role of
the party in the repressions of the 1930's. I write there that **the
party itself became a victim of those mass repressions, that 80
percent of the members of the party with pre-October party
membership were arrested, that 75 percent of the members of
the Central Committee who were elected at the 17th party**

congress were physically annihilated, as well as 60 percent of the delegates of this same party congress. All told in the 1930's about 1.2 million party members were arrested. This is more than one-third of the membership of the party at the beginning of 1937.

But it should also be taken into account that in the years 1935-1936, many hundreds of thousands of party members were expelled from its ranks and also later arrested. So that, if we have in mind the membership of the VKP(b) [Communist Party (Bolshevik)] at the beginning of 1934, it is not difficult to calculate that about 50 percent of the Bolsheviks were repressed and that an overwhelming part of them was immediately shot or died in camps at the end of the 1930's and in the 1940's.

Moreover, the party was placed under the control of the NKVD [People's Commissariat of Internal Affairs]. Punitive organs received the right to arrest not only rank and file Communists, but members of the Central Committee also, and even members of the Central Committee Politburo and the secretariat without any sanctions by the Central Committee. This was an usurpation of authority by Stalin and his apprentices, and the real authority in the country belonged to a small group of persons who were supported principally by the punitive organs. It was not until the years 1953-1954, after the arrest of Beriya and those around him, that the control of these organs over the party was eliminated and that the former extrordinary power of the MVD-MGB [Ministry of Internal Affairs-Ministry of State Security] was abolished. I do not know in which of my works something else can be read into them.

Summarizing my analysis, I wrote: "Our party was ready to meet any danger face to face. But it was defenseless against a strike in the back. Our party was prepared to struggle with any enemies but it turned out for a while to be defenseless against strikes delivered by the hands of its own leaders."

Repression and terror have specific guilty parties, and it would be wrong to speak about the blame of the whole party or even about all of the people, as has become fashionable in certain circles. Lenin was a realist, and he wrote for Central Committee members in March 1922: If we are not to close our eyes to reality, then we must acknowledge that at the present time the party's proletarian policy is determined not by its membership (there is no doubt that a majority of the membership of our party is insufficiently proletarian. . . .), but by a huge indivisible authority of that thin layer which can be called the old party guard.

All it takes is a small internal struggle in this layer and its authority will be, if not undermined, then in any case weakened to the extent that a decision will not depend on it.

The War Was Won by the People
by Ales Adamovich, *Moscow News*, February 28, 1988

"It was at his feet that the fascist colours were dropped during the Victory Parade in front of the Mausoleum. It was he who planned all the operations at the front. It was he who knew about every motor vehicle sent to the front. It was Stalin's voice that could be heard on the hot line at any hour of day and night."

—From a letter by A. Khamafitova (Leningrad)

Newspapers receive letters like this. And not just *Moscow News*. I, for one, was taken to court by a veteran of the Patriotic War because of an interview I gave to *Literaturnaya Gazeta*, in which I talked about Stalin's crimes. The plaintiff's main argument was this: We won the war thanks to Stalin and his name. The court dismissed the suit. Nevertheless, this case suggests to me that the times of the cult are still weighing heavily upon us. Stalin's organizational ability or some other ability often over-shadows his mistakes and crimes, and relegates to the background those who really bore the brunt of, and won, the war. The war was won by the people.

Let's imagine an aircraft is flying on course when a terrorist bursts into the cockpit, kills the pilots, members of the crew and some of the passengers. The aircraft continues on course thanks to the automatic pilot but the terrorist has to land it somehow—he wants to live after all. A few members of the crew are still alive, so, after consulting them, the terrorist manages a crash landing during which other passengers are killed. But a few passengers survive. What is the reaction? Instead of seizing the terrorist, everyone rushes up to thank and praise him. Something similar happened in our life as well. But Stalin even praised us (out of surprise?). You remember—for exceptional patience. It is not yet known, Stalin averred, how another nation in our position would have behaved. . . .

Indeed, the people had to muster all their strength and pay with their own blood, the greatest amount of blood, for the sake of victory. And yet there are some who insist on glorifying Stalin and not the people—notwithstanding?! We are surprising people! It is time we understood that so long as Stalin remains the "banner of victory" in the eyes of many, his flesh and blood need not fear any reforms or revolutions. Shall we imperil perestroyka today just for the sake of Stalin?

We still remember the loud oration in honour of Stalin's ten strikes against the enemy. Today we know well enough which of our military leaders prepared them. The Battle of Stalingrad, Operation Bagration, and others. However, we also know of at least ten other strikes by Stalin . . . against his own army.

First. In 1937-1939 thousands of the most experienced Red Army commanders were labeled "enemies of the people" and wiped out.

Second. We still refer to it mildly as "Stalin's miscalculation" —Stalin's order, after signing the nonaggression pact with Hitler, to undo all our military preparations—for which the Army and the country paid so dearly.

And when Stalin abandoned the Army, going into seclusion for ten days in Kuntsevo, either frightened or "offended" (it would be interesting to understand this). Much has already been told about those horrible days: the collapsed fronts and lines of advance, the calls from everywhere to the "centre" in the belief that he who had taken all power into his own hands should be in the right place, should be aware of the situation and, of course, should be taking steps. . . . There are many things for which Stalin mustn't be forgiven, those ten days especially.

Thus, one after the other: new "strikes by Stalin" against his own men, against victory.

Near Kiev, Stalin prevented the armies from withdrawing in time to escape encirclement. . . .

Near Kharkov, Stalin insisted on mounting an offensive, desregarding the views of military experts. Again there was defeat and more prisoners of war. . . .

In the Crimea, he entrusted the offensive to Mekhlis, a high-handed functionary who had earned his stripes solely by inflating the Stalin cult. . . .

And what was the cost of his "miscalculation" not in 1941, but in 1942: the concentration of our troops and hardware near Moscow, instead of in the south.

If the people continue to cherish the lie-illusion about Stalin— "There was order! Prices were lowered! With his name we worked to win and won"—a stronghold will be preserved for the enemies of perestroyka.

The first thing that must be done: remove, at last, the cut-and-dried portrait of Stalin in uniform from our films at least. Enough of Liberations, Victories, Battles near Moscow—it is time to speak about Stalin as honestly as our finest literary works speak about the war.

It is possible to respect, forgive and cherish feelings of long affection for a far from ideal person (how many ideal ones are there?) for definite services which are also credited to Stalin. But this person slandered so many that even 35 years after his death we have not yet been able to acquit all those innocent people ruined by him. How is it possible to have any reservations about such a person? But to convince everyone, we need to have facts. We need books, films and documentary works (or written on a documentary basis)—and then many things in our present-day intellectual and social life will acquire a much needed clarity.

Who Were Our Executioners?
Letter to the editor of *Radyanska Ukraina*, October 26, 1988

The *Radyanska Ukraina* article entitled "Where is That Street Then," which correctly raised the question of renaming some streets, has reopened old sores in my heart. I did not request Donetsk Gorispolkom to rename Mekhlis and Zhdanov Streets, but fully seconded the veterans who did. Moreover, a new name should also be found for the city district named after Voroshilov.

As we all know, in the years of Stalinism these public figures were responsible for repressions and stained their conscience with the blood of innocent victims, of honest and blameless people. It is impossible to forget that. And since we all, the entire country led by the party, have chosen the line of restructuring, of cleansing our lives from the effects of the cult of Stalin and his hangmen, we must not forget anything. The reason I am saying this is that I was among those who happened to enjoy the "kind" attention of the "father of peoples," and it was only by a miracle that I remained alive. After all, of every 100 inmates of Kolyma, only 2 or 3 survived. My lot was typical of that generation decimated by firing squads and tormented in Kolyma camps.

I come from Lebedin, in Sumy Oblast. In response to the nationwide call, I joined the aviation service. A party member since 1930, I was secretary of a squadron party organization in Zhitomir aviation brigade. I went through the 1933 purge and, when arrested in 1937, I was a squadron technician whose honest and blameless service consistently gained the command's acknowledgement. And yet I was accused of complicity with Polish spies and of spreading rumors about the 1933 famine in the Ukraine. I was not a spy, and did not say anything about the famine, although I myself and all my colleagues had seen the horrible pictures of the famine when at Zhitomir railway station people were swelling up and dying of starvation by the hundreds.

I was sentenced by a team of three in accordance with Article 58, as they say, without any court hearing or investigation. To be more specific, there was an investigation, but is was a parody of the administration of justice.

In Zhitomir prison, I was one of the 160 crammed into cell No 8, which was intended for 8 prisoners. We were standing pressed up against each other. Five or six died every day. The bodies were not removed immediately, and so they continued to stand because there was no room for them to fall down.

Then we were transported under guard to Vladivostok. In transit camps we were called out by alphabet to be told how long each of us had to serve. I got 7 years.

I was taken to Kolyma. I cannot recall that calmly. I am nearly 80. I have had two heart attacks, and every recollection of those times causes pain in my heart. To be more exact, I carry this pain constantly, because it has never stopped. The conditions in the "Shturmovaya" and the "Burkhala" mines under the northern ore mining administration were horrible. There were executions by shooting, cruelties, and hunger. They had nothing whatsoever to do with the ideals for the sake of which true Leninist Bolsheviks accomplished the revolution. At Kolyma, I saw the wives and children of prominent party figures and statesmen. In Vladivostok transit camp, I met Postyshev's son, Viktor. He said that his mother was also there. I remember having met Hlushko in the "Burkhala" mine; he was military attache under Primakov in England. I will never forget the desperate sobbing of the Kremlin physician, Ivanov. Like myself, none of them could believe that this could happen to us, in our own country, under people's rule. Many of us then began to see things clearly, but it was impossible to do anything.

For failure to cope with the daily quota—to wheel out of the pit 200 to 250 barrows full of gold-bearing ore—the inmates used to be delivered up "to the mosquitoes," that means stripped and exposed to the stings of blood-thirsty midges, and then sent to the so-called units with aggravated conditions. It was death that awaited them there. Awful thin soup was served once a day.

Dying people, roped, used to be carted, along with dead bodies, to the pit to die. People were shot dead just for entertainment. I have experienced all kinds of suffering. I do not even know how I survived, because also real criminals tormented us, used us as stakes to win or lose in gambling. We did not know anything that was going on outside. We learned about the war when the Germans were close to Kiev.

Having served my term, I was kept in Kolyma for an additional 2 years. Then, new afflictions followed. Just when it seemed I had found a job in Kharkov, a militiaman came to inform me that I would not be allowed to stay in the city. Finally, I landed in Donetsk. Here I have spent nearly 30 years working at a metallurgical plant, and for my work have repeatedly won recognition. However, even after the rehabilitation in 1960 I was frequently summoned by the "organs" to be told that what had happened to me and to the thousands of my compatriots was a state secret. If it remains a secret, something similar could occur again! This must not be forgotten, and nothing must be forgiven! Otherwise we are not human, and restructuring will fail. "Teams of three" will again make short work of honest people.

I was luckier, but even so my life was ruined; I never lived in the way I should have in my prime.

I keep a certificate dated 29 February 1960, saying that "In view of newly found evidence, the sentence passed by the military tribunal of Rifle Corps 13 on 2 November 1937, as well as the sentence passed by the military bench of the USSR Supreme Court on 5 March 1938 concerning F.V. Kovalenko have been abolished and the legal action has been terminated. F.V. Kovalenko has been rehabilitated." The writ bears the signature of Major General of Justice A. Kostromin, bench chairman in the USSR Supreme Court.

I have been rehabilitated, but some people would like to brand me again with the mark of a convict. Why? I have tried to explain, and have appealed to the authorities to end the persecution. I fully agree with all honest people who came up with the idea to build a monument to the victims of the repressions carried out by Stalin and his cohorts. However, it is essential to bear in mind not those who died, but also those who survived. This also applies to compensation that should be granted to Stalin's victims who are still living. Why do they not even now have drugs at reduced prices? Why must such people be deprived of coal and suffer from cold in their dwellings? After all, the assigned 2.5

metric tons of coal are far from sufficient. I find sympathy at the plant, people know me there and frequently assist me, but they are unable to meet all my needs. For this reason let me repeat: It is necessary to remember not only those who died, to cherish their memory in order to preclude the repetition of this tragedy, but also to pay back, even if only a little, that which is due to those innocent victims of repression who are still alive. It is good that your paper discusses the need to cleanse our society of the phenomena which are alien to us, but it is also essential to strive for the triumph of truth in all its forms. Moreover, it is necessary to finally isolate the handful of criminals from the great Lenin's party which has been and is the leader of the people.

—Yours sincerely, F. Kovalenko, labor veteran, former flight technician, CPSU member since 1930.

The city of Donetsk.

P.S.: I would like to ask—where are those who were killing and tormenting us? Why have they not been brought to the people's trial? Who defends them, and who needs them now? Are the present bureaucrats who offend the victims of repression and who treat people with contempt not their spirtual heirs? As a disabled person of Group 2 I was assigned, for example, to Branch 33 of the Kalininskiy District provision store in order to at least be able to buy a piece of meat without much effort since I am unable to stand in line. However, I enjoyed the privilege for 6 months only. Last May the assignment was canceled. I probably displeased someone else, although no one calls me a Polish spy any longer. Who is interested in this? I went to the oblispolkom, and the officials there told me that they fully sympathized with me, but were unable to help.

The End of "The Doctors' Plot"
by David Gai, *Moscow News*, February 7, 1988

. . . On Jan. 13, 1953, *Tass* carried news of the arrest of a group of doctors.[1] It reported that a terrorist group of physicians had set themselves the goal of shortening the lives of active Soviet state officials by means of harmful medical treatment. "A. A. Zhdanov and A. S. Shcherbakov fell victims of this band of monsters in

[1] [See CDSP, Vol IV, No. 51, p. 3.]

human form," the report noted, and it went on: "It has been established that all the participants in this terrorist group of doctors were in the pay of foreign intelligence services, sold them their bodies and souls, and were their hired, paid agents. Most of the members of the terrorist group—Vovsi, B. Kogan, Feldman, Grinshtein, Etinger and others—were bought by the American intelligence service. They were recruited by a branch of American intelligence—the international Jewish bourgeois nationalist organization, 'Joint'.*** Other participants in the terrorist group (Vinogradov, M. Kogan, Yegorov) are long-time agents of British intelligence."

The report came like a bolt out of the blue. Could leading medical researchers and practicing physicians—consultants to the Kremlin hospital—be spies and murderers? At first, people refused to believe it. Many came around to believing it, however, with the consequence that clinics were soon deserted and hospital patients refused to take their medicine. The doctor's white gown became an object of fear.

How did "the doctors' plot" begin? What were its origins? Some light has been shed on this by Yefim Smirnov, member of the Academy of Medicine and Hero of Socialist Labor, who served as USSR Minister of Public Health after the war. In one interview he recalled:

"Not long before Jan. 13, 1953, I was visiting Stalin at a dacha not far from Sochi. We were walking in an orchard and talking. Pointing to trees on which lemons and oranges were growing, Stalin spoke about the care that they required. Suddenly, without any transition, he asked:

" 'Comrade Smirnov, do you know who the doctor was who treated Dimitrov and Zhdanov?'

" 'Yes,' I answered and gave the name.

" 'It's odd that the same doctor treated them, and they both died.'

" 'Comrade Stalin, the doctor wasn't to blame for that.***'

" 'How do you mean—not to blame?'

" 'I went over the history of Dimitrov's illness and the coroner's conclusion. I can assure you that there was nothing that could have been done. I know, incidentally, that Dimitrov himself recommended this doctor to Zhdanov. He considered him to be a well-educated and tactful person and a well-qualified specialist.'

"Stalin said nothing. But I had the feeling that I had not convinced him. He was always suspicious by nature, and by the end of his life this trait had become simply pathological."

Professor Yakov Rapoport, who was arrested in connection with "the doctors' plot" (his memoirs are being prepared for publication in the magazine *Druzhba narodov*),[2] recalls what Vladimir Vinogradov told him at one time:

"On his last visit to Stalin, Professor Vinogradov found that his patient's condition had worsened precipitously, and he made a note in the medical record concerning the need for a strict regimen of complete rest from activity of any sort. It must be noted that after Stalin's death, Vinogradov's diagnosis was fully confirmed. But while the 'leader of peoples' was still alive, the outstanding physician's political naivete cost him his freedom and could have cost him his life: His recommendation was seen as an attempt to remove Stalin from active involvement of any sort, including active involvement in political matters, of course.

"When Beria, who was overseeing the doctors attending to Stalin, told him about Vinogradov's conclusion, Stalin went into an indescribable rage, shouting: 'Put him in irons! Put him in irons!' "

The angry outburst was apparently no mere coincidence. It is quite possible that Stalin remembered the time of Lenin's illness and his own role in isolating the leader of the Revolution—in the guise of concern for his health—from Party affairs. Now it turned out that he himself had landed in a similar situation, and his attending physician was urging total rest and a stop to all activity.

Professor Vinogradov was arrested shortly thereafter.

The arrests of the first, most authoritative group of doctors took place in November 1952.

Architect Leonid Kogan, the son of Professor Boris Kogan, recalls:

"While still a student at the architectural institute, I came home late one day and suddenly heard loud voices in the apartment. We were being searched. My father, I learned, had already been taken away. The search went on all night: They tapped on the walls, searching for guns, poison and the like. My father, a Party member since February 1917, was one of the organizers of Soviet rule in the Volyn area. Devoting himself subsequently to medicine, he became one of Moscow's leading therapists. He was responsible for the health of prominent Comintern figures

[2][*Druzhba narodov*, No. 4, April, pp. 222–245, published Rapoport's memoirs, with an introduction by editor in chief Sergei Baruzdin. *Yunost*, No. 4, April, pp. 76–81, published reminiscences by Rapoport's daughter, Natalia Rapoport, who was 14 at the time of her father's arrest.]

and treated Dimitrov in particular (it was B. Kogan whom Stalin had in mind in the aforementioned conversation with the then Minister of Public Health, Smirnov). My father and Dimitrov were bound by friendship. How preposterous it was for him to be charged at the first interrogation with working as a foreign agent." . . .

The monstrous accusations against people who had been highly respected just a short time before were shocking. Shortly thereafter the name of Lidiya Timashuk, a rank-and-file doctor at the Kremlin hospital, became famous—it was she, it turned out, who was to play the key role in exposing the "band of criminals." By decree of the Presidium of the USSR Supreme Soviet she was awarded the Order of Lenin. We read from a newspaper of those days: "Until quite recently, none of us knew about this woman, and now the name of Doctor Lidiya Feodosyevna Timashuk has become a symbol of Soviet patriotism, high vigilance and uncompromising, courageous struggle against the enemies of our homeland. She helped to unmask the Americans' hirelings—monsters who used the doctor's white coat to kill Soviet people."

In mid-January 1953, the wives of the "enemies of the people" were arrested, and their children were subjected to persecution—fired from their jobs and expelled from the Party and Young Communist League.

Today, no one who was on the main list of participants in the "terrorist group" is still living. The last one died quite recently, at age 90—Vladimir Vasilenko, Hero of Socialist Labor and a member of the USSR Academy of Medicine. They were extremely reticent when it came to sharing recollections of what they had endured in prison. The pain had not passed with the years, it had merely been dulled; they did not like it when someone attempted to reopen the old wounds with questions. It is probably for that reason that their relatives do not have many memories of episodes from the "prison period."

The interrogations were conducted at night. The hardest thing was going without sleep for days on end. Powerful lamps were shone in the suspect's face during interrogations. Ever since then, Vovsi's wife, Vera, has found bright light to be an irritant.

They demanded that Miron Vovsi confess to having been linked to Hitler Germany's intelligence service. Miron Semyonovich retorted to the investigator: "You have made me an agent of two intelligence services, at least don't assign me to German intelligence—my father and my brother's family were tortured by the fascists in Dvinsk during the war." The investigator replied: "Don't try to profit from the blood of your relatives."

Ryumin, chief of the Ministry of State Security's investigative unit for especially important cases, was personally responsible for "the doctors' plot." A totally immoral, cynical and power-hungry careerist, Ryumin knowingly falsified the materials of the investigation. He had begun "undermining" the doctors long before their arrest. Even before the news about the "terrorist group" appeared in the press, Sofya Karpai, head of the Kremlin hospital's electrocardiography office, and Professor Yakov Etinger, a consultant at the same hospital, had fallen victim to his efforts. They were accused of deliberately misreading Andrei Zhdanov's electrocardiogram. Etinger was unable to withstand the prison conditions and died.

The circle of arrests expanded. Ryumin looked forward to a highly publicized trial, a promotion and honors. But then Stalin died. The imprisoned doctors were not informed of his death. The interrogations continued, although at a less active pace, as if by inertia.

For many of those who had been jailed—children and relatives of the arrested—the reaction was: "Now there's no one to help our loved ones." They had viewed Stalin as a savior and defender.

And then came the night of April 3. All of the arrested doctors and their wives were suddenly escorted out of the prison, put in cars and driven home. Only then, after being set free, did the doctors learn what the newspapers had written about them and hear of Stalin's death.

The next morning the newspapers published a report stating, among other things: "A check has shown that the accusations***
are false and that the documentary data on which the investigation relied are unfounded. It has been ascertained that the testimony of those arrested—testimony that allegedly confirmed the accusations leveled against them—was obtained by employees of the investigative unit of the former Ministry of State Security through the use of investigative methods that are impermissible and strictly prohibited under Soviet law."

Below that was an announcement voiding the decree awarding Timashuk the Order of Lenin. She herself worked only a short time longer at the hospital and then retired. It is doubtless just as well that this also be reported because, to this day, some people still believe and are circulating rumors to the effect that Timashuk was killed in an automobile accident in the mid-1950s, a victim of someone's intrigues. No, she managed to live to a ripe old age.

With honor restored to their names, Vovsi, Vinogradov, Kogan, Yegorov, Feldman, Vasilenko, Grinshtein, Zelenin, Preobrazhensky, Popova, Zakusa, Shereshevsky, Maiorov and the others returned to productive work in the medical field.

As for Ryumin, a government report stated: "In view of the extreme dangers posed by his activities and the grave consequences of the crimes he committed, the Military Tribunal of the USSR Supreme Court sentenced Ryumin to the highest measure of punishment—death by firing squad." This stern punishment was also meted out to the other employees of the former Ministry of State Security who took part in the forgeries and were among those pressing for false accusations.

Thus was written the final page in "the doctor's plot."

Every Day in This Spot: Marble Gorge
by V. Sungorkin, *Komsomolskaya Pravda*, January 29, 1989

We are now reading about Stalin's camps, and we are horrified by the scale of the repressions, by the millions and millions of our compatriots who were persecuted. We, who did not live in those dim and distant times, today voice our indignation out loud: How could the people tolerate this? But now I look at the photograph and recall: Even 14 years ago both I and many of my young peers already knew a great deal about what is common knowledge today. . . .

We are now looking for documents of that time, and we hear complaints about the inaccessibility of NKVD and MGB [People's Commissariat for Internal Affairs and Ministry of State Security] archives. We saw enough "documents" in the mid-1970's when we were on the Baykal-Amur Main railroad [BAM]. During Khrushchev's "thaw," the camps in the more populous areas were removed and assiduously razed to the ground. The diligent teams of "purgers" of our country's history did not reach the taiga and the mountains through which the "zeks" [slang for camp inmates] of the "BAM camp" had laid the route. And the empty camps still stood, right through the optimistic 1970's. Komsomol detachments were set down by helicopter in the taiga hamlets and discovered that the proud modern word "BAM worker" had long been synonymous with "robber" in the lexicon of old timers (their mothers used to frighten them with the word in their childhood). They saw the embankment, on which trees had now grown, the granite supports of bridges towering, solitary, over the deserted river, a postwar tunnel filled to the ceiling with ice, and over it a bas-relief of Iosif Vissarionovich reaching almost to the sky. And everywhere rusty barbed wire, half-ruined barracks, and rickety towers. The camps.

Japanese bulldozers plowed up the barbed wire and the posts and pushed them into a pile. The barracks were burnt down, and the towers were dragged onto the same bonfire so that not a trace remained—the dry wood burned brightly. New rails were laid on the old ties. Sometimes the excavators brushed against a layer of human skeletons, and then the men would swear and drive off somewhere else. The old timers talked fearfully and in whispers about mass executions—they said that almost everyone in the camp at Murtygit was killed. The Evenki reindeer breeders from the "Zarya" sovkhoz recalled the generous reward offered for the head (the head—literally) of a fugitive. But generally it was not done to talk about these subjects—it was considered very indecent. People did not even dream of writing about it. For some reason.

So this picture lay around for 10 years, and no one even thought of publishing it. We did not live during the "personality cult" years, but the "system of bans" was easily and conveniently lodged in our minds. Or is it true that the fear is passed on in our genes?

The Komsomol Central Committee Bureau resolution on the work of Komsomol organizations to rehabilitate Komsomol members repressed in the personality cult years, published in yesterday's *Komsomolskaya Pravda,* and the constituent conference of the "Memorial" association, which opened yesterday in Moscow, forced people to recall a film shot in the Transbaykal ranges in the north of Chita Oblast.

That camp has been preserved to this day. Possibly because it is located high on the Kodar Ridge. We got there in a few days on foot. I do not know a lot about the camp. Tens of thousands of people worked there. First they laid a temporary railroad more than 1,000 km long from the Transsiberian. It ran through mountains and along swamped river valleys. Then they built an airstrip. They carved galleries in the wall of the mountain cirque and began extracting ore. . . .

It is well known that one of the camps here was called "Sinilga" (Shishov's "Ugryum River" is not far away). It is believed that no prisoner ever escaped from there. For hundreds of miles around there are only bare mountains and glaciers. The snow melts toward the end of July, and starts falling at the beginning of September. The climate here—high in the mountains—is very dry. Perhaps this is why everything has been preserved: Utensils, clothing, placards on the hut walls: "The drillers of X column challenge X drillers." An ancient Studebaker lay stuck among the rocks. The guardroom: "Guard! You must! . . ." The bridge across the river has survived, power line supports and the enriching factory on the bank are still standing. The "zeks" did a quality job. The cemetery is preserved. The paper-thin barracks are still standing. In 60 degrees of frost only those who were closest to the stove survived . . .

I have not managed to find out what happened to these prisoners. The camps on the Kodar were ultra-secret—in the nearby village of Chara I heard in the pre-BAM times that all the prisoners were driven into the mine galleries and the entrances were blown up. If that is not the truth, then I ask you to respond: Who is still alive from among the prisoners of Mramornoye Ushchelye [Marble Gorge]? Write to me at the *Komsomolskaya Pravda* editorial office. I hope that there will be a sequel to this article.

I am writing this piece and it suddenly occurs to me that someone will read this in the quiet of his office, and he will slowly pick up the telephone: "Did you read it? Mmm-yes. This question ought to be cleared up somehow." And a helicopter will land—the barracks will be burned down . . . Why does such an "odd thought" spring to mind? I would like to know, why?

Certainly, in principle, all the documents about the repressions can be burned and Stalin's camps can be wiped off the face of the earth. History, in principle, can be successfully falsified—we have already seen it happen. And once again veterans and teenagers will write to the editorial office: "We do not believe you. Stalin advocated order. Where is the evidence for the repressions?" The camp in Mramornoye Ushchelye is the evidence.

I propose that we preserve those Stalinist camps which still remain in remote places. Declare them historical monuments. Make Mramornoye Ushchelye a museum area—it is only 60 km in a direct line from the BAM route. The Chita youth newspaper's editorial office is one of the initiators of the "Memorial" movement. Well, folks, perhaps you will support the idea? Surely you have also heard about Mramornoye Ushchelye. I have made the same suggestion to the Komsomol Central Committee headquarters on the BAM. Around 100,000 victims of repression worked in the BAM camp system, and there were thousands of Komsomol members among them. . . . The administration was located in a city with a symbolic name—Svobodnyy [Freetown].

The Death. From the Memoirs of A.L. Myasnikov, One of the Medical Consultants Who Attended I.V. Stalin.
by L. Myasnikov, *Literaturnaya Gazeta*, March 1, 1989

THE LETTERS we receive often ask about Stalin's last days and his death. We present here excerpts from an unpublished manuscript by member of the USSR Academy of Sciences Professor A.L. Myasnikov (1899–1965). He was a very eminent therapist, pupil of D.D. Pletnev and G.F. Lang, director of the USSR Academy of Sciences Institute of Therapy, winner of the international "Golden Stethoscope" award. From 1960 he was working on a book of memoirs entitled *My Life*, which he completed 3 months before his death. The professor's grandson sent the manuscript to the editorial office, and we thank him for thinking of the newspaper.

Late in the evening of 2 March 1953 an official of the special department in the Kremlin hospital came to our apartment: "I have come to fetch you to treat a sick boss." I quickly said my good-byes to my wife (it was not clear where I was going or when I would be back). We traveled along Kalininka Street, where professors N.V. Konovalov (a neuropathologist) and Ye.M. Tareyev were waiting for us, and we hurried off to Stalin's dacha in Kuntsevo (opposite the new university). We went up to the gate in silence; there was barbed wire on both sides, with a trench and fence; and dogs.

Finally we were in the house (a large pavilion with spacious rooms furnished with long ottomans; the walls were decorated with polished panels). The minister of health (the new one, A.F. Tretyakov; Ye.I. Smirnov had been removed in December in connection with an audit of the ministry conducted by a government commission, and had been transferred to a military department in his earlier line of business as chief of the military sanitation directorate), Professor P.Ye. Lukomskiy (chief therapist at the Ministry of Health), Roman Tkachev and Filimonov, and Ivanov-Neznamov (footnote: Professors R.A. Tkachev and I.N. Filimonov were eminent neuropathologists; docent V.I. Ivanov-Neznamov was a therapist in the medical and sanitary administration in the Kremlin) were already in one of the rooms.

The minister told us that during the night of 2 March Stalin had suffered a cerebral hemorrhage with loss of consciousness, loss of speech and paralysis of the right arm and leg. The previous day Stalin had been working late into the night in his office. The duty officer of the guards had seen him behind his desk at 0300 (he had looked in through a peephole). The light had been left burning even later, but that was as usual. Stalin slept in another room but there was a divan in his office on which he often rested. At 0700 the guard had again looked through the keyhole and seen Stalin prostrate on the floor between the desk and the divan. He was unconscious. The patient was moved to the divan, where he had been ever since. . . .

The consulting physicians were interrupted by the appearance of Beriya and Malenkov (subsequently they always came and went only as a twosome). Beriya addressed us with some words about the misfortune that had befallen the party and our people and expressed the conviction that we would do everything within the power of medicine and so forth. "Bear in mind," he said, "that the party and government have absolute trust in you and you will have everything you need, and for our part we will offer you nothing but complete agreement and help."

These words were probably uttered because at that time some of the professors—the "doctor-murderers"—were in prison awaiting the death sentence. The next day the first government bulletin on Stalin's illness was published: "The best medical efforts are being applied to treat comrade Stalin," followed by a list of our names and titles; mention was also made of the fact that "Comrade Stalin's treatment is under the constant observation of the CPSU Central Committee and Soviet Government."

Stalin was lying awkwardly, short and somewhat fat, with his face distorted; his right extremities lay like limp stalks. The respiration was difficult, periodically quiet, and then stronger (Cheyne-Stokes respiration). The blood pressure was 210/110. There was intermittent arrhythmia. The leukocyte count was up to 17,000. Temperature was elevated at 38 degrees or higher. . . . Auscultation and percussion of the heart revealed no particular impairment, and in the lungs nothing pathological was found in the lateral and frontal lobes. The diagnosis, God help us, seemed

clear enough: hemorrhage in the left cerebral hemisphere resulting from hypertension and arteriosclerosis. Plenteous treatment
was indicated. . . .

The consulting physicians decided to remain, and they telephoned their homes. We spent the night in a nearby house. Each
of us took his turn over the patient's bed. Someone from the
Central Committee Politburo was always at the patient's side,
mostly Voroshilov, Kaganovich, Bulganin, and Mikoyan.

On the third morning the consulting physicians had to give
Malenkov an answer to his question about the prognosis. Our
answer could only be a negative one; death was inevitable.
Malenkov gave us to understand that he had expected this conclusion even though he had hoped that the medical treatment
might still save his life or prolong it for an adequate period. We
understood: It was a question of the essential background for
making preparations for the organization of a new authority, and
at the same time preparing the public for it.

So then we issued the first bulletin on I.V. Stalin's state of
health (0200 on 4 March). It contained ambiguous language: "A
number of therapeutic steps have been taken aimed at restoring
the body's vital functions." This, as it were, expressed in guarded
form a certain hope of "restoration," that is, it was calculated to
calm the country. Meanwhile messages were sent to all the
members of the central committee and to the leaders of other
party and soviet organs to come urgently to Moscow in order to
discuss the situation in connection with the forthcoming death
of the head of state.

Stalin's illness, of course, was commented on extensively both
in our country and abroad. But as they say, only one step sepa-
rates tragedy from comedy. In the medical institutions—the
scientific council of the ministry, the presidium of the Academy, and some of the institutes—meetings were convened to
discuss how to help in Stalin's treatment. Proposals were put
forward for these or those methods, which it was suggested be
forward to the consulting physicians. For example, in order to
manage the hypertension, advice was given on treatment methods developed at the Institute of Therapy (and it was strange to
read the recommendations that were sent to me—my own).
Later they sent a description of a method for drug-induced sleep;
but the patient was deeply unconscious, in sopor, that is, a deep
sleep. Professor Negovskiy suggested that the respiratory disorder be treated with an artificial breathing apparatus that he had
developed for resuscitating drowned patients and patients who

had breathed poisonous gas; they even brought his apparatus to the house, but after he had seen the patient he agreed not to insist on his method (and then he "stuck" to the consulting physicians, which for him, as a party person, was interesting; however, he did not get to sign the bulletins and so his name never appeared in the newspapers).

Touching appeals and letters arrived in the mail. There were assurances of faith that the consulting physicians could save the life of the General Secretary, their father and teacher, entreaties to do the same, sometimes in a threatening tone but more often in a spirit of trust and faith in the strength of Soviet medicine. Junior officers and Red Army people offered their blood for transfusion—to the last drop—and some wrote that they were quite prepared to donate their own hearts ("Just let the surgeons cut out my young heart and put it into Comrade Stalin").

It should be noted that before his illness, at least for the last 3 years, Stalin had not consulted with physicians for medical care; in any event, that is what the chief of the Kremlin medical and sanitary administration told us. Several years before, when living at his own dacha at Matsestaya, Stalin fell ill with influenza and was attended by N.A. Kipishidze (from Tbilisi) and M.M. Shikhov, who was working at the Balneology Institute in Sochi. They said that he was stern and mistrusting. In Moscow he had evidently avoided medicine. At his large dacha in Kuntsevo there was not even a pharmacy with first aid necessities; there was, among other things, no nitroglycerin, and if he had had an attack of angina pectoris he could have died from the spasms that two drops of the medicine would have prevented. Even so, they brought nurses in disguised as chamber maids and a doctor disguised as a colonel—72 people in a single year! No one knew how long he had been suffering from hypertension (and he was never treated for it). Svetlana his daughter, the intelligent and sympathetic young wife of Yu.A. Zhdanov, son of Zhdanov (a docent and chemist and a department chief in the central committee science department) told how to all requests to see the doctors "Papa categorically refused." Here I remembered the words said by Stalin to G.F. Lang when the latter lived with the sick Gorkiy: "Doctors do not know how to treat people. Down in Georgia we have many centenarians and they treat themselves with dry wine and wear a warm felt cloak."

Svetlana Yosifovna invited us to lunch and supper and tried with her simplicity and restrained courtesy not to make things excessively strained or to allow gloomy silences. K.Ye. Voroshilov also dined with us; he seemed to be sympathetic, like an old father, and concerned about the illness of a man close to him.

Stalin's respiration was labored, and he sometimes groaned. Only for one brief moment did it seem that he was consciously looking at those surrounding him. Then Voroshilov leaned toward him and said: "Comrade Stalin, we are all here, your true friends and companions-in-arms. How do you feel, my dear?" But Stalin's glance expressed nothing and he again lapsed into sopor. In the night it seemed many times that he was dying. The next morning, 4 March, someone got the idea that on top of everything there might have been a heart attack. A young physician arrived from the hospital with an EKG machine and stated peremptorily, "Yes, an infarct." There was a commotion. Already a deliberate failure to diagnose a myocardial infarct had figured in the doctors' plot in the state leaders they had supposedly finished off. Now it was probably our turn . . . For up to now in our medical conclusions we had not indicated the possibility of a heart attack. And everyone in the world knows about this. Since he had been unconscious, of course, Stalin had been unable to complain of the pain that is so typical a symptom of a heart attack. The leukocyte count and the elevated temperature could also have indicated infarction.

The consulting physicians were undecided. I was the first to decide to take the bull by the horns: "The EKG changes are too regular for an infarct; they show up on all leads. These are cerebral pseudo-infarcts on the EKG. My colleagues from the Naval Medical Academy have also obtained these kinds of tracings in experiments involving open trauma to the skull. Perhaps they can also occur in insults."

The neuropathologists supported this; cerebral insult was in any event their main diagnosis—a cerebral hemorrhage—and it was clear enough to them. Despite the self-confident treble of the woman operating the EKG machine, the consulting physicians did not recognize an infarct. However, the diagnosis was now made to include a new feature: possible localized hemorrhage in cardiac muscle resulting from severe cardiovascular disorders against a background of hemorrhage in the cerebral basal ganglia.

On the morning of 5 March Stalin suddenly started to vomit blood; the vomiting led to a drop in the heart rate and the blood pressure fell. This symptom somewhat perplexed us: how could it be explained?

In order to maintain the falling pressure various drugs were

(Mikhail Serebryakov, *Soviet News*)

administered. All the consulting physicians crowded round the patient and in the next room, and there was alarm and speculation. From the central committee, N.A. Bulganin was on duty. I noticed that he was looking at us suspiciously and perhaps with hostility. He looked splendid with his marshal's stars on his epaulettes; his face was a little puffy, the tuft of his beard jutting forward—a beard somewhat similar to the beard of Tsar Romanov, or perhaps a general of the period of the Russo-Japanese war. Standing at the divan he turned to me: "Professor Myasnikov, why is he vomiting blood?" I answered: "Perhaps it is the result of small hemorrhages in the wall of the stomach of a vascular nature, connected with the hypertension and the insult." "Perhaps . . ." he mimicked unpleasantly. "And perhaps he has a cancer of the stomach, Stalin. Look," he added with the suggestion of a threat, "with you everything is vascular, but the main thing you mis . . ." (he obviously wanted to say "misled" or "mistook" but he suddenly caught himself up short and finished up saying "missed").

We spent all day on 5 March injecting various drugs, writing up the diary and composing the bulletin. Meanwhile, the members of the central committee were gathering on the second floor: The members of the Politburo came in to see the dying man and people peered in through the door according to rank, reluctant to approach any closer even to their half-dead "boss." In any event I remember N.S. Khrushchev, also standing back at the doors, for even at that time the hierarchy was observed: first Malenkov and Beriya, then Voroshilov, then Kaganovich, then Bulganin and Mikoyan. Molotov was sick with influenzal pneumonia but he still came two or three times for a short visit.

An explanation for the gastrointestinal bleeding was written up in the diary and was also entered in a detailed epicrisis written up at the end of the day, when the patient was still breathing but expected to die at any hour.

Finally that hour came at 2150 on 5 March.

It was, of course, a very protentous moment. As soon as we had established that the pulse had stopped, breathing had ceased and the heart stopped, the leading figures of the party and government filed into the spacious room, with the daughter Svetlana, the son Vasiliy, and a guard. Everyone stood motionless for a long time in solemn silence, I do not really know for how long—about 30 minutes or more. A great historical event was undoubtedly taking place. A leader had died, a leader before whom the entire country trembled, and essentially, to one degree or other, the entire world. A great dictator, just recently all-powerful and inaccessible, transformed into a poor, pitiful corpse, that on the morrow would be cut to pieces on the pathologist's table ... Then it would be transformed to ashes, like the corpses of other ordinary folk. Standing there in silence each of us probably had his own thoughts, but there was a common sense of the changes that must, that had to come in the life of our state and our people ...

Something was going to have to change in our lives, probably for the better. For did not this ending bring to our lives a spirit of freedom and normal safety? ...

STRIKES

"We have a working people's state here, and who would ever dream of striking against himself?"

—*Pravda*

"Mass refusals to work, hunger strikes, unsanctioned meetings and demonstrations and even strikes have become realities of our life."

—Vladimir I. Melnikov
Komi Party Chief

"(A trade union committee) has the right to stop work at an enterprise in an organization when the procedure established by law for considering a labor dispute is being violated, or when management does not live up to an agreement that has been reached."

—draft of new law

TELEPHONES

"01"
by Konstantin Melikhan, *Ogonyek*, January 1988

I don't know about your telephone company, but with ours, you can never predict what it's going to do next. For example, you try calling the laundromat and you get the printing office. Or you call a restaurant and you get the hospital.

One evening, my neighbor comes running in.

"Quick," she shouted. "Call 01, I think we have a fire."

I rush to dial 01. Someone picks up the phone and on the other end I hear my supervisor.

"Oh," I say, "I'm sorry. I think I've got the wrong number." I hang up and dial 01 again, and again I hear my supervisor. He says, "Orlov, did something happen?"

I say, "Yes. But it's none of your business."

"So why are you calling me?"

He hangs up. I dial again, and again it's my supervisor. He says, "Orlov, why don't you get a good night's sleep, and tomorrow, come into my office."

He hangs up again. With a trembling hand, I carefully dial 01 again. I hear, "This is the fourth time you are getting me out of bed."

This is where I lost my patience.

"Well," I say, "don't pick up the phone when no one is calling you."

"So whom is this that you are calling," he says. "The only other person here is my wife."

"I'm trying to call 01," I answer. "We have a fire here."

"That," he says, "does not surprise me for a moment. Thank God you don't have a fist fight over there."

He hangs up again.

My neighbor runs in again, shouting, "So why are you not calling 01?"

"I am," I say. "I am trying to call 01, only I keep getting my supervisor."

"So then," she says, "call your supervisor and you'll get 01."

So now I purposely call my supervisor.

"Look," he says, "what are you dialing with?"

"I didn't dial 01 this time." I say. "I dialed your number on purpose."

"Well," he says, "that became clear to me a long time ago."

He hangs up.

My neighbor says to me, "You call yourself a real man? You can't even dial 01 properly."

So she dials the number herself. Suddenly I hear, "No. Orlov is nobody to me. I am simply an acquaintance."

I grab the phone from her and shout, "I am sorry, sir. This is not my fault. The lady wanted to call you herself, because I am not a real man."

Suddenly I hear, "I am not 'sir.' I am his wife."

I ask, "Where are you?"

She says, "What I would like to know is where this "firewoman" got our telephone number?"

"Well," I say, "everyone already knows it."

So she says, "Thank you, Comrade Orlov, for calling me."

"That's no problem," I say. "If you want, I can call again."

She says, "And as for your supervisor, he'll be right over. He just has to pack a few of his things."

She hangs up.

I say to my neighbor, "Everything is all right. They'll be here right away."

She says, "It's too late. The fire went out. All by itself. Call them and tell them not to come."

I call the wife of my supervisor. A sleepy voice answers: "Fire department?"

"I am not calling you," I say. "I am calling the wife of my supervisor."

They ask, "What's the address?"

I give them the address of my supervisor. They say, "We'll be there right away."

In two minutes I get a call from my supervisor and his wife and I hear, "Is this the police?"

I looked at my watch and said, "The time is 3:01 . . . The time is 3:01."

TRAVEL

An Italian Adventure
Moscow News,1989

Much has changed in this country in recent times, including the Soviet citizens' attitude to foreign travel. But that of some officials, like those who made ridiculous charges against Yelena Vargina, remains unchanged. Yelena's father, Igor Vargin, wrote about it to *Moscow News* and our correspondent Marina Levashova went to Tula to investigate.

In 1986 Yelena Vargina, working at the Rosmyasomoltorg association in Tula (an industrial city about 200 km off Moscow), went on a fortnight's tour of Italy visiting Rome, Florence, Venice, Milan, and San Marino to see the famous plazas, fountains, beaches and other tourist attractions. Her group was taken around by a young Italian called Francesco, the coach owner and driver. Little did he know at the time how much attention his smiling face in Yelena's photographs of the Adriatic would draw in some offices in far-away Tula.

Two months after her return from Italy at the district Party committee in Tula, Yelena was accused of "sounding out the Italian Francesco for political motives." "Sounding out" apparently meant that she had asked him "too pointed" political questions, such as: Is it difficult to obtain political asylum in Italy? How many Russians defect to Italy?

Secretary Kalugin of the district Party committee demanded an immediate report on Communist Vargina's conduct in that capitalist country. Yelena, much bewildered, wrote one explanatory note after another—giving a minute-by-minute description of her movements.

"What rubbish!" the group interpreter Krutilina would later remark both orally and in her written statement to the Party committee. "It was me who asked all those questions. They just confused the two of us!"

Nevertheless Vargina's "file" continued to grow with excerpts from verbatim records of various meetings and conferences, some of them stamped "classified", to say nothing of the evidence given by Yelena's fellow travellers. "Yelena was absent three times from her hotel room during night hours", **"Yelena repeatedly posed"** for pictures, **"dressed garishly, enjoyed herself and smiled a lot"**—these vague hints in the report made by the tour leader Starostina (who incidentally did not reprove Yelena once during the tour) formed the basis of the verdict passed by the bureau of the district Party committee which read: ". . . Having lost her political vigilance and forgotten her Party membership Comrade Vargina flagrantly violated the instruction that tête-a-tête contacts with foreign citizens are inadmissible, as had been duly pointed out to her. Vargina does not understand the danger of what happened, is unable to evaluate the event correctly and behaves insincerely."

Vargina was not, however, expelled from the Party, but received a "serious reprimand" written down in her Party card.

The whole episode looks ludicrous and absurd today, in 1989, but the "reprimand" still mars her Party card, and some people still insist that Yelena has been punished properly.

And doesn't the remark by Nikolai Solntsev, chief of Tula's branch of the international youth travel bureau Sputnik, who said that the penalty imposed on Yelena in 1986 would have been less severe (!) today, imply that she would still have been penalized? Perhaps, instead of a "strong written reprimand" she would only be reprimanded orally? . . .

I think that, for years, Yelena will shiver at the very mention of foreign travel and prefer press reports about friendly relations with other nations to personal experience. And yet, from all the reports, records and statements in Yelena's file I failed to understand how the Party committee estimated the actual depth of her fall. But comrades from Tula prefer to remain loyal to notorious instructions dating back to the unidentified past.

. . . Before leaving Tula I decided to ask people in the street how they would have treated Yelena. Out of the few dozen passersby I interviewed only one girl said she would have reprimanded Yelena. A militiaman said he would have punished her for talking politics. "But one cannot be punished for saying the usual things," he smiled.

I hope we shall all live to see the time when the idea of penalty incurred for talking politics will evoke nothing but a smile.

Like a Poor Relation;
Report on Foreign Business Trip
Letter to the editor of *Pravda*, January 13, 1989

Kiev—I am going on a foreign business trip. In recent years I have had over 25 invitations to various international congresses and conferences but the USSR Ministry of Health has given me permission to go to only eight. On each occasion this permission arrived at the very last moment. How can I prepare properly and edit my report in a foreign language in these circumstances?

And how many ordeals I have to suffer to receive "blessing" in my own institute. Although people everywhere are speaking of the simplification of the procedure, even now the cart is creaking and only just moving forward. On instructions from above, the character reference and recommendation is "compiled" and discussed first in the department, then at the faculty party bureau, then at a faculty party meeting. Then there is the trade union committee and the institute party committee, and only after that is the paper signed by the rector. But why can he not sign it immediately, without all the procrastination? The reason is to play it safe, the desire to make as many people as possible responsible for my trip, just in case. Of course this approach is a legacy of the notorious times when every scientist (and not just the scientist) was suspected of every mortal sin, including the intention to remain abroad.

But having received all the documents, I went on a scientific trip abroad. Because of the poverty of the USSR Ministry of Health my pockets were almost empty. I know from experience that in the eyes of foreign scientists we Soviet scientists look like poor relations.

I have recently received invitations from Australia and France. I very much wanted to travel to the remote continent. I had something to share with scieintists there, and there is no harm in borrowing from their experience. But the absurd rule which exists—a scientist can travel to the capitalist countries only once every 5 years—made it impossible for me to visit Australia. I think the number of trips should be determined by how useful each trip is to the development of science in the USSR.

Now about what would seem to be trivia: The congress of symposium organizers concern themselves with my food, hotel, transport problems, and return ticket abroad. But whenever I am ready to leave Kiev the question of how to get a ticket arises. There are enormous waiting lines at the "Intourist" booking offices and I have to stand in line and spend time and nervous and physical energy. Yet it would probably be possible to open a separate booking office for people traveling abroad on business.

Finally, one last point: After the forum or conference, ties and contacts are made and the participants in professional meetings and scientific discussions write letters to each other. In May last year I received a report from a foreign colleague: He had received my letter which had taken . . . 6 months to arrive. Supposing this to be a misunderstanding, he soon sent a letter to me. But this letter took from June to November to reach Kiev. And why? Because although the letter had my home address on it, some communications worker had had the "idea" to send it to my institute, where it was opened and read by many people before reaching me.

I was admitted to the party in 1942. For many years I have been a professor in charge of a department. As a Soviet scientist I am far from indifferent to the way my party and my motherland look in the eyes of foreign scientific representatives. I am not indifferent to what they think about our science, health care, our censorship procedures, and communications system. Superfluous obstacles and barriers must be removed on the path of those who travel abroad to establish contacts and exchange scientific experience. This is a demand of the times.

—Doctor of Medical Sciences
Professor Yu. Bernadskiy,
Kiev Institute department chief

TRUST

An Atmosphere of Trust

IVANOV: (To Petrov) I trust you.

PETROV: (To Ivanov) And I trust you.

SIDOROV: (To Ivanov and Petrov) And I trust you both. Do you trust me?

IVANOV and PETROV: (To Sidorov in unison) Of course we do! (In walks Yevdokimov.)

YEVDOKIMOV: My friends! I have trusted you before but now I will trust you even more. That is if you will trust me.

IVANOV: What kind of question is that! Will we trust you? Of course we will!

PETROV: I personally will. I don't know about the others.

SIDOROV: I will.

YEVDOKIMOV: Now really, if we don't have a feeling of trust for each other, how will we ever learn to trust each other?

IVANOV: Precisely. Therefore, I trust.

PETROV: And I trust. But of course it is my feeling. What if someone does not trust me? Let them tell me then.

SIDOROV: I, personally, trust you like no one else.

IVANOV: And I trust you like no one else.

YEVDOKIMOV: (Hurt, to Ivanov) So what are you saying? You trust Petrov more than you trust me or do I count for nothing?

SIDOROV: You worry for no reason. We do not trust you any less.

IVANOV: I trust you even more.

PETROV: (Hurt, to Ivanov) It's interesting to know that you trust Yevdokimov more than me? Am I not worthy of your trust?

IVANOV: No, of course you are worthy of trust. And if you don't trust me when I tell you this then may everyone here punish me by his mistrust!

PETROV: (Scared) What are you talking about? I trust you.

SIDOROV and YEVDOKIMOV: (Scared. In unison.) And we trust you too!

DIRECTOR: (Claps his hands) This is not believable! Not believable at all! Let's do the scene one more time . . .

UNEMPLOYMENT

Man and Work: Finding One Another
by Yu. Krasnopolskiy, *Trud*, February 7, 1989

For more than a half century—since the middle of the thirties when it was declared that there was no more unemployment in the country—we have been satisfied with this optimistic formula. Although things were far from that simple. There have always been people who were not working for one reason or another. They exist today as well. "Idleness," "labor surplus," and other terms invented by science do not exhaust the essence of the phenomenon. Its scope, of course, is incommensurable with what is happening in the West. But here is something to think about: Labor productivity in our country is less by a factor of 2.5 than, say, in the United States, and the work that is performed by two people there, in our country takes—five. . . .

Under the new management conditions there is a reduction of management personnel and collectives are working with fewer people. But at the same time not a single person should go without work. Here our position is firm. But is our economy as a whole and our labor agencies in particular prepared for the changes that have already begun and are gathering force? How in general do we envision the rearrangment of the country's labor potential? This was the subject published recently in *Trud* entitled "They have Cut Back. What Next?" and the discussion of the subject was continued in a roundtable meeting conducted by the editorial staffs of the newspaper *Trud* and the journal *Sotsialisticheskiy Trud*. Its participants were scholars, trade union workers, and specialists. And—in absentia—the readers: those who have had occasion to encounter the phenomenon, which is real, although we are not fully aware of it—the absence of work.

The "Average" Temperature

Yu. Yakovets, professor, department head of the Academy of the National Economy:

What is our employement situation like? It is very complicated. In economically developed regions (the Baltic area and Belorussia, for example) the birth rate is low and consequently the level of employment of the population is high. In Central Asia the growth of the population is high but the economy is less developed. Tajikistan, for example, has the highest birth rate and the lowest per capita national income.

What is the reason for this? There are many people who are not working. In our day we were not concerned about a moderate, socially substantiated approach to the development of the region's economy with its specific peculiarities: families with many children, a low level of migration of the population, and so forth. **We constructed giants of industry while what we needed were small enterprises located as close as possible to the places of residence.** The Nurekskaya GES and the aluminum plant are good and necessary, but they are just a facade. Behind the facade 27 percent of the able-bodied population are unemployed: every fourth person—even a capitalist would not dream of this. Regions with a "labor surplus" are a direct reproach and problem number one for the country's Gosplan, the local planning agencies, and the Union and territorial labor agencies. We need an efficient program of priority directions for the development of their economies, taking all peculiarities and the way of life into account. We understand this, but so far we do not have a unified statewide program of action.

Ye. Antosenkov, professor, director of the Scientific Research Institute of Labor:

. . . There is also another problem: moral. In the editorial mail there are many letters about "superfluous" people who have become this way exclusively because of life circumstances. Let us say that an elderly person finds it much more difficult to find employment than his younger colleague does. Here is what is written, for example, by P. Timchenko from Kharkov Oblast:

"I am 58 years old. I was released from my job to care for my sick mother, and when she died I was unable to find another job

**anywhere: They blame staff cutbacks. And just imagine—I had
to resort to making moonshine just to feed myself. I myself do
not drink. . . ."**

Or another letter:

"When I was on leave to care for my child my position as an
engineer was eliminated and they offered me the job of a cleaning lady. I had to agree to it: they will not hire you anywhere if
you have a child. I wash the floors at night so that my colleagues
will not see me. It is a disgrace: after all, I am an engineer."

N. Shchebbenok, Maritime Kray

Can we fail to take notice of cases like this?

A Mop for the Engineer

Yu. Tigalev, sector chief of the division for mass production
work and wages of the AUCCTU: We say that everyone has the
right to work but not to a specific job. If the job he wants is
unavailable, he must take another one according to his capabilities. But this brings up a sea of new problems. It is not permitted
to fire a woman with small children—her position is eliminated.
In terms of form everything is legal—they have offered her another job and she has agreed to take it, but what about what is
really happening? There are social guarantees in the Constitution, but in life—alas, not always. Trade unions here frequently
back away from their protective functions and business executives take advantage of the moment to get rid of "undesirables."
So far these are only individual cases, but when the economy is
completely changed over to the new conditions, the cutbacks
will begin on a large scale.

The labor agencies have an immense amount of responsibility
here. They must take charge of the situation and efficiently
reorient people for different kinds of employment. This is inevitable, but I do not think that we are ready for this yet. **Workers
are being released at many enterprises but nobody knows where
or how they find new jobs.** . . . It seems to me that it is necessary to take a close look at the way we are implementing the
decree adopted a year ago by the CPSU Central Committee, the
USSR Council of Ministers, and the AUCCTU concerning providing for effective employment of the population, improvement
of the system of labor placement, and strengthening of social
guarantees for the workers. Is this not a case where the decision
is good but its implementation is absolutely unacceptable?

UNITED STATES

When You Wander, You Come Back Home
by Nikolai Moykin, *Literaturnaya Gazeta*, March 1, 1989

Every morning for 5 years I would enter the imposing UN Secretariat building in New York, and every evening I would leave it after work, passing a man in a smoky blue uniform—an American police officer. However, during the 5 years of my posting in the United States, not a single police officer ever required me (or any other UN employees) to show my pass to the headquarters of this most impressive international organization.

I later learned that the police who guarded the UN Secretariat had developed a special system for recognizing its workers through photographs. An observer of this system, in service at the Secretariat, must keep in his head the photos of all the workers (and there are thousands of them), so thoroughly that he can unerringly distinguish UN workers from visitors.

It was also explained to me that this system of control without verification of identification documents was thought up with the single purpose of avoiding inconvenience and fuss for people.

In short, it was thought up in order to provide elementary respect for man.

I returned from over the ocean long ago; for 12 years now, every morning I enter no less imposing, but not as tall, a building as the one in New York, a building in the center of Moscow, and in the evening after work I leave it, passing by a man in a smoky gray uniform—the police of my native land. And every time I must present my identification (pass). The guard knows me for some time now, by face and even by name. And I do not work out of some "post office box," but in an institution as strictly civilian and peaceful in its aim and mission as the UN Secretariat.

For what purpose was such a system of controlled pass checking thought up in my organization? Naturally, not to free people from extra inconvenience, fuss or annoyance. It was thought up for only one reason: to thwart accidents. Basic respect of the

individual is of no matter here. But does not our society, including our department, consist entirely of individuals?

The evidence of the disrespect to our fellow countrymen becomes even more clear and is accepted with even more offense
and bitterness when we compare it with the facts which I observed in similar situations in others states.

I am certain that any one of us has experienced inconvenience
and gotten nervous upon encountering a sign: break from 13:00
to 14:00; lunch from 14:00 to 15:00; cleaning 16:00 to 17:00,
etc. This is convenient and good for a small group of tradespeo-
ple, but what an inconvenience and disrespect toward tens of
millions of people across the country, all at once!

In America, the lunch hour essentially does not exist. There is
no lunch hour in supermarkets, trade centers, restaurants, pharmacies, banks and other public institutions. In the big cities,
grocery stores and even movie theaters open 24 hours a day can
always be found.

And doesn't the fact that in the States, a commuter train
passenger who did not have time to purchase a ticket at the
window is not fined testify to a respect for man? He buys his
ticket while the train is moving, not getting out of his seat; the
conductor himself sells it to him. Here, an unticketed rider is a
"malefactor," and is immediately dragged away by two or three
controllers, and they exact some ungodly fine from him. The
average Soviet public transport "freeloader" pays an even higher
price for "crime:" public humiliation and nervous scolding.

Incidentally, not everyone is in a hurry here. During the international forum, "For a nuclear-free world, for the survival of
mankind" which took place in Moscow in 1987, I was asked to
accompany two Canadian guests to the theater, and then to a
restaurant. The delegates were being fed at the hotel "Kosmos."
We sat down at a small table in the "Galaktika" restaurant, but
had to wait 20-30 minutes before our order was taken. Thirty
more minutes passed before we got our first course. The restaurant was almost empty.

After supper, one of the Canadian guests, writer B. Broadfoot,
a gray-haired old man, a former journalist who has traveled all
over the the world, said, "What disrespect for people! If a Canadian waiter had served us in Vancouver or Montreal the way we
were served here today, he would not have to get up early the
next day—he would have been fired the night before."

In my observation, in any government, the citizen always
stands in the forefront. When I first landed in New York at John

F. Kennedy International Airport, the pilot announced over the intercom, "Your attention, please, ladies and gentlemen. You have arrived in the United States of America. Welcome to our country! American citizens will exit first." At the Sydney airport, I noted the special signs which separated holders of Australian passports from other arriving passengers. They go through all customs procedures more quickly, without mixing with foreigners.

Of course, such privileges extended to fellow countrymen do not presuppose inhospitality, or a disrespectful attitude toward representatives of other countries. The thing is, there should be no obsequious attitudes toward foreigners without respecting oneself.

Here, for example, the best hotels are built and set aside for foreigners. And for citizens with passports bearing the hammer and sickle, entry to the luxe hotels of "Intourist" is almost always and everywhere closed.

But no, incidentally, sometimes they do let our own in. For example, in off-season. They let us in reluctantly, as if doing us a great favor. And the doorman conducts himself as if he were a member of some elite special forces, dressed in civvies (so as not to scare off the foreigners), as if he were guarding the country's most secret site (from his fellow countrymen).

One of my first discoveries in the United States was that there are no foreigners there. Not in the literal sense, of course. It is simply that no one is set apart, that they themselves don't set themselves apart from the general ethnic conglomeration of America.

As far as I know, Americans never opened special stores for foreigners like our "Berezki," have not built for them separate hotels, restaurants, offices, hospitals and clinics. They have not leased the homeland's best passenger ships to foreign companies, as we do; they have not created great companies such as "Intourist" for servicing the "overseas guests," or entire departments like our UPDK (department for diplomatic corps service), as we have.

Thus, the situation is that foreigners have access to the Bolshoy Theater and the Armory on any day, and the poorly connected Muscovite or visitor to the capital can only dream about them. We put almost all of Yalta and Pitsunda at the disposal of foreigners, and our "savage" compatriots fill up the sweltering municipal beaches of Sochi and Alushta in greater numbers every year. A foreigner can get any internal flight on Aeroflot without waiting, while a Soviet citizen cannot get a ticket even with a certified telegram on the death of a relative.

Our rich country is experiencing a shortage of many products, services, specialists, etc. Yet among all these types of deficits is one which cannot be inventoried or manufactured. This is the deficit of respect for the individual.

WOMEN

We Are Tired of . . . Believing
Letter to the editor of *Tiesa*, March 8, 1989

We are already tired of writing various appeals: tired of reading, in all the newspapers and magazines, scads of articles which deal with this sad theme. Finally, we are even tired of believing. We are tired, for we hear only words. Even now, we see, nothing is being done in actuality. Perhaps this is due to the fact that we parents are viewed by the government not as people, but manpower. Five square meters of living space suffice for manpower.

Manpower is supposed to sleep within those couple of square meters, and throw oneself into work with renewed vigor in the morning. Everyone in his little spot, where a 12-13-year-old is doing his homework and "meaningfully" spending his free time, while the 5-year-old is raging within "his" square meters—he requires space, and often usurps it from others; from the first grader, for instance, who is concentrating in trying to learn the alphabet. Nearby, within his 5 square meters, gurgles the newborn; here, too, one dries the diapers, and bustles around with baby bottles and medicines. . . .

Doctors always give the very nice instructions to separate the patient . . . at least, by hanging up a sheet, in order to prevent the spread of infection. Doctors, in particular, should speak out, on what type of individual will grow up under such conditions.

One laughs through tears, a mother's tears. We mothers are written off, not unlike the worn looms are written off at our enterprises.

Were it not for that eternal word "mama," who knows how we would get up, how we would proceed, and how one would believe. . . . Whenever small hands embrace us and little dishevelled heads cuddle up to us, we rise again and proceed. We proceed on their behalf. We proceed to ask, to beg, to receive. . . . We proceed, clutching a bunch of certificates, in order to get an allowance attesting how poor the family is, to get school assistance, to get an allowance after the birth of the fourth child (R4); we carry our papers to the trade administration in order to obtain a towel or a child's fur jacket and we look for shoes, hats, coats, and dresses. Without a certificate you often come back with nothing. Only families with four children get certificates. If there are three children in the family you do not receive a certificate. However, does not the voice of sanity dictate, that even if there is one child in the family, who constitutes a representative of our elevated, only, "privileged" class, privileges should be given him? Supposing the family happens to be thrice so "privileged. . . ."

Our melancholy thoughts are perhaps not suitable for the *Tiesa* newspaper. We are addressing this to you, anyway, since this subject is written about in your paper.

—Terese Staponiene, Virginija Sadauskiene, Galina Cirvinskiene, Janina Joksiene, Dalia Stoniene, and Stefa Mikalauskiene.

Stepdaughters of the Big City
by Special Correspondents Yury Osipov, Aleksandr Mikhailovsky and Pavel Krivtsov, *Ogonyek*, No. 41, October 1988

Despite the fact that Moscow is significantly "overfulfilling its plan" for population growth, it also had an acute manpower shortage. How can the problem be resolved?

"Certainly not by recruiting 'above-limit' workers [*limitchiki*—outside workers with nonresident status]," said Doctor of Economics Yevgeny Grigoryevich Antosenkov, Director of the Research Institute of Labor. "They are by no means a panacea."

Procrastination in solving socioeconomic problems ends up costing billions of rubles. Just look at the huge number of Moscow dormitories that have become permanent places of residence for so many. The women suffer the most.

According to figures cited at the June 19, 1986, plenary session of the Moscow City Party Committee, in the past 15 years over 700,000 outside workers have been recruited to work in Moscow (at a cost of roughly 10 billion rubles). At the same time, factory modernization and the elimination of manual labor was proceeding slowly. Industrial managers were "corrupted" by this approach and slacked off in their efforts to accelerate scientific and technical progress. Labor discipline and public order grew lax, labor turnover increased. Approximately 50% of all those who had been enlisted to work in Moscow's economy left the enterprises that had hired them.

The Pyotr Alekseyev Fine Fabric Mill is one of Moscow's oldest enterprises (next year it will mark its 150th anniversary). It operates around the clock, the equipment is dilapidated and the ventilation is poor. It's obvious why there's no way you could get some Muscovites to work there. Over 90% of the factory's 2,000 workers come from outside Moscow; most are young women. But they live a bit better than most such workers; the mill has just built a modern new dormitory with accommodations for 520. Child care is also provided.

Recently, however, the management decreed that husbands would no longer be permitted to live in the dormitories. When asked, "What are we supposed to do, get divorced?" the director merely replied that this was not management's concern and that women shouldn't get married until they have housing. And this response from an enterprise that supposedly looks after its workers!

Economic managers say that without outside workers Moscow's industry would have ground to a halt long ago. But one can't help wondering: "Why does the capital even allow the construction of enterprises for which there is not enough manpower? And isn't the expansion of such industry in Moscow an antistate practice that only serves the interests of individual ministries? Why is it necessary to tear tens of thousands of young men and women away from their homes and create chaos in so many spheres of life?

Provincial young people are lured by the bright lights of the big city; not all of them are keen to improve themselves culturally, get an education and become skilled specialists. The majority want a good salary and a separate apartment—that's the limit of their dreams. Well, they also want a good marriage, of course (with a Muscovite, even though the statistics show that this is unlikely).

Removed from familiar surroundings and left to their own devices in a huge, strange city, many of the newly arrived female workers are doomed to casual encounters that fail to bring them happiness. And no matter what—next morning they face the rumble of the machines and the arduous monotony of their labor. After work they return to the boredom, crowding and incessant noise of the dormitory. All this causes conflicts and mutual hostility among dormitory residents. Not long ago a young single mother died in a shared room, her baby in her arms. She was afraid to ask for help from her neighbors on the other side of the chintz curtain, who had come to hate her because of the baby's annoying cries.

Many of the girls adapt poorly to the rhythm of Moscow life and suffer from nervous disorders. Doctors note that the young women who get pregnant usually have complications and more often than not suffer miscarriages or are compelled to seek abortions.

Those who succeed in getting a Moscow residence permit try to find a husband. But even if they do, where will the young family live? Usually the couples have only their beds in dormitories meant for single workers. Intentionally or not, enterprise managers keep people from starting families. From their viewpoint, marriage is followed by children, which means that the woman will leave her job for at least 18 months. And she'll also need accommodations in a family dormitory.

If women don't marry by age 30, some have babies anyway, "for themselves." They don't want to miss the joy of motherhood. On the other hand, there are those who view their children merely as a means of obtaining a separate apartment—but it proves to be of little help.

In one family dormitory, eight single mothers and their children live together in four small rooms. When one child comes down with an infectious disease, eight machines are idle. And the children we saw were very nervous and sickly. It's no wonder!

How long must young women live as "single girls" in these dormitories? An outside worker will normally obtain a permanent residence permit in five or six years, and she can put her name on the waiting list for housing after 10 years' residence in Moscow. This means that 20-year-old women can expect to get housing when they are nearly 40, provided that they are good workers. Until then they are supposed to live in a dormitory!

For over 50 years attempts have been made—in vain—to prohibit or at least limit the construction of new industrial enterprises within the Moscow city limits. The 1971 general plan envisaged the construction of 327 enterprises and organizations outside the capital, but only a small number have been built. Moreover, Moscow's plants are being modernized mainly by increasing the number of workplaces, because an enterprise's status and the salaries of its executives are determined by the size of the work force. This vicious circle only aggravates the problem of outside labor.

So what should we do? Abolish the system of hiring outside workers once and for all? V. V. Tulyakov, senior inspector of the Moscow City Soviet Executive Committee's labor administration, opposes approving any further recruitment of workers from other cities and also points with concern to the covert hiring of outside workers through the vocational-technical schools.

But Ye. G. Antosenkov, Director of the Research Institute of Labor, is against purely administrative solutions and argues that only efficient production and the improvement of the economy as a whole—and not just in Moscow—can effect a radical change in the situation. He sees encouraging signs, however. With enterprises everywhere now shifting to full economic accountability and reducing their work forces by 5% to 7%, the problem of recruiting labor for Moscow and other cities will eventually be replaced by a new concern—ensuring full employment.

WORLD WAR II (GREAT PATRIOTIC WAR)

Stalin Gave an Order
by R. Ignatyev, *Izvestiya*, August 15, 1988

"Not One Step Back!" This is the name by which Order No. 227, signed by People's Commissar of Defense J. Stalin on July 28, 1942, is popularly known. The document was never secret. It was, however, stamped "Not for Publication." Therefore, for all practical purposes this document remained confidential for 46 years. Now, for the first time, it has been included in an exhibition—the one that opened Aug. 11 at the Soviet Culture Pavilion of the Exhibition of Economic Achievements of the USSR.

"I tried to publish this dreaded order while I was working on my monograph, 'The Battle of Stalingrad,' " says the well-known

Soviet historian Academician A. Samsonov. "But at that time I was allowed to do nothing more than make reference to it. In later editions of the book I was allowed to publish portions of the document. And now, at long last—in the glasnost period, when history has been made accessible and documents labeled 'Secret' have begun to circulate, my article has appeared in print with the text of Order No. 227. Unfortunately, however, 'questionable' passages were removed."

Q: Which ones, for example?

A: Mainly those where the creation of so-called barrier detachments is mentioned and compared with stern measures taken by Hitler's army. The fact is, after the battle for Moscow the German soldiers' fighting morale had fallen, and so the Fascists took repressive measures: They posted barrier detachments. And so, as if with this in mind, Headquarters decided to introduce the same thing in our Army. The order notes that the Germans formed special detachments as barriers, placed them behind unstable divisions, and ordered them to shoot on the spot anyone who panicked and attempted either to abandon the position or surrender. It goes on to say: "These measures have had their effect, and now German troops are fighting better than they were during the winter.*** Shouldn't we take a lesson from our enemies on this score?"

Of course, by that time our situation at the front was becoming grave. As stated in the order, we had lost more than 70 million people (left on territory occupied by the fascists—R. I.) and more than 800 million poods of grain [1 pood equals 36 lbs.—*Trans.*]. . . . "Every position, every meter of Soviet territory must be defended down to the last drop of blood. Every patch of Soviet ground must be clung to and defended in every way possible. . . ."

Q: As is evident from the document, some of the forces on the southern front did panic, leaving Rostov and Novocherkassk unable to offer resistance and bringing shame to their banners.

A: I'm a war veteran myself, and I know about it other than through hearsay. Yes, anything could happen at the front, and so I can say that what made Order No. 227 particularly severe was that it excluded the possibility of taking the specific situation into account, including those instances when forces had gotten into hopeless positions, when only falling back could save them. After all, the essence of the dreaded document was this: Any retreat whatsoever was categorically forbidden without special permission from the high command. The penalty for failing to comply was execution, even though in a war of maneuver, giving up a position can also be a tactical move, as we know. . . .

Q: Which wartime documents classified as "Secret" would you personally like to present to the court of public opinion?

A: First of all, Order No. 270, issued Aug. 16, 1941.

Q: What are its essential elements?

A: It is similar to Order No. 227 in its harshness of tone and in a number of its provisions. No. 270 appeared at a time when our forces were in retreat along the entire front. Many units and formations had been surrounded. Order No. 270 gives an assessment of the situation. All Soviet prisoners of war were declared traitors and turncoats. The families of commanders and political officers who had been taken prisoner were subjected to repression, and soldiers' relatives were deprived of the benefits enjoyed by the families of participants in the war. A number of other prominent people besides Stalin signed this terrible document. The last to affix his signature was G. K. Zhukov. It is impossible to understand why this attitude was taken toward all prisoners of war. After all, the majority of them displayed courage and heroism, even in prison. About 4 million people perished just in the concentration camps located on Hitlerite-occupied Soviet territory. And so many vanished without a trace. They cannot all be declared traitors. . . . Order No. 270 imposed suffering on millions of families, as well as on those who returned from prison. The stigma of traitor was passed along from one generation to the next, causing pain to a great number of innocent people. *Izvestiya* raised this serious issue, and I fully support the paper's position.

Q: Doubtless, had there been no mistakes and oversights on the part of the leadership, there would have been fewer situations in which soldiers were taken prisoner.

A: Entire armies, corps and divisions were surrounded. Many were taken prisoner during the fighting around Moscow. But, of course, our troops did not capitulate then. They stopped 28 fascist divisions, but had they surrendered, Moscow would have fallen. . . . Sometimes entire units were surrounded because of miscalculations by the Supreme Military Commander. When, for instance, it became obvious that Kiev could not be held, Zhukov suggested to Stalin that our armies be moved across the Dnepr to the banks of the Psel. Stalin screamed at him and said: "How dare you suggest surrendering Kiev!" As a result, Zhukov was removed as Chief of the General Staff, Kiev was lost, and armies were surrounded. The commander of the front was killed. Thousands and thousands of soldiers and officers fell on the field of battle. Tens of thousands were taken prisoner. They too were stigmatized by a suspicion of treason. And who is to blame? The leadership, of course, who, despite the clear military necessity, refused to move its forces out of Kiev. Numerous examples of this sort could be cited.

Q: One last thing, Alexander Mikhailovich: Are there many of these blank pages left in the history of the Great Patriotic War?

A: Yes, many. The attempt to smooth over and varnish reality followed from highly questionable theses, which do explain why the blank pages appeared. They must not be allowed. Documents must be declassified. Archives must be made accessible. I am certain that if the materials of the Supreme Headquarters were made public, many things would fall into place.

B. YELTSIN

Let Us Not Forget Man
by Pavel Voshchanov, *Komsomolskaya Pravda*,
   December 31, 1988

ECONOMIC OBSERVER Pravel Voshchanov conducted this interview with Boris Nikolayevich Yeltsin, first deputy chairman of the USSR Gosstroy and USSR minister.

Your own stance, an original way of thinking, an unusual view of the urgent problems of life . . . You can agree or disagree with people like that, you can accept them or reject them. But one thing is impossible—you cannot be indifferent to their stance and convictions. The name of one such person is Boris Nikolayevich Yeltsin, first deputy chairman of the USSR Gosstroy and a USSR minister. On the eve of the New Year, our economic observer Pavel Voshchanov met with him.

VOSHCHANOV: Boris Nikolayevich, during the year now ending

Komsomolskaya Pravda has received many letters in which the same request crops up: Please tell us what Yeltsin thinks about this. Of course, we will not be able to discuss all the issues, and indeed a newspaper page is limited in size. What if we confine our discussion to questions of the economy and social justice?

YELTSIN: Agreed. The link between them is itself very important to me. After all, it is no secret that for many years people tried to ignore that link. They shrugged it off. Slogans and actual deeds were not infrequently "on opposite sides of the barricades." The peasant, for instance, was called upon to increase agricultural productivity, but at the same time he was deprived of the opportunity to sell surpluses on the market, his land and livestock were taken away from him, and he was driven away from familiar places to the remotest corners of the country. And the worker? He too was "spurred on" to labor feats, but at the same time wage rates were cut, leaving wages permanently at a low level. People were constantly told that in our humane country everything is done exclusively for their benefit. But what did they see in practice? Waiting lines of many years for any kind of housing. Empty counters. Extortion, corruption, and money-grubbing. The self-satisfied flourishing of bureaucracy. And the result? People stopped listening to the slogans and lost enthusiasm for labor feats. It all began to seem deceitful and economically unjustified. It is no accident that when the idea of restructuring was born, many people shrugged it aside through habit. That is a fact. Only after 3 years did people begin to understand that it is not a question of supporting a new leader. It is all considerably more profound. It is a matter of restructuring man himself, faced as he is today with a difficult choice. He has a chance to win the battle for the dignity that was lost some time ago, for everything we call social justice.

VOSHCHANOV: It is no secret that many economic decisions are made without taking into account people's opinions and interests. They are drafted, as a rule, in secret, in the quiet of ministerial offices. Then the public wastes considerable effort in trying to revoke them. What form should social control of the adoption of the most important economic decisions take, in your view?

YELTSIN: **Recently we have talked a great deal about referendums. But we have yet to use even once this instrument for the expression of the people's will! The bureaucracy has invented a very curious substitute for it—"nationwide discussion." There is** nothing wrong with such discussion in itself. But the technique prompts objections. How does it work? Tens, hundreds of thousands of proposals are conveyed from below to the relevant institutions that are preparing the document. What happens to them there? Who discusses them, and in what way? Why are some accepted, while others are rejected? Today these questions remain a mystery to us. But it should be totally clear. Otherwise strange things can happen: There are thousands of proposals, but only dozens of amendments are made. Consulting with the people means not only telling them what it is proposed to do and how. It also means listening to them and acting in accordance with their wishes. But at the moment some of our apparatchiks seem to look at the problem like this: "Let them amuse themselves, we will have our way all the same!" But the people should have their way. The majority of the people. The voters should therefore be given the right to demand, through their deputies, the holding of referendums on any issues that are causing the concern. And another observation: In drafting economic programs, we should get away from those unfortunate averages. Too many decisions are made on the basis of the "statistically average" citizen. I think that in order to represent the full gravity of a particular decision and assess all its consequences, in economic policy we consider most important the poorly off person, he who makes the minimum wage or is on pension. I am sure many decisions would look completely different then.

VOSHCHANOV: In their letters readers often express concern: How realistic is th task of providing every Soviet family with an individual apartment by the year 2000? After all, a similar task was set before, in 1965. Then it was suggested that every family would have a well-appointed apartment by 1980. Are we repeating the old mistake, are we setting a task that is impossible in the first place? How could you, as the minister responsible for the development of the construction sector, answer that question?

YELTSIN: First of all, I will not deny the difficulty of resolving this task. That is the most important thing. **As for people's concern, unfortunately it is true that we often proclaim a slogan, and only later begin to calculate and think how to put it into practice.** In this way we ourselves sow distrust in many plans and initiatives. Did we assess the potential on this occasion? Yes. Tasks were defined for each 5-year plan: It was proposed to commission 700 million square meters of housing during this one, and 800 million in the next. At first it looked as if that would be enough. But when people began to do more thorough calculations, with the help of demographers, sociologists, and economists, then it emerged, to the construction workers' horror, that in order to resolve the task it is necessary to commission in the 13th 5-Year Plan not 700 million, but 1 billion square meters of housing. As you see, the task has grown more difficult. Especially since as of today we do not even have a base for construction on that scale. We must create a base. But that is not easy to do. Judge for yourself, when the construction boom started in Khrushchev's day, it took 15 years to create the capacities for house-building enterprises to the tune of 60 million square meters. And today we have to create 2.5 times that figure in a maximum of 4 years. Difficult? Incredibly. But there is no other way. We are now beginning to speed up the development of this work. We are establishing precisely what reserves we have today. We propose the construction of several hundred additional plants. In a word, colossal efforts are needed. But I simply have no right not to believe that the task is realistic. If I did not believe that, I would not work at the Gosstroy for a single day.

VOSHCHANOV: Many letters addressed to you touch on questions of the benefits and privileges enjoyed by certain categories of our citizens. Why is this particular problem central in many of your speeches?

YELTSIN: With regard to special rations and other nomenklatura privileges, my position is well known. I have always advocated their total abolition. But I am not in favor of leveling! No way. I am opposed to "hierarchical" benefits. Why? Because this is not in accordance with the economic law of the socialist society, "to each according to his labor." "According to his labor" means wages, not goods and services! Otherwise a system of double privileges emerges in society: On the one hand you have higher wages, and on the other you have more goods for those wages. Is that not economic nonsense? I think material benefits should be identically accessible to everyone. **In other words, a minister's ruble should be no different from a cleaner's ruble. That is of fundamental importance.**

It cannot be denied that today our ruble is rather devalued. Alas, there are not enough goods to back it up. So can it be fair to some people to obtain full value for their money, and thus for their labor, while others do not? Today we are trying to lure our young people to the far north. How? With high wages. Yet they cannot fully "convert into goods" their honestly earned "fast" rubles. There is only one possibility: to keep them "under the mattress." Yet someone who has a special ration, or, as they call it today, a special order, receives full value for his labor. That, it seems to me, is the economic essence of social injustice.

VOSHCHANOV: At the 19th All-Union CPSU Conference you proposed that efforts be concentrated on the development of three spheres of the economy: trade and public catering, consumer goods production, and the service sphere. But some economists think this would inevitably lead to a decline in the pace of the country's economic development. We may gain today, they say, but we will lose tomorrow . . .

YELTSIN: **But what is the point of a fast pace today, if it does not make life any better or easier for people? For whom are we actually investing money in economic development? For future generations?** They are supposed to reap all the benefits of our selfless labor. But are we not making a mistake? After all, if the economy turns away from people, then sooner or later people turn away from the economy. They have already done so; you cannot fail to notice it. And if we are talking about future generations, where will they come from, healthy and happy, if their parents are constantly living in a state of debilitating shortages?

I think there is a political aspect to this problem too. We must ensure that people feel immediately what restructuring really has to offer them. So that everyone can say: "I have begun to live better!"

VOSHCHANOV: But it is no secret that the social sphere of our economy is in an extremely neglected state today. That means considerable resources are needed. Where are they to come from?

YELTSIN: I think it is quite possible to slightly cut some of our programs in other areas. For instance, to postpone for a time the fulfillment of the most costly space programs. Or to cut some things in the defense sphere. And the majority of production sectors should be looked at from precisely this standpoint. In short, I am in favor of tilting the economy sharply in the direction of people. What results that could yield! All the costs would be more than recouped! We should realize today that unless people feel the real benefits of restructuring, it will not work. It will remain only a slogan or, as Lenin said, a "hollow bureaucratic rattle."

VOSHCHANOV: To conclude our conversation: What would you like to wish the newspaper and its readers?

YELTSIN: That they get rid of indifference. Get rid of the fear that still drives us to this day. Get rid of the innate fear of fighting for your convictions. Do not lose faith in restructuring, despite all the difficulties we encounter in putting it into practice. Without that faith, without a staunch, daily struggle for social justice, we could once again find ourselves hostages to bureaucracy.

Boris Yeltsin on Leadership, Reform, Other Issues
by Ezio Mauro, *La Repubblica*, January 7, 1989

EZO MAURO CONDUCTED this interview with former Moscow Gorkom First Secretary Boris Yeltsin in Moscow.

Moscow—"I have faith in restructuring. Sooner or later restructuring will have faith in me again." The old fighter is ready. A year after his excommunication from the party, with his defeat by the conservatives who expelled him from the Moscow CPSU leadership, Boris Yeltsin feels that his political purgatory is about to come to an end; condemns the lag in restructuring; urges Gorbachev not to leave the reform unfinished; attacks his major adversary, Yegor Ligachev; and meanwhile intends to participate in the campaign for elections to the new parliament. Above all, as he returns to the fray Yeltsin recounts the stages, secrets, and conflicts of the past year of restructuring, marked by an open conflict between reformists and conservatives within the Soviet leadership. It is the exciting story of a political battle that is not yet over, that affects the empire's future, and that also involves personal relations between the CPSU's leaders.

"I believe Gorbachev and I will soon achieve a rapprochement," Yeltsin announced. "I know he regretted condemning me, and even then he was my most loyal comrade. The time has come to say that this split between us was caused entirely by Yegor Ligachev. Now, even though he is still afloat, I do not believe that Ligachev can continue this work. I am waiting, but at the next congress, unless I obtain justice before then, I will again request my political rehabilitation. I want the cancellation of the two words defining my position as 'politically erroneous.' The facts show that this is not so." The large office of the deputy chairman of Gosstroy is gleaming and empty, as though Yeltsin were just passing through. On the bare desk there lay only a copy of the "Publishing Digest" ["Rassegna editoriale"] with the following headline underlined in red: "Yegor, You Are Absolutely Wrong."

MAURO: Boris Nikolayevich Yeltsin, Western papers call you the kamikaze of restructuring. You attacked and lost, but have not surrendered. What is your assessment now of this past year of clashes within the Soviet leadership? Has restructuring grown stronger?

YELTSIN: I must answer "no"—unfortunately. Of course there have been many changes and steps forward in democracy, glasnost, and reforms, but the results are not those hoped for and needed. We must not forget that restructuring is entering its 4th year. And 4 years on we would have liked to be much further forward than we are.

MAURO: Is Gorbachev not stronger than he was a year ago?

YELTSIN: On the personal level, yes. Now the conservatives have concealed themselves against the background of restructuring and are awaiting the right moment. The latest reshuffle rewarded the Gorbachevian leaders. Foreign policy is successful—certainly more so than domestic policy, and this is a paradox worth pondering. Combining all these points, it can be concluded that Gorbachev is stronger—but in his personal positions more than in his policy.

MAURO: Are you saying that restructuring's future is not dependent on Gorbachev's future?

YELTSIN: I am simply saying that the specific results of the new course are smaller than people expected.

MAURO: Where do you believe the greatest lag has occurred?

YELTSIN: The economic reform has in fact ground to a halt. On the social plane little has been achieved; in the field of democratization that which should be proceeding swiftly is barely moving; the media are going into decline, concentrating as they do on the thirties instead of today's problems; and even with regard to cadres policy not everything necessary is being done for a real reform.

MAURO: From what you say, you do not seem to regret at all the criticisms that cost you your post a year ago. Is this so?

YELTSIN: Why should I regret them? In the social sphere I see no changes that can convince me that I was wrong in my condemnation. Indeed as a result of some of the issues I raised—from food supplies to services—decisions have been made with which I agree. However, they are precisely decisions: People expect results, and there is a long way to go. So after a year events threaten to corroborate a speech I delivered to the October plenum, which was never published.

MAURO: But now that even *Pravda* criticizes democratic centralism can you say whether it is true that you criticized Raisa Gorbacheva in that speech?

YELTSIN: It is untrue. I do not believe that matters relating to the general secretary's wife are a topic for a plenum.

MAURO: On that occasion you were accused of having criticized the "party leadership." Can you now clarify whether you criticized Ligachev alone or others too in your speech?

YELTSIN: Others too.

MAURO: A month later Gorbachev said that you have undermined "the unity of all forces" necessary for the success of restructuring. Now that unity has exploded following the public clash between conservatives and progressives. When do you believe the leadership pact began to falter?

YELTSIN: I believe that speech of mine gave a jolt to the leadership, revealing the latent conflict within it. The leadership had never before been challenged at a plenum. In fact it has not happened since either. So people had to be shown the uniformity of the leadership group at all costs. **I know, for instance, that after Nina Andreyeva's article was published by *Sovetskaya Rossiya* Gorbachev and Ligachev stopped talking to one another.** On Lenin's "birthday," however, they appeared side by side talking at length in front of the television cameras. This is politics and this is what politics demanded.

MAURO: Do you believe that the pro-Stalinist manifesto written by Nina Andreyeva was intended to weaken Gorbachev in order to influence him or did she actually want to establish an alternative to the secretary?

YELTSIN: In order to answer that I would have to be inside the mind not only of the article's author but of whoever organized the operation and planned the attack. The fact that there was an attack proves that somebody did nurture the hopes you mentioned.

MAURO: Boris Nikolayevich, you usually talk frankly; Was Ligachev the organizer?

YELTSIN: I will answer you as diplomatically as I know how: It cannot be ruled out. No, it really cannot.

MAURO: Is this why Gorbachev unexpectedly allowed you to speak at the latest party conference? Was it to let you attack Ligachev?

YELTSIN: Actually it was I who took the initiative to speak. You were unable to see what happened in the hall. If Gorbachev had wanted to have me speak he could have done so before, since I had sent the Presidium two notes asking to speak. Without success. So from the floor, where I had been confined with delegates from Karelia, I arose and, brandishing my papers in front of everyone, declared: I want to speak. Whether my speech was useful to Gorbachev is another matter.

MAURO: Was it useful because it forced Ligachev to reply, thus revealing himself as the conservatives' leader?

YELTSIN: Yes, but not only him. He had to reply to me and thus revealed himself to the party and the country for what he really is. The least that can be said is that his was an unintelligent speech that marked the beginning of his misfortune.

MAURO: For that matter, the misfortune was greater for Gromyko and Solomentsev, lauded by Ligachev in his speech as Gorbachev's "kingmakers" but now expelled from the Politburo. Where do you believe Gorbachev found the strength to redesign the party leadership, after so many compromises?

YELTSIN: I am still wondering why he did not find his strength sooner. The renewal should have happened earlier and been much more thorough. When it actually happened no special courage was needed any longer; everything was already very much overdue. If Ligachev too had been expelled from the Politburo there would have been no resistance.

MAURO: You still place much emphasis on Ligachev, but was it not precisely he, as he revealed at the conference, who recommended Boris Yeltsin to the Politburo?

YELTSIN: It is untrue. When the Politburo decided that I should transfer from Sverdlovsk to Moscow in 1985 I was informed of it by telephone by Dolgikh. I said "no." So the next day Ligachev phoned me on Gorbachev's instructions. I repeated my "no" so he invoked party discipline.

MAURO: Why did you turn down Moscow?

YELTSIN: Let us say that I liked the work in the Urals, after 10 years. Let us also say that workers there do not swing from one thing to another. If they are to support Yeltsin, they support him. So much so that they still do so.

MAURO: What was the origin of your dispute with Ligachev?

YELTSIN: It was a political dispute. Apart from that, we would just exchange greetings. The clash was chiefly over social justice. He told me that when it comes to people I was too left-wing and that otherwise I was too right-wing. I have always judged him insincere, even toward the general secretary. I did not believe him, even though he says he built socialism in a single region, or some such. . . .

MAURO: Do you now regard it as a personal victory that Ligachev has been demoted, losing his ideology post and being transferred to argiculture?

YELTSIN: Quite honestly, it is still not enough. It is necessary to go all the way.

MAURO: How far is that?

YELTSIN: Look, if I had been in his shoes I would have resigned some time ago, immediately after the conference. He covered himself in shame when he decided to announce to everyone that it was they four who created Gorbachev. It was an attempt to take the secretary hostage, but also to compromise him. I believe it took a great deal of self-control on Gorbachev's part not to react. I had never heard such cynical talk from anyone. People realized this, as shown by the hundreds of letters I receive. They ask: When is Ligachev leaving?

MAURO: There is one point you should clarify: In your opinion, was Ligachev demoted or not?

YELTSIN: I would talk in terms of semi-punishment. He tried to personalize the battle and was put in his place in time. But he is still there. I would call it a kind of conditional sentence.

MAURO: Can the conservatives be identified with Ligachev? Was he, and is he, really on his own?

YELTSIN: If you mean that the leadership has not yet been entirely renewed, I would reply that it is true.

Truth Is Very Important for People
by V. Ivanov, *Sovetskaya Estoniya*, February 19, 1989

V. IVANOV conducted this interview with USSR Minister B.N. Yeltsin, first deputy chairman of the USSR Gosstroy, on 1 February 1989, datelined Tallinn-Moscow-Tallinn.

People are still talking about Boris Nikolayevich Yeltsin. One often comes across both written and verbal questions like: What is he doing now? What are his plans? The editorial office decided to obtain the answers at first hand. Our correspondent interviewed USSR Minister B.N. Yeltsin, first deputy chairman of the USSR Gosstroy.

IVANOV: Boris Nikolayevich, the situation today is such that some *OBVIOUS* economic changes for the better are needed for successful advances in restructuring. But this also requires rather a lengthy period of time and major efforts. There is, at the same time, another way: *POLITICAL* reforms which do not require immediate material expenditure of capital investments. . . . But is there not some danger of putting the cart before the horse? In other words, of "rushing" so far ahead on the political plane as to make it that much harder for the economic rear services to catch up?

YELTSIN: First, I would not set the one in opposition to the other. It is obviously necessary to implement simultaneously both political and economic reforms. And even though I have stood corrected on numerous occasions, I would still affirm time and again my commitment to the view I expressed both at the 19th party conference and beforehand—namely: **Generally speaking there was no well thought-out concept of restructuring with its stage-by-stage implementation and an indication of the results at every stage. This is why I would describe its nature as spasmodic—halfway political and halfway economic. . . . On the whole, without any result.**

IVANOV: But was it actually possible to compile so detailed a program for such a gigantic country like ours and in such a complex situation as the one in which we found ourselves in the mid-eighties?

YELTSIN: Not only was it possible, it was also necessary. I am not talking about long-term prospects through the 3d millennium. We are talking about the next 15 years at most! And what should have been done without fail was to forecast the development of the situation and define priorities for the first 3-4 years.

I perceive as nothing more than a mistake the fact that no target for raising the people's living standards was set as the paramount task. Apart from anything else, this represents so much time lost—3½ years. Only recently have program resolutions been adopted on improving supplies of food, commodities, services, and housing. Yet this should have been done at the very beginning. Not to conduct restructuring **on a broad front** as was said at the time—since we have neither the resources, nor the manpower, nor the potential to do this—but to concentrate along the main avenues of meeting people's essential needs. How should this have been funded? **By cutting back or putting** off for 5 years a series of our space programs. **By cutting back funds for defense needs.** Also, of course, at the expense of some other sectors. But in any case to ensure that, within these 3–4 years, people would sense that living standards had risen and supplies had improved. Then they would have associated this directly with restructuring: "You see, we were offered yet another slogan, like the ones we got so used to, but this time the slogan was matched by deeds."

This is not a question of total abundance of everything people's hearts desired. This is still a long way away. But people must sense something **tangible**, they must personally experience changes for the better. This could have been achieved.

To continue: The "feedback" would have come into operation, and people would have given 50 percent and 100 percent more work and efforts in factor of restructuring—that would have been the time to launch the "offensive" on a broad front.

This, in my view, is where a tactical mistake was committed, and this is where I disagreed with many others.

IVANOV: Boris Nikolayevich, some people today are inclined to perceive the real way out of the economic blind alleys as lying through the development of the cooperative movement, which would force the state sector to "shake itself up" by competing against it; through an activation of the market mechanism. What do you think about it?

YELTSIN: I believe that the cooperative movement is perfectly entitled to exist, like the multiplicity of other forms of economic development. But even here: Hitherto the government has failed to find the best possible way (whether by legislative acts or by other means) to, on the one hand, prevent excessive enrichment by "newly hatched cooperative members . . ."

IVANOV: . . . And not always honestly acquired!

YELTSIN: . . . Yes. But also, on the other hand, not to kill off people's desire to engage in cooperative or individual labor activity. There is also a third aspect: It is also necessary to give state enterprises more rights, to bring them in this regard closer to cooperatives, which today enjoy a relatively greater freedom in their choice of partners and in the solution of questions of supply and the marketing of output.

IVANOV: In this context, how do you appraise the recent government document which restricts cooperatives' activity in many sectors? Does it not seem to you that, having taken a step forward, we are then taking two or three steps back?

YELTSIN: **Perfectly correct. There have already been five or six** resolutions adopted on cooperatives, and we simply cannot find a way out. We are lurching from one side to the other . . . Allow it!—Prohibit it! And the justification is: lack of experience . . . All very well if it were a matter of months. But we are talking about *years*. It is time to start accumulating experience and applying it.

IVANOV: A question closely related to the same topic: The farmsteading system of land management is being gradually revived here in Estonia. Many peasants have already been presented with special land deeds confirming their inalienable right over a certain land parcel which they can bequeath. Some people are even inclined to perceive this as a return to private property. Briefly speaking, private ownership of the means of production and the legitimacy of its existence in our conditions are being discussed perfectly openly, and not just in the context of farmsteads. What would you say about this?

YELTSIN: It seems to me that the main point of the farmsteading system—whether you call it private property, termless lease, or 999-year lease—is that it really gives people back their sense of being masters of their own land. To people and to their children.

Just look at the expression itself—"private property." . . . You see, stereotypes are rather too strong in our country, and the majority perceive it as a return to capitalism, which is something altogether more terrifying. I would not use it. People's mentality must be taken into account. In my view, "long-term lease" or "termless lease" are more acceptable and less confusing word collocations, even though the meaning is the same in principle. But the form is certainly viable. It makes it possible **to get down to work with confidence.**

IVANOV: Yes, but peasants in general and Estonian peasants in particular still remember situations when they were first given land for termless and free use, and this was later followed by numerous resolutions and instructions which, in actual fact, annulled all their rights over that land . . .

YELTSIN: But this right of theirs must be CONSTITUTIONALLY enshrined, by means of a law.

IVANOV: It is evidently necessary to also take into account the historical and other specific features of the country's various regions?

YELTSIN: Absolutely. This is, after all, the root cause of our greatest mistake as regards the nationalities question. In other words, we believed for a long time that we had solved it—finally, irreversibly, once and for all times. This is why we paid it no attention at all—either from the viewpoint of science or an analysis of processes occurring in regions, national communities, and republics, or from the practical viewpoint. This is a very painful question. But this neglect by leaders who should have been dealing with it ultimately resulted in arrogance toward some nations, and at times even in insults against entire peoples. And this is, of course, simply impermissible!

IVANOV: Just as a matter of dotting the "i's": What do you consider to be the primary element in our state's structure—the republics voluntarily united within the USSR but remaining, under the Constitution, sovereign states which only delegate part of their powers to the union government, or the union which grants (or does not grant) certain rights to the republics?

YELTSIN: My opinion: The republics are primary. From the viewpoint of the very concept of democracy and democratization—any centralization always strives for bureaucratization and, therefore, tends to reduce the level of society's democratic nature.

This is why I believe that the opinion of **the people,** and therefore the opinion of a republic representing a given people, ought to be primary.

IVANOV: Is it altogether possible to talk about some faceless and inert mass which is dubbed the "apparatus"?

YELTSIN: As regards my statements, they are published only by local press organs which are sufficiently independent of the center. My name has not been mentioned in the central press for 1 year now (apart from *Moskovskiye Novosti*, which does not reach the mass readership—V.I.). As for the apparatus. . . .

It certainly exists as a mechanism. Even though it is composed of separate individuals. Maybe some of its components would like to change a few things or slightly amend a few things, but the corporate interest always prevails.

IVANOV: Do you believe that it is the apparatus which opposes you today?

YELTSIN: First and foremost. It is, of course, certain individuals who direct and prompt the apparatus. . . .

This is easy to explain. A fair proportion of cadres fear for their positions and privileges. Rather too many good things may be lost. By the way, I am being charged (and these accusations were also heard at the party conference) with supposedly advocating some faceless "leveling." But this is not so. I simply believe that only **wages** should be strictly differentiated, according to every person's contribution to society's cause. As for all the rest, bearing access to benefits in mind, let people be brought to the same level regardless of the office they hold—from top leaders down to workers and street cleaners. This, in my view, is one of the fundamental principles and ideals of socialism. But even this is lacking in our country. **In other words, all that has been left of socialism is the public ownership of the means of production. And a plant worker neither senses nor understands this.**

IVANOV: In other words, "If it belongs to everybody it belongs to nobody. . . ."

YELTSIN: Exactly.

The Boris Yeltsin Phenomenon
by Vitaly Tretyakov, *Moscow News*, April 23–30, 1989

"WHY DOES a Party committee's dislike of a deputy whom the apparatus doesn't sympathize with, suddenly give rise to powerful support from the people (B. N. Yeltsin's example)?"

(From the article "The People Have Made Their Choice," *Pravda*, April 1, 1989.)

The problem of the popularity of politicians and political leadership, which has always existed everywhere, has always been studied everywhere in the civilized world with care and without servility towards those who laid claims to this popularity or leadership. For dozens of years we excluded ourselves from the civilized world on this count as well. Life, however, takes its revenge. The interests of perestroika demand that the phenomenon of Yeltsin's popularity should no longer be ignored.

In the above quote from a *Pravda* editorial I was surprised by the word "suddenly". No, it's not all of a sudden. The situation which existed on March 26—the election day—offers a logical confirmation of the fact that the Yeltsin phenomenon has not only been born of perestroika, but is part of it. That is why I would like to find the reasons for his popularity and examine some components of "Yeltsin's image" in the masses' social awareness.

It stands to reason that this image does not coincide with either the political or everyday reality of Boris Yeltsin. It is better for someone else who knows Boris Yeltsin well to judge the extent of these discrepancies. The overwhelming majority of electors, whose votes ensured Yeltsin's landslide victory in the elections, do not have a good and intimate knowledge of him either. The electors decided on the basis of the candidates' image as happens most often in the battle of the hustings. What was in that "image" that generated the most sympathy? In an attempt to answer these questions I shall try—to the extent to which this is possible—to avoid introducing my own evaluation of the "Yeltsin image" which has taken shape in mass mentality.

Yeltsin's birth as a political leader, enjoying, according to *Pravda*, "powerful support from the people", has been recorded with absolute precision. It was that moment on February 26, 1986, at the 27th CPSU Congress, when he uttered the following words, with the accent on the last phrase: "The untouchability of authorities, the infallibility of leaders, and the 'dual-track morality' are intolerable and impermissible in present-day conditions. A system of periodic accountability must at last be worked out at the CPSU Central Committee for leaders at all levels ... Delegates may ask me: why didn't I say this when addressing the 26th Party Congress? Well, I can reply and do it frankly: at that time apparently I still lacked courage and political experience."

Having said this, Yeltsin was one of the **first** to accept responsibility for the "accomplishments" of the stagnation period, although he was by far not the first among the culprits of these "accomplishments". The initial stage of any revolutionary process is a period of searching for answers to the question "Who is to blame?" Whoever found the courage to say "I am to blame" immediately received powerful moral support in the eyes of millions of people eager to hear precisely from "above" the words about personal, and not only collective responsibility for what happened.

Since Yeltsin's example was not followed by the majority of those who needed to do this, in the people's opinion, he retained moral leadership, specifically in the right to reply to the next question of perestroika: "What is to be done?" And people started listening to his replies, the more so that, in his post as the leader of the Moscow City Committee of the CPSU, Yeltsin passed over more quickly than the others from words about perestroika to real perestroika as he understood it.

First and foremost, he constantly accentuates the problems confronting perestroika, using examples from everyday life which are easily understood by the ordinary person.

Yeltsin honestly exposed the "techniques" of perestroika, especially in the methods of work with people. The idea of cutting down the Party apparatus was still only being discussed, but he got down to business in Moscow's City and District Party committees which came under his jurisdiction. While yet another discussion of the food supply problem was going on, the First Secretary of the Moscow City CPSU Committee used his own power and authority to bring about abundance at Moscow's fairs and collective farm markets. He took perestroika—and he is not alone in this—literally. Glasnost? He speaks about everything. Struggle against red tape? He looks for it at all institutions. The electoral struggle? Yeltsin straightforwardly seeks to win support from the people, as did certain other candidates. And he succeeded where others failed.

Lastly, Yeltsin constantly serves as a reminder about the slow pace of perestroika, saying that people don't want results tomorrow, but today, that tomorrow will possibly be too late.

These are some of the methods which, to all appearances, Yeltsin tried to use in his actions. At times he succeeded, and he always had the support of those who, during the stagnation years, became fed up with promises instead of actions.

As a result, the majority feels that Yeltsin speaks on behalf of at least those who are still powerless to affect developments. When in 1987 Yeltsin, having quit the "upper echelon", found himself back up there, the crest of his popularity rose so high that his planned exile into the political wasteland did not materialize. This was also corroborated by the March 26 elections, as a result of which Yeltsin became a people's deputy of the USSR.

Before this, the impression of Yeltsin's personal unity with the people was daily reinforced in popular opinion both by the deeds of Yeltsin himself and by the words and deeds of those who criticize him.

He exists in popular opinion as a normal person and as a man of action. Yeltsin was the first to tear from himself the shroud of secrecy which usually veils personal acts by representatives from the "upper crust." The image of a destroyer of secrets always has a great appeal to people. It is also satisfying to confirm what I guessed a long time ago: the shroud of secrecy hides no secrets at all. He delivered many of the insulting meaning imposed by the tradition of secrecy: that the actions of those on top are inaccessible to rank-and-file persons in both meanings of the word "inaccessible"—no access and none of your business. Yeltsin made access free and showed that the same human beings sit "at the top". They are like all the others—they argue, err, make rash steps, get excited and furious, disagree with each other on small and occasionally big things. By so doing, as it seems to people, Yeltsin brought big-time politics down from the Olympic heights and put them at the feet of rank-and-file citizens.

Moreover, Yeltsin himself tried to come down from these heights to his rank-and-file co-citizens, and risked departing from the bureaucratic traditions: he was the first to go by street-car, give up rations and sign up at a district polyclinic. Some said that all of this was done as a pose. But so far there are simply no other leaders who would have done the same even as a pose.

He started addressing the broadest audiences not with speeches, but with answers to hundreds of questions—moreover, any questions. He started giving interviews to journalists, telling them not only about his decisions, but also his doubts, failures and the personal threats against him. It is, of course, possible to be ironical. It is possible to assert that after exposing the store-rooms of food stores over-stuffed with goods, Yeltsin did not solve the problem of shortages, but merely created an illusion that the solution was around the corner. But just recall the name of Caliph Harun al-Rashid. He is remembered because he studied the real life of rank-and-file people of Baghdad without any suite and in ordinary dress.

In his speeches Yeltsin calls for solving not all the problems facing society, but precisely those which have a direct bearing on the ordinary life of ordinary people: food, housing, social justice, and crime—especially in trade. Needless to say, in so doing he does not touch upon the strategic track of perestroika along which the entire load of problems must be pulled without getting stuck in the past of any of them. He owes his strength to his accuracy in hitting the sorest points. And it is this that has a hypnotic effect—it's the same as Dr. Kasyan, working with the strength of his fingers and hands, who attracts thousands of patients who have lost faith in the miracles of modern medical science.

Moreover, in his numerous statements—especially those made after his departure from the top echelon of the leadership—Yeltsin asks people to understand and support him. The feeling that remains after hearing such statements is unusual and grati-fying: it is not us, the people, that a leader helps find the right road. It is he who asks us for help in the search for this road.

Thus, people identify with Yeltsin. He is a victim of dislike on the part of higher-ups—who of us hasn't been in the same posi-

tion? And he is being slighted for refusing to look for their approval—who hasn't dreamed of doing this? And the main thing—he speaks with everyone, those below and those above, in a similar way and on equal terms, crushing the hierarchical barriers which everyone, especially those below, is fed up with.

The overall impression is that he is not fighting for power for his own sake: he resigned from his post in 1987, and announced his readiness to give up his ministerial post in the event of his being elected a people's deputy. He is accused of being power-hungry, but everyone is accustomed to believing that the most logical thing to do in this case would be not to resign and not to publicly express his disagreement with colleagues at the top, but something precisely the opposite. True, this is the logic of common sense. A subtle political strategy, however, can be built on much more intricate tactical manoeuvers. This is all quite hypothetical, but the fact remains that we strongly miss people behaving like he does.

Is it really the case or does it only seem that he is not fighting for power for his own sake? One thing is self-evident—Yeltsin is fighting for himself, for his honour: he demands political rehabilitation during his lifetime in defiance of tradition. He doesn't confess his sins, but stands up for himself everywhere. He may have delusions—but his own, not borrowed from someone else. He is expelled from the highest political circles but, refusing to resign himself to this, comes up again and again to the rostrum, becoming a target for criticism. Glasnost is his assistant, but after all he uses it to the fullest—something which many others do not dare to do.

He proves to be right more often than it may seem. Yesterday he alone said what everyone is discussing now. When the verbatim report of the October 1987 Plenary Meeting of the CPSU Central Committee was published at long last, it became clear that the rumours we heard were false. Readers even ask: "Hasn't the verbatim report been cut?"

Of course, this may be the "effect of being late" to which political documents are very sensitive. In March 1989 we read what was said in October 1987. The 19th Party Conference shifted a number of accents in the CPSU Central Committee's activities and introduced changes into the Secretariat's work, which had been criticized by Yeltsin. The September 1988 Plenary Meeting of the Central Committee modified the composition of the Politburo, which we know today but which we couldn't have anticipated in 1987.

Ironically, even those who criticize Yeltsin never tire of mentioning his positive features and businesslike qualities, and his ability and desire to work. Whatever he is accused of, and whatever he is guilty of, can be said about any Soviet boss—everything, down to his difficult character. But then his positive qualities are unusual, they betray a figure which may even be contradictory, but is likeable in a human way even in its errors and delusions.

Relations with the apparatus are a special component of the Yeltsin phenomenon. This phenomenon could originate only in the apparatus because so far the apparatus has been a real and stable part of power—people need stability. But the stability and strength of the officialdom irk people and restrict their freedom. Therefore sympathies are given to those who shatter this apparatus. However, any serious shattering of the apparatus is feasible so far only on the part of those who themselves constitute its part and therefore are a real force. The circle closes—the Yeltsin phenomenon moves in this circle. I am sure that had Yeltsin run for the post of director of some research institute or factory, his success could not be guaranteed. On March 26, 1989, Yeltsin was voted in by the overwhelming majority not as a "boss for the people", but as a "boss for the bosses". The unanimity in voting for Yeltsin was the people's reply to the apparatus for its arrogant use of power.

A mishap and a lucky one—he falls and rises again. This is Yeltsin—personalized glasnost and perestroika with their advances and reverses. For long people have wanted such a leader to make an appearance. And he did appear. People said: if a man like this comes, he will be removed. And he didn't hold out.

The usual collapse of an ideal. It not only frightens us, but makes us rise to defend it, because faith in the ideal remains.

Of course, an element of idealization is in evidence here. An additional proof of this is the rich campaign folklore from the election period associated with Yeltsin. **The main thing, however, which attracts people's sympathy is the fact that he has been doing everything which perestroika and glasnost permit, but which dozens of people above him and millions of others below him have not dared to do.** He is a product of perestroika, which is why he is so popular. Each time, he continues whatever Mikhail Gorbachev begins. He continues it, sharpening it to the extreme and boldly throwing it onto the altar of "people's love" or into the face of those who were not yet prepared even for the delicate formulations of the General Secretary (or who hoped that words would not be followed by deeds). It is hard for a leader with a real policy to retain the sympathies of everyone, because a real policy never bears golden fruit all at once and for everyone. Of course, Yeltsin has the advantageous position of a "shadow leader", a critic of whatever is being poorly done as a result of that real policy. The majority of his admirers engage in the same kind of criticism, lacking—in contrast to Yeltsin—just one thing: the possibility of being heard. And they support a person who elevates their thoughts to the level of decision making.

His real value as a politician can come to a head only when he gets real political responsibilities instead of the portfolio of a sectoral minister. They say that he had one during the period of his Party leadership in Moscow and he couldn't cope. That may be. But the other less open people must still prove that they cope better. Until they prove this, even Yeltsin's failures will be blamed not on him, but on the command system or on some of his critics. Moreover, if perestroika takes a turn for the worse in comparison with the present-day situation, Yeltsin's popularity will increase. If for the better, it will diminish because the success will then be attributed to other active leaders of perestroika as well.

Yeltsin himself, of course, may not even last in political life. But as long as perestroika is alive, his place will not be vacant. It shouldn't be consigned to the back of the hall. There is a need to understand why many want Yeltsin to be their spokesperson in discussing the country's problems.

Politicaly this phenomenon arose thanks to the Party, but today it exists thanks to the people—and it's impossible not to reckon with this. Supporting perestroika as a whole and in its separate parts, people take an extremely critical attitude towards its slow (or seemingly slow) pace. In this Yeltsin is at one with the people.

S. ZALYGIN

A Person of No Twists or Turns
by Irina Dementyeva, *Moscow News*, 1989
*A talk with Sergei Zalygin, people's deputy of the USSR
and editor of* Novy Mir

Q: You are not a member of the Party. You are a non-Party editor of a literary monthly, a non-Party writer. Now you are a non-Party people's deputy. Could the fact that you are not a Communist be an obstacle or an advantage in your activities?

A: Suppose a person comes to me—I don't ask him whether or not he is a Party member. The main thing is what he thinks and does. Yes, the work of a deputy is political work. But very often the work of a writer also happens to be political. I have always kept aloof of organizations as a means of making my career. I've been more interested in creative work, especially individual endeavour. But our times also call for a different approach.

Q: The Congress is to be made up of 2,250 people's deputies. Your leverage as a deputy—is it one-2,250th?

A: I would like it to weigh more than that. But I've never been a deputy and there has never been such gathering of deputies as there will be now. So I can't assess my part. Nor am I worried about this. I'm concerned with what, all things considered, I shall be able to do. My platform is well known. I'm writing a lot, and I hope that my readers and listeners understand what I want. In my programme I'm not proposing anything new either for them or for myself. I agreed to run for election solely because I believed that this would offer fresh possibilities for old intentions and objectives.

Q: In the process of nominating candidates for deputies many active supporters of perestroika ran into difficulties, sometimes even dramatic ones. You were nominated practically without a struggle and elected with a minimum number of votes cast against you. How can this be explained? Fame? Indifference? The fact that your programme suits everyone? Or because it is specific and you have shown that you can secure what you want?

[432]

A: The percentage of votes against me was not that small. I didn't get through straight away at the first round. But this isn't the point. I still believe that our *Novy Mir* magazine enjoys recognition among readers, hence also its editor.

Q: Well, and your struggle for the preservation of nature.

A: Yes, this as well: nature-protection interests are not alien to anyone, hence the trust, if it exists.

How would I work if I felt that I was not trusted. I know there are people who look for mistrust, they flare up on encountering resistance. There are such people . . .

Q: At your meetings with voters what question did you find the most difficult?

A: I had only one meeting with voters. But I receive such a lot of mail. Questions become difficult when you can't help, and when you haven't found an answer to them yourself. There are many difficult questions on ecology, on the magazine and on the articles which I write and print. People often send me newspaper clippings. Thirty-seven persons have sent me the same clipping from a Stavropol newspaper about the Volga-Chograi canal. Everyone deems it necessary to tell me about this abnormal construction project as if I can reverse the whole thing. But if these 37 people joined hands where they are, they would already amount to a force. Instead, we have accepted this method—you ease your soul in a letter, so to speak, and you feel good.

Q: At major forums it has become kind of a tradition to criticize the press. One miner who didn't manage to speak out on this occasion in Moscow, spoke in Donetsk specially for Mikhail Gorbachev. Why do you think, when criticizing the press, people more often than not confine themselves to general statements and practically never oppose a concrete action? And second: don't you find that the attacks against the press are guided by someone?

A: There is little doubt that this is the case in the localities, on a regional level. I have hundreds of letters to prove this. Local journalists, and even correspondents of central newspapers are assembled at the regional Party committee and told whom they should criticize and whom they should praise, what to appraise with a plus sign and what with a minus sign.

The central press, I believe, is much freer. But no newspaper is completely free of pressure, even if it is called completely free. The whole point is how far it can resist this pressure. I shall be specific. In our magazine we have long been waging an uphill fight for two or three authors and we hope to win. As for the rest

I feel no pressure. Occasionally, people are not happy with our articles. But why should I count on them being liked?

Q: Judging by the heat of the electoral struggle, people have come to believe in elections. There is the opinion that compromises are permissible in politics. Do you agree with this? If so, on what point of your programme are you ready to compromise?

A: I am not against compromises. Quite often I look for them. The important thing is not to step across some line drawn by yourself, beyond which compromises are impossible.

When I started taking an interest in the activities of the Ministry of Land Improvement and Water Conservation, I was very tactful and hoped all the time that we would find a common language. It took me probably a year or even longer to understand that we would never find this. And now I am saying for everyone to hear that crimes are being perpetrated there. I'll stand on trial if I'm not right.

Sometimes it seems that certain people are attempting to come to a mutual understanding with me, but later it becomes clear that this was only a trap. A play. I had already conceded all I could concede, but no concession was made to me on anything.

You asked on what point of my programme I was prepared to compromise. On none.

Q: The Ministry of Land Improvement and Water Conservation has spent billions of roubles on the project for reversing the flow of rivers and on other "transformations of nature". But no one has taken personal responsibility for this. What do you think is the matter?

A: Honestly, I myself don't understand what the reason is. Maybe it lies in the fact that we are trained to carry out orders, which frees a person of personal responsibility for whatever he does. This phenomenon is much broader and more dangerous than we think sometimes, because we've got used to it.

Let us bear in mind not Lake Baikal and not the Aral Sea, but an ordinary region, say, the Novgorod Region. There are no "great construction projects" there, but land improvers have left their pernicious trace on Novgorod soil as well: overgrown littered canals and drainage systems, dried up arable land. Land improvement is the costliest method of increasing yields. It should be applied when all other methods have failed. Land improvement can be effective only where agricultural land is good—not where it has grown barren, or where it has been tilled in a haphazard way, with the wrong machinery . . . It's mad! We are starting with land improvement, when we should be finishing with it.

The present ruiners of nature hope that they will get off scot-free. They will not be made answerable for the Aral Sea. For the Karabogaz Gulf. For the Non-Black Earth Area. For the Poltava chernozems. For anything at all on earth.

But what they have been doing is also a crime against man and humanity, and it is not yet known whether more lives will be ruined than under the personality cult. At that time two or three generations suffered, but these excutives encroach upon the existence of all coming generations, by deciding for them what bread they will have to eat, what water they will have to drink, to what extent it is poisoned. . . .

I understand that these considerations of universal human importance are not for government departments, which have their own worries: how to use their money, how to employ people, how to fulfil and overfulfil the plan and budget. Two million specialists in land reclamation—they must be used somewhere if the "profile" and direction of work are changed. But if they were not only executives, but also citizens, they would know where to use them. Suppose they build not canals but roads, considering that land improvement machinery permits this or dealing not with hydroreclamation, where there is no need, but with afforestation or with the entire irrigation project. Then people would also be employed, and in a neccesary job.

As things stand now: a state commission of experts has closed down a construction project, but work continues. The experts have said their word, but there is still no decision from the Council of Ministers, so roofless houses are still being built. **When we dream about a state committed to the rule of law, we usually think of how to protect the citizen and his rights, and this is good. But there is still no Code to protect the state and the people against the follies and greed of government departments.** There must also be the citizen's responsibility to the state, the more so when this citizen is a high-ranking leader, a minister. We have mixed up all of these relations. Relations between man and state. Relations between man and society.

Q: But isn't it the same thing?

A: **No, it isn't. The state should trust and follow the conclusions of specialists, shouldn't it? But given all the distorted connections and relations in our society, the voice of common sense is muffled and state initiatives are intercepted by those of government departments.**

And then not everything can be made contingent upon the law. Centuries must pass before an atmosphere of legality permeates society. But we have been experimenting for seven decades in this context, and increasingly in the wrong direction. After all, the British have allotted to their state the role of a "night watchman" guarding them. But our statesmen decide what buttons must be sewn on at what factory and to what jacket. As a result, there are neither buttons nor jackets.

Don't foist upon the state what should be dealt with by citizens themselves, don't distract it from the duties of a "night watchman". Maybe even our state committed to the rule of law could be built at a faster rate if the executives acted as politicians and legislators instead of as authors of instructions on how we should live, what we should eat, read, whom we should love and hate.

Q: I heard that the struggle against reversing the flow of northern rivers, persistently and successfully waged by you, borders on national egoism, that the northern rivers could save the Aral Sea and the Karakalpak people from extinction and the traditional economic mode of life of Kazakhs and Uzbeks. We, say the advocates of such views, speak for the country. Some people must sacrifice something for the sake of others. How do you view this kind of reasoning? Are political compromises possible here?

A: You asked about difficult questions. Here is perhaps one of the most difficult. If changing the flow of rivers could save the Aral Sea, I would behave differently. But I don't believe that it will. Many Uzbek and Kazakh scientists and writers share my conviction. And then this plan threatens us with catastrophe. In the same Republics huge sums are threatened which could, for instance, considerably improve the medical service and pensions.

Q: Traditionally, Russian journalism takes a definite stand. With your magazine, either there was a leading publicist or a group of writers adhering to the same platform, as in Tvardovsky's *Novy Mir.* You willingly publish critics and ideologues belonging to different trends. Aren't you afraid that the magazine may lose face?

A: I'm not a bit afraid. I am often accused of being neither a right-winger nor a left-winger, of being no one knows what. But I want to take no part in squabbles. I want to participate in perestroika. It is very difficult to stick to this line, because there is no support from either right or left, but this amounts to what is the true face of the magazine. I think that our perestroika lacks culture on each of its "floors"—in personal relations, in public discussions, in discussions in the press, in relations between state and society, and among statesmen. There must be some who can support precisely the **culture of perestroika.**

I came with this thought to the magazine, yet even here I was not understood at once. But from readers' comments we see that many people are of the same mind as ourselves. It is no accident that our magazine has the biggest circulation.

Q: You are a natural heir to Tvardovsky's *Novy Mir.* Which of his traditions would you like or are forced to give up?

A: None at all.

Simply the *Novy Mir* of the 1960s was in a different position from today. It was more lonely. But today I follow with interest the line taken by *Druzhba Narodov*, which I find to be close in spirit to *Novy Mir.* Today it is no longer, "I", but "we"—many magazines and newspapers.

Q: You have passed through NEP and experienced the rise, triumph and condemnation of the command system, you have written several wonderful, clever and profound books, you have fought against the project to reverse the flow of Siberian rivers and you won, you have become a people's deputy and assumed your share of responsibility for the country. Have you decided the two equations which the hero of the novel "After a Storm" remembered in his letter to the author: What is good? What is bad?

A: No, I haven't.

Paradise on earth, I think, is impossible. Hell . . . Hell, after all, is hell only because there is no good in it, and this is the only way it differs from paradise. The unclear distinction between "good" and "bad" is what makes up the problem which every individual decides for himself all his life. As soon as he ceases to decide, his thought comes to a halt, and everything else. This is a matter of spiritual life and spiritual death, an eternal question for man and humanity. It cannot be solved. But it moves life because it is in the process of perpetual motion and perpetual solution. The only perpetuum mobile, if you like.

GLOSSARY

Aktiv. The most "active" part of an organization; the decision-makers.

Artel. A group of people organized into units for producing, anything from agriculture to shoes.

Bich. A homeless person or a person who does odd jobs, usually around large port cities.

FRG. Federal Republic of Germany (West Germany).

Gorkom. The main party organ for an individual city.

Great Patriotic War. World War Two.

Ispolkom. Executive Committee of a regional soviet.

Kolkhoz. Collective farm (belongs to members).

Kray. A territorial unit, the next size up from *oblast*.

Kuban. The main wheat and grain-growing area in the Ukraine.

Kulak. Landed peasant. Millions were either shot or starved under Stalin; the rest were forced into collective farms.

MGB. Ministry for State Security.

MVD. Ministry of Internal Affairs.

NKVD. Predecessor of KGB.

Nomenklatura. The government or ruling party elite.

Obkum. The main party organ of an *oblast*.

Oblast. A territorial unit, second smallest in size, consisting of *rayons*.

Okrug. An election district.

Raykom. Regional Committee of Communist Party.

Rayon. A district.

Smolniy. Pre-1917 Revolution, an expensive school for ruling class; then headquarters of the revolution; now HQ for Leningrad Party organization.

Sovkhoz. A state farm (owned by the state rather than members).

Soviet. Organ of power or government, also popularly elected organ of government, now in the process of re-empowerment.

TIME LINE: THE SECOND
RUSSIAN REVOLUTION

Date Line: March 1985

Mikhail Gorbachev becomes General Secretary of the Communist Party of the USSR and begins to promote and implement reform he calls *glasnost* (openness) and *perestroika* (restructuring). He pursues a twin-track policy of accommodation with the West together with a movement toward democracy in the USSR. He is in favor of greater autonomy for Soviet national republics, including Estonia, Latvia, and Lithuania, and allows a loosening of the reins of control over satellite countries like Hungary, Czechoslovakia, and East Germany. Ironically, four years later, East Germany will ban some publications from the USSR as being "too liberal."

Date Line: November 1985

Gorbachev and Ronald Reagan meet in Geneva. This is the first meeting of the heads of state of the US and the USSR in six years. They issue a joint statement supporting a 50 percent reduction in strategic nuclear arms.

Date Line: April 1986

The explosion and consequent release of deadly radiation from the nuclear power plant at Chernobyl prompt outcries of indignation, especially after the USSR is silent about the disaster for three days. Gorbachev uses Chernobyl as a first step toward rectifying relations with the West by publicly admitting full culpability and then by inviting international inspection. This begins the first series of cracks in the wall of secrecy that has surrounded events in the USSR for more than fifty years. Phil Donahue is invited to broadcast from the scene and the first of a series of live telecasts originating simultaneously from the US and the USSR begins. The world begins to edge away from confrontation.

Also in 1986 comes the publication of Chingiz Aitmatov's *Plakha (The Executioner's Block)*, a depiction of the amorality in the society at large. It broaches such subjects as environmental desecration in the name of socialist "development," decentralization of management, drug trade, press censorship, and the individual's relationship with God. It is the first Soviet novel since Bulgakov's *The Master and Margarita* to include a literary treatment of Jesus.

On March 1, 1986, comes the official promulgation of glasnost as policy: it is quickly tested, and this continues to be the case. Various "unofficial" groups are formed, meet, and begin to voice their "unofficial" thoughts and actions in the form of protest and calls for greater democratic rights.

Date Line: August 1986

The appointment of Sergei Zalygin as editor-in-chief of *Novy Mir*, one of the largest and most influential monthly periodicals. It is the first time in Soviet history that a non-Party member is appointed to this position at any major magazine.

Date Line: December 1986

The appeal by the Byelorussian activists for the revival of the Byelorussian national culture, thus beginning the open expression of nationalistic ferment for greater independence and in some cases outright secession from the USSR. Senior Soviet policy makers including Y. Ligachev, considered the number-two man in the hierarchy, begin to agitate against glasnost. Ligachev will be replaced by Alexander Yakovlev, a close ally of Secretary General Gorbachev, and Ligachev will be shifted to the head of the Ministry for Agriculture.

Date Line: December 1986

Andrei Sakharov, Nobel Prize-winning physicist and leading critic of the repressions of the regime, and his wife, Yelena Bonner, are released from internal exile in Gorky. Their release is followed by the release of numerous other dissidents, and the Soviet Union begins to announce that henceforth there will be no more political prisoners or "prisoners of conscience." Jewish emigration to Israel and the US is liberalized, a process that continues through 1989 when Charles Vanik, the US congressman whose work inspired trade restrictions on the USSR in the 1950s, calls for liberalized trade with the USSR, including "most favored nation" status.

That same year sees the release of Tanguz Abuladze's film *Pokayaniye* (Repentance), depicting the terror and the paranoia of the Stalin era. The main character is a composite of Stalin,

Beria, and Mussolini. Soviet audiences are shocked and pleased as glasnost begins to be taken seriously as a means of releasing long-held fears and frustrations. The bureaucracy and its "command and administer" structure is denounced with full permission from "the top." One wag complains that "Gorbachev has given us more freedom but he hasn't told us what to do with it yet."

Date Line: June 1987

Novy Mir becomes the first Soviet magazine to publish the poetry of Joseph Brodsky, previously convicted of "parasitism." Elem Klimov is appointed as first secretary of the Film Makers Union, resulting in the release of scores of previously banned films. The Supreme Soviet passes a law ratifying perestroika, ordering competition, "accountability," and self-financing for state-owned enterprises—and a phase-out of a great deal of central control over planning and pricing. *Moscow News* along with the journal *Ogonyek*, begins to assume a leading role in the publication of new and revealing stories about the quality of life in contemporary USSR, including previously banned stories about crime, drugs, and the military involvement in Afghanistan.

Date Line: November 1987

Gorbachev's commemorative speech on the 70th anniversary of the October Revolution denounces Stalin. "The guilt of Stalin is enormous and unforgiveable," he says. This speech paves the way for an honest and critical examination of the Soviet past, a process that continues to the present day. History examinations of Soviet students are canceled and a nationwide teach-in ensues in its place until the history texts can be rewritten with accuracy. Censorship is loosened across the board and glasnost moves into high gear.

Date Line: December 1987

Gorbachev, in a triumphal tour of the US, signs the INF treaty with Reagan, eliminating short- and medium-range missiles.

Date Line: January-April 1988

Novy Mir begins publication of *Doctor Zhivago*, the long-banned novel by Nobel laureate Boris Pasternak. Tentative first steps taken to rehabilitate Stalin victims Leon Trotsky, Bukharin, and others. Matthias Rust, a West German young flying student, pilots a single-engine Cessna from Finland to Moscow and lands the plane in Red Square, creating a sensation, and an excuse for Gorbachev to reshuffle his military high command, replacing hard-liners with his own people.

Religious revival begins in earnest with the return of dozens of churches and cathedrals to various religious congregations. Teaching of Hebrew and Judaic studies is no longer persecuted.

Date Line: June 1988

Unofficial art returns from the world of the proscribed, and the Arbat, the "art quarter" of Moscow, begins to flourish, mounting exhibits of art from outside the "socialist realism" camp. In the US a CBS documentary on the new developments in the Soviet Union draws an audience of thirty million.

Gorbachev, in a major speech to a Party conference, calls for important changes in the structure of the Soviet government, including a new presidency limited to two five-year terms, multi-candidate elections, a diminished role for the Party in the economy, and a diminished role for the bureaucracy everywhere.

Date Line: December 1988

At the UN Gorbachev presents a "new world agenda" against environmental predations, drugs, poverty, and war. He announces a 500,000-man troop cut and his intentions to further reduce tensions in Europe and elsewhere. This begins a more than token troop and arms withdrawal from Eastern Europe as well as from the Chinese border. Clearly aware of Western skepticism, Gorbachev matches words with actions and invites the West to match his initiatives, relishing his rising popularity in western Europe and elsewhere.

At home Gorbachev battles successfully with his rivals in the Central committee, Ligachev being the most notable leader of the hard-line conservatives. Ligachev is given the portfolio for agriculture.

Date Line: 1988

The Soviet Union begins a dramatic troop withdrawal from Afghanistan, site of the USSR's longest-running war. Gorbachev announces that the USSR will be out of Afghanistan by February 15, 1989, and he meets his deadline. Much to the surprise and chagrin of the Western powers, the Soviet-supported government of Najibullah hangs on after the Soviet withdrawal, rather than falling immediately after to the guerilla opposition. Afghanistan, however, is nearly destroyed.

Date Line: 1989

In March Gorbachev announces the complete failure of Stalinist collectivization of farming and the beginnings of a leasehold system, whereby farmers can lease their farms in perpetuity from the government and return to family farming. Meantime, the cooperative movement spreads as an alternative to state socialism. Limited introduction of free enterprise begins to have effect on a lagging and sluggish economy but also accentuates the problem of gangsterism, as co-ops are sold "protection" and are frequently vandalized and harassed. The country struggles with the problem of taxation of the co-ops, as some laws encourage their development while others impede it.

For the first time in seventy years, the Soviet Union holds free elections for its new parliament. Boris Yeltsin and a host of other reformers and dissidents are elected. Yeltsin's return marks the first time in Soviet history when a "disgraced" party official is "rehabilitated" in his own lifetime.

In April comes Gorbachev's major party purge, resulting in the ouster of more than one-third of all the members of the Central Committee. More agitation for reform comes from nearly all sectors of Soviet society, including the "captive nations" of Eastern Europe. In Soviet Georgia there is a riot by the military in which more than forty people are killed by poison gas after soldiers storm a peaceful protest. In Lithuania, Latvia, and Estonia, nationalist movements for independence demonstrate their staying power; representatives are elected to the Moscow Congress, which convenes in June.

In May Gorbachev flies to Beijing for a summit with Chairman Dung and is met with more than a million Chinese demonstrating against their government for more reform, democracy, freedom of the press, and an end to corruption. Many of the protestors carry banners with Gorbachev's words and picture, but he is upstaged by the enormity of the protest.

Also in May, a chapter of PEN, the international organization of writers and editors devoted to literary and press freedom, is established in the USSR.

Aleksandr N. Aksenov is relieved of his duties as head of the State Committee for Television and Radio Broadcasting concidentally with the broadcast of a program on which a talk-show guest suggested that "it was time to take Lenin's remains from their case in the Red Square mausoleum and bury them like those of other mortals." Aksenov publicly acknowledged that the comment was "rude" and that on television "political mistakes are especially inadmissible," a further instance of some of the limits of glasnost.

Gorbachev proposes token cuts of five hundred short-range nuclear missiles in Europe, propelling already strong currents in NATO committed to negotiating nuclear arms reductions. The Bush administration comes under pressure domestically as well as internationally to respond to this move. When it vacillates, Gorbachev proposes massive reductions in conventional arms and troops—up to one and a half million troops and commensurate weapons and weapons systems, deflating American government reasons for "hanging tough." NATO begins to look increasingly like an alliance in disarray as Gorbachev seeks to integrate the USSR into mainstream Europe.

Meanwhile, on the "nationalities front," Lithuania votes itself "sovereignty" and awaits Moscow's response.

The Congress of People's Deputies meets for the first time to elect standing members to the new Legislature (Supreme Soviet) and a new president. Gorbachev, unsurprisingly, is elected president, although he is grilled publicly and on national television. Two days later liberals, reformers, and dissidents, including Boris Yeltsin, are defeated as the apparatus decimates the opposition; the new Legislature is termed a "Stalinist-Brezhnevite Supreme Soviet" for its monolithic character by the defeated side.

This quick, thumbnail summary of events in the USSR since 1985 makes no pretense of being in any way complete, but it does trace some of the highlights that are developed in this book. The Gorbachev-inspired second Russian Revolution has thus far proven to be as durable as it is positive in initiating "democracy from the top." If Gorbachev has given the Soviet people freedom, but "hasn't told them what to do with it yet," they are learning quickly as they struggle with the task of overcoming the terrible scars of their Stalinist legacy.

Still, for every revolution there is a counter-revolution, and the "forces of stagnation" have not been altogether complacent and have been able to prevent the implementation of reform on numerous levels in numerous instances.

Stay tuned.

—June, 1989

A NOTE ON SOURCES

Much of the material that comprises *The Glasnost Reader* is drawn from the following sources: The *Daily Report*, published in Washington by FBIS (the *Daily Report* publishes translations of various articles from the Soviet press), and *Moscow News*, a leading journal of *glasnost*—lively, informative, courageous.

Special thanks to Alexander Amerisov, editor and publisher of the *Soviet American Review*, perhaps the best journal published in the United States covering "inside" politics and contemporary history in the Soviet Union.

Subscriptions to all these journals are available in the United States.